*Using*

# Peachtree® Complete

**FOR ACCOUNTING**

## 2012

## Glenn Owen

*Allan Hancock College*

## SOUTH-WESTERN
CENGAGE Learning®

Australia • Brazil • Japan • Korea • Mexico • Singapore • Spain • United Kingdom • United States

## SOUTH-WESTERN
CENGAGE Learning·

**Using Peachtree® Complete 2012
for Accounting**
Glenn Owen

Vice President of Editorial, Business:
Jack W. Calhoun

Editor-in-Chief: Rob Dewey

Senior Acquisitions Editor: Matthew Filimonov

Senior Developmental Editor: Ted Knight

Editorial Assistant: Ann Loch

Marketing Manager: Heather Mooney

Senior Content Project Manager: Tim Bailey

Media Editor: Bryan England

Manufacturing Planner: Doug Wilke

Senior Marketing Communications Manager:
Libby Shipp

Production Service: Cenveo® Publisher
Services

Senior Art Director: Stacy Jenkins Shirley

Internal Designer: Juli Cook/Plan-It Publishing

Cover Designer: Kathy Heming

Cover Image: iStock Photo

Rights Acquisitions Specialist: Sam Marshall

For product information and technology assistance, contact us at
**Cengage Learning Customer & Sales Support, 1-800-354-9706**

For permission to use material from this text or product, submit all requests online at **www.cengage.com/permissions**
Further permissions questions can be emailed to
**permissionrequest@cengage.com**

Peachtree screenshots and product logos © 2011 Sage Software, Inc. and its affiliated entities. All rights reserved.

Library of Congress Control Number: 2011943938

Student Edition ISBN 13: 978-1-133-62748-7
Student Edition ISBN 10: 1-133-62748-X
Student Edition with CD ISBN 13: 978-1-133-62728-9
Student Edition with CD ISBN 10: 1-133-62728-5

**South-Western Cengage Learning**
5191 Natorp Boulevard
Mason OH 45040
USA

Cengage Learning products are represented in Canada by Nelson Education, Ltd.

For your course and learning solutions, visit **www.cengage.com**
Purchase any of our products at your local college store or at our preferred online store **www.cengagebrain.com**

Printed in the United States of America
1 2 3 4 5 6  15 14 13 12

# Brief Contents

# Contents

## What If?

What if you could integrate a popular computerized accounting program into your classroom without using complicated and confusing manuals? What if your students could use this program and reinforce basic accounting concepts in an interactive case setting? What if you could accomplish both without spending a fortune and a vast amount of time preparing examples, cases, and illustrations? In fact, *Using Peachtree Complete 2012 for Accounting* by Owen is a textbook that fulfills and expands upon all three of these "what ifs."

## Why Is This Textbook Needed?

The first course in accounting has evolved significantly over the last several years. Educators are responding to the demands of accounting and nonaccounting faculty who rely on this course to lay a foundation for other courses. Moreover, the accounting profession relies on this course to attract the "best and the brightest" to become accounting majors. The evolution of this course has also put pressure on instructors to integrate computers into the classroom and, in so doing, develop students' skills in intelligently using and interpreting accounting information.

Faculty often want to incorporate computerized accounting into the first course but are reluctant to invest the time and effort necessary to accomplish this laudable goal. Existing materials are often "preparer" driven in that they focus on the creation of financial reports only. Students are often discouraged in their use of computers in the first accounting course because of the confusing and complicated accounting software manuals that concentrate on accounting mechanics.

This text responds to all of these needs. It provides a self-paced, step-by-step environment in which students use Peachtree Complete 2012 to create financial statements and other financial reports to reinforce the concepts they learn in their first course and to see how computer software can be used to make business decisions.

## Notable New Features in Peachtree Complete 2012 for Accounting

*Peachtree Complete 2012 for Accounting* has several new features.

Users can now quickly and easily create a new transaction based on a previously saved one. This feature is available on seven screens: Quotes, Sales Orders, Proposals, Sales Invoicing, Purchase Orders, Purchase Invoices, and General Journal Entries.

Sage Advisor now helps customers experience the full value of their software investment. Through personalized dashboards, engaging "show me how" videos, on-screen help, and other business resources. Sage Advisor helps customers learn more about their Sage Peachtree product, discover new ways to simplify their processes, and obtain valuable business advice.

Sage Peachtree Business Intelligence now has a reporting and analysis solution integrated with Sage Peachtree. Using the familiar interface of Excel, it enables more robust reporting and easier access to Sage Peachtree data.

The new Vendor Management System gives the user greater visibility into all the information needed for a specific vendor on one manageable dashboard.

While all of these new features help the commercial user of Peachtree, none of them has a significant impact on the basic accounting model, so students who are familiar with the previous versions of Peachtree won't see many changes in the functionality of the software.

## New Features of the Textbook

*Video Demonstration*

In this and the previous editions, we created two new resources, one for students and one for instructors. Student demonstration videos throughout the text help students visualize Peachtree processes. These demonstrations are referenced by a demonstration video icon in the margin (see example icon in the margin). These demonstrations are stand-alone, full-action videos with audio showing step-by-step illustrations of business processes explained in this text. All of these are available via the text's companion Website http:// which is best located by navigating your web browser to www.cengage.com/us and then typing the author's name (Glenn Owen) in the search text box, selecting Higher Education Catalog from the drop-down list, and then clicking the Search button. Select the Peachtree 2012 text and then click the Students: Access Free Companion Content text. The second resource is rubrics for instructors to grade all cases in the end-of-chapter material. These rubrics link each case requirement and events to a specific student-learning outcome. These rubrics are available on the instructor companion Website to this text, which is best accessed by locating the text Website (see above) and clicking the Instructor Companion Site text.

Also included are two additional comprehensive problems in Chapters 7 and 11: Bridgette Sweet Photography and Crystal Clear Pools. Both of these are service-related companies for which the student creates a new Peachtree file and adds business events to produce financial statements and reports. These also present excellent assessment opportunities.

Two important features are included in this edition. The first is a business events summmary, which appears at the ends of Chapters 6 through 11. This table identifies the various business events addressed in the chapter, the process steps to record the business event, and a page reference in the text where these steps are explained. Second, we added a series of short exercises at the ends of Chapters 6 through 11. These exercises require students to make small changes to a company file. The new company, which is created in Chapter 6, is Boston Catering, a firm in Cambridge, Massachusetts, which provides catering services to businesses in the Cambridge and Boston areas. Each exercise stands by itself and is not cumulative, except exercise 1 in Chapter 6. In that exercise, the student creates a new file. The exercises that follow in Chapter 6 require the use of the file created in exercise 1 but do not rely on any previous exercise. Thus, students and instructors can focus on specific tasks. For example, in Chapter 6 exercise 2, students add customers. In exercise 3 they add vendors, in exercise 4 they add items, and in exercise 5 they add employees. Students can complete all or just some of the exercises because each is independent of the others. In each successive chapter, a beginning student file is provided and each exercise adds business events. For example, Chapter 7, exercise 1 requires the student to add some cash-oriented financing activities, exercise 2 requires the student to add some cash-oriented investing activities, exercise 3 requires the student to add some cash-oriented operating activities like sales, etc. Once again, students can complete all or just some of the exercises because each is independent of the others.

## What Are the Goals of This Textbook?

The text's first and foremost goal is to help students learn or review fundamental accounting concepts and principles by using Peachtree and the analysis of business events. The content complements the first course in accounting and, therefore, may be used in conjunction with a core text on accounting.

A second goal is to enable students to build a foundation for understanding financial statements. After an initial tour of Peachtree, students learn how to use Peachtree to understand and interpret financial statements.

A third goal of the text is to provide students a means to investigate the underlying source documents that generate most financial accounting information, such as purchase orders, sales invoices, and so on. Students will experience this process by entering a few business events for later inclusion in financial reports.

A fourth goal is to provide students a means of exploring some managerial aspects of accounting by performing financial analysis and comparisons. Budgets are created and compared to actual operating results, and receivables and payables are aged for analysis of cash management and cash flow projections.

A fifth goal of this text is to reduce the administrative burdens of accounting faculty by providing a self-paced environment, data sets, cases, and a correlation table describing how this text might be used with a variety of popular accounting texts.

Finally, this textbook takes a user perspective by illustrating how accounting information is both used and created. Peachtree is extremely user friendly and provides point and click simplicity with excellent, sophisticated accounting reporting and analysis tools. The textbook uses a proven and successful pedagogy to demonstrate the software's features and elicit student interaction.

## What Are the Key Features of This Textbook?

This text is designed to work with *Peachtree Complete 2012*. It can be used with other versions of Peachtree, but the screen shots and instructions are based entirely on *Peachtree Complete 2012*. The text is broken down into two parts. Part 1 is designed to help you navigate through Peachtree. It provides a foundation for Part 2, which will show you how to create a new Peachtree file and record a variety of operating, investing, and financing transactions. This part is divided into five chapters—each with its own set of questions, assignments, and case problems.

All chapters in Part 1 revolve around Century Kitchens, a remodeling contractor. Century specializes in remodeling existing homes and is well known in town for its quality construction and timely completion of projects. You've answered an ad for a part-time administrative assistant and are about to learn more about what Peachtree can do for a business. Chapter 1 gives you a quick interactive tour of Peachtree, in which you will become familiar with

Peachtree's essential features. Chapters 2, 3, 4, and 5 introduce you to creating and preparing the balance sheet, the income statement, the statement of cash flows, and supporting reports.

Part 2 is designed to teach you how to use Peachtree and the accounting methods and concepts you've learned in your introductory accounting course. This part is divided into six chapters, each with its own set of questions, exercises, assignments, and case problems. You will follow the adventures of Donna and Karen at Wild Water Sports, who have hired you to help them set up their business in Peachtree, capture various business transactions, make adjusting entries, set up and use budgets, and generate key business reports. You will use Peachtree Setup to establish accounts, customers, vendors, items, and employees and then record business transactions using key source documents like sales receipts, invoices, bills, deposit forms, and checks. You will learn how to create journal entries in Peachtree to accrue revenues and expenses, adjust deferred assets and liabilities, and record depreciation of long-lived assets. Finally, you will learn how Peachtree's budgeting and reporting process can help Wild Water Sports plan and control its business activities.

A tested, proven, step-by-step methodology keeps students on track. Students enter data, analyze information, and make decisions all within the context of the case. The text constantly guides students, letting them know where they are in the course of completing their accounting tasks. Numerous screen shots include callouts that direct students' attention to what they should look at on the screen. On almost every page in the book, you will find examples of how steps, screen shots, and callouts work together.

*Trouble?* paragraphs anticipate the mistakes that students are likely to make or problems they are likely to encounter, and then help students recover and continue with the chapter. This feature facilitates independent learning and frees you to focus on accounting concepts rather than on computer skills. With very few exceptions, Peachtree does not require the user to record journal entries to record business events. An appendix on traditional accounting records gives you the flexibility to teach journal entries at your discretion. It provides the information necessary for students to make journal entries to record the events described in Chapters 6–11. Questions begin the end-of-chapter material. They are intended to test students' recall of what they learned in the chapter.

Assignments follow the questions. In the first five chapters, the assignments involve continuing your exploration of Peachtree by viewing Century Kitchens' information. Additional cases (Kelly Jennings, Sierra Marina, and Jason Galas Attorney at Law PC) are used to extend your practice and exploration of Peachtree files.

In Chapters 6–11 exercises follow the questions. Three assignments follow the exercises. Each assignment in Chapters 7–11 includes a beginning backup data file that is used to get the student started. This includes an extension of the Wild Water Sports continuing business problem used in the chapter, followed by the Central Coast Cellular and Santa Barbara Sailing assignments. Three additional cases follow these assignments. None of these cases includes a beginning data file. Students continue the case from the previous chapter. These include the Forever Young, Ocean View Flowers, and Aloha Properties cases. Five comprehensive problems appear at the end of Chapters 7 and 11. These problems provide an opportunity for students to demonstrate their comprehensive understanding of Peachtree procedures and accounting knowledge. Your instructor might consider using these as assessments.

The Student version of the text Website includes multiple-choice quizzes for each chapter. All beginning data files for each chapter and for each assignment are also provided for downloading.

The Instructor's Manual includes solutions to all questions, assignments, cases, and comprehensive problems. Completed Peachtree backup files are provided for the assignments, cases, and comprehensive problems to enable instructors to see what the student-completed data file should look like after each chapter. The instructor's section of the text Website also includes multiple choice quizzes, student data files, instructor-completed data files, and exhibit PowerPoints of all the screen shots in the printed text. The text Website is located at www.cengagebrain.com.

## Dates

Peachtree, as all accounting programs, is extremely date sensitive. This follows from the accounting periodicity concept, which requires accounting information to be organized by accounting periods such as months, quarters, or years. It is very important that while using this text you be aware of entering the proper dates to record business transactions or to view business reports. For example, the Century Kitchens case, used in Chapters 1–5, is based in 2011. If you are working on this case in 2012 you should change the System Date, from within Peachtree, to a date within 2011. Not doing so may cause you to accidentally record transactions in the wrong accounting period. Some of the exercises, assignments, cases, and comprehensive problems are presented in 2007, 2008, 2009, 2010, 2011, 2012, or 2013. The quality of these assessments and learning tools is unaffected by dates.

# About the Author

**Glenn Owen** is a tenured member of Allan Hancock College's Accounting and Business faculty, where he has lectured on accounting and information systems since 1995. In addition, he was a lecturer at the University of California at Santa Barbara, teaching accounting and information systems courses from 1980 until his retirement in 2011. He has also been a lecturer at the Orfala College of Business at California Polytechnic State University, San Luis Obispo, teaching financial and managerial accounting courses. His professional experience includes five years at Deloitte & Touche, vice-president of finance positions at Westpac Resources, Inc., and Expertelligence, Inc. He has authored many Internet-related books and accounting course supplements and is currently developing online accounting instruction modules for his Internet-based financial accounting courses. Mr. Owen published the third edition of his *Excel and Access in Accounting* text in 2011. It is tailored to Office 2010, which gives accounting students specific, self-paced instruction on the use of spreadsheets (Excel) and database applications (Access) in accounting. He has authored the *Using QuickBooks Pro for Accounting* text every year for the last 15 years. His most recent version for Quickbooks Pro 2011 was published in the summer of 2011. His innovative teaching style emphasizes the decision maker's perspective and encourages students to think creatively. His graduate studies in educational psychology and his 36 years of business experience combine for a balanced blend of theory and practice.

# Dedication

I would like to thank my wife Kelly for her support and assistance during the creation of this and previous editions of this text. While our boys are now out of the house and pursuing their own interests, she continues to listen to my often crazy ideas for new cases and experiences with college students, providing an excellent sounding board and reality check. You and the boys continue to be what life is all about.

# Acknowledgments

I am grateful to the many adopters and colleagues who provided substantial and meaningful advice and suggestions. Their many comments shaped this book and made me a better author and educator. In particular, I would like to thank those who served as reviewers and who provided comments and valuable suggestions in the planning and writing of this book:

Linda Bressler — University of Houston–Downtown

Patti Lopez — Valencia Community College

Josephine M. Mathias — Mercer County Community College

Jeanne Miller — Cypress College

P. N. Saksena — Indiana University South Bend

Howard Smith — Texas State University

Larry Stoffel — Taylor University

Bob Urell — Irvine Valley College

Ralph Bocock — Allan Hancock College

Nancy Shafer — Allan Hancock College

# Note to Student and Instructor

## Peachtree Version and Payroll Tax Tables

The text and related data files created for this text were constructed using *Peachtree Complete 2012* Build: 19.0.00.0906. To check your build, select "About Peachtree Accounting" from the Help menu. To check for updates, go to Peachtree's Website at www.peachtree.com. The files accompanying this text can be used in any version of *Peachtree Complete 2012* or higher. If you are using a higher version, Peachtree will automatically offer to update your file when you try to restore from the Data Files CD.

In this version of Peachtree, Sage continues its use of a basic payroll service. This is a requirement in order to use the Peachtree payroll features that automatically calculate taxes due to federal or state agencies. Initially, Peachtree comes with the current tax tables; however, they become out of date, which can occur within a month of purchase, and the payroll feature is disabled unless the user subscribes to the payroll service. Some previous versions of this text utilized whatever tax tables were in effect at the time of publication. Users who had different tax tables often noted differences in solutions as a result. This new requirement solves that problem. The author decided to use the manual payroll tax feature, which requires that students manually enter the tax deductions. This alleviates the discrepancies between the solutions manual and the students' data entry and lifts the burden of having to purchase the tax table service for each copy of Peachtree installed in a lab environment.

Instructions on how to set up payroll for manual calculation of payroll taxes are provided in the text. For more information, see your Peachtree documentation. All reports have a default feature which identifies the basis in which the report was created, such as accrual or cash, and the date and time the report was printed. The date and time shown on your report will, of course, be different from that shown in this text.

# Getting Started with Peachtree

*In this Part, you will:*

- **Take an interactive tour of Peachtree.**
- **Create a balance sheet and modify its presentation.**
- **Create an income statement and modify its presentation.**
- **Create a statement of cash flows and modify its presentation.**
- **Create supporting reports and modify their presentation.**

Part 1 is designed to help you navigate through Peachtree. It provides a foundation for Part 2, which will show you how to create a new Peachtree file and record a variety of operating, investing, and financing transactions.

This part is divided into five chapters—each with its own set of questions, assignments, and case problems. Chapter 1 gives you a quick interactive tour of Peachtree, in which you will restore Peachtree backup files and become familiar with Peachtree's essential features. Chapters 2, 3, 4, and 5 introduce you to creating and preparing the balance sheet, the income statement, the statement of cash flows, and supporting reports.

# An Interactive Tour of Peachtree

## Learning Objectives

*In this Chapter, you will:*

- Install Peachtree on your computer.
- Restore Peachtree backup files from your text CD.
- Back up a Peachtree file for later use.
- Work with Peachtree's Lists, Maintain, Tasks, Analysis, and Reports menus/functions.
- Work with Peachtree's desktop and Navigation Centers.
- Examine the system date and accounting period.
- Work with Peachtree's record and task windows.
- Launch and exit Peachtree in Windows.
- Open and close a Peachtree file.
- Use Peachtree to help make business decisions.
- Print in Peachtree.
- Use various facets of Peachtree Help.

## *Case:* **Century Kitchens**

You've been working in a part-time job at a restaurant, and today you decide that you've served your last hamburger. You want a new part-time job—one that's more directly related to your future career in business. As you skim the want ads, you see an ad for an administrative assistant at Century Kitchens, a remodeling contractor. Century specializes in remodeling existing homes and is well known in town for its quality construction and timely completion of projects. The ad says that job candidates must have earned or be earning a business degree, have some computer skills, and be willing to learn on the job. This looks promising. And then you see the line "Send a résumé to Scott Montalvo." You know Scott! He was in one of your marketing classes two years ago; he graduated last year with a degree in business. You decide to send your résumé to Scott right away.

A few days later, you're delighted to hear Scott's voice on the phone. He remembers you well. He explains that he wants to hire someone to help him with clerical and other administrative tasks in support of his new company, Century Kitchens. He asks if you could start right away. When you say yes, he offers you the job on the spot! You start next Monday.

When you arrive Monday morning, Scott explains that the first thing he needs you to learn is how to use a software package called Peachtree. You quickly remind Scott that you're not an accounting major. Scott laughs as he assures you that you'll have no problem with Peachtree because it is so user oriented. He chose Peachtree exactly for that reason and has been using it for about three months. Scott wants accurate, useful, and timely financial information to help him make sound business decisions, and he's not an accountant.

Scott explains that Century Kitchens incorporated on January 1, 2011, and he's been using Peachtree since then. Since January 1, 2011, he's been entering each transaction, but he's become so busy at Century that he needs someone else in the office who can enter transactions, generate reports for the managers, and so on. So he says that today he will give you a tour of Peachtree and teach you some of the basic features and functions of this package. You tell him that you're familiar with Windows and you're ready to start.

## Using This Text Effectively

Before you begin the tour of Peachtree, note that this textbook assumes you are familiar with the basics of Windows: how to control windows, how to choose menu commands, how to complete dialog boxes, and how to select directories, drives, and files. If you do not understand these concepts, please consult your instructor. Also note that this book is designed to be used with your instructor's and/or another textbook's discussion of essential accounting concepts.

The best way to work through this textbook is to carefully read the text and complete the numbered steps, which appear on a shaded background, as you work at your computer. Read each step carefully and completely before you try it.

As you work, compare your screen with the figures in the chapter to verify your results. You can use Peachtree with any Windows operating system. The screen shots you will see in this book were captured in different Windows environments. Depending on which operating system you are using (Windows 7, Vista, or XP), you may see some minor differences between your screens and the screens in this book. Any significant differences that result from using the different operating systems with Peachtree will be explained.

Don't worry about making mistakes—that's part of the learning process. The *Trouble?* paragraphs identify common problems and explain how to correct them or get back on track. Follow the suggestions *only* if you are having the specific problem described.

After you finish a chapter, you can complete the questions, assignments, and case problems found at the end of each chapter. They are carefully structured so that you will review what you have learned and then apply your knowledge to new situations.

## Demonstrations

*Video Demonstration*

Demonstrations are available throughout this text and are referenced by a DEMO icon in the margin. These demonstrations are stand-alone full-action videos with audio showing step-by-step illustrations of business processes explained in this text.

All of these are available via the text's companion website at www.cengage. com/us. Locate the Using Peachtree Complete 2012 for Accounting text and then click on the text Students: Access Free Companion Content and then click the Access Now button. To view a list of demonstrations available, click Demonstrations. Read the Read Me First file first.

## Installing Peachtree on Your Computer

If you are completing this assignment in your school's computer lab where Peachtree is already installed you may skip this section. Included on a CD located on the inside back cover of this book is an Educational Version of the Peachtree software. Insert the CD into your computer and follow instructions provided as the CD loads. For additional information and instruction see Appendix 2 Installing and Registering the Peachtree Application Software.

## Restoring Peachtree Backup Files from Your CD

To complete the chapters and exercises in this book, you must have access to data files. The CD located inside the back cover of this book contains backups of all the practice files you need for the chapters, the assignments, and the case problems.

*Video Demonstration*

*DEMO 1A - Restoring and opening up a file*

You will need to restore the backup files to their original format in new folders.

Working from your computer's hard drive is the most efficient way to use the Peachtree program. However, if you are in a lab environment and want to take your file with you when you leave, you'll need to make a backup copy of the file and save it to a removable disk (ideally a portable USB drive).

To restore the .ptb file you just created to a different computer, follow the restore procedures described previously, but instead of restoring from the Data CD, you'll be restoring from your USB drive.

---

### To restore a backup file (file labeled with a .ptb extension):

1 Insert your Data Files CD into your computer's CD or DVD drive.

2 Launch Peachtree. Close the What's New in Peachtree window if it appears and then close the Setup Guide if it appears as well. (We'll review these later.)

3 Click **File** and then click **Restore**.

4 Click the **Browse** button. Navigate your window to the location of the file you want to restore by clicking in the Look in text box until you locate the drive containing the Data Files CD. Select a file, Century Kitchens, for example, and then click **Open**.

5 Click the **Next** button and then choose to have your backup restored to a New Company folder. See the example in Figure 1.1. *Note:* Your location will be different from that shown in the figure.

### Figure 1.1

Restore Company Backup Window

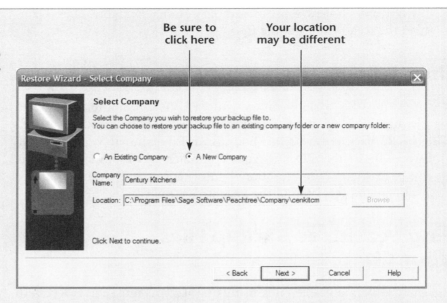

**6** Click **Next**. Check the **Company Data** check box and then click **Next**.

**7** Click **Finish** in the Peachtree Confirmation window. Your restored company will appear in a few minutes.

**8** Continue this process for all the backup files on your Data Files CD as you need them.

### To create a backup file (file labeled with a .ptb extension):

**1** Attach your portable USB drive (in this case labeled F:\).

**2** Launch Peachtree (if not already running).

**3** Open the file you want to back up (once again, only if it is not already open).

**4** Click **File** and then click **Back Up**.

**5** Place a check in the **Include company name** check box and then click **Back Up**.

**6** Change the backup location to your disk. See the example in Figure 1.2. The file name provided should be Century Kitchens—followed by the date you're making the backup, for example 070611, meaning July 6, 2011.

**Figure 1.2**

Peachtree Backup Window

**7**  Click **Save** to begin the backup process.

**8**  Click **OK** to begin the process. After a few seconds, your file has been backed up.

# What Is Peachtree?

Scott is excited about using Peachtree since it is the best-selling small business accounting software on the market today. He explains that Peachtree is an automated accounting information system that describes an entity's financial position and operating results and that helps managers make more effective business decisions. He also likes Peachtree's reports and graphs, which quickly and easily organize and summarize all the data he enters.

Scott says he especially likes Peachtree because it can handle all of Century Kitchens' needs to invoice customers and maintain receivables, as well as pay bills and maintain payables. It can track inventory and create purchase orders using Century Kitchens' on-screen forms—all without calculating, posting, or closing. Scott can correct all transactions he's recorded at any time, while an audit trail feature automatically keeps a record of any changes he makes.

Scott explains further that Peachtree has five key menus/functions that, when combined, help manage the financial activity of a company. The five menus/functions—Lists, Maintain, Tasks, Analysis, and Reports & Forms—work together to create an accounting information system. He decides to explain these without yet opening the Peachtree software.

*Video Demonstration*

*DEMO 1B - Peachtree overview and introduction*

## Lists

The Lists menu/function gives you access to current information on customers and sales, vendors and purchases, employees and payroll, inventory and services, and accounts, to name a few. Lists are created and edited either from a list window or while completing a form, such as an invoice, a bill, or a timesheet. Figure 1.3 shows a list of Century Kitchens' customer names and balances owed.

## Maintain

The Maintain menu/function gives you the ability to add, delete, and edit customers, vendors, employees, inventory, etc. You access an existing vendor by

**Figure 1.3**

A Customer List from Century
Kitchens

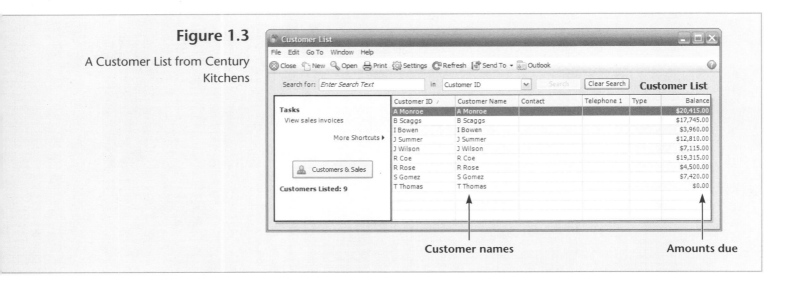

selecting its Vendor ID. From there, you can add, edit, or delete existing information. A typical vendor record is shown in Figure 1.4. The address, city, state, zip, and phone number fields provide unique information for this vendor. Additional tabs provide you access to purchase defaults, custom fields, and history. More on the specifics of record windows will be discussed later.

## Tasks

The Tasks menu/function is where you access the various accounting functions of Peachtree for your business. This is where you would access invoices to bill your customers, bills to recognize a liability to your vendors and record receipt

**Figure 1.4**

A Maintain Vendor Window from
Century Kitchens

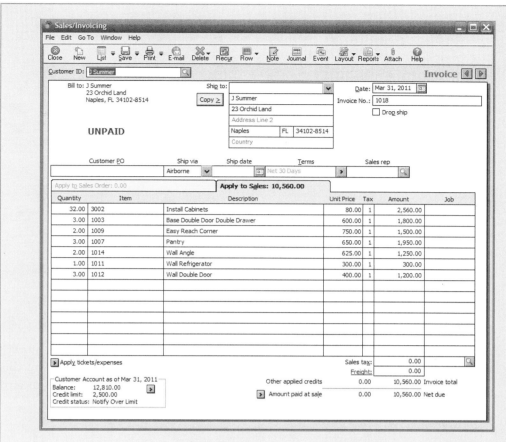

**Figure 1.5**

A Sales/Invoicing Window from Century Kitchens

of inventory, payroll records to account for your employees' time and effort, cash receipts records to account for payments received from your customers, and checks to pay your vendors and employees.

Figure 1.5 illustrates one of those tasks—invoicing your customer. The invoice requires a Customer ID, date, invoice number, terms, quantity of items sold, and an Item ID, which specifies what was sold to the customer. The Customer ID links to the customer list referred to previously so that the Bill To: information is automatically provided. Terms are also linked to the customer file and are input automatically. Upon entering the Item ID, the item description, unit price, tax code, and amount are automatically provided as well. The specifics of this task window will be discussed in more detail later.

## Analysis

The Analysis menu/function helps you analyze the state of your business from four different facets. Each allows you to view information from either a graphic or a numeric perspective. The cash flow manager analyzes your projected cash flows, the collections manager analyzes your accounts receivable, the payment manager analyzes your accounts payable, and the financial manager provides a business summary of key ratios and amounts as shown in Figure 1.6.

## Reports & Forms

The Reports & Forms menu/function presents the financial position and the operating results of a company in a way that makes business decision making easier. The income statement report in Figure 1.7 shows the revenues and

**Figure 1.6**

A Financial Manager Window from Century Kitchens

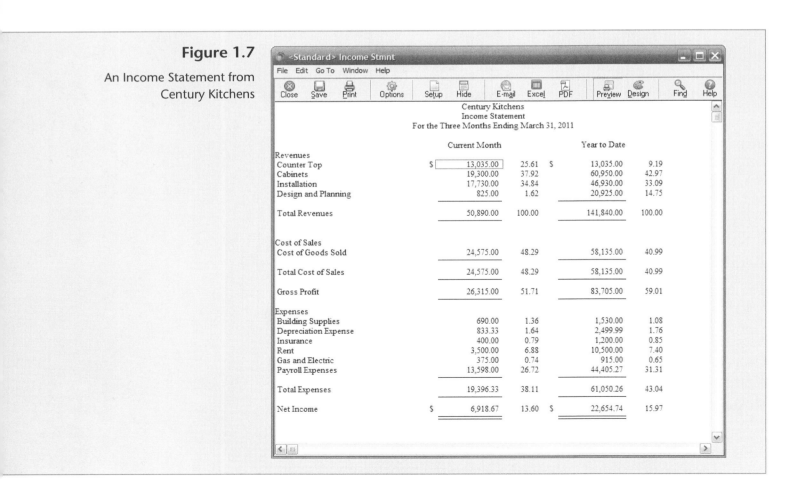

expenses of Century Kitchens for a specific period of time. You can modify reports in many ways, such as by comparing monthly periods, comparing this year with prior years, or examining year-to-date activity. Other standard

**Figure 1.7**

An Income Statement from Century Kitchens

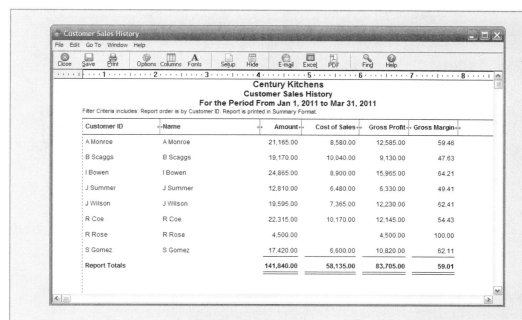

**Figure 1.8**

A Customer Sales History from Century Kitchens

financial reports such as the balance sheet, statement of cash flows, and statement of retained earnings are also available.

Peachtree can also produce reports that help support the business decision-making process in the areas of accounts receivable, accounts payable, payroll, and inventory. Sample reports include a customer sales history for the period 1/1/11 to 3/31/11 (shown in Figure 1.8), an aging of accounts payable, payroll tax report, and inventory valuation report, to name a few.

## The Peachtree Desktop

Scott explains that Peachtree operates like most other Windows programs, so most of the Peachtree window controls will be familiar to you if you have used other Windows programs. He reaches for the mouse and quickly clicks a few times until his screen looks like Figure 1.9, the Peachtree desktop. The desktop is the starting point for accessing all of Peachtree's key features. The main components of the Peachtree desktop are shown in this figure. Let's take a look at these components so you are familiar with their location and use.

The title bar at the top of the window tells you that you are in the Peachtree program and identifies the company file currently open. The menu bar contains the command menus, which open windows within Peachtree. The File, Edit, Window, and Help menus are similar to other Windows programs in that they allow you to perform such common tasks as open, save, copy, paste, find, and get help.

The Lists menu gives you access to all lists, including the chart of accounts, customers, vendors, employees, and inventory items, to name a few. The Lists, Maintain, Tasks, and Reports & Forms menus provide easy access to the previously mentioned functions as well as common tasks unique to that menu. Remember, in the Lists menu, you can access lists of customers, vendors, employees, and inventory items. The Maintain menu will allow you to add new customers, vendors, employees, and inventory items. The Tasks menu will allow you to create invoices, enter cash sales, create credit memos, receive payments, etc. The Reports menu will give you quick access to common reports for easy

*Video Demonstration*

*DEMO 1C - Using Navigation Centers*

**Figure 1.9**

Peachtree's Opening Screen from
Century Kitchens

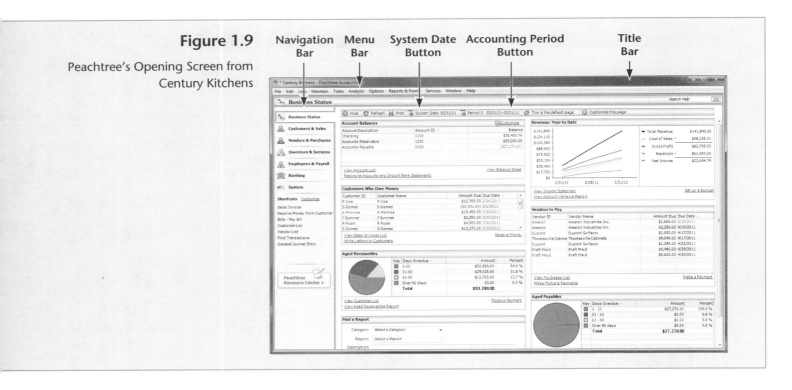

creation. Finally, the Help menu will give you immediate access to an index of help topics.

The navigation bar on the left gives you one-click access to the Navigation Centers and shortcuts to common business tasks. The Navigation Centers themselves provide useful access to tasks unique to whichever center you've opened. Figure 1.10 illustrates a partial view of the Customers & Sales Navigation Center. At the top, you have quick icon access to customers, jobs, and sales taxes. Below those icons are more icons simulating the flow of business events in the sales process: providing a customer a quote, then sales order, sales invoice, cash collection, etc.

At the top of all Navigation Centers is the button control bar. Two critical components of the button control bar are the System Date and Accounting Period buttons as shown in Figure 1.9. Clicking the System Date button allows you to change the system date for all Peachtree applications. See Figure 1.11. It does not change the system date of your computer or other applications you may be running. If the system date falls within the current accounting period, that date is used as the default date for entering business transactions like invoices, cash receipts, and checks, for example. Setting the system date is critical to your success in this course. Since many of you will be entering Peachtree information on dates other than that specified by the assignment or case problem you're working on, *it's critical that you specify a system date within a particular assignment or case's date range*. Otherwise, you may accidentally enter a business event on a date outside the range of dates for the assignment of a case, which will make it appear that an event you know you recorded has disappeared.

Clicking the Accounting Period button allows you to change the accounting period. This informs users of the current fiscal year and allows them to move between accounting periods to enter or view business events occurring in that period. Figure 1.12 illustrates the various accounting period options open to the user for Century Kitchens.

**Figure 1.10**

Peachtree's Customers & Sales Navigation Center from Century Kitchens

**Figure 1.11**

Changing Peachtree's System Date

## Peachtree Records and Tasks Windows

Scott explains that you'll spend most of your time in Peachtree working with Records and Tasks. Records are lists of information such as the customer list referred to previously. Remember, you'll use the Maintain menu/function to add, delete, and access these records. A typical record is shown in Figure 1.13. The toolbar provides access to common processes unique to a record such as New for adding a new record, Save for saving the record, and Delete for deleting the record. Clicking the arrows next to the Customer ID moves between records, and clicking the different tabs provides access to unique information for each customer such as terms and credit, sales defaults such as the general ledger account most often affected when entering a transaction for this customer, etc. The current balance owed by this customer is also displayed based on the system date you've specified.

Tasks include transactions such as sales invoices, cash receipts, purchase orders, etc. Remember, you'll use the Tasks menu/function to record new business transactions. A typical task, recording a cash receipt transaction, is shown in Figure 1.14. The toolbar provides access to common processes unique to a record such as New for adding a new cash receipt, Save for saving the transaction, and Delete for deleting the transaction. Clicking the arrows next to Receipt moves the user between various cash receipt transactions. Clicking the Apply to Revenues tab is appropriate when the cash receipt is from a cash sale. The receipt shown in Figure 1.14 was used to pay an existing invoice.

**Figure 1.12**

Changing Peachtree's Accounting Period

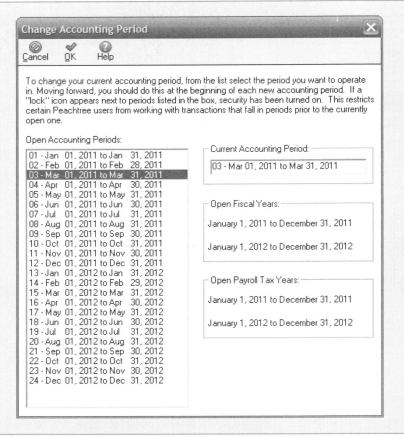

**Figure 1.13**

Customer Record Window from Century Kitchens

Tabs contain specific information on each customer

Scroll to view different customers

Toolbar

Current balance based on system date specified

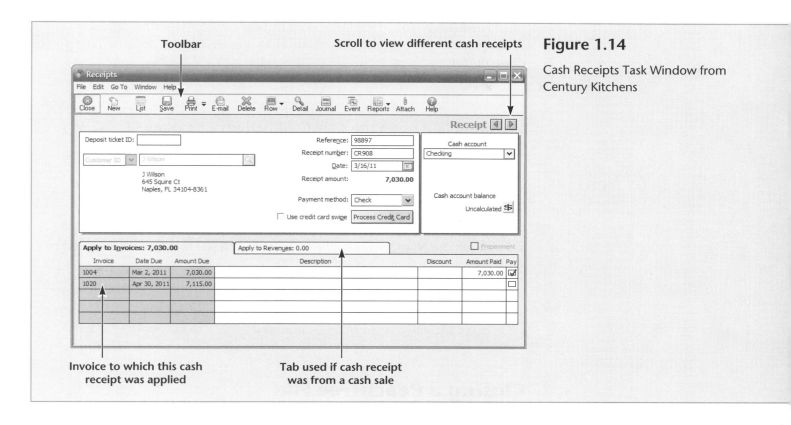

**Figure 1.14**

Cash Receipts Task Window from Century Kitchens

## Launching Peachtree

Now that you know about the lists, maintain, tasks, analysis, and reports functions, you are ready to launch Peachtree. Scott invites you to join him in his office and use his large-screen monitor to start your tour. You open Windows, and Scott tells you how to launch Peachtree.

### To launch Peachtree in Windows:

1 Click the **Start** button.

2 Select the **Programs** menu and look down the list for Peachtree.

3 Once you've located the Peachtree program, click and release the Peachtree Complete Accounting 2012 icon or name.

Now that you have launched Peachtree, you can begin to learn how to use it.

## Restoring and Opening a Peachtree File

Scott hands you a CD and tells you to restore the backup file he made last night at home called Century Kitchens.ptb. He took the file home last night to get it ready for your discussion today. The file on the office computer has the data before his effort last night, and he wants to restore it onto the office computer today. (You will find this file included on your Data Files CD.)

*Trouble?* If your Peachtree Application window does not already fill the desktop, click the Application window **Maximize** button, located next to the **Close** button.

### To restore and open the Century Kitchens Company file:

1   Insert your Data Files CD into your CD-ROM drive.

2   Launch Peachtree.

3   Click **File** and then click **Restore**.

4   Click the **Browse** button. Select **Century Kitchens** and then click **Open**.

5   Click the **Next** button and then choose to have your backup restored to a New Company folder.

6   Click **Next**. Check the **Company Data** check box and then click **Next**.

7   Click **Finish** in the Peachtree Confirmation window. Your restored company file will appear in a few minutes.

## Closing a Peachtree File

Now that you have seen the components of the Peachtree screen, Scott wants to show you how to close a file, so that you will always be able to save your work and exit Peachtree. He explains that to close a Peachtree file, you can do one of three things:

•   Exit Peachtree using the Exit command on the File menu.

•   Open another company file using the Open Company command.

•   Close the file using the Close Company command on the File menu.

### To close the Century Kitchens Company file:

1   Click **File**.

2   Click **Exit**.

Then Scott tells you something very unusual. He says that, unlike other Windows programs, Peachtree *does not have a Save command*. In other words, in Peachtree you cannot save a file whenever you want. You stare at Scott in disbelief and ask how that can be possible. Scott explains that *Peachtree automatically saves all of the data you input and the changes you make as soon as you make them and click OK.* Scott admits that when he first used Peachtree, he was uneasy about exiting the program until he could find a way to save his work. But he discovered that there are no Save or Save As commands on the Peachtree File menu as there are on most other Windows programs. He reassures you that, as unsettling as this is, you'll get used to it when you become more familiar with Peachtree.

## Peachtree's Menus, Navigation Centers, and Shortcuts

Scott explains that to enter sales receipts, create invoices, pay bills, receive payments, and so on, you can use Peachtree menu commands. Some of these functions are also available from buttons in the Peachtree Navigation Centers or the Shortcuts list. While having multiple ways of accomplishing the same thing is often confusing, what matters is that you get the business transaction or event recorded accurately.

Some Peachtree menus are dynamic; in other words, the options on the menu change depending on the form, list, register, or report with which you are working. For instance, when you enter sales receipts information, the File and Edit menus change to include menu commands to print the sales receipts or to edit, delete, memorize, or void the sales receipts.

Because this is all new to you, Scott suggests that first you become familiar with how managers at Century Kitchens use Peachtree to make business decisions.

## Using Peachtree to Help Make Business Decisions: An Example at Century Kitchens

Once transactions are entered into the Peachtree accounting information system, they can be accessed, revised, organized, and reported in many ways to aid business decision making. This ability is what makes a computerized accounting information system so valuable to managers.

While you're sitting with Scott, he receives a phone call from Laurie McConnell. Laurie needs some information on whether any accounts are past due. You know from your accounting course that Laurie is really asking for information about Century Kitchens' accounts receivable, or amounts due from customers from previously recorded sales. Laurie wants to know how much is due from customers and how current those receivables are; specifically, she wants to know which customers owe Century Kitchens and when their payments were due. Scott tells Laurie he'll look into this immediately and call her right back.

Be aware that dates are critical to retrieving relevant information in Peachtree. In most cases when you ask for a report, Peachtree will give you that report as of the system date (today's date, whatever that might be). For example, if you are working on this assignment on January 5, 2012, and you request a report on receivables, Peachtree will give you a report of receivables as of January 5, 2012. If you want a report as of March 31, 2011, you will need to change the date on the report and then refresh the report to see that information. Alternatively, you can set Peachtree's system date to a date within the accounting period you're working with as explained previously.

Scott calls Laurie back and tells her that $93,280.00 is due from customers. He explains that $29,625.00 of that amount is 31 to 60 days old and $12,765.00 is 61 to 90 days old. Further, the oldest invoice is 1005, from R Coe. Laurie would like to know specifically when payments were made, if any, and in what amounts. Scott knows he can easily get this information from the windows he just reviewed.

### To identify the customers who owe Century Kitchens money and the total amount of receivables due from these customers:

1 Launch the Peachtree 2012 application.

2 Click the **System Date** button.

3 Type **3/31/11** into the Date text box and then click **OK**.

4 Click the **Accounting Period** button.

5 Select accounting period **Period 3 – 03/01/11 – 03/31/11** and then click **OK**.

6 Click **No** if asked if you would like to print reports.

7 Click **Analysis** and then click **Collection Manager**.

8 Select the **Graph** option button.

9 Select **Pie** from the drop-down edit box. Your window should look like Figure 1.15.

**Figure 1.15**

Graphic Collection Analysis from Century Kitchens

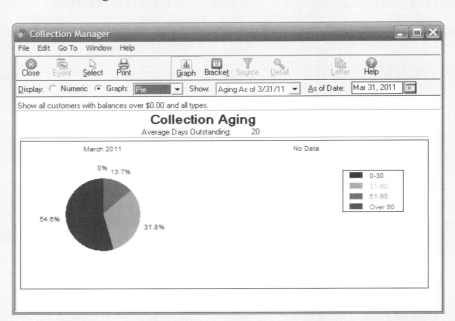

10 Select the **Numeric** option button. Your window should look like Figure 1.16.

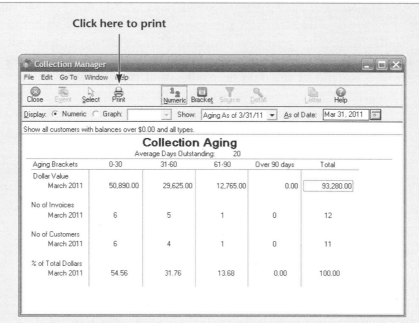

**Figure 1.16**

Numeric Collection Analysis from Century Kitchens

**11**  Double-click the **29,625.00** balance in the 31–60 day column to view the detail of what makes up that balance. See Figure 1.17.

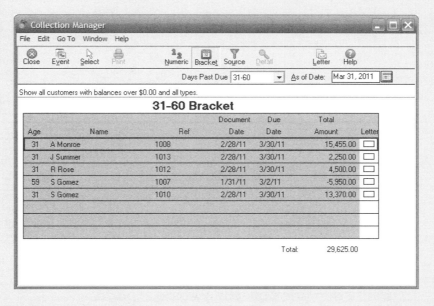

**Figure 1.17**

Detail of Balances 31 to 60 Days Old

**12**  Change the Days Past Due from 31–60 to 61–90, and then double-click the oldest invoice, **1005**, due from R Coe.

**13**  Double-click invoice **1005** again in the following customer detail window to view invoice 1005.

**14**  Maximize the invoice window and then use the scroll bar to move down through the invoice detail. (*Note:* Depending on the size of your screen, some of the invoice detail may be hidden from view as shown in Figure 1.18.)

He tells her that the invoice date was 1/27/11 for $15,240 and that a credit of $2,475 was applied to that invoice. He has quickly and easily accessed financial information from the company's Peachtree data, and Laurie thanks him. She is grateful for his quick response so she can make her decision. She asks if, before the end of the day, he would print out a copy of the numeric collection aging report and leave it on her desk. Scott is happy to oblige.

**Figure 1.18**

Invoice 1005 from Century Kitchens

## Printing in Peachtree

Scott suddenly remembers a meeting he must attend. But before exiting Peachtree, you remind him that he promised to print a numeric collection aging report for Laurie.

**To print a numeric Collection Aging report:**

1   If you have closed the numeric collection aging report, click **Analysis** and then click **Collection Manager**.

2   Select the **Numeric** option button.

3   Click the **Print** button located on the button bar to print this window.

4   You've opened several windows and not closed them. Close all open windows and return to the Peachtree desktop.

Scott asks you to drop off this report at Laurie's desk sometime after lunch.

# Using Peachtree Help

Scott suggests you explore Peachtree's Help features while he is at his meeting. He tells you that Peachtree Help has the standard features and functions of Windows Help and, in addition, has other help features specific to Peachtree. These other features are listed in the main Help menu shown in Figure 1.19.

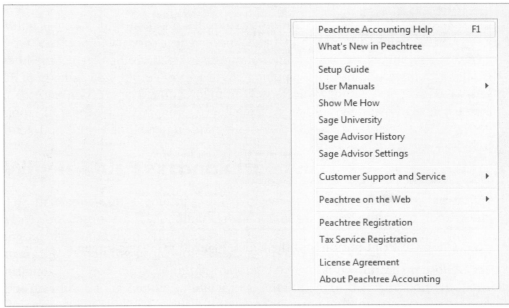

| | |
|---|---|
| Peachtree Accounting Help | F1 |
| What's New in Peachtree | |
| Setup Guide | |
| User Manuals | ▶ |
| Show Me How | |
| Sage University | |
| Sage Advisor History | |
| Sage Advisor Settings | |
| Customer Support and Service | ▶ |
| Peachtree on the Web | ▶ |
| Peachtree Registration | |
| Tax Service Registration | |
| License Agreement | |
| About Peachtree Accounting | |

**Figure 1.19**

Help Menu

As with other Windows programs, you can access Help by clicking the Help menu or by pressing F1. Peachtree Help is context sensitive—that is, different help screens appear depending on where you are in the program. You can get help for a specific topic by choosing the Help Index menu item.

You decide to follow up on Scott's suggestion to look at a help feature he finds very useful, the Help Index. You are specifically interested in how Peachtree uses accounts.

**To use the Help Index:**

**1** Click **Help** from the menu bar.

**2** Click **Peachtree Accounting Help** on the menu (see Figure 1.19) and then click the **Index** tab.

**3** Type the word **add** as a keyword.

**4** Double-click **new accounts to chart of accounts** to view the Peachtree Help window. You should see the window as shown in Figure 1.20.

**Figure 1.20**

Peachtree Help

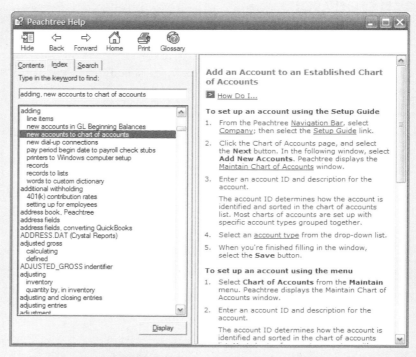

5   Click the **Print** button and then click **Print** to print this screen.

6   Close this window.

You will have an opportunity to use most of these options in this and later chapters. Scott had also mentioned something about Peachtree's Guided Tour, which leads you through basic transactions in Peachtree Accounting. It also provides overviews of new features in the current release.

## Peachtree Essentials Course

Sage, the developer of Peachtree Complete, has created video instruction in its Peachtree Essentials Course. These videos will help you get started right away.

### To use the Peachtree Essentials Course:

1   Navigate your web browser to http://cdn.bestsoftware.com/FTP/ SagePeachtree/SageAdvisorVideos/player.html.

2   The initial website should look similar to Figure 1.21, but remember web pages change constantly to provide you current information and recent updates. Choose one of the topics located on the left-hand side of the window and view the demo. View others at your leisure.

**Figure 1.21**

Peachtree Essentials Course

You will get a "big picture" overview of important concepts in Peachtree, as well as step-by-step instructions for key tasks.

## What's This?

Scott returns from his meeting. He asks if you've used the What's This? feature in Peachtree. He's found this an effective way to quickly access information anywhere in Peachtree. The What's This? feature is accessed by right-clicking most anywhere in a Peachtree window. Right-clicking an area in a window gives you quick access to a description of what that area of the window is asking for or expecting.

**To see how the What's This? feature can help you use Peachtree:**

1   Click **Vendors & Purchases** to open the Vendors & Purchases Navigation Center.

2   Click **Write Checks** and then click **New Check** to open the Write Checks window.

**3** Right-click inside the Check Number text edit box and then click **What's This?**. The What's This? answer should pop up as shown in Figure 1.22. (Windows 7 and Vista users: The Help for this program was created in Windows Help format, which depends on a feature that is not included in Windows 7 or Vista. However, you can download a program that will allow you to view Help created in the Windows Help format from the Microsoft website.)

**Figure 1.22**

Check Number What's This?
Answer

> **Check Number**
> Leave the check number blank if you want to print a check.
> Enter a number only if the check has already been written.
> This will ensure that a second check is not written to the
> vendor because Peachtree Accounting will print the word
> "DUPLICATE" on the check. You can enter any number, using
> up to 20 alphanumeric characters.
> If the **Electronic Payment** box is selected for this payment,
> the **Check Number** box will read "Electronic" since there is
> no check number for a payment handled electronically (
> *Peachtree Complete* and *Peachtree Premium Accounting*
> only).

**4** Close the Write Checks window.

## How Do I

Scott then asks if you've discovered the How Do I feature of Peachtree. He finds all of Peachtree's features very useful, but he particularly recommends that you use the How Do I feature as you begin to work with Peachtree. The How Do I feature provides a list of common procedures to accomplish various tasks in the context of where you activate the How Do I menu. Scott offers to demonstrate this feature of Peachtree.

The How Do I menu item appears in the Help menu of every window in Peachtree. The resulting list provides access to various sections of Peachtree Help, including step-by-step procedures and other context-sensitive help.

**To see how the How Do I feature can help you use Peachtree:**

**1** Open the **Customers & Sales** Navigation Center and then click the **Sales Invoices** button and then click **New Sales Invoice**.

**2** Click **Help** from the menu bar and then click **How Do I. . .** to reveal the How Do I: Customers, Sales, and Receipts section of Peachtree Help as shown in Figure 1.23.

**3** Scroll down the help listing shown on the right side of the window until you find the Receipts section. Click **Receive payment from a customer** to reveal Peachtree's description of how to apply a customer payment to an invoice as shown in Figure 1.24.

**Figure 1.23**

How Do I Feature

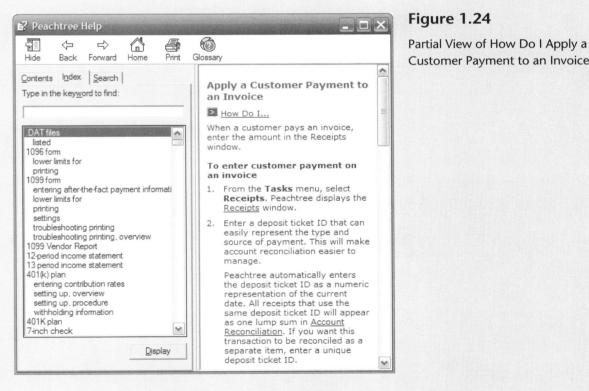

**Figure 1.24**

Partial View of How Do I Apply a Customer Payment to an Invoice

**4**   Close all open windows to return to the Navigation Center.

## Exiting Peachtree

You thank Scott for taking the time to introduce you to Peachtree as he rushes off to yet another meeting. You know you can probably exit Peachtree on your own, using standard Windows commands. You choose to use the Exit command on the File menu.

**To exit Peachtree:**

1    Click **File** on the Peachtree menu bar to display the File menu.

2    Click **Exit**. Good accounting practice encourages backing up data files, but backup is not necessary now with these sample files.

## End Note

Scott has shown you some of the features of Peachtree, how to navigate these features, and how business decisions can be aided by the reporting and analysis of accounting information afforded by Peachtree. You are impressed by the speed at which information is made available and are anxious to learn more.

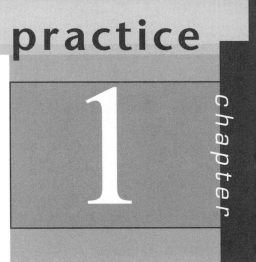
## Chapter 1 Questions

**1** Describe, in your own words, the various uses of Peachtree.

**2** List the five important menus/functions in Peachtree.

**3** Describe the Lists menu/function.

**4** Describe the Maintain menu/function.

**5** Describe the Tasks menu/function.

**6** Describe the Analysis menu/function.

**7** Describe the Reports & Forms menu/function.

**8** Describe the Peachtree desktop and Peachtree Navigation Centers.

**9** Describe the importance of setting the system date.

**10** Describe the How Do I and What's This? help features available in Peachtree.

## Chapter 1 Assignments

**1** *Working with Files and Printing a List*

Use the Century Kitchens file to practice opening, closing, and printing. Be sure to set the System Date to 1/31/11. Change the accounting period to Period 1. Open the Customers & Sales Navigation Center. Click **Print** next to Customer Sales History in the Recently Used Customer Reports section and accept the defaults provided.

*merchandising*

**2** *Practice Using Peachtree Help Features*

Use the Peachtree Help menu to learn more about Peachtree.

a. From the Help menu, select **Peachtree Accounting Help**. Type **Customer List** as the keyword to find, then double-click **Customer List report**, and print this topic.

b. Go to the Inventory & Services Navigation Center. Click the **Purchase Orders** button and then click **New Purchase Order**. Right-click the **Quantity** section and select **What's This?**. Right-click the window that appears and then click **Print Topic. . . .**

c. Open the **Employees & Payroll** Navigation Center, click the **Employees** button, and then click **New Employee**. Click **Help** and then click **How Do I. . .** to reveal the How Do I: Employees and Payroll section of Peachtree Help. Click **Set up an employee**. Click **Print** to print this topic.

**3** *Using the Peachtree Demos*

Navigate your web browser to http://cdn.bestsoftware.com/FTP/ SagePeachtree/SageAdvisorVideos/player.html. Choose a couple of the Getting Started Tutorials videos like "New Company Setup Guide" or "Peachtree Setup Guide" located in the Peachtree Setup folder. Comment on what you liked and what you didn't like about this demonstration created by Sage.

**✗4**    *Accessing Inventory Data*

Scott Montalvo wants to know the amount and nature of inventory on hand as of January 31, 2011. Remember to set the system date to 1/31/11 and the accounting period to Period 1. Open the Inventory & Services Navigation Center. View the Inventory listing on the right-hand side of the window.

a.    What is Item 1003?

b.    How many of this item were on hand on that date?

c.    How many of these units were sold as of that date?

**✗5**    *Accessing Sales Data*

Scott also wants to know the company's sales for the period February 1 through February 28, 2011. Remember to set the system date to 2/28/11 and the accounting period to Period 2. Open the Customers & Sales Navigation Center. View the Customers listing on the right-hand side of the window.

a.    How much did J Wilson owe Century Kitchens?

b.    What is I Bowen's street address?

c.    Use the Collections Manager in the Analysis section to determine how much was owed to Century Kitchens in the 31–60 days outstanding category.

# Preparing a Balance Sheet Using Peachtree

*Learning Objectives*

*In this Chapter, you will:*

- Create and print a standard balance sheet.
- Create a balance sheet with ratios using the Financial Statement Wizard.
- Create a comparative balance sheet using the Design feature.
- Investigate details supporting balance sheet items.

## *Case:* Century Kitchens

It's your second day at your new job, and you arrive early. Scott is already hard at work at the computer. He tells you he is preparing for Century Kitchens' quarter year ending on March 31, 2011. Since this is the first time he will prepare financial statements using Peachtree, he's a little nervous.

You recall from your accounting course that a balance sheet reports the assets, liabilities, and owners' equity of a company at a specific point in time. As part of your continued training on Peachtree, Scott asks you to watch what he does as he prepares the balance sheet. He explains that his immediate goals are to familiarize himself with how to prepare a balance sheet using Peachtree and to examine some of the valuable features Peachtree provides to help managers analyze and interpret financial information.

## Creating and Printing a Balance Sheet

You know from your business courses that the information on a balance sheet can be presented in many ways. Scott tells you that Peachtree provides one preset way to present a balance sheet. However, Peachtree also allows him to

---

**To create and print a Standard Balance Sheet report:**

1  Open Century Kitchens.

2  Set the system date to **3/31/11** and the accounting period to **Period 3**.
   "*Trouble?* Occasionally, when you change system dates or accounting periods, you will be asked if you want to print reports or run an internal accounting review. If this occurs simply click No."

**3**  Click **Reports & Forms** and then click **Financial Statements**.

**4**  Double-click <**Standard**> **Balance Sheet** as shown in Figure 2.1.

**Figure 2.1**

Select a Report or
Form Window

**5**  Be sure the **Print Page Numbers** and **Show Zero Amounts** check boxes
are unchecked.

**6**  Click **OK**. The resulting standard balance sheet is shown in
Figure 2.2.

**Figure 2.2**

Peachtree's Standard Balance
Sheet for Century Kitchens

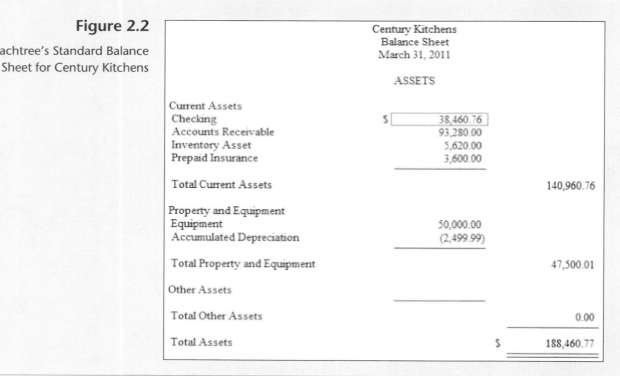

**Figure 2.2**

Continued

```
                        LIABILITIES AND CAPITAL

Current Liabilities
   Accounts Payable                    $        27,270.00
   Payroll Liabilities                            13,536.03
                                               _____

   Total Current Liabilities                                        40,806.03

Long-Term Liabilities
                                               _____

   Total Long-Term Liabilities                                          0.00
                                                               _____

   Total Liabilities                                               40,806.03

Capital
   Common Stock                                125,000.00
   Net Income                                   22,654.74
                                               _____

   Total Capital                                                  147,654.74
                                                               _____

   Total Liabilities & Capital          $       188,460.77
                                                               ═══════════
```

**7**  Click the **Print** button on the report button bar.

**8**  Click **OK** to print your report.

**9**  Click **Close** to close the <Standard> Balance Sheet window.

**10**  Click **Close** to close the **Select a Report or Form** window.

customize the way he presents the information. He decides to examine the preset balance sheet first. He chooses what Peachtree calls the Standard Balance Sheet report.

"Why did Peachtree create the March balance sheet and not the January or February balance sheet?" you ask.

"Peachtree initially creates a balance sheet for the period you've specified," Scott answers. "Remember, one of our first steps was to specify the accounting period as Period 3. If you wanted to create a balance sheet for the end of February, you would have selected Period 2."

Scott is amazed at how rapidly Peachtree created this balance sheet compared to how long it's taken him to create one manually in the past. As you both look over this balance sheet, Scott comments that because he generated this information so quickly with so little effort he might now be able to add information to balance sheets that he didn't have time to include before. For example, he has always wanted to include ratio information on balance sheets to help him make better business decisions.

## Creating Balance Sheets with Ratios Using the Financial Statement Wizard

By using the Help function of Peachtree, Scott discovered how easy it is to create a balance sheet that shows a ratio column. He learns that he can either use Peachtree's Financial Statement Wizard or modify the existing balance sheet with Peachtree's Design feature. He decides to use the Wizard this time to add a ratio column. The ratio column will divide each line item on the balance sheet like cash, accounts receivable, inventory, etc. by total assets. This ratio column on a balance sheet is commonly referred to as a common-sized balance sheet.

## To create a balance sheet with a ratio column using the Financial Statement Wizard:

**1**   Click **Reports & Forms** and then click **Financial Statements**.

**2**   Click the **Financial Statement Wizard** button and then click **Next**.

**3**   Select <**Standard**> **Balance Sheet** from the drop-down list of Financial Statement templates.

**4**   Type **Common-Sized Balance Sheet** as the name of the newly created financial statement. Your screen should look like Figure 2.3.

**Figure 2.3**

Financial Statement Wizard

**5**   Click **Next** three times to accept the default information.

**6**   Select **Ratio** from the Contents column 3 section drop-down list.

**7**   Select **Column 2** from the Use Column drop-down list. Your screen should look like Figure 2.4.

**Figure 2.4**

Financial Statement Wizard
Column Properties

"What is meant by the term *balance* when it appears in the contents section of a column properties window?" you ask.

"This type of column displays the balance amount—net, budget, credit, or debit—of the accounts appearing on the statement," Scott responds. "Peachtree used net since it wanted the net debit/credit balance shown for each balance sheet account."

**8**  Click the **Account Range** button. Choose from account **1100** to account **1890** as the range of accounts in the ratio and then press [Tab] as shown in Figure 2.5 since you want to include the total of all asset accounts.

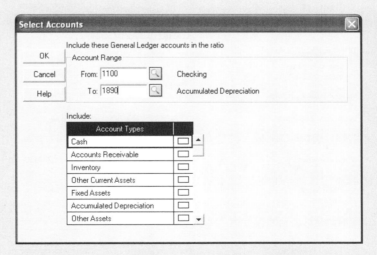

**Figure 2.5**

Financial Statement Wizard Select
Accounts

9   Click **OK** to accept this range of accounts for the denominator of the ratio.

10  Click **Next** four more times to select the defaults provided.

11  Choose the **Display your new financial statement** option button and then click **Finish**.

12  Make sure the **Print Page Numbers** and **Show Zero Amounts** check boxes are unchecked and then click **OK**. The resulting balance sheet is shown in Figure 2.6.

**Figure 2.6**

Asset Section of the Balance Sheet with a Ratio Column

Century Kitchens
Balance Sheet
March 31, 2011

ASSETS

| | | | |
|---|---|---|---|
| Current Assets | | | |
| Checking | $    38,460.76 | | 20.41 |
| Accounts Receivable | 93,280.00 | | 49.50 |
| Inventory Asset | 5,620.00 | | 2.98 |
| Prepaid Insurance | 3,600.00 | | 1.91 |
| Total Current Assets | | 140,960.76 | 74.80 |
| Property and Equipment | | | |
| Equipment | 50,000.00 | | 26.53 |
| Accumulated Depreciation | (2,499.99) | | (1.33) |
| Total Property and Equipment | | 47,500.01 | 25.20 |
| Other Assets | | | |
| Total Other Assets | | 0.00 | 0.00 |
| Total Assets | | $    188,460.77 | 100.00 |

LIABILITIES AND CAPITAL

| | | | |
|---|---|---|---|
| Current Liabilities | | | |
| Accounts Payable | $    27,270.00 | | 14.47 |
| Payroll Liabilities | 13,536.03 | | 7.18 |
| Total Current Liabilities | | 40,806.03 | 21.65 |
| Long-Term Liabilities | | | |
| Total Long-Term Liabilities | | 0.00 | 0.00 |
| Total Liabilities | | 40,806.03 | 21.65 |
| Capital | | | |
| Common Stock | 125,000.00 | | 66.33 |
| Net Income | 22,654.74 | | 12.02 |
| Total Capital | | 147,654.74 | 78.35 |
| Total Liabilities & Capital | | $    188,460.77 | 100.00 |

13  Close the **Just created report** and **Select a Report or Form** windows.

# Creating a Balance Sheet with Peachtree's Design Feature

Scott wonders if Peachtree has a preset report that compares balance sheet information—in other words, one that provides ending balances for several months. Such a comparison in annual reports is useful to external financial statement users who are usually interested in how accounts change over time. Scott again consults Help and learns that there is no preset report but that he can create one using Peachtree's Design Feature. He decides to introduce you to the Design Feature by creating comparative balance sheets for the months of January, February, and March. Peachtree does not have a preset report like that. Alternatively, he has learned that instead of using the Financial Statement Report Wizard, he can modify an existing report using the Design feature of Peachtree and customize his report even more.

*Video Demonstration*

*Demo 2 - Creating a balance sheet with the design feature*

---

**To create a comparative balance sheet report using the Design feature of Peachtree:**

**1** Click **Reports & Forms** and then click **Financial Statements**. (*Note:* Your recently created common-sized balance sheet is now a part of the financial statement list.)

**2** Double-click <**Standard**> **Balance Sheet** from the drop-down list of Financial Statement templates.

**3** Select **Current 3 Periods** from the Time Frame drop-down list and then click **OK**.

**4** Click **Design** from the Report button bar.

**5** The design view of the standard balance sheet, shown in Figure 2.7, presents the top of the report.

**Click here to save changes**

**Click here to preview the resulting financial statement**

**Click here to enter the Design mode**

**Figure 2.7**

Design View of a Report

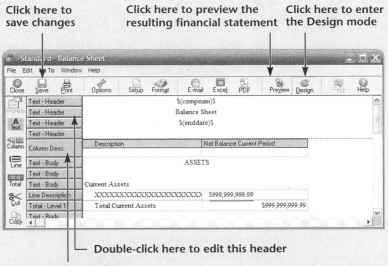

**Double-click here to edit this header**

**Double-click here to edit what appears in columns**

**6** Double-click the second **Text – Header** button and type **Comparative Balance Sheets** as the name of your new financial statement instead of Balance Sheet as shown in Figure 2.8 and then click **OK**.

**Figure 2.8**

Modifying a Text Header

Delete old text and then type new header here

**7** Double-click the third **Text – Header** button and replace the current text by typing **For the Month Ended** and then click **OK**.

**8** Double-click the **Column Desc.** button.

**9** Add column 3 by clicking on the third line below the Column heading; then enter the boldface information where indicated: Contents = **Balance**, Title = **$(EndDate 2)$**, Width = **18**, Format/$ = ✓ (checked), Align Title = **Center of Column**, Qualifier = **Net**, Time Frame = **Current Period – 2**, Round = **Whole Dollars**, Alignment Options: **Data and Totals aligned**. (*Hint:* Be sure to place a space after EndDate and before 2.) Finally, make sure the **Print** check boxes to the left of the column numbers are checked. The resulting window is shown in Figure 2.9.

**Figure 2.9**

Modifying Column Descriptions

This is a special code reflecting the end of the period date – 2 months prior to the current period

Select Current – 2 which means back 2 months from the current period (Make sure you have already set the current period = Period 3 on the navigation (desktop) page, as instructed earlier)

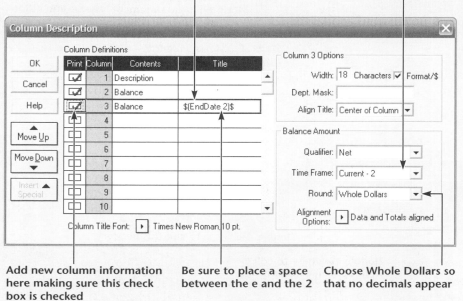

Add new column information here making sure this check box is checked

Be sure to place a space between the e and the 2

Choose Whole Dollars so that no decimals appear

"What did you mean by selecting Current – 2 in the Time Frame section of the Balance Amount section of the Column Properties window?" you ask.

"The Time Frame section specifies what accounting period data you want in this column relative to the current period," Scott comments. "For example, since we specified Period 3 before we started this exercise, Peachtree knows that is our current period, in this case March 11. Thus, in a separate column, we told Peachtree to place balances in one column two periods before Period 3, or Period 1 (January 11). Thus, Current – 2 means two periods before the current period."

**10** Add column 4 with Contents = **Balance**, Title = **$(EndDate 1)$**, Width = **18**, Format/$ = **Yes** (checked), Align Title = **Center of Column**, Qualifier = **Net**, Time Frame = **Current Period – 1**, Round = **Whole Dollars**, Alignment Options: **Data and Totals aligned**. Finally, make sure the **Print** check box is checked.

**11** Set Title = **$(EndDate)$** as the title of column 2, set Width = **18**, set Round = **Whole Dollars**, Alignment Options: **Data and Totals aligned**.

**12** Select column 2 and then click the **Move Down** button twice so that it ends up at column 4. Modify your screen to look like Figure 2.10.

Check this checkbox to format this column with $

Once you select a column click Move Up or Move Down to reorient the columns

**Figure 2.10**

Further Modification of Column Descriptions

"What do $(EndDate)$ and $(EndDate 1)$ mean?" you ask.

"$(EndDate)$ and $(EndDate 1)$ are special codes that can be inserted in Peachtree reports," Scott answers. "The $ signs bookend special data fields that are used to put information on reports depending on the accounting period selected. In this case, the special data field

EndDate means the last day of the current accounting period. In our current case, that would be March 31, 2011, since we've selected to be in accounting period 3. The data field EndDate 1 means the last day of the previous accounting period. In our current case, that would be February 28, 2011."

"Would EndDate 2 translate to January 31, 2011?" you ask.

"Exactly," Scott responds.

**13**   Click **OK**.

**14**   Double-click the text body button for ASSETS (which is just below the Column Desc. button) and change the alignment to **Left of Column** and then click **OK**.

**15**   Double-click the text body button for LIABILITIES AND CAPITAL and change the alignment to **Left of Column** and then click **OK**.

**16**   Click the **Preview** button from the button bar and then after making sure the **Print Page Numbers** and **Show Zero Amounts** check boxes are unchecked, click **OK**. The asset portion of the new balance sheet should look like Figure 2.11. (*Note:* The statement heading position moves when the screen is resized so your heading may not be in the same position as that shown in the figures.)

**Figure 2.11**

New Balance Sheet for Century Kitchens

| | | Century Kitchens<br>Comparative Balance Sheets<br>For the Month Ended | | | |
|---|---|---|---|---|---|
| | | January 31, 2011 | February 28, 2011 | | March 31, 2011 |
| ASSETS | | | | | |
| Current Assets | | | | | |
| Checking | $ | 48,329 | $ 43,064 | $ | 38,461 |
| Accounts Receivable | | 36,795 | 68,750 | | 93,280 |
| Inventory Asset | | 0 | 0 | | 5,620 |
| Prepaid Insurance | | 0 | 4,000 | | 3,600 |
| Total Current Assets | | 85,124 | 115,814 | | 140,961 |
| Property and Equipment | | | | | |
| Equipment | | 50,000 | 50,000 | | 50,000 |
| Accumulated Depreciation | | (833) | (1,667) | | (2,500) |
| Total Property and Equipment | | 49,167 | 48,333 | | 47,500 |
| Other Assets | | | | | |
| Total Other Assets | | 0 | 0 | | 0 |
| Total Assets | $ | 134,291 | $ 164,147 | $ | 188,461 |

**Century Kitchens**
**Comparative Balance Sheets**
**For the Month Ended**

| | | January 31, 2011 | | February 28, 2011 | | March 31, 2011 |
|---|---|---|---|---|---|---|
| LIABILITIES AND CAPITAL | | | | | | |
| Current Liabilities | | | | | | |
| Accounts Payable | $ | 0 | $ | 14,220 | $ | 27,270 |
| Payroll Liabilities | | 4,911 | | 9,191 | | 13,536 |
| Total Current Liabilities | | 4,911 | | 23,411 | | 40,806 |
| Long-Term Liabilities | | | | | | |
| Total Long-Term Liabilities | | 0 | | 0 | | 0 |
| Total Liabilities | | 4,911 | | 23,411 | | 40,806 |
| Capital | | | | | | |
| Common Stock | | 125,000 | | 125,000 | | 125,000 |
| Net Income | | 4,381 | | 15,736 | | 22,655 |
| Total Capital | | 129,381 | | 140,736 | | 147,655 |
| Total Liabilities & Capital | $ | 134,292 | $ | 164,147 | $ | 188,461 |

**Figure 2.11**

Continued

**17**  Click **Save** to save your changes.

**18**  Type **Comparative Balance Sheets** as the name of your newly created financial statement. Replace the existing description with the one shown in Figure 2.12.

**Type new name here**

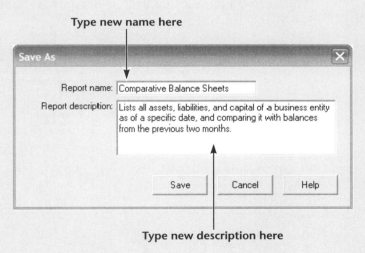

**Type new description here**

**Figure 2.12**

Saving Your New Financial Statement Design

**19**  Click **Save**.

**20**  Close all windows.

## Investigating the Balance Sheet

Now that Scott knows he can generate the types of reports he wants, he decides to drill down to the underlying general ledger report that supports each financial statement he creates. You know that this is a helpful feature because managers often need to be able to quickly explain report balances; thus, knowledge of the underlying detailed transactions is essential. Scott decides to practice drilling down by analyzing the transactions that make up the accounts receivable balance.

### To investigate accounts receivable:

1   Click **Reports & Forms** and then click **Financial Statements**.

2   Double-click <**Standard**> **Balance Sheet** from the drop-down list of Financial Statement templates.

3   Select **Current 3 Periods** from the Time Frame drop-down list and then click **OK**.

4   Place the cursor over the Accounts Receivable balance of 93,280.00. A cursor shaped like a magnifying glass and containing a "Z" appears. This cursor indicates that drilling down is available for this amount. See Figure 2.13.

**Figure 2.13**

Drilling Down

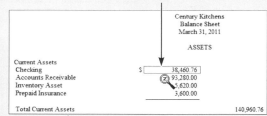

When you click on this amount a box surrounds the amount. This indicates it is available for the drill down process

Double-click to view the general ledger report that supports this amount

5   Double-click the amount **93,280.00**. The general ledger report for account 1200 (Accounts Receivable) appears but lists only one month's transactions. That's because this report is showing only the events that took place during Period 3 (March). See Figure 2.14.

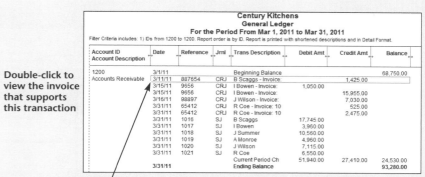

**Figure 2.14**

General Ledger Report for Account 1200

**6** Double-click invoice **1016** to examine one of the actual invoices that increased accounts receivable during March. This is referred to, in general, as a support document. See Figure 2.15.

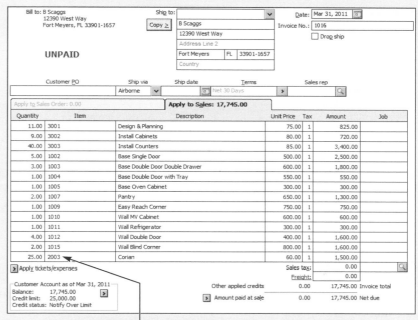

**Figure 2.15**

Invoice 1016

**7** Close the Sales/Invoicing window. The general ledger report, which was hidden while you examined invoice 1016, reappears.

**8** Double-click anywhere on the row containing the payment for **$2,475** made by R Coe and posted 3/31/11. A Receipts window appears. See Figure 2.16. Note that this payment was a payment on account for $3,000 and was applied to invoices 1002 and 1005.

**Figure 2.16**

Customer Payment Received from
R Coe on 3/31/2011

**9** Close all windows.

## End Note

Scott is pleased with the drill-down capability of Peachtree because it allows him to quickly and easily investigate any of the balances reported. He's seen that accounts receivable is supported by the general ledger report for that account and that accounts receivable are affected by the sales journal (SJ) and related sales invoice source documents and by the cash receipts journal (CRJ) and related cash receipts source documents. He explains to you that only those items shown with a box around them are available for the drill-down process. He feels much more confident about using Peachtree. You are quickly becoming more comfortable with Peachtree as well.

In the next chapter, you will expand your Peachtree knowledge to include the creation, modification, and printing of another useful financial statement—the income statement.

## Chapter 2 Questions

**1** How many preset ways does Peachtree provide for a balance sheet?

**2** What alternatives exist for creating a customized balance sheet or any other financial statement for that matter?

**3** List the steps you would take to create a balance sheet for a different accounting period than currently indicated.

**4** What does *balance* mean when defining the contents of a column?

**5** How do you enter the Design mode to modify a current financial statement?

**6** How do you edit what appears in the columns for any financial statement?

**7** How do you force amounts in a column to be rounded to whole dollars?

**8** What is meant by Current – 2 in the column properties Balance Amount section? Explain.

**9** What is meant by *drill down*?

**10** Identify two source documents that might be found when drilling down accounts receivable.

## Chapter 2 Assignments

**1** *Prepare and print the following reports using the Century Kitchens Peachtree files. Set the current accounting period to **Period 2**. (Place your name in the footer of each report. To do so, scroll to the bottom of any report in Design mode, double-click the **Text – Footer**, type your name, and click OK. This will help you locate your report as opposed to any other student's report when using computer labs. After you add your name in the footer you'll be prompted to provide a revised name for the report. Simply add a number to the end of the standard report name like Standard Balance Sheet 1 unless otherwise directed.)*

*merchandising*

a. A standard balance sheet as of the current period.

b. Modify the standard balance sheet using Peachtree's Design feature to create a balance sheet comparing balances for the previous period and the current period exactly as you did in the chapter except with just two months. Save it as **Comparative Balance Sheets 2**. (*Hint:* Set the system date to 2/28/11 and the period to Period 2.) The asset portion of the new balance sheet should look like Figure 2.17.

c. Modify the balance sheet you just created in (b) using Peachtree's Design feature to create a balance sheet comparing balances at 1/31/11 and 2/28/11 with a ratio column for each month. Save it as **Comparative Balance Sheets 3**. The asset portion of the new balance sheet should look like Figure 2.18.

## Figure 2.17

### Comparative Balance Sheet

| | Century Kitchens Comparative Balance Sheets For the Month Ended | | |
|---|---|---|---|
| ASSETS | January 31, 2011 | | February 28, 2011 |
| **Current Assets** | | | |
| Checking | $ | 48,329 | $ 43,064 |
| Accounts Receivable | | 36,795 | 68,750 |
| Prepaid Insurance | | 0 | 4,000 |
| Total Current Assets | | 85,124 | 115,814 |
| **Property and Equipment** | | | |
| Equipment | | 50,000 | 50,000 |
| Accumulated Depreciation | | (833) | (1,667) |
| Total Property and Equipment | | 49,167 | 48,333 |
| **Other Assets** | | | |
| Total Other Assets | | 0 | 0 |
| Total Assets | $ | 134,291 | $ 164,147 |

## Figure 2.18

### Comparative Balance Sheet with Ratios

| | Century Kitchens Comparative Balance Sheets For the Month Ended | | | | |
|---|---|---|---|---|---|
| ASSETS | January 31, 2011 | | | February 28, 2011 | |
| **Current Assets** | | | | | |
| Checking | $ | 48,329 | 35.99 | $ 43,064 | 26.24 |
| Accounts Receivable | | 36,795 | 27.40 | 68,750 | 41.88 |
| Prepaid Insurance | | 0 | 0.00 | 4,000 | 2.44 |
| Total Current Assets | | 85,124 | 63.39 | 115,814 | 70.56 |
| **Property and Equipment** | | | | | |
| Equipment | | 50,000 | 37.23 | 50,000 | 30.46 |
| Accumulated Depreciation | | (833) | (0.62) | (1,667) | (1.02) |
| Total Property and Equipment | | 49,167 | 36.61 | 48,333 | 29.44 |
| **Other Assets** | | | | | |
| Total Other Assets | | 0 | 0.00 | 0 | 0.00 |
| Total Assets | $ | 134,291 | 100.00 | $ 164,147 | 100.00 |

d. A general ledger report of those transactions recorded in February 2011 that affected accounts receivable.

e. A general ledger report of those transactions recorded in February 2011 that affected accounts payable.

**2** *Answer the following questions using the Century Kitchens Peachtree files.*

  a. Drill down from the accounts receivable balance due at 2/28/11. Locate invoice 1008. What did Century Kitchens sell on the first line of this invoice? Whom is it billing? What was the total invoice amount?

  b. Drill down from the accounts receivable balance due at 2/28/11. Locate the $10,000 payment received on 2/5/11. From whom was the payment received? What invoice number was the payment applied to?

  c. Drill down from the accounts payable balance owed at 2/28/11. Locate a bill dated 2/16/11 from Thomasville Cabinets. What is the first item listed on the bill? What was the total cost for this item?

  d. Drill down from the accounts payable payments made on 2/28/11. Who was the payee? What invoice of the payee's is being paid?

## Chapter 2 Cases

### Chapter 2 Case Problem 1

## KELLY JENNINGS ADVERTISING

*service*

Kelly Jennings has just started working full time in her new business—an advertising agency named Kelly Jennings Advertising located in San Martin, California. Like many eager entrepreneurs, she started her business while working full time for another firm. At first, her billings were quite small. But as her client base and billings grew, she decided to leave her job and set out on her own. Two of her colleagues and friends—Cheryl Boudreau and Diane Murphy—see Kelly's eagerness and dedication and decide the time is right for them, too. Kelly agrees to have them join her sole proprietorship as employees, and so together they leave the traditional corporate agency environment.

Kelly set up an accounting system for her business using Peachtree and has recorded beginning balances as of 12/31/08 and transactions for the months of January and February with help from an accounting friend. She has just received a request from her banker to submit a balance sheet as documentation for a business loan.

**1** *Prepare and print the following reports using Kelly Jennings Advertising Peachtree files. Set the period to* **Period 2** *and the system date to* **2/29/08.** *(Remember, you'll need to restore this file from your Data Files CD. Also be sure to place your name in the footer of each report. To do so, scroll to the bottom of any report in Design mode, double-click the* **Text – Footer** *and then type your name. This will help you locate your report as opposed to any other student's report when using computer labs. After you add your name in the footer you'll be prompted to provide a revised name for the report. Simply add a number to the end of the standard report name like* **Standard Balance Sheet 1** *unless otherwise directed.)*

a. A standard balance sheet as of the current period.

b. Use the Financial Statement Wizard to create a balance sheet with ratios as you did in the chapter as of the current period. Save it as **Balance Sheet with Ratios**.

c. Modify the standard balance sheet using Peachtree's Design feature to create a balance sheet comparing balances at the current and previous month exactly as you did in the chapter except with just two months. Save it as **Comparative Balance Sheets**.

d. A general ledger report of those transactions recorded in January 2008 that affected accounts receivable. (*Hint:* You need to be in Period 1.)

e. A general ledger report of those transactions recorded in February 2008 that affected accounts payable. (*Hint:* You need to be in Period 2.)

**2**  *Answer the following questions:*

a. Drill down from the accounts receivable balance due at 1/31/08. Locate invoice 3. What did Kelly Jennings Advertising sell on this invoice? Whom is it billing? What was the total invoice amount?

b. Drill down from the accounts receivable balance due at 1/31/08. Locate the $600 payment received on 1/29/08. The payment was applied to what invoice?

c. Drill down from the accounts payable balance owed at 2/29/08. Locate a bill dated 2/19/08 from Rex's Film Supply. What did Kelly Jennings Advertising purchase on this bill? What was the total cost?

d. Drill down from the accounts payable balance owed at 2/29/08. Locate a payment made on check 1003 for $150. The payment was applied to what invoice?

## Chapter 2 Case Problem 2

# SIERRA MARINA

Meagan Casey is the sole proprietor and owner of Sierra Marina, located at the north end of Shaver Lake in the California Sierra Mountains. She has been in business for a few years and decided on July 1, 2010, to automate her accounting using Peachtree. Meagan has already entered the June 30, 2010 ending balances from her previous accounting system as well as all transactions for July and August 2010, and she has asked you to help her prepare some basic financial reports related to the company's assets, liabilities, and equities.

**1**  *Prepare and print the following reports using Meagan's Sierra Marina Peachtree file. Set the period to Period 1 and the system date to 7/31/2010. (Remember, you'll need to restore this file from your Data Files CD. Also be sure to place your name in the footer of each report. To do so, scroll to the bottom of any report in Design mode, double-click the* Text – Footer *and then type your name. This will help you locate your report as opposed* *to any other student's report when using computer labs. After you add your name in the footer you'll be prompted to provide a revised name for the report. Simply add a number to the end of the standard report name like Standard Balance Sheet 1 unless otherwise directed.)*

   a.   A standard balance sheet as of the current period.

   b.   Use the Financial Statement Wizard to create a balance sheet with ratios as you did in the chapter as of the current period. Save it as Balance Sheet with Ratios.

   c.   A general ledger report of those transactions recorded in July 2010 that affected accounts receivable.

   d.   A general ledger report of those transactions recorded in July 2010 that affected accounts payable.

**2**   *Answer the following questions:*

   a.   Drill down from the accounts receivable balance due at 7/31/10. Locate invoice 3. Who is the customer? What item numbers were billed to this customer? What amount was paid at the sale?

   b.   Drill down from the accounts receivable balance due at 7/31/10. Locate a cash receipt on 7/30/10. Who is the customer making payment? What is this payment for?

   c.   Drill down from the accounts payable balance owed at 7/31/10. Locate a bill dated 7/26/10 from Fresno Bee. What did Sierra Marina purchase on this bill? What was the total cost?

## Chapter 2 Case Problem 3

# JASON GALAS, ATTORNEY AT LAW, PC

Jason Galas has a well-deserved reputation as a leader in innovative and cutting-edge corporate tax planning with over 20 years of experience. His firm's diverse practice extends beyond ordinary tax issues. Jason decided to automate his accounting using Peachtree. His bookkeeper has already entered the December 31, 2011 ending balances from the previous manual accounting system as well as all transactions for January and February 2012, and they have asked you to help them prepare some basic financial reports related to the company's assets, liabilities, and equities.

**1**   *Prepare and print the following reports using the Jason Galas, Attorney at Law, PC Peachtree file. Set the period to Period 1 and the system date to 1/31/12. (Remember, you'll need to restore this file from your Data Files CD. Also be sure to place your name in the footer of each report. To do so, scroll to the bottom of any report in Design mode, double-click the* **Text – Footer** *and then type your name. This will help you locate your report as opposed to any other student's report when using computer labs. After you add your name in the footer you'll be prompted to provide a revised name for the report. Simply add a number to the end of the standard report name like Standard Balance Sheet 1 unless otherwise directed.)*

    a.    A standard balance sheet as of 1/31/12.

    b.    Use the Financial Statement Wizard to create a balance sheet with ratios as you did in the chapter as of 1/31/12. Save it as Balance Sheet with Ratios.

    c.    A general ledger report of those transactions recorded in January 2012 that affected client fees receivable.

    d.    A general ledger report of those transactions recorded in January 2012 that affected accounts payable.

**2**    *Answer the following questions:*

    a.    Drill down from the accounts receivable balance due at 1/31/12. Locate invoice 563. Who is the client? What items were billed to this client?

    b.    Drill down from the accounts receivable balance due at 1/31/12. Locate a cash receipt on 1/27/12. Who is the client making the payment? What is this payment for?

    c.    Drill down from the accounts payable balance owed at 1/31/12. Locate a bill dated 1/26/12 from Randol Leasing. What is this bill for? What is the amount due?

# Preparing an Income Statement and Statement of Retained Earnings Using Peachtree

**3**

*In this Chapter, you will:*

- Create and print a standard income statement and statement of retained earnings.
- Create an income statement without ratios and year-to-date information using the Financial Statement Wizard.
- Create a comparative income statement using the Design feature.
- Investigate details supporting income statement items.

## *Case:* Century Kitchens

Now that Scott has created a balance sheet, he is ready to create an income statement and a statement of retained earnings for the period January 1, 2011, through March 31, 2011. You may recall from your accounting course that the income statement reports revenues and expenses for a specific period and that the statement of retained earnings reports beginning retained earnings plus net income less dividends, equaling ending retained earnings for a period.

Again, as part of your training with Peachtree, Scott asks you to watch how he prepares the income statement. He expects to use many of the same functions and features to prepare an income statement that he used to prepare the balance sheet.

## Creating an Income Statement and a Statement of Retained Earnings

The income statement can be presented in four preset ways and can be customized. Scott decides to examine one of the preset income statement formats first—the format called Standard Income Stmnt (Statement).

## To create a standard income statement:

**1**  Open Century Kitchens.

**2**  Set the system date to **3/31/11** and the accounting period to **Period 3**.

**3**  Click **Reports & Forms** and then click **Financial Statements**.

**4**  Double-click <**Standard**>**Income Stmnt**.

**5**  Be sure the **Print Page Numbers** and **Show Zero Amounts** check boxes are unchecked.

**6**  Click **OK**. The resulting standard income statement is shown in Figure 3.1.

**Figure 3.1**

Income Statement for the Three Months Ending March 31, 2011

Century Kitchens
Income Statement
For the Three Months Ending March 31, 2011

| | Current Month | | | Year to Date | |
|---|---|---|---|---|---|
| **Revenues** | | | | | |
| Counter Top | $ 13,035.00 | 25.61 | $ | 13,035.00 | 9.19 |
| Cabinets | 19,300.00 | 37.92 | | 60,950.00 | 42.97 |
| Installation | 17,730.00 | 34.84 | | 46,930.00 | 33.09 |
| Design and Planning | 825.00 | 1.62 | | 20,925.00 | 14.75 |
| Total Revenues | 50,890.00 | 100.00 | | 141,840.00 | 100.00 |
| **Cost of Sales** | | | | | |
| Cost of Goods Sold | 24,575.00 | 48.29 | | 58,135.00 | 40.99 |
| Total Cost of Sales | 24,575.00 | 48.29 | | 58,135.00 | 40.99 |
| Gross Profit | 26,315.00 | 51.71 | | 83,705.00 | 59.01 |
| **Expenses** | | | | | |
| Building Supplies | 690.00 | 1.36 | | 1,530.00 | 1.08 |
| Depreciation Expense | 833.33 | 1.64 | | 2,499.99 | 1.76 |
| Insurance | 400.00 | 0.79 | | 1,200.00 | 0.85 |
| Rent | 3,500.00 | 6.88 | | 10,500.00 | 7.40 |
| Gas and Electric | 375.00 | 0.74 | | 915.00 | 0.65 |
| Payroll Expenses | 13,598.00 | 26.72 | | 44,405.27 | 31.31 |
| Total Expenses | 19,396.33 | 38.11 | | 61,050.26 | 43.04 |
| Net Income | $ 6,918.67 | 13.60 | $ | 22,654.74 | 15.97 |

**7**  Close all open windows.

Scott comments that this version of the standard income statement presents the current period, which he defined as Period 3 (3/1/11–3/31/11), and a year-to-date column showing income statement data from January 1, 2011, through March 31, 2011. It also shows ratio information commonly referred to as a common-sized income statement. Each ratio item is that line item divided by sales.

"What are the other preset income statements?" you ask.

"Well, there is the income 2 yrs. (years) statement, which shows comparative information between the current month and the same month in the previous fiscal year," he answers. "Then there is the income/budget statement, which compares actual income statement data for the current month and year to date with budget amounts and computes a variance. Finally, the income/earnings statement adds retained earnings information to the standard income statement we just prepared."

Scott explains that since we don't yet have budget information entered into Peachtree and we don't have prior-year data to compare to, it makes no sense to prepare those statements right now. Instead, he suggests you create the income/earnings preset income statement.

---

### To create and print a standard income/earnings income statement:

1 Open Century Kitchens.

2 Set the system date to **3/31/11** and the accounting period to **Period 3**.

3 Click **Reports & Forms** and then click **Financial Statements**.

4 Double-click **<Standard>Income/Earnings**.

5 Be sure the **Print Page Numbers** and **Show Zero Amounts** check boxes are unchecked.

6 Click **OK**. The resulting combined income and retained earnings statement is shown in Figure 3.2.

Century Kitchens
Statement of Income and Retained Earnings
For the Three Months Ending March 31, 2011

| | Current Month | | Year to Date | |
|---|---|---|---|---|
| **Revenues** | | | | |
| Counter Top | 13,035.00 | 25.61 | 13,035.00 | 9.19 |
| Cabinets | 19,300.00 | 37.92 | 60,950.00 | 42.97 |
| Installation | 17,730.00 | 34.84 | 46,930.00 | 33.09 |
| Design and Planning | 825.00 | 1.62 | 20,925.00 | 14.75 |
| **Total Revenues** | 50,890.00 | 100.00 | 141,840.00 | 100.00 |
| **Cost of Sales** | | | | |
| Cost of Goods Sold | 24,575.00 | 48.29 | 58,135.00 | 40.99 |
| **Total Cost of Sales** | 24,575.00 | 48.29 | 58,135.00 | 40.99 |
| **Gross Profit** | 26,315.00 | 51.71 | 83,705.00 | 59.01 |
| **Expenses** | | | | |
| Building Supplies | 690.00 | 1.36 | 1,530.00 | 1.08 |
| Depreciation Expense | 833.33 | 1.64 | 2,499.99 | 1.76 |
| Insurance | 400.00 | 0.79 | 1,200.00 | 0.85 |
| Rent | 3,500.00 | 6.88 | 10,500.00 | 7.40 |
| Gas and Electric | 375.00 | 0.74 | 915.00 | 0.65 |
| Payroll Expenses | 13,598.00 | 26.72 | 44,405.27 | 31.31 |
| **Total Expenses** | 19,396.33 | 38.11 | 61,050.26 | 43.04 |
| **Net Income** | 6,918.67 | 13.60 | 22,654.74 | 15.97 |
| Beginning Retained Earnings | 15,736.07 | | 0.00 | |
| Adjustments To Date | 0.00 | | 0.00 | |
| **Ending Retained Earnings** | $ 22,654.74 | | 22,654.74 | |

**Figure 3.2**

Income and Retained Earnings Statement for the Three Months Ending March 31, 2011

7 Click **Print** from the button bar and then click **OK** to print this report. Close all open windows.

Scott comments that preparing a statement of retained earnings by itself is just as easy.

**To create a standard retained earnings statement:**

1 Open Century Kitchens.

2 Set the system date to **3/31/11** and the accounting period to **Period 3**.

3 Click **Report & Forms** and then click **Financial Statements**.

4 Double-click <**Standard**> **Retained Earnings**.

5 Be sure the **Print Page Numbers** and **Show Zero Amounts** check boxes are unchecked.

6 Click **OK**. The resulting retained earnings statement is shown in Figure 3.3.

**Figure 3.3**

Retained Earnings Statement for the Three Months Ending March 31, 2011

| Century Kitchens | | |
| --- | --- | --- |
| Statement of Retained Earnings | | |
| For the Three Months Ending March 31, 2011 | | |
| Beginning Retained Earnings | $ | 0.00 |
| Adjustments To Date | | 0.00 |
| Net Income | | 22,654.74 |
| Subtotal | | 22,654.74 |
| Ending Retained Earnings | $ | 22,654.74 |

7 Click **Print** from the button bar and then click **OK** to print this report. Close all open windows.

"What if we wanted an income statement without those ratios and year-to-date information?" you ask.

"We would have to create one using Peachtree's Financial Statement Wizard or Design feature. I'll have you create a basic income statement like that using Peachtree's Financial Statement Wizard," Scott answers.

## Creating a Basic Income Statement Using the Financial Statement Wizard

Previously, Scott had discovered how easy it was to create a balance sheet that showed a ratio column. He learned that he could either use Peachtree's Financial Statement Wizard or modify the existing balance sheet with Peachtree's

Design feature. He decides to use the Wizard this time to create an income statement without ratios and without a year-to-date column.

## To create and print a basic income statement using the Financial Statement Wizard:

1  Open Century Kitchens.

2  Set the system date to **3/31/11** and the accounting period to **Period 3**.

3  Click **Reports & Forms** and then click **Financial Statements**.

4  Click the **Financial Statement Wizard** link and then click **Next**.

5  Select <**Standard**> **Income Stmnt** from the drop-down list of Financial Statement templates.

6  Type **Basic Income Statement** as the name of the newly created financial statement and change the description as shown in Figure 3.4.

**Figure 3.4**

Financial Statement Wizard

7  Click **Next**, delete the existing Header 3, and type **For the Month Ending $(enddate)$** as Header 3 instead. (The $ tells Peachtree that the text in between them is a special data field. Be sure to type this exactly. More on special data fields later.)

8  Click **Next** two times to accept the default information.

9  Delete all titles except Current Month for column 2.

10  Select <**Not Used**> from the Contents column 3, 4, and 5 section drop-down lists. Your screen should look like Figure 3.5.

**Figure 3.5**

Column Properties

11  Click **Next** three times to accept the defaults provided.

12  Uncheck the **Print Page Numbers** and **Show Zero Amounts** check boxes.

13  Click **Next**, click **Finish**, and then click **OK** to view your new income statement as shown in Figure 3.6.

**Figure 3.6**

Basic Income Statement

Century Kitchens
Income Statement
For the Month Ending March 31, 2011

|  | Current Month |
|---|---|
| Revenues | |
| Counter Top | $ 13,035.00 |
| Cabinets | 19,300.00 |
| Installation | 17,730.00 |
| Design and Planning | 825.00 |
| | |
| Total Revenues | 50,890.00 |
| | |
| Cost of Sales | |
| Cost of Goods Sold | 24,575.00 |
| | |
| Total Cost of Sales | 24,575.00 |
| | |
| Gross Profit | 26,315.00 |
| | |
| Expenses | |
| Building Supplies | 690.00 |
| Depreciation Expense | 833.33 |
| Insurance | 400.00 |
| Rent | 3,500.00 |
| Gas and Electric | 375.00 |
| Payroll Expenses | 13,598.00 |
| | |
| Total Expenses | 19,396.33 |
| | |
| Net Income | $ 6,918.67 |

**14**    Click **Print** from the button bar and then click **OK** to print this report.

**15**    Close all windows.

# Creating an Income Statement with Peachtree's Design Feature

*Video Demonstration*

*Demo 3 - Creating an income statement with the design feature*

Scott decides to revise the previously created income statement to make it a month-by-month income statement for the periods February and March of 2011. In fact, what he will create is an income statement that will display the current and previous months' amounts depending on the accounting period selected.

## To create and print a comparative income statement report using the Design feature of Peachtree:

**1**    Open Century Kitchens.

**2**    Set the system date to **3/31/11** and the accounting period to **Period 3**.

**3**    Click **Reports & Forms** and then click **Financial Statements**.

**4**    Double-click **Basic Income Statement**.

**5**    Select **Current Period** from the Time Frame drop-down list and make sure the **Print Page Numbers** and **Show Zero Amounts** check boxes are unchecked and then click **OK**.

**6**    Click **Design** from the Report button bar.

**7**    Figure 3.7 shows the top of the report. Each line or column of the report can be edited by double-clicking the buttons on the left like **Text – Header**, **Column Desc.**, etc.

**8**    Double-click the third **Text – Header**. Remove the existing text and then type **For the Months Ending**. Click **OK** to accept changes and close the Text window.

**9**    Double-click **Column Desc.**

**10**    In column 3, select **Activity** from the Contents section and type **$(End-Date 1)$** as the title.

**11**    Set Width=**18** and select **Right of Column** from the Align Title drop-down list.

**12**    Check the **Format/$** check box.

**13**    Select **Current–1** from the Time Frame drop-down list and **Whole Dollars** from the Round drop-down list.

*[handwritten margin note: Activity - summary activity for period time. Balance - Bal. in acct on specific date]*

**Figure 3.7**

Design View

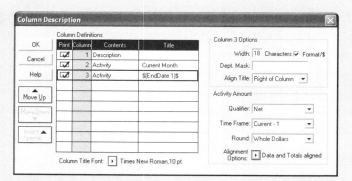

**14** Set the Alignment Options to **Data and Totals Aligned**. Your screen should look like Figure 3.8. Be sure the **Print** check box is checked for all three columns.

**Figure 3.8**

Column Description

**15** Select column 2 and then change the title from Current Month to **$(EndDate)$**.

**16** Select **Whole Dollars** from the Round drop-down list and set Width=**18**. The **Format/$** check box should already be checked, the Time Frame text box should indicate **Current**, and the Alignment

Options should indicate **Data and Totals Aligned**. Now click **OK** to close the window.

**17** Click **Preview** and then click **OK** to view your new income statement as shown in Figure 3.9.

Century Kitchens
Income Statement
For the Months Ended

| | March 31, 2011 | | February 28, 2011 |
|---|---|---|---|
| Revenues | | | |
| Counter Top | $  13,035 | $ | 0 |
| Cabinets | 19,300 | | 26,300 |
| Installation | 17,730 | | 17,280 |
| Design and Planning | 825 | | 9,375 |
| Total Revenues | 50,890 | | 52,955 |
| Cost of Sales | | | |
| Cost of Goods Sold | 24,575 | | 21,200 |
| Total Cost of Sales | 24,575 | | 21,200 |
| Gross Profit | 26,315 | | 31,755 |
| Expenses | | | |
| Building Supplies | 690 | | 675 |
| Depreciation Expense | 833 | | 833 |
| Insurance | 400 | | 800 |
| Rent | 3,500 | | 3,500 |
| Gas and Electric | 375 | | 375 |
| Payroll Expenses | 13,598 | | 14,216 |
| Total Expenses | 19,396 | | 20,399 |
| Net Income | $    6,919 | $ | 11,356 |

**Figure 3.9**

Comparative Income Statement

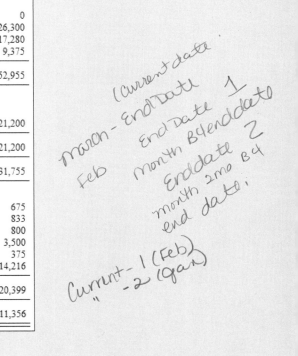

**18** Click **Save** from the button bar and then type **2 Mo Comparative Income Stmt** as the name of the newly created statement.

**19** Click **Save**.

**20** Click **Print** from the button bar and then click **OK** to print this report.

**21** Close all windows.

"What do $(EndDate)$ and $(EndDate 1)$ mean?" you ask.

"$(EndDate)$ and $(EndDate 1)$ are special codes that can be inserted in Peachtree reports," Scott answers. "The $ signs bookend special data fields that are used to put information on reports depending on the accounting period selected. In this case, the special data field EndDate means the last day of the current accounting period. In our current case, that would be March 31, 2011, since we've selected to be in accounting period 3. The data field EndDate 1 means the last day of the previous accounting period. In our current case, that would be February 28, 2011."

"Would EndDate 2 translate to January 31, 2011?" you ask.

"Exactly," Scott responds.

Scott suggests you add one more column to your new income statement that computes the percentage of the current month compared to the prior month. You offer to read through the Help function of Peachtree to figure it out.

## To add a percentage column to your income statement:

**1** Open Century Kitchens.

**2** Set the system date to **3/31/11** and the accounting period to **Period 3**.

**3** Click **Reports & Forms** and then click **Financial Statements**.

**4** Double-click **2 Mo Comparative Income Stmt**. (If you didn't save it last time, you'll need to recreate it!)

**5** Select **Current Period** from the Time Frame drop-down list and make sure the **Print Page Numbers** and **Show Zero Amounts** check boxes are unchecked and then click **OK**.

**6** Click **Design** from the Report button bar.

**7** Double-click **Column Desc**.

**8** Add a fourth column with Contents = **Percentage**, Title = **Pct of Prior Mo**, Width = **20**, and Align Title = **Right of Column**.

**9** Select **2** as the numerator of the percentage and then select **3** as the denominator of the percentage. Your Column Description window should look like Figure 3.10.

**Figure 3.10**

Adding a Percentage

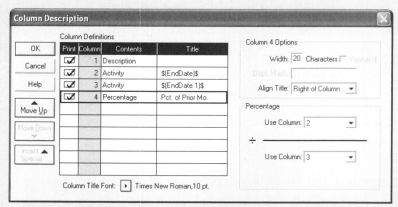

**10**   Click **OK** and then click **Preview** on the button bar and then **OK** to view your new statement as shown in Figure 3.11.

**Figure 3.11**

Income Statement with Percentages

Century Kitchens
Income Statement
For the Months Ended

| | March 31, 2011 | February 28, 2011 | Pct of Prior Mo |
|---|---|---|---|
| Revenues | | | |
| Counter Top | $ 13,035 | $ 0 | 0.00 |
| Cabinets | 19,300 | 26,300 | 73.38 |
| Installation | 17,730 | 17,280 | 102.60 |
| Design and Planning | 825 | 9,375 | 8.80 |
| Total Revenues | 50,890 | 52,955 | 96.10 |
| Cost of Sales | | | |
| Cost of Goods Sold | 24,575 | 21,200 | 115.92 |
| Total Cost of Sales | 24,575 | 21,200 | 115.92 |
| Gross Profit | 26,315 | 31,755 | 82.87 |
| Expenses | | | |
| Building Supplies | 690 | 675 | 102.22 |
| Depreciation Expense | 833 | 833 | 100.00 |
| Insurance | 400 | 800 | 50.00 |
| Rent | 3,500 | 3,500 | 100.00 |
| Gas and Electric | 375 | 375 | 100.00 |
| Payroll Expenses | 13,598 | 14,216 | 95.65 |
| Total Expenses | 19,396 | 20,399 | 95.08 |
| Net Income | $ 6,919 | $ 11,356 | 60.93 |

**11**   Click **Save**, type **2 Mo Comp Income Stmt w Pct** as the name of your new statement, and then click **Save**. Don't close the statement window as you're going to do some more work!

"I thought the percentage column added would show increases or decreases but instead the percentage column showed what percentage a line item was compared to the same item the previous month," you comment.

"You're right," Scott says. "I prefer a statement that shows whether a line item increased or decreased from the previous month. I'll try that next by adding a column showing the changes from the previous period to the current period and then a percentage change column as well."

**To add an increase or decrease column to your income statement and remove the percentage column:**

**1**   Click **Design** (assuming you kept the 2 Mo Comp Income Stmt w Pct report open from above; if not, you'll have to open it now).

**2**   Double-click **Column Desc**.

**3** Change column 4 so that Contents = **Formula**, Title = **Inc/Dec**, Width = **16**, Round = **Whole Dollars**, and Align Title = **Right of Column**.

**4** Change the Formula Activity on your screen to match that shown in Figure 3.12.

**Figure 3.12**

Column Description for Column 4

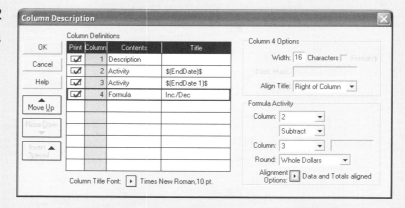

**5** Add a new column 5 with Contents = **Percentage** Title = **Pct Change**, Width = **16**, and Align Title = **Right of Column**.

**6** Change the Formula Activity on your screen to match that shown in Figure 3.13.

**Figure 3.13**

Column Description for Column 5

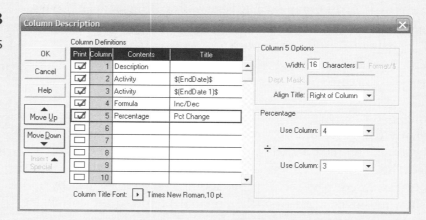

**7** Click **OK** to close the Column Description window.

**8** Click **Preview** on the button bar, and then click **OK** to view your new statement as shown in Figure 3.14.

| | | | | | | |
|---|---|---|---|---|---|---|
| | Century Kitchens | | | | | |
| | Income Statement | | | | | |
| | For the Months Ended | | | | | |
| | | March 31, 2011 | | February 28, 2011 | Inc/Dec | Pct Change |
| **Revenues** | | | | | | |
| Counter Top | $ | 13,035 | $ | 0 | 13,035 | 0.00 |
| Cabinets | | 19,300 | | 26,300 | (7,000) | (26.62) |
| Installation | | 17,730 | | 17,280 | 450 | 2.60 |
| Design and Planning | | 825 | | 9,375 | (8,550) | (91.20) |
| Total Revenues | | 50,890 | | 52,955 | (2,065) | (3.90) |
| **Cost of Sales** | | | | | | |
| Cost of Goods Sold | | 24,575 | | 21,200 | 3,375 | 15.92 |
| Total Cost of Sales | | 24,575 | | 21,200 | 3,375 | 15.92 |
| Gross Profit | | 26,315 | | 31,755 | (5,440) | (17.13) |
| **Expenses** | | | | | | |
| Building Supplies | | 690 | | 675 | 15 | 2.22 |
| Depreciation Expense | | 833 | | 833 | 0 | 0.00 |
| Insurance | | 400 | | 800 | (400) | (50.00) |
| Rent | | 3,500 | | 3,500 | 0 | 0.00 |
| Gas and Electric | | 375 | | 375 | 0 | 0.00 |
| Payroll Expenses | | 13,598 | | 14,216 | (618) | (4.35) |
| Total Expenses | | 19,396 | | 20,399 | (1,003) | (4.92) |
| Net Income | $ | 6,919 | $ | 11,356 | (4,437) | (39.07) |

**Figure 3.14**

Income Statement with Increases and Decreases

**9** Click **Save**, type **2 Mo Comp Income Stmt IncDec** as the name of your new statement, and then click **Save**.

**10** Close all windows.

# Investigating the Income Statement

Scott had been concerned about the company's performance in March, and now he can see how things differed between March and February. His most immediate concern is the drop-off in Design and Planning revenues since he knows that will correlate to future reductions in revenues for cabinet and counter purchases and installations. Further, he sees that his expenses seem fairly consistent between periods, making his biggest concern the decrease in revenues. He is, however, a bit curious about payroll expenses and decides to use Peachtree's drill-down capabilities to investigate like he did previously with the balance sheet.

To investigate payroll expenses for March, Scott uses the drill-down capabilities of Peachtree to examine the underlying general ledger report and paycheck details. He explains that the paycheck in this example is referred to as a source document and will prove helpful in his analysis.

## To investigate payroll expenses:

**1** Open Century Kitchens.

**2** Set the system date to **3/31/11** and the accounting period to **Period 3**.

**3** Click **Reports & Forms** and then click **Financial Statements**.

**4** Double-click **2 Mo Comparative Income Stmt**. (If you didn't save it last time, you'll need to re-create it!)

**5** Select **Current Period** from the Time Frame drop-down list, make sure the **Print Page Numbers** and **Show Zero Amounts** check boxes are unchecked, and then click **OK**.

**6** Click once on the March Payroll Expenses amount of **13,598**. Note how a box appears around the amount, indicating you can drill down from this number.

**7** Double-click the **13,598** amount to reveal a general ledger report for March payroll expenses as shown in Figure 3.15.

**Figure 3.15**

General Ledger Report for Account 6560 for March 2011

**Century Kitchens**
**General Ledger**
**For the Period From Mar 1, 2011 to Mar 31, 2011**

Filter Criteria includes: 1) IDs from 6560 to 6560. Report order is by ID. Report is printed with shortened descriptions and in Detail Format.

| Account ID / Account Description | Date | Reference | Jrnl | Trans Description | Debit Amt | Credit Amt | Balance |
|---|---|---|---|---|---|---|---|
| 6560 | 3/1/11 | | | Beginning Balance | | | 30,807.27 |
| Payroll Expenses | 3/16/11 | 127 | PRJ | Jessie Landon | 1,309.00 | | |
| | 3/16/11 | 127 | PRJ | Jessie Landon | 3.27 | | |
| | 3/16/11 | 127 | PRJ | Jessie Landon | 10.47 | | |
| | 3/16/11 | 127 | PRJ | Jessie Landon | 18.98 | | |
| | 3/16/11 | 127 | PRJ | Jessie Landon | 81.16 | | |
| | 3/16/11 | 128 | PRJ | Juan Gomez | 24.17 | | |
| | 3/16/11 | 128 | PRJ | Juan Gomez | 1,666.67 | | |
| | 3/16/11 | 128 | PRJ | Juan Gomez | 13.34 | | |
| | 3/16/11 | 128 | PRJ | Juan Gomez | 4.17 | | |
| | 3/16/11 | 128 | PRJ | Juan Gomez | 103.35 | | |
| | 3/16/11 | 129 | PRJ | Laurie McConnell | 50.22 | | |
| | 3/16/11 | 129 | PRJ | Laurie McConnell | 810.00 | | |
| | 3/16/11 | 129 | PRJ | Laurie McConnell | 6.48 | | |
| | 3/16/11 | 129 | PRJ | Laurie McConnell | 11.75 | | |
| | 3/16/11 | 129 | PRJ | Laurie McConnell | 2.03 | | |
| | 3/16/11 | 130 | PRJ | Scott Montalvo | 193.75 | | |
| | 3/16/11 | 130 | PRJ | Scott Montalvo | 45.31 | | |
| | 3/16/11 | 130 | PRJ | Scott Montalvo | 3,125.00 | | |
| | 3/31/11 | 137 | PRJ | Jessie Landon | 544.00 | | |
| | 3/31/11 | 137 | PRJ | Jessie Landon | 7.89 | | |
| | 3/31/11 | 137 | PRJ | Jessie Landon | 33.73 | | |
| | 3/31/11 | 138 | PRJ | Juan Gomez | 24.17 | | |
| | 3/31/11 | 138 | PRJ | Juan Gomez | 103.35 | | |
| | 3/31/11 | 138 | PRJ | Juan Gomez | 1,666.67 | | |
| | 3/31/11 | 139 | PRJ | Laurie McConnell | 2.76 | | |
| | 3/31/11 | 139 | PRJ | Laurie McConnell | 345.00 | | |
| | 3/31/11 | 139 | PRJ | Laurie McConnell | 5.00 | | |
| | 3/31/11 | 139 | PRJ | Laurie McConnell | 0.86 | | |
| | 3/31/11 | 139 | PRJ | Laurie McConnell | 21.39 | | |
| | 3/31/11 | 140 | PRJ | Scott Montalvo | 3,125.00 | | |
| | 3/31/11 | 140 | PRJ | Scott Montalvo | 193.75 | | |
| | 3/31/11 | 140 | PRJ | Scott Montalvo | 45.31 | | |
| | | | | Current Period Ch | 13,598.00 | | 13,598.00 |
| | 3/31/11 | | | Ending Balance | | | 44,405.27 |

**8** Double-click any of the 3/16/11 entries for Jessie Landon. For example, double-click the **10.47** entry shown in Figure 3.15.

**9** Check number 127 should appear. This is the source document for this payroll entry as shown in Figure 3.16.

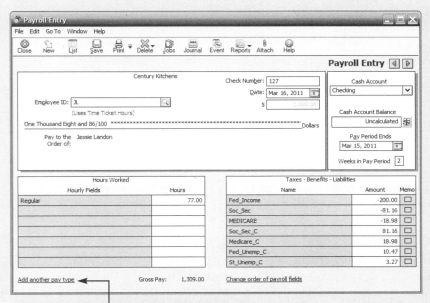

**Figure 3.16**

Payroll Check for Jessie Landon

**Text in this location may be different in your window**

**10** Note that the $10.47 payroll expense is the employer's cost for FUTA (federal unemployment).

**11** Close all windows.

Scott is satisfied that payroll entries for March are reasonable. However, he's still curious about the drop-off in Design and Planning revenues. He decides to investigate February revenues.

## To investigate February revenues:

**1** Open Century Kitchens.

**2** Set the system date to **3/31/11** and the accounting period to **Period 3**.

**3** Click **Reports** and then click **Financial Statements**.

**4** Double-click **2 Mo Comparative Income Stmt** from the drop-down list of Financial Statement templates.

**5** Select **Current Period** from the Time Frame drop-down list, make sure the **Print Page Numbers** and **Show Zero Amounts** check boxes are unchecked, and then click **OK**.

**6** Click once on the February Design and Planning revenue amount of **9,375**. Note how a box appears around the amount, indicating you can drill down from this number. Note that all of the transactions affecting this revenue account are invoices.

**7** Double-click the **9,375** amount to reveal a general ledger report for Design and Planning revenues as shown in Figure 3.17.

**Figure 3.17**

General Ledger Report

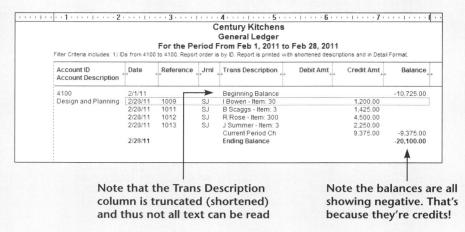

**8** Note how the Trans (Transaction) Description column of the report cuts off some of the information.

**9** To increase the column size, click and drag the blue arrows to the right of Trans Description until the column is wide enough to show all of the text. (You would click and drag to the left to reduce the column size.) Note that the report won't fit on one page as evidenced by the red dotted line showing the page break. See Figure 3.18.

**Figure 3.18**

Modifying Column Widths in a Report

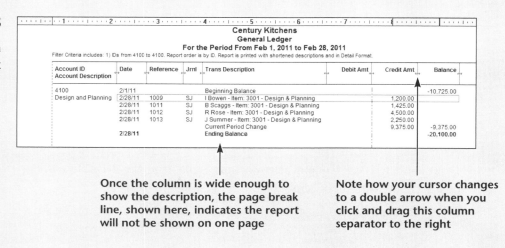

**10**  Click **Setup** from the button bar, choose the **Landscape** orientation, and then click **OK**. (This is the most common and easiest way to make your reports print one page wide.)

**11**  The report may still not fit on one page. If not, then change the column size of the Ref column, the Debit Amt column, and the Credit Amt column until the dotted red vertical line on the right side of the screen disappears, indicating the report will fit on one page.

**12**  Click **Print** on the button bar and then click **OK** in the Print window to print this resized report.

**13**  Click **Close** to close this window but don't save the changes.

**14**  Alternatively, Peachtree lets you turn off the truncating feature for this report, thereby wrapping text around a column. Reopen the general ledger report for revenue account 4100 (Design and Planning), click **Options** from the button bar.

**15**  Uncheck the **Shorten Description** check box and then click **OK**.

**16**  Click **Print** on the button bar to print this reconfigured report. Note how this makes the report longer but no wider.

**17**  Click **Close** to close this window but don't save the changes.

**18**  Scott notices three different invoices on the printed report, all of which were recorded on 2/28/11. He's almost certain the J Summer invoice actually was done in March, not February. Reopen the general ledger report for revenue account 4100 and then double-click invoice **1013** to view the actual invoice shown in Figure 3.19.

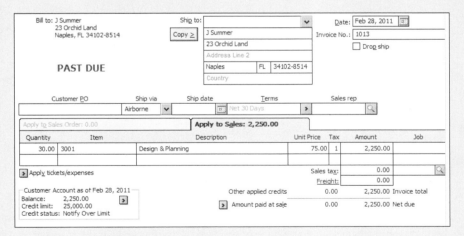

**Figure 3.19**

Invoice 1013

**19**  Close all windows.

Scott's certain that the work shown on invoice 1013 was performed in March and not in February as reported. He chooses to leave it recorded as is, but that does explain some of the drop-off in revenues.

## End Note

Now that you have completed Chapters 2 and 3, you can see how easily Peachtree creates the two financial reports—the balance sheet and the income statement—most commonly used to communicate accounting information to external users. In Chapter 4, you will continue your quick overview of Peachtree by creating a statement of cash flows.

# Chapter 3 Questions

**1** What information is included in the Standard Income Stmnt report option?

**2** How is the ratio included in the Standard Income Stmnt calculated?

**3** How do you access Peachtree's Design feature to modify or create reports?

**4** What do $(EndDate)$ and $(EndDate 1)$ mean?

**5** How do you know if a report amount can use the drill-down capability of Peachtree?

**6** What happens when you double-click a number on a report that can use the drill-down capability?

**7** What happens when you double-click a particular transaction in a general ledger report?

**8** How do you modify the column width of a general ledger report?

**9** What is the most common and easiest way to make your reports print one page wide?

**10** What source document would you expect to see when you drill down from a revenue general ledger report?

# Chapter 3 Assignments

**1** *Prepare and print the following reports using the Century Kitchens Peachtree files. Set the accounting period to* **Period 1.** *(Place your name in the footer of each report. To do so, scroll to the bottom of any report in Design mode, double-click the* **Text – Footer,** *then type your name, and click* **OK.** *This will help you locate your report as opposed to any other student's report when using computer labs.)*

*merchandising*

   a. A basic income statement (like you prepared in the chapter) for the current period (with the accounting period set to Period 1).

   b. Modify a basic income statement using Peachtree's Design feature to create an income statement comparing three accounting periods (with a system date of 3/31/11 and with the accounting period set to Period 3). For example, you could use 1/31/11, 2/28/11, and 3/31/11, exactly as you did in the chapter except with three months instead of two. Save it as **3 Mo Comparative Income Stmt**. The new statement should look like Figure 3.20.

**Figure 3.20**

Three-Month Comparative Income Statement

Century Kitchens
Income Statement
For the Months Ended

| | March 31, 2011 | February 28, 2011 | January 31, 2011 |
|---|---|---|---|
| **Revenues** | | | |
| Counter Top | $ 13,035 | $ 0 | $ 0 |
| Cabinets | 19,300 | 26,300 | 15,350 |
| Installation | 17,730 | 17,280 | 11,920 |
| Design and Planning | 825 | 9,375 | 10,725 |
| Total Revenues | 50,890 | 52,955 | 37,995 |
| **Cost of Sales** | | | |
| Cost of Goods Sold | 24,575 | 21,200 | 12,360 |
| Total Cost of Sales | 24,575 | 21,200 | 12,360 |
| Gross Profit | 26,315 | 31,755 | 25,635 |
| **Expenses** | | | |
| Building Supplies | 690 | 675 | 165 |
| Depreciation Expense | 833 | 833 | 833 |
| Insurance | 400 | 800 | 0 |
| Rent | 3,500 | 3,500 | 3,500 |
| Gas and Electric | 375 | 375 | 165 |
| Payroll Expenses | 13,598 | 14,216 | 16,591 |
| Total Expenses | 19,396 | 20,399 | 21,254 |
| Net Income | $ 6,919 | $ 11,356 | $ 4,381 |

c.  Modify the income statement you just created in (b) using Peachtree's Design feature to create an income statement showing increases/decreases for each month. Save it as **3 Mo Comp Income Stmt IncDec**. It should look like Figure 3.21.

**Figure 3.21**

Comparative Income Statement with Increases/Decreases

Century Kitchens
Income Statement
For the Months Ended

| | March 31, 2011 | Inc./Dec. | February 28, 2011 | Inc./Dec. | January 31, 2011 |
|---|---|---|---|---|---|
| **Revenues** | | | | | |
| Counter Top | $ 13,035 | 13,035 | $ 0 | 0 | $ 0 |
| Cabinets | 19,300 | (7,000) | 26,300 | 10,950 | 15,350 |
| Installation | 17,730 | 450 | 17,280 | 5,360 | 11,920 |
| Design and Planning | 825 | (8,550) | 9,375 | (1,350) | 10,725 |
| Total Revenues | 50,890 | (2,065) | 52,955 | 14,960 | 37,995 |
| **Cost of Sales** | | | | | |
| Cost of Goods Sold | 24,575 | 3,375 | 21,200 | 8,840 | 12,360 |
| Total Cost of Sales | 24,575 | 3,375 | 21,200 | 8,840 | 12,360 |
| Gross Profit | 26,315 | (5,440) | 31,755 | 6,120 | 25,635 |
| **Expenses** | | | | | |
| Building Supplies | 690 | 15 | 675 | 510 | 165 |
| Depreciation Expense | 833 | 0 | 833 | 0 | 833 |
| Insurance | 400 | (400) | 800 | 800 | 0 |
| Rent | 3,500 | 0 | 3,500 | 0 | 3,500 |
| Gas and Electric | 375 | 0 | 375 | 210 | 165 |
| Payroll Expenses | 13,598 | (618) | 14,216 | (2,375) | 16,591 |
| Total Expenses | 19,396 | (1,003) | 20,399 | (855) | 21,254 |
| Net Income | $ 6,919 | (4,437) | $ 11,356 | 6,975 | $ 4,381 |

d. A general ledger report of those transactions recorded in January 2011 that affected revenue account 4060 Installation. (Make sure it fits on one page and that all items are visible by adjusting the width of each column and printing in landscape view. Don't save changes!)

e. A general ledger report of those transactions recorded in January, February, and March 2011 that affected expense account 6150 Depreciation Expense. (Make sure it fits on one page and that all items are visible by turning off the truncating feature. Don't save changes!)

**2** *Answer the following questions using the Century Kitchens Peachtree files after opening a standard income statement for the three-month period:*

a. Drill down from the Counter Top revenue account. Locate invoice 1019. What did Century Kitchens sell on the first line of this invoice? Who is it billing? What was the total invoice amount?

b. Drill down from the Rent expense account. What check numbers were used to pay rent for the three months? To whom was rent paid?

c. Drill down from the Building Supplies expense account. What check numbers were used to pay for this expense during the three months? To whom were these checks written?

## Chapter 3 Cases

### Chapter 3 Case Problem 1

## KELLY JENNINGS ADVERTISING

Kelly Jennings (see Chapter 2 Case Problem 1) requires some additional financial reports.

**1** *Prepare and print the following reports using Kelly Jennings Advertising Peachtree files. (Use the file you updated in Chapter 2 or restore this file from the Data Files CD. Be sure to include your name in the Extra Footer Line of each report when possible. Set the system date to 2/29/08 and the accounting period to* **Period 2.***)*

a. A standard income/earnings statement as of 2/29/08 with no page numbers and no zero amounts.

b. Modify the income statement you just created in (a) using Peachtree's Design feature to create an income statement comparing two accounting periods with no ratios rounded to whole dollars in $ format and a column width of 18 for all numbers. For example, you could use 1/31/08 and 2/29/08, exactly as you did in the chapter. Save it as **2 Mo Comparative Income Stmt**.

c. Modify the income statement you just created in (b) using Peachtree's Design feature to create an income/earnings statement comparing two accounting periods with a column showing increases/decreases rounded to whole dollars and a column showing percentage increases/decreases. Save it as **2 Mo Comp Income Stmt IncDec**.

d. A general ledger report of those transactions recorded in January 2008 that affected the Radio revenue account. (Make sure it fits on one page and that all items are visible by adjusting the width of each column and printing in landscape view. Don't save changes!)

e. A general ledger report of those transactions recorded in January 2008 that affected expense account 6172 Film expenses. (Make sure it fits on one page and that all items are visible by turning off the truncating feature. Don't save changes!)

**2**  *Answer the following questions:*

a. Drill down from account 4523 Television revenue in January 2008. Locate invoice 7. What did Jennings sell on the first line of this invoice? Whom is it billing? What was the total invoice amount?

b. Drill down from the TV Commercial Spots expense account in January 2008. What is the amount owed and to whom is the payment due? What was the invoice number?

c. Drill down from the Depreciation expense account in January 2008. What source document was used to create this expense? What is the expense for?

## Chapter 3 Case Problem 2
# SIERRA MARINA

Sierra Marina (see Chapter 2 Case Problem 2) requires some additional financial reports.

**1**  *Prepare and print the following reports using Meagan's Sierra Marina Peachtree file. (Use the file you updated in Chapter 2 or restore this file from the Data Files CD. Be sure to include your name in the Extra Footer Line of each report where possible. Set system date to 8/31/10 and the accounting period to Period 2.)*

a. A standard income statement as of 8/31/10 with no page numbers and no zero amounts.

b. Modify the income statement you just created in (a) using Peachtree's Design feature to create an income statement comparing July and August with no ratios rounded to whole dollars in $ format and a column width of 18 for all numbers. Delete all references to Cost of Sales and Gross Profit by right clicking **Text – Body**, Line Description, etc. and clicking delete. You'll also need to double-click the **Total-Level 2** section to change it to total Level 1. Your modified income statement should look like Figure 3.22 below. Save it as **2 Mo Comparative Income Stmt**.

**Figure 3.22**

Modified Income Statement for Sierra Marina

Sierra Marina
Income Statement
For the Month Ended

| Revenues | | August 31, 2010 | July 31, 2010 |
|---|---|---|---|
| Equipment Rental | $ | 6,000 | 2,960 |
| Fishing Boat Rental | | 3,000 | 1,050 |
| Personal Watercraft Rental | | 43,000 | 34,600 |
| Pontoon Boat Rental | | 15,000 | 17,320 |
| Slips/Storage Rental | | 1,000 | 98 |
| Wake/Ski Boat Rental | | 42,000 | 38,000 |
| | | | |
| Total Revenues | | 110,000 | 94,028 |
| | | | |
| Expenses | | | |
| Advertising | | 4,000 | 3,500 |
| Automobile | | 4,000 | 0 |
| Computer | | 6,000 | 0 |
| Depreciation | | 17,000 | 17,000 |
| Fuel | | 19,000 | 18,000 |
| Office Supplies | | 700 | 500 |
| Payroll | | 20,800 | 13,530 |
| Professional Fees | | 0 | 1,500 |
| Repairs | | 21,000 | 18,544 |
| Taxes | | 0 | 1,000 |
| Telephone | | 900 | 0 |
| Utilities | | 4,000 | 7,763 |
| | | | |
| Total Expenses | | 97,400 | 81,337 |
| | | | |
| Net Income | $ | 12,600 | 12,691 |

**Figure 3.23**

Income Statement for Sierra Marina with Two New Columns

Sierra Marina
Income Statement
For the Month Ended

| Revenues | | August 31, 2010 | July 31, 2010 | Inc./Dec | Percent Change |
|---|---|---|---|---|---|
| Equipment Rental | $ | 6,000 | 2,960 | 3,040 | 102.70 |
| Fishing Boat Rental | | 3,000 | 1,050 | 1,950 | 185.71 |
| Personal Watercraft Rental | | 43,000 | 34,600 | 8,400 | 24.28 |
| Pontoon Boat Rental | | 15,000 | 17,320 | (2,320) | (13.39) |
| Slips/Storage Rental | | 1,000 | 98 | 902 | 920.41 |
| Wake/Ski Boat Rental | | 42,000 | 38,000 | 4,000 | 10.53 |
| | | | | | |
| Total Revenues | | 110,000 | 94,028 | 15,972 | 16.99 |
| | | | | | |
| Expenses | | | | | |
| Advertising | | 4,000 | 3,500 | 500 | 14.29 |
| Automobile | | 4,000 | 0 | 4,000 | 0.00 |
| Computer | | 6,000 | 0 | 6,000 | 0.00 |
| Depreciation | | 17,000 | 17,000 | 0 | 0.00 |
| Fuel | | 19,000 | 18,000 | 1,000 | 5.56 |
| Office Supplies | | 700 | 500 | 200 | 40.00 |
| Payroll | | 20,800 | 13,530 | 7,270 | 53.73 |
| Professional Fees | | 0 | 1,500 | (1,500) | (100.00) |
| Repairs | | 21,000 | 18,544 | 2,456 | 13.24 |
| Taxes | | 0 | 1,000 | (1,000) | (100.00) |
| Telephone | | 900 | 0 | 900 | 0.00 |
| Utilities | | 4,000 | 7,763 | (3,763) | (48.47) |
| | | | | | |
| Total Expenses | | 97,400 | 81,337 | 16,063 | 19.75 |
| | | | | | |
| Net Income | $ | 12,600 | 12,691 | (91) | (0.72) |

c. Modify the income statement you just created in (b) using Peachtree's Design feature to create an income statement comparing two accounting periods with a column showing increases/decreases and a column showing percentage increases/decreases rounded to whole dollars. Your modified income statement should look like Figure 3.23 below. Save it as **2 Mo Comp Income Stmt IncDec**.

d. General ledger report of account 40300 Personal Watercraft Rental for the month of July.

**2** *Answer the following questions:*

a. Drill down from the Equipment Rental account in July. What did Sierra Marina sell on 7/30/10? Whom is it billing? What was the total invoice amount?

b. Drill down from the Fuel expense account in July. What is the amount owed and to whom is the payment due? What was the invoice number?

## Chapter 3 Case Problem 3
# JASON GALAS, ATTORNEY AT LAW, PC

Jason Galas (see Chapter 2 Case Problem 3) requires some additional financial reports.

**1** *Prepare and print the following reports using the Jason Galas, Attorney at Law, PC Peachtree file. (Use the file you updated in Chapter 2 or restore this file from the Data Files CD. Be sure to include your name in the Extra Footer Line of each report, where possible. Set system date to 2/29/12 and the accounting period to* **Period 2.***)*

a. A standard income statement as of 2/29/12 with no page numbers and no zero amounts.

b. Modify the income statement you just created in (a) using Peachtree's Design feature to create an income statement comparing January and February with no ratios rounded to whole dollars in $ format and a column width of 18 for all numbers. Delete all references to Cost of Sales and Gross Profit by right-clicking Text – Body, Line Description, etc. and clicking Delete. You'll also need to double-click the **Total-Level 2** section to change it to Total Level 1. Your modified income statement should look like Figure 3.24 below. Save it as 2 Mo Comparative Income Stmt.

c. Modify the income statement you just created in (b) using Peachtree's Design feature to create an income statement comparing two accounting periods with a column showing increases/decreases and a column showing percentage increases/decreases rounded to whole dollars. Your modified income statement should look like Figure 3.25 below. Save it as 2 Mo Comp Income Stmt IncDec.

**Figure 3.24**

Modified Income Statement for Jason Galas, Attorney at Law, PC

Jason Galas Attorney at Law PC
Income Statement
For the Months Ended

|  | February 29, 2012 | January 31, 2012 |
|---|---|---|
| **Revenues** |  |  |
| Fee Income-Taxation | $        35,600 | $        43,300 |
| Total Revenues | 35,600 | 43,300 |
|  |  |  |
| **Expenses** |  |  |
| Advertising Expense | 5,000 | 0 |
| Maintenance Expense | 1,800 | 1,800 |
| Office Expense | 300 | 1,200 |
| Payroll Tax Expense | 2,179 | 1,876 |
| Rent or Lease Expense | 5,600 | 5,600 |
| Salaries Expense | 14,500 | 14,500 |
| Wages Expense | 5,040 | 2,324 |
| Telephone Expense | 1,450 | 1,300 |
| Travel Expense | 1,800 | 2,700 |
| Utilities Expense | 4,000 | 1,800 |
| Total Expenses | 41,669 | 33,100 |
| Net Income | $        (6,069) | $        10,200 |

**Figure 3.25**

Income Statement for Jason Galas, Attorney at Law, PC with Two New Columns

Jason Galas Attorney at Law PC
Income Statement
For the Months Ended

|  | February 29, 2012 | January 31, 2012 | Inc./Dec. | Pct. Change |
|---|---|---|---|---|
| **Revenues** |  |  |  |  |
| Fee Income-Taxation | $      35,600 | $      43,300 | (7,700) | (17.78) |
| Total Revenues | 35,600 | 43,300 | (7,700) | (17.78) |
|  |  |  |  |  |
| **Expenses** |  |  |  |  |
| Advertising Expense | 5,000 | 0 | 5,000 | 0.00 |
| Maintenance Expense | 1,800 | 1,800 | 0 | 0.00 |
| Office Expense | 300 | 1,200 | (900) | (75.00) |
| Payroll Tax Expense | 2,179 | 1,876 | 303 | 16.15 |
| Rent or Lease Expense | 5,600 | 5,600 | 0 | 0.00 |
| Salaries Expense | 14,500 | 14,500 | 0 | 0.00 |
| Wages Expense | 5,040 | 2,324 | 2,716 | 116.87 |
| Telephone Expense | 1,450 | 1,300 | 150 | 11.54 |
| Travel Expense | 1,800 | 2,700 | (900) | (33.33) |
| Utilities Expense | 4,000 | 1,800 | 2,200 | 122.22 |
| Total Expenses | 41,669 | 33,100 | 8,569 | 25.89 |
| Net Income | $      (6,069) | $      10,200 | (16,269) | (159.50) |

d.  A general ledger report of account Fee Income-Taxation for the month of February.

**2   *Answer the following questions:***

a.  Drill down from the Advertising Expense account in February. Whom did they pay? How much was paid?

b.  Drill down from the Salaries Expense account in January. Who was paid in January? What was their gross pay?

# Preparing a Statement of Cash Flows Using Peachtree

**4**

*In this Chapter, you will:*

- Create and print a standard cash flow statement.
- Create a comparative cash flow statement using the Design feature.
- Investigate details supporting cash flow items.

## *Case:* Century Kitchens

One of the main financial statements used by businesses is the statement of cash flows. Your previous experience with this statement has not always been good so the thought of the computer preparing this one for you is quite enticing. You recall that this statement reports cash flows from operating, investing, and financing activities for a specific period.

Once again, as a part of your training with Peachtree, Scott asks you to work with him as he prepares a statement of cash flows for the period January 1, 2011, through March 31, 2011.

## Creating a Statement of Cash Flows

The statement of cash flows in Peachtree is presented in only one format, although it can be modified after it is created. There is another report for cash flows, called Stmnt Changes, which creates a statement of changes in financial position and is not addressed in this text. Scott decides to create the statement of cash flows and modify it later.

**To create a standard cash flow statement:**

1 Open Century Kitchens.

2 Set the system date to **3/31/11** and the accounting period to **Period 3**.

3 Click **Reports & Forms** and then click **Financial Statements**.

4 Double-click <**Standard**> **Cash Flow**.

**5**  Be sure the **Print Page Numbers** and **Show Zero Amounts** check boxes are unchecked.

**6**  Click **OK**. The resulting standard cash flow statement is shown in Figure 4.1.

**Figure 4.1**

Standard Statement
of Cash Flow

| | Century Kitchens<br>Statement of Cash Flow<br>For the three Months Ended March 31, 2011 | |
|---|---|---|
| | Current Month | Year to Date |
| Cash Flows from operating activities | | |
| Net Income | $        6,918.67  $ | 22,654.74 |
| Adjustments to reconcile net<br>income to net cash provided<br>by operating activities | | |
| Accumulated Depreciation | 833.33 | 2,499.99 |
| Accounts Receivable | (24,530.00) | (93,280.00) |
| Inventory Asset | (5,620.00) | (5,620.00) |
| Prepaid Insurance | 400.00 | (3,600.00) |
| Accounts Payable | 13,050.00 | 27,270.00 |
| Payroll Liabilities | 4,344.94 | 13,536.03 |
| Total Adjustments | (11,521.73) | (59,193.98) |
| Net Cash provided by Operations | (4,603.06) | (36,539.24) |
| Cash Flows from investing activities<br>Used For | | |
| Equipment | 0.00 | (50,000.00) |
| Net cash used in investing | 0.00 | (50,000.00) |
| Cash Flows from financing activities<br>Proceeds From | | |
| Common Stock<br>Used For | 0.00 | 125,000.00 |
| Net cash used in financing | 0.00 | 125,000.00 |
| Net increase <decrease> in cash | $        (4,603.06)  $ | 38,460.76 |
| Summary | | |
| Cash Balance at End of Period | $        38,460.76  $ | 38,460.76 |
| Cash Balance at Beg of Period | (43,063.82) | 0.00 |
| Net Increase <Decrease> in Cash | $        (4,603.06)  $ | 38,460.76 |

**7**  Scroll down this report as shown in Figure 4.1 and notice the three sections: operating activities, investing activities, and financing activities. Notice at the bottom of the statement the net cash increase for the period is reported. It is then added to the cash at the beginning of the period to yield cash at the end of the period. Do not close this window.

In your examination of the statement of cash flows, you notice in the operating activities section that several adjustments are made to reconcile net income to net cash provided by operations. Scott points out that one of the more common adjustments is depreciation, since it reduces income but does not use cash. In the Peachtree report, this is derived from the changes in the accumulated depreciation type of accounts. From your accounting classes, you remember this as usually being described as depreciation expense, not accumulated depreciation. Scott decides not to bother with semantics and just leave it as is.

"How about modifying the statement of cash flows to reflect comparative amounts like prior months? Is there a preset previous-month comparative report available?" you ask.

"Well, no," Scott explains. "Not only is there no preset comparative report in Peachtree, there is no Financial Statement Wizard to create one. Maybe Peachtree will have one in the next version."

## Creating a Statement of Cash Flows with Peachtree's Design Feature

Scott decides to revise the previously created statement of cash flows to make it a month-by-month statement of cash flows for three periods—January, February, and March—with no year-to-date column. In fact, what he will create is a statement of cash flows that will display the current and previous two months' amounts depending on the accounting period selected. Creating this comparative statement of cash flows will give the company some insight into how cash flows change over several months.

*Video Demonstration*

***Demo 2 - Creating a statement of cash flows with the design feature***

**To create and print a comparative statement of cash flows report using the Design feature of Peachtree:**

1 Continue from the previous section.

2 Click **Design** from the Report button bar.

3 The following design view of the standard statement of cash flows (Figure 4.2) shows the top of the report. Each line or column of the report can be edited by double-clicking the buttons on the left like **Text – Header, Column Desc.**, etc.

4 Double-click the third **Text – Header**. Remove the existing text and then type **For the Months Ended**. Click **OK** to accept changes and close the Text window.

5 Double-click the first **Column Desc.** button from the top.

6 Select column 3 (Year to Date), set Contents = **Activity**, type **$(End-Date 1)$** as the Title, set Width = **18**, select **Center of Column** from the Align Title drop-down list, check the **Format/$** check box, select

**Figure 4.2**

Design View

First Column Descriptor – Double-click here to edit what appears in columns

Click here to save changes

Click here to preview the resulting financial statement

Click here to enter the Design mode

Double-click here to edit this header

Second Column Descriptor – Double-click here to edit what appears in these particular columns

Line Description – If you double-click here, you'll find the only account analyzed is accumulated depreciation

Third Column Descriptor – Double-click here to edit what appears in these particular columns

The column is qualified as only credit activity, meaning only credits to the accounts specified in the line description are included

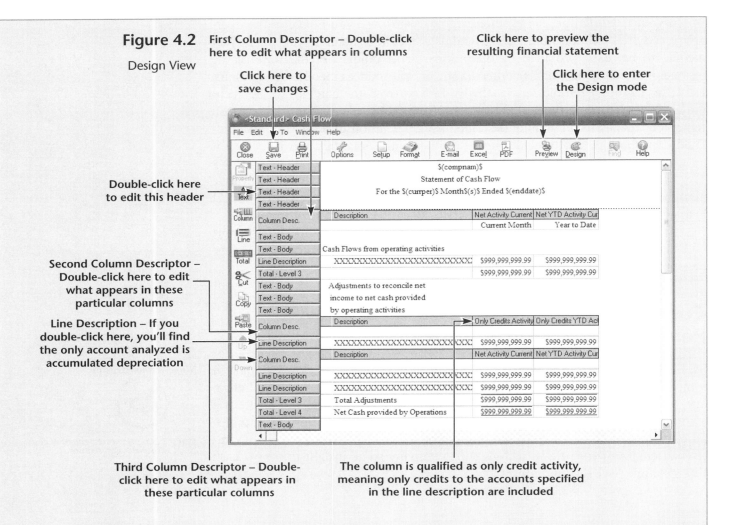

**Current – 1** from the Time Frame drop-down list and **Whole Dollars** from the Round drop-down list, and set the Alignment Options to **Data and Totals Aligned**. Be sure the **Print** check box is checked for all three columns.

**7** Select column 4 and check the **Print** check box, then set Contents = **Activity**, type **$(EndDate 2)$** as the Title, set Width = **18**, select **Center of Column** from the Align Title drop-down list, check the **Format/$** check box, select **Current – 2** from the Time Frame drop-down list and **Whole Dollars** from the Round drop-down list, and set the Alignment Options to **Data and Totals Aligned**.

**8** Select column 2 and make sure the Print check box is checked, then change the title from Current Month to **$(EndDate)$**. Select **Whole Dollars** from the Round drop-down list, set Width = **18**, and select **Center of Column** from the Align Title drop-down list. Your screen should look like Figure 4.3.

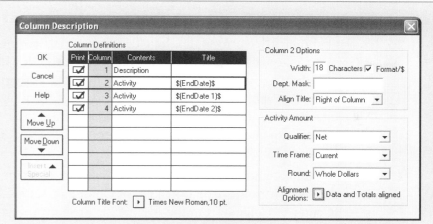

**Figure 4.3**

Column Description

**9** Click **OK** to close the Column Description window.

**10** Double-click the second **Column Desc.** button from the top.

**11** Select column 3 (Year to Date), set Contents = **Activity**, set Width = **18**, select **Center of Column** from the Align Title drop-down list, select **Only Credits** from the drop-down list of Qualifiers, check the **Format/$** check box, select **Current – 1** from the Time Frame drop-down list and **Whole Dollars** from the Round drop-down list, and set the Alignment Options to **Data and Totals Aligned**. Be sure the **Print** check box is checked for all three columns.

**12** Select column 4 and check the **Print** check box, set Contents = **Activity**, select **Only Credits** from the drop-down list of Qualifiers, set Width = **18**, select **Center of Column** from the Align Title drop-down list, check the **Format/$** check box, select **Current – 2** from the Time Frame drop-down list and **Whole Dollars** from the Round drop-down list, and set the Alignment Options to **Data and Totals Aligned**.

**13** Select column 2 and then select **Whole Dollars** from the Round drop-down list and set Width = **18**. Your screen should look like Figure 4.4.

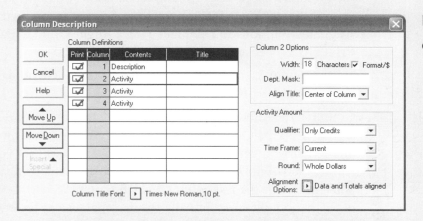

**Figure 4.4**

Column Description

**14** Click **OK** to close the Column Description window.

**15** Double-click the third **Column Desc**. button from the top.

**16** Select column 3 (Year to Date), set Contents = **Activity**, set Width = **18**, select **Center of Column** from the Align Title drop-down list, select **Net** from the drop-down list of Qualifiers, check the **Format/$** check box, select **Current − 1** from the Time Frame drop-down list and **Whole Dollars** from the Round drop-down list, and set the Alignment Options to **Data and Totals Aligned**. Be sure the **Print** check box is checked for all three columns.

**17** Select column 4 and check the **Print** check box, set Contents = **Activity**, select **Net** from the drop-down list of Qualifiers, set Width = **18**, select **Center of Column** from the Align Title drop-down list, check the **Format/$** check box, select **Current − 2** from the Time Frame drop-down list and **Whole Dollars** from the Round drop-down list, and set the Alignment Options to **Data and Totals Aligned**.

**18** Select column 2, select **Whole Dollars** from the Round drop-down list, set Width = **18**, and make sure the Qualifier is **Net**. Click **OK** and then close the window.

**19** Double-click the fourth **Column Desc**. button from the top. (This one is for the top of the investing section.)

**20** Select column 3 (Year to Date), set Contents = **Activity**, set Width = **18**, select **Center of Column** from the Align Title drop-down list, select **Only Debits** from the drop-down list of Qualifiers, check the **Format/$** check box, select **Current − 1** from the Time Frame drop-down list and **Whole Dollars** from the Round drop-down list, and set the Alignment Options to **Data and Totals Aligned**. Be sure the **Print** check box is checked for all three columns.

**21** Select column 4, check the **Print** check box, set Contents = **Activity**, select **Only Debits** from the drop-down list of Qualifiers, set Width = **18**, select **Center of Column** from the Align Title drop-down list, check the **Format/$** check box, select **Current − 2** from the Time Frame drop-down list and **Whole Dollars** from the Round drop-down list, set the Alignment Options to **Data and Totals Aligned**, and make sure the **Print** box is checked.

**22** Select column 2, select **Whole Dollars** from the Round drop-down list, and set Width = **18**.

**23** Continue the same process down the statement of cash flows, being sure to keep the Qualifier the same for the current and previous periods. When you get to the last two columns, notice that you switch from the contents being an activity to the contents being a balance. Also, note that the last column, which represents cash at the beginning of the period (which is actually the cash balance at the end of the previous period), has a bit different time frame than the previous columns. Column 2's time frame should be **Current − 1**, column 3's time frame should be **Current − 2**, and column 4's time frame should be **Total Last Year** as shown in Figure 4.5.

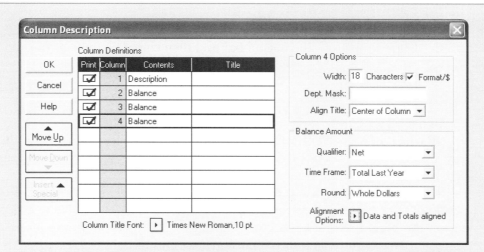

**Figure 4.5**

Column Descriptions for the Net Increase <Decrease> in Cash

**24**  Click **OK** to close the Column Description window.

**25**  Click **Preview** and then click **OK** to view your new statement of cash flows as shown in Figure 4.6.

**Figure 4.6**

Comparative Statement of Cash Flows

Century Kitchens
Statement of Cash Flow
For the Months Ended

| | March 31, 2011 | February 28, 2011 | January 31, 2011 |
|---|---|---|---|
| Cash Flows from operating activities | | | |
| Net Income | $ 6,919 | $ 11,356 | $ 4,381 |
| Adjustments to reconcile net income to net cash provided by operating activities | | | |
| Accumulated Depreciation | 833 | 833 | 833 |
| Accounts Receivable | (24,530) | (31,955) | (36,795) |
| Inventory Asset | (5,620) | 0 | 0 |
| Prepaid Insurance | 400 | (4,000) | 0 |
| Accounts Payable | 13,050 | 14,220 | 0 |
| Payroll Liabilities | 4,345 | 4,280 | 4,911 |
| Total Adjustments | (11,522) | (16,622) | (31,051) |
| Net Cash provided by Operations | (4,603) | (5,266) | (26,670) |
| Cash Flows from investing activities | | | |
| Used For | | | |
| Equipment | 0 | 0 | (50,000) |
| Net cash used in investing | 0 | 0 | (50,000) |
| Cash Flows from financing activities | | | |
| Proceeds From | | | |
| Common Stock | 0 | 0 | 125,000 |
| Used For | | | |
| Net cash used in financing | 0 | 0 | 125,000 |
| Net increase <decrease> in cash | $ (4,603) | $ (5,266) | $ 48,330 |
| Summary | | | |
| Cash Balance at End of Period | $ 38,461 | $ 43,064 | $ 48,329 |
| Cash Balance at Beg of Period | (43,064) | (48,330) | 0 |
| Net Increase <Decrease> in Cash | $ (4,603) | $ (5,266) | $ 48,329 |

**26**  Click **Save** from the button bar and then type **3 Mo Comparative Cash Flows** as the name of the newly created statement.

27   Click **Save**.

28   Click **Print** from the button bar and then click **OK** to print this report.

29   Close all windows.

"That was a lot of work!" you comment.

"Right you are," Scott answers, "but once complete, you can use this for any accounting period you'd like, and it will always show a comparison between the current and prior two months of cash flow."

Scott reminds you that typing $(EndDate)$ as a title inserts the end of the period date of the period selected, which makes the report flexible and dependent on the period selected. Selecting Current − 2 as the time frame inserts data requested two periods before the current accounting period selected. This also makes the report flexible and dependent on the period selected.

Upon further inspection of his newly created comparative statement of cash flows, Scott notices that the two net increases in cash for January don't agree. He realizes that this is the consequence of rounding to whole dollars.

## Investigating the Statement of Cash Flows

Scott had been concerned about the company's performance in March, and now he can see how cash flow differed each month by looking at his newly created comparative cash flow statement. His most immediate concern is the cash used by operations. He notes that the loss generated in March certainly didn't help his cash flow and that increases in accounts receivable and inventory seem to be exacerbating the problem.

You remember from your accounting classes that changes in accounts receivable are one of the adjustments to net income to arrive at operating cash flow. You also remember that accounts receivable increases are subtracted from net income to arrive at operating cash flow since the revenues from some sales aren't collected in cash immediately. Thus, as accounts receivable increase, the revenue (reflected in net income under accrual accounting) is not realized (i.e., not received in cash yet). He decides to use Peachtree's drill-down capabilities to investigate the changes in accounts receivable for the last three months.

**To investigate the adjustment to the statement of cash flows from changes in accounts receivable:**

1   Open Century Kitchens.

2   Set the system date to **3/31/11** and the accounting period to **Period 3**.

3   Click **Reports & Forms** and then click **Financial Statements**.

4   Double-click **3 Mo Comparative Cash Flows** from the drop-down list of Financial Statement templates. (If you didn't save it last time, you'll need to re-create it!)

**5** Select **Current Period** from the Time Frame drop-down list, make sure the **Print Page Numbers** and **Show Zero Amounts** check boxes are unchecked, and then click **OK**.

**6** Click **(36,795)** from the January column. Note the box that surrounds this amount indicates a drill-down value.

**7** Double-click the **(36,795)** value to reveal a general ledger report for accounts receivable explaining the net increase in accounts receivable for the month of January. See Figure 4.7.

**Figure 4.7**

Change in Accounts Receivable for January

Century Kitchens
General Ledger
For the Period From Jan 1, 2011 to Jan 31, 2011
Filter Criteria includes: 1) IDs from 1200 to 1200. Report order is by ID. Report is printed with shortened descriptions and in Detail Format.

| Account ID Account Description | Date | Reference | Jrnl | Trans Description | Debit Amt | Credit Amt | Balance |
|---|---|---|---|---|---|---|---|
| 1200 | 1/1/11 | | | Beginning Balance | | | |
| Accounts Receivable | 1/7/11 | 1001 | SJ | J Wilson | 450.00 | | |
| | 1/7/11 | 1002 | SJ | R Coe | 525.00 | | |
| | 1/10/11 | 1003 | SJ | A Monroe | 750.00 | | |
| | 1/27/11 | 1005 | SJ | R Coe | 15,240.00 | | |
| | 1/29/11 | 23987 | CRJ | J Wilson - Invoice: 1001 | | 450.00 | |
| | 1/29/11 | 283 | CRJ | A Monroe - Invoice: 1003 | | 750.00 | |
| | 1/31/11 | 1004 | SJ | J Wilson | 12,030.00 | | |
| | 1/31/11 | 1006 | SJ | I Bowen | 4,950.00 | | |
| | 1/31/11 | 1007 | SJ | S Gomez | 4,050.00 | | |
| | | | | Current Period Change | 37,995.00 | 1,200.00 | 36,795.00 |
| | 1/31/11 | | | Ending Balance | | | 36,795.00 |

**8** Place the cursor next to the R Coe invoice. Double-click anywhere on the **R Coe invoice 1002** from the sales journal (SJ) to reveal this source document (an invoice) explaining that particular increase in accounts receivable.

**9** Look over the invoice and then close the Sales/Invoicing window.

**10** Double-click the **750.00** amount from the cash receipts journal (CRJ) to reveal this source document (a cash receipt) explaining that particular decrease in accounts receivable.

**11** Look over the cash receipt and then close that window and the General Ledger Report window.

**12** Double-click **(5,620)** in the March column of the statement of cash flows to reveal a general ledger report explaining the increase in inventory during March.

**13** Scroll to the bottom of that report, noting the total debits to the account of 30,195 and the net credits to the account of 24,575 resulting in the 5,620 net increases.

**14** Double-click the 3/31/11 credit of **1,600.00** to reveal the underlying source document (invoice) supporting this credit. (The invoice does not actually show the $1,600 since that is the cost of the goods sold, but the invoice does reflect 32 units sold.)

**15** Look over this invoice and then close the Invoice window.

**16**  Scroll back up the general ledger report and double-click the **2,250.00** amount recorded on 3/11/11.

**17**  This action reveals a source document (purchase receipt of granite counter) from a vendor (i.e., an inventory purchase).

**18**  Close all open windows.

"After looking over this general ledger report on inventory in March, can you explain the reason for the increase?" Scott asks.

"Yes," you reply. "Inventory is increased by purchases as shown by the purchase receipt and decreased by the cost of goods sold as shown by the sales invoice. We must have purchased more inventory than we sold."

"Exactly," Scott responds.

## End Note

You've now seen how all three of the key financial statements, the balance sheet, income statement, and statement of cash flows, can be easily created, modified, and printed from within Peachtree. In Chapter 5, you will complete your overview of Peachtree by creating supporting reports for accounts receivable, inventory, and accounts payable.

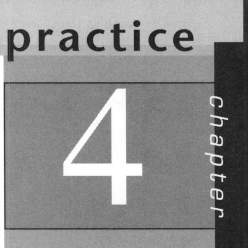
## Chapter 4 Questions

**1** What accounting periods are included in the standard statement of cash flows?

**2** What are the three sections called in the standard statement of cash flows?

**3** Why is depreciation an adjustment to net income in the operating activities section of the standard statement of cash flows?

**4** Why would you create a comparative statement of cash flows for several months?

**5** Why type $(EndDate)$ as a title for a new statement of cash flows?

**6** Why select Current – 2 as the time frame when creating a new statement of cash flows?

**7** What's the risk of using Whole Dollars as your choice for rounding?

**8** What report appears when you double-click the change in accounts receivable in the statement of cash flows?

**9** What source documents are typically shown in the accounts receivable general ledger report?

**10** What causes inventory to show a net increase?

## Chapter 4 Assignments ✓

**1** *Prepare and print the following reports using the Century Kitchens Peachtree files. (Place your name in the footer of each report. To do so, scroll to the bottom of any report in Design mode, double-click the* **Text – Footer**, *and then type your name. This will help you locate your report as opposed to any other student's report when using computer labs.)*

*merchandising*

    a. A standard cash flow statement for the current period (with a system date of 2/28/11 and with the accounting period set to Period 2 rounded to whole dollars).

    b. Modify the cash flow statement you created in (a) using Peachtree's Design feature to create a comparative cash flow statement comparing two accounting periods. For example, you could use 1/31/11 and 2/28/11, exactly as you did in the chapter except with two months. Save it as **2 Mo Comparative Cash Flows**. The new statement should look like Figure 4.8.

    c. A general ledger report of those transactions recorded in February that affected prepaid insurance.

    d. A general ledger report of those transactions recorded in February that affected accounts payable.

**Figure 4.8**

Two-Month Comparative
Cash Flows

Century Kitchens
Statement of Cash Flow
For the Months Ended

| | | February 28, 2011 | | January 31, 2011 |
|---|---|---|---|---|
| Cash Flows from operating activities | | | | |
| Net Income | $ | 11,356 | $ | 4,381 |
| Adjustments to reconcile net income to net cash provided by operating activities | | | | |
| Accumulated Depreciation | | 833 | | 833 |
| Accounts Receivable | | (31,955) | | (36,795) |
| Prepaid Insurance | | (4,000) | | 0 |
| Accounts Payable | | 14,220 | | 0 |
| Payroll Liabilities | | 4,280 | | 4,911 |
| Total Adjustments | | (16,622) | | (31,051) |
| Net Cash provided by Operations | | (5,266) | | (26,670) |
| | | | | |
| Cash Flows from investing activities | | | | |
| Used For | | | | |
| Equipment | | 0 | | (50,000) |
| Net cash used in investing | | 0 | | (50,000) |
| | | | | |
| Cash Flows from financing activities | | | | |
| Proceeds From | | | | |
| Common Stock | | 0 | | 125,000 |
| Used For | | | | |
| Net cash used in financing | | 0 | | 125,000 |
| Net increase <decrease> in cash | $ | (5,266) | $ | 48,330 |
| | | | | |
| | | | | |
| Summary | | | | |
| Cash Balance at End of Period | $ | 43,064 | $ | 48,329 |
| Cash Balance at Beg of Period | | (48,330) | | 0 |
| Net Increase <Decrease> in Cash | $ | (5,266) | $ | 48,329 |

**2**   *Answer the following questions using the Century Kitchens Peachtree files after opening a standard cash flow statement (with accounting period set to Period 3).*

   a.   Drill down from the year-to-date accounts payable account. Locate check 135. What did Century Kitchens pay for with this check? What was the date of the purchase?

   b.   Drill down from the year-to-date accounts payable account. What was purchased on 3/11/11? Who invoiced Century? What was the invoice number?

   c.   Drill down from the year-to-date accounts receivable account. What happened on 3/16/11?

# Chapter 4 Cases

## *Chapter 4 Case Problem 1*
## KELLY JENNINGS ADVERTISING

service

**1**   *Kelly Jennings (see Chapter 2 and 3 Case Problem 1) requires some additional financial reports. Prepare and print the following reports using Kelly Jennings Advertising Peachtree file. (Use the file you updated in Chapter 3 or restore this file from the Data Files CD. Be sure to include your name in the Extra Footer Line of each report, where possible. Set system date to 2/29/08 and the accounting period to* **Period 2.***)*

   a.   A standard cash flow statement as of 2/29/08 with no page numbers and no zero amounts.

   b.   Modify the cash flow statement you just created in (a) using Peachtree's Design feature to create a cash flow statement comparing two accounting periods with no rounding, 18 character widths, and aligned to the right column. Save it as **2 Mo Comparative Cash Flows**.

   c.   A general ledger report of those transactions recorded in January 2008 that affected the accounts receivable account. (Make sure it fits on one page and that all items are visible by turning off the truncating feature. Don't save changes!)

   d.   A general ledger report of those transactions recorded in January 2008 that affected the inventory account. (Make sure it fits on one page and that all items are visible by turning off the truncating feature. Don't save changes!)

**2**   *Answer the following questions:*

   a.   Drill down from the year-to-date accounts payable account. Locate check 1253. What did Jennings pay for with this check?

   b.   Drill down from the year-to-date accounts payable account. What was purchased on 1/28/08? Who invoiced Jennings? What was the invoice number?

   c.   Drill down from the year-to-date accounts receivable account. What happened on 2/26/08?

## *Chapter 4 Case Problem 2*
## SIERRA MARINA ✓

**1**   *Sierra Marina (see Chapter 2 and 3 Case Problem 2) requires some additional financial reports. Prepare and print the following reports using Sierra Marina's Peachtree file. (Use the file you updated in Chapter 3 or restore this file from the Data Files CD. Be sure to include your name in the Extra Footer Line of each report, where possible. Set system date to 8/31/10 and the accounting period to* **Period 2.***)*

   a.   A standard cash flow statement as of 8/31/10 with no page numbers and no zero amounts.

   b.   Modify the cash flow statement you just created in (a) using Peachtree's Design feature to create a cash flow statement comparing two accounting periods rounded to the nearest whole dollar, 18 character widths, and aligned to the right column. Save it as **2 Mo Comparative Cash Flows**.

   c.   A general ledger report of those transactions recorded in July 2010 that affected the accounts receivable account. (Make sure it fits on one page and that all items are visible by turning off the truncating feature. Don't save changes!)

   d.   A general ledger report of those transactions recorded in July 2010 that affected the accounts payable account. (Make sure it fits on one page and that all items are visible by turning off the truncating feature. Don't save changes!)

**2**   *Answer the following questions:*

   a.   From the general ledger report you created in 1 c above, locate the transaction occurring on 7/16 (Invoice 9). What customer was involved with this transaction? What service item was sold?

   b.   From the general ledger report you created in 1 d above, locate the transaction occurring on 7/19. What vendor was involved with this transaction? What GL Account was affected?

### Chapter 4 Case Problem 3
## JASON GALAS, ATTORNEY AT LAW, PC

Jason Galas (see Chapter 2 and 3 Case Problem 3) requires some additional financial reports.

**1**   *Prepare and print the following reports using the Jason Galas, Attorney at Law, PC Peachtree file. (Use the file you updated in Chapter 3 or restore this file from the Data Files CD. Be sure to include your name in the Extra Footer Line of each report, where possible. Set system date to 2/29/12 and the accounting period to* **Period 2**.*)*

   a.   A standard cash flow statement as of 2/29/12 with no page numbers and no zero amounts.

   b.   Modify the cash flow statement you just created in (a) using Peachtree's Design feature to create a cash flow statement comparing January and February rounded to whole dollars in $ format and a column width of 18 for all numbers. Save it as 2 Mo Comparative Cash Flows.

   c.   A general ledger report of those transactions recorded in January 2012 that affected the client fees receivable account. (Make sure it fits on one page and that all items are visible by turning off the shorten description feature. Save it as A/R cash flows. Note this is saved in the General Ledger report group.)

d.  A general ledger report of those transactions recorded in February 2012 that affected the accounts payable account. (Make sure it fits on one page and that all items are visible by turning off the shorten description feature. Save it as A/P cash flows. Note this is saved in the General Ledger report group.)

**2**   *Answer the following questions:*

a.  From the general ledger report you created in 1 c above, locate the transaction occurring on 1/10/12 (Invoice 561). What customer was involved with this transaction? What service item/items was/were sold?

b.  From the general ledger report you created in 1 d above, locate the first transaction in February. What vendor was involved with this transaction? What was the amount of the transaction? What GL account was affected?

# Creating Supporting Reports to Help Make Business Decisions

*In this Chapter, you will:*

- Review the Business Status Center.
- Create, print, and analyze a detailed and summary aged receivables report.
- Create, print, and analyze an inventory valuation report.
- Create, print, and analyze a detailed and summary aged payables report.

## *Case:* Century Kitchens

You arrive at work, and two phones are ringing. As Scott hangs up from one call and is about to answer another, he quickly explains what's happening—he's thinking about expanding the business and needs to borrow from the bank, and the bank is requesting up-to-the-minute information. You quickly answer a phone and write down the banker's request for some information on inventory. As you hang up from the call, Scott asks you to come into his office. You compare notes—he has requests for information on accounts receivable and accounts payable. You show him your note requesting information on Century Kitchens' inventory.

Scott has shown you that Peachtree can easily generate transaction reports, but you can see that the banker's requests require more detailed information. You remember from your accounting course that accountants frequently use what are called supporting schedules—reports that provide the underlying details of an account. You ask Scott if Peachtree can help. He smiles and says, "You bet. Peachtree calls these schedules 'reports,' but they are the same thing. Let's get to work."

Scott reminds you that usually when you start Peachtree and open the Century Kitchens data file, the first screen you see is the Business Status Center. He suggests you start with a review of what's available in the Business Status Center.

## Reviewing the Business Status Center

The Peachtree Business Status Center displays a variety of general business information, including account balances, revenue figures, receivables and payables data, and action items. It also includes a feature that lets you find, display, and/or print a Peachtree report.

Some of the information that appears in the Business Status Center can be drilled down on to investigate the underlying source documents that created that information.

The default settings in Peachtree reveal an Account Balances section first. This section provides account balances as of the end of the accounting period

*Video Demonstration*

*Demo 5 - Using the business status center*

**Figure 5.1**

Account Balances

| Account Balances | | 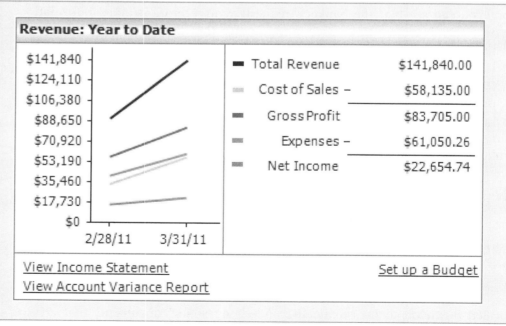Customize |
|---|---|---|
| Account Description | Account ID | Balance |
| Checking | 1100 | $38,460.76 |
| Accounts Receivable | 1200 | $93,280.00 |
| Accounts Payable | 2000 | ($27,270.00) |
| | | |
| | | |
| | | |
| View Account List | | View Balance Sheet |
| Reconcile Accounts and Import Bank Statements | | |

you've specified. For system date 3/31/11 and accounting period 3, the Account Balances section looks like Figure 5.1. Note that if you change the system date and accounting period, the information displayed in the Business Status Center changes. The blue text indicates the ability to drill down for further information. In this case, you can drill down on Account ID to reveal a specific account register, which shows transactions for the day, month, period, quarter, year, or week to date, month to date, period to date, quarter to date, year to date, or all. The blue text also indicates reports or lists you might want to see related to this section. For Century Kitchens, that would include an account list or balance sheet. Lastly, common tasks are also provided; in this case, reconciling accounts or importing bank statements can be activated quickly and easily.

The second section, on the right, reveals Revenue: Year to Date. This section reveals a chart of revenues by period and a quick income statement as well as drill-down ability to view a full income statement, budget, or account variance report as shown in Figure 5.2.

**Figure 5.2**

Revenue Year to Date

**Revenue: Year to Date**

| | |
|---|---|
| Total Revenue | $141,840.00 |
| Cost of Sales – | $58,135.00 |
| Gross Profit | $83,705.00 |
| Expenses – | $61,050.26 |
| Net Income | $22,654.74 |

View Income Statement                    Set up a Budget
View Account Variance Report

The next section, titled Customers Who Owe Money, reveals a list of—you guessed it—customers who owe the company money. By default, this list is in order of due dates as shown in Figure 5.3. This list will prove helpful to Scott when he investigates accounts receivable balances. The red dates indicate a past due amount and when double-clicked reveal the underlying source document creating that receivable. The same document can also be found by single-clicking the Customer ID. You remember that the due dates are determined by the invoice date and the terms afforded each customer. Once again, the blue text reveals access to common lists or tasks. As you can see, not all balances are shown in Figure 5.3. Depending on the size of your monitor, you may need to use the scroll bar to scroll down the list. When you do, you'll notice that the current receivable due dates are in black, not red.

**Figure 5.3**

Customers Who Owe Money

The section below, also related to the amounts customers owe, is titled Aged Receivables. It shows a graph of accounts receivable as of the end of the accounting period and a table of amounts by days overdue as shown in Figure 5.4. This blue text again indicates common lists, reports, and tasks you can access from this section.

**Figure 5.4**

Aged Receivables

To the right is a section titled Vendors to Pay, which reveals amounts owed to vendors sorted by due date as shown in Figure 5.5. Again, in this case, the red due dates indicate past due amounts, and the black due dates indicate current payments due. Again, you remember that the due dates are determined by the purchase date and the terms afforded you by each vendor. Individual source documents are accessed by double-clicking on specific due dates or a click on the Vendor ID.

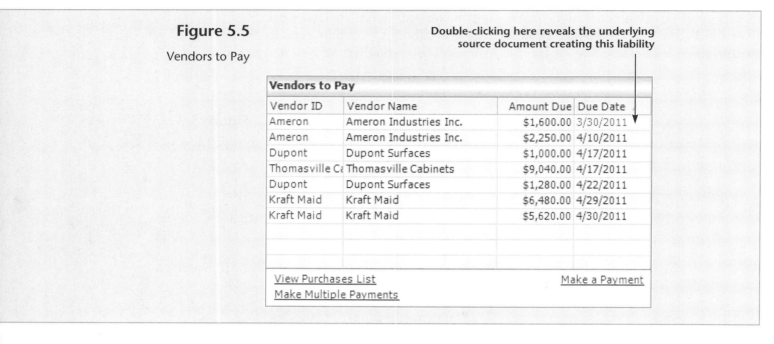

**Figure 5.5**

Vendors to Pay

The next section, titled Aged Payables, stratifies accounts payable like the Aged Receivables section discussed previously. A graph and table of accounts payable amounts by days overdue are shown in Figure 5.6. Access to common lists, reports, and tasks is also provided.

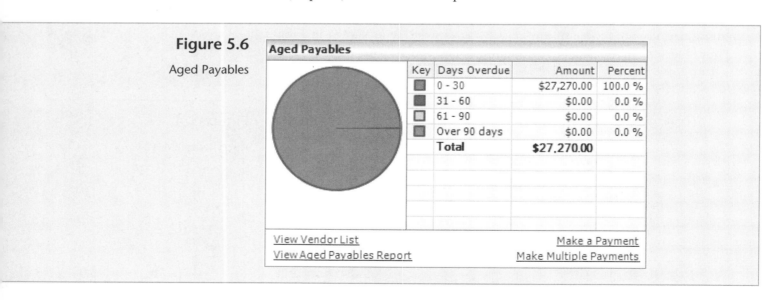

**Figure 5.6**

Aged Payables

The last section in the Business Status Center provides the user the ability to find a report based on specific categories. Knowing Scott was interested in a report that provided information on receivables from customers, you searched for a report under the category of Customers & Sales and found an Aged Receivables report along with a description of what that report provides. See Figure 5.7.

**Click here to reveal a list
of categories available**

**Figure 5.7**

Find a Report

**Find a Report**

Category: Customers & Sales

Report: Aged Receivables

Description: Customers with outstanding invoices sorted by aging category.

Print    Display

**Click here to reveal a
list of reports available
for a specific category**

This section gives the user the ability to print or display the report.

"The Business Status Center looks like it can be very helpful to us as we try and answer the bank's questions," you comment.

"Quite true," Scott responds. "Let's investigate this aged receivables report."

## Create, Print, and Analyze an Aged Receivables Report

You know from your accounting course that accounts receivable represent amounts due from customers for goods or services they have received but for which they have not yet paid. Peachtree provides several preset accounts receivable reports that anticipate the information managers most often need.

The banker wants information on a particular customer's past due account balance, and she wants to know the total amount due from customers as of today.

Scott tells you that the best way to get information on past due accounts is to create a schedule that Peachtree calls an "Accounts Receivable Aging report"—but what you learned in your accounting course is usually called an "accounts receivable aging schedule." You remember that an aging schedule is a listing of how long each receivable has been uncollected. He wants it short and to the point.

### To create an aged receivables report:

1  Open Century Kitchens.

2  Set the system date to **3/31/11** and the accounting period to **Period 3**.

3  Click **Reports & Forms** and then click **Accounts Receivable**.

4  Double-click **Aged Receivables** from the Report List. (Alternatively, you could access this report from the Aged Receivables section of the Business Status Center or by searching for reports as described earlier.)

5  Click the **Columns** button.

**6** Uncheck the **Show** check boxes for the Customer ID, Bill to Contact, and Telephone 1 fields as shown in Figure 5.8.

**Figure 5.8**

Aged Receivables Fields

Click here to uncheck or check a field. Removing the check causes the report to not show a field

**7** Click **OK** to accept changes.

**8** Click **Print** and then click **OK** in the Print window to print it. Your printed version should look like Figure 5.9.

**Figure 5.9**

Aged Receivables Report

**Century Kitchens**
**Aged Receivables**
**As of Mar 31, 2011**
Filter Criteria includes: 1) Includes Drop Shipments. Report order is by ID. Report is printed in Detail Format.

| Customer | Invoice/CM # | 0-30 | 31-60 | 61-90 | Over 90 days | Amount Due |
|---|---|---|---|---|---|---|
| A Monroe | 1008 | | 15,455.00 | | | 15,455.00 |
| | 1019 | 4,960.00 | | | | 4,960.00 |
| **A Monroe** | | **4,960.00** | **15,455.00** | | | **20,415.00** |
| | | | | | | |
| B Scaggs | 1016 | 17,745.00 | | | | 17,745.00 |
| **B Scaggs** | | **17,745.00** | | | | **17,745.00** |
| | | | | | | |
| I Bowen | 1017 | 3,960.00 | | | | 3,960.00 |
| **I Bowen** | | **3,960.00** | | | | **3,960.00** |
| | | | | | | |
| J Summer | 1013 | | 2,250.00 | | | 2,250.00 |
| | 1018 | 10,560.00 | | | | 10,560.00 |
| **J Summer** | | **10,560.00** | **2,250.00** | | | **12,810.00** |
| | | | | | | |
| J Wilson | 1020 | 7,115.00 | | | | 7,115.00 |
| **J Wilson** | | **7,115.00** | | | | **7,115.00** |
| | | | | | | |
| R Coe | 1005 | | | 12,765.00 | | 12,765.00 |
| | 1021 | 6,550.00 | | | | 6,550.00 |
| **R Coe** | | **6,550.00** | | **12,765.00** | | **19,315.00** |
| | | | | | | |
| R Rose | 1012 | | 4,500.00 | | | 4,500.00 |
| **R Rose** | | | **4,500.00** | | | **4,500.00** |
| | | | | | | |
| S Gomez | 1007 | | -5,950.00 | | | -5,950.00 |
| | 1010 | | 13,370.00 | | | 13,370.00 |
| **S Gomez** | | | **7,420.00** | | | **7,420.00** |
| | | **50,890.00** | **29,625.00** | **12,765.00** | | **93,280.00** |

**9** Click **Save** on the button bar, type **Aged Receivables 1** as the name of this report, and then click the **Save** button.

You can see that this report gives Scott an up-to-date listing of customers and their balances. It tells him how long each receivable has been uncollected so he can take appropriate action.

You ask Scott the name of the customer about whom the banker requested information. He says the customer's name is R Coe and that the banker wants to know the status of his account and his payment history. He says that, as you have done with other reports, you can drill down to gather this information.

**To investigate a particular receivable on an aged receivables report:**

**1** Double-click the **12,765.00** amount owed by R Coe from invoice 1005.

**2** Invoice 1005 appears as shown in Figure 5.10.

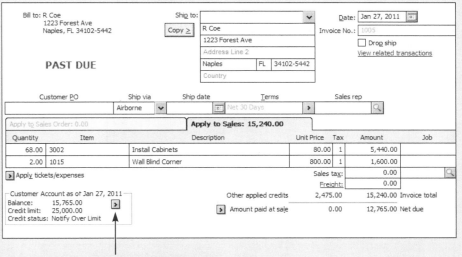

Click here to reveal this customer's ledger

**Figure 5.10**

Invoice 1005

**3** Expand the invoice if necessary to view all items including the Net Due of $12,765, which matches the aging balance.

**4** Click the **right arrow** button in the lower left-hand corner of the invoice in the box labeled Customer Account as of Jan 31, 2011. A customer ledger appears for the month of January.

**5** Click **Options** from the button bar, change the range by changing the To: date to Mar 31, 2011, and then click **OK**. A revised customer ledger for R Coe appears as shown in Figure 5.11.

**Figure 5.11**

R Coe Customer Ledger for the Period January 1, 2011, to March 31, 2011

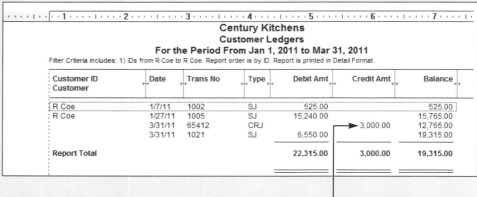

Double-click here to reveal this cash receipt

**6** Note that the ending receivables balance due is $19,315.00, which is made up of three invoices and one payment on account.

**7** Double-click the **3,000.00** payment received on 3/31/11. A receipt source document should appear as shown in Figure 5.12.

**Figure 5.12**

Receipt Source Document

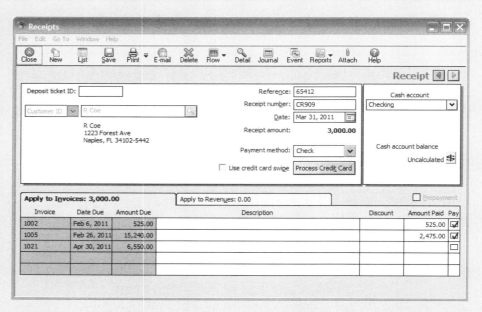

**8** Notice that the $3,000.00 check was received from R Coe on 3/31/11. Of this payment, $525.00 was applied to pay off invoice 1002. The balance of the $3,000.00—$2,475.00—was applied to invoice 1005. This explains why the balance due and the invoice amount were different. (See Figure 5.10, bottom right.)

Scott has copied down the information the banker requested—R Coe is 44 days past due on invoice 1005, he owes $12,765.00 on that invoice, and invoice 1002 was paid off on 3/31/11. He has a current invoice, 1021, for $6,550.00. He is now ready to fulfill the banker's other requests for a summary report for all receivables.

---

**To create and print a summary aged receivables report:**

**1**    Click **Reports & Forms** and then click **Accounts Receivable**.

**2**    Double-click **Aged Receivables 1** from the Report List. (This, of course, is the report you just created and saved.)

**3**    Click **Options** from the button bar and then check the **Summarize report** check box.

**4**    Click **OK** to reveal the newly modified aged receivables report as shown in Figure 5.13.

**Century Kitchens**
**Aged Receivables**
**As of Mar 31, 2011**

Filter Criteria includes: 1) Includes Drop Shipments. Report order is by ID. Report is printed in Summary Format.

| Customer | 0-30 | 31-60 | 61-90 | Over 90 days | Amount Due |
|---|---|---|---|---|---|
| A Monroe | 4,960.00 | 15,455.00 | | | 20,415.00 |
| B Scaggs | 17,745.00 | | | | 17,745.00 |
| I Bowen | 3,960.00 | | | | 3,960.00 |
| J Summer | 10,560.00 | 2,250.00 | | | 12,810.00 |
| J Wilson | 7,115.00 | | | | 7,115.00 |
| R Coe | 6,550.00 | | 12,765.00 | | 19,315.00 |
| R Rose | | 4,500.00 | | | 4,500.00 |
| S Gomez | | 7,420.00 | | | 7,420.00 |
| | 50,890.00 | 29,625.00 | 12,765.00 | | 93,280.00 |

**Figure 5.13**

Summary Aged Receivables Report

**5**    Click **Save** on the button bar, type **Aged Receivables 2** as the name of this report, and then click the **Save** button.

**6**    Close all windows.

# Create, Print, and Analyze an Inventory Valuation Report

Scott asks you about the request you took over the phone. You show him your notes; you spoke to Kim Hui, one of the company's investors. He stopped by the other day and noticed a lot of cabinet inventory in the shop and wondered why we had so much.

Scott explains that in his business he never places a purchase order to a cabinet or counter top manufacturer unless it's been signed off by a customer. "We hold the inventory until we can schedule it for installation. Once installed, we then bill the customer, and the inventory becomes cost of goods sold."

He suggests that you use Peachtree to show, via an inventory valuation report, just exactly what inventory you have as of 3/31/11.

## To create an inventory valuation report:

**1** Click **Reports & Forms** and then click **Inventory**.

**2** Double-click **Inventory Valuation Report**. You note that the report is quite long and has truncated (shortened) item descriptions and lots of items for which there is no quantity on hand.

**3** Click **Columns** from the button bar.

**4** Click the **Filters** button.

**5** Uncheck the **Shorten description** and **Include items** with no quantity on hand check boxes.

**6** Click **OK** to view the inventory valuation report shown in Figure 5.14.

**Figure 5.14**

Inventory Valuation Report

Century Kitchens
Inventory Valuation Report
As of Mar 31, 2011

Filter Criteria includes: 1) Stock/Assembly. Report order is by ID.

| Item ID Item Class | Item Description | Stocking U/M | Cost Method | Qty on Hand | Item Value | Avg Cost | % of Inv Value |
|---|---|---|---|---|---|---|---|
| 1002 Stock item | Base Single Door | | Average | 3.00 | 1,200.00 | 400.00 | 21.35 |
| 1003 Stock item | Base Double Door Double Drawer | | Average | 2.00 | 960.00 | 480.00 | 17.08 |
| 1006 Stock item | Base Lattice | | Average | 3.00 | 960.00 | 320.00 | 17.08 |
| 1008 Stock item | Chopping Block Table | | Average | 1.00 | 360.00 | 360.00 | 6.41 |
| 1012 Stock item | Wall Double Door | | Average | 5.00 | 1,600.00 | 320.00 | 28.47 |
| 1014 Stock item | Wall Angle | | Average | 1.00 | 540.00 | 540.00 | 9.61 |
| | | | | | 5,620.00 | | 100.00 |

**7** Scroll around this report to familiarize yourself with its contents. It describes the inventory on hand as of 3/31/11.

**8** Click **Print** on the button bar to print this report.

**9** Click **Save** on the button bar, type **Inventory Valuation Report 1** as the name of this report, and then click the **Save** button.

**10** Close all windows.

## Create, Print, and Analyze an Aged Payables Report

The last request to which you and Scott need to respond is from Juan Gomez, who handles all inventory purchase orders, pays bills, and monitors accounts payable. He wants two reports so he can plan next month's cash flow.

You quickly ask if Peachtree handles accounts payable aging the same way it handles accounts receivable aging. Scott smiles, "You catch on fast," he says. "Let's start with an aged payables report. It provides the detail Juan needs."

### To create an aged payables report:

**1** Click **Reports & Forms** and then click **Accounts Payable**.

**2** Double-click **Aged Payables** from the Report List. (Alternatively, you could access this report from the Aged Payables section of the Business Status Center or by searching for reports as described earlier.)

**3** Click **Columns**.

**4** Uncheck the **Show** check boxes for the Vendor ID, Contact, and Telephone 1 fields as shown in Figure 5.15.

**Figure 5.15**

Aged Payables Fields

— **Click here to uncheck the show box so that the Vendor ID is not shown in the report**

**5**    Click **OK** to accept changes. Your report should look like Figure 5.16.

**Figure 5.16**

Aged Payables Report

Note that in Detail Format each invoice creating a vendor balance is shown

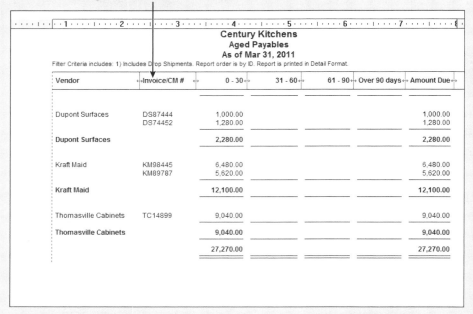

**6**    Click **Print** and then click **OK** in the Print window to print it.

**7**    Click **Save** on the button bar, type **Aged Payables 1** as the name of this report, and then click the **Save** button.

After Scott prints this report for Juan, you look it over. You notice a large outstanding balance to Thomasville Cabinets, and you suggest using drill down to investigate it further. You and Scott both decide to investigate this liability for which Century Kitchens owes $9,040.00.

### To investigate a particular payable on an aged payables report:

**1**    Double-click the **9,040.00** balance owed to Thomasville Cabinets.

**2**    Invoice TC14899 appears as shown in Figure 5.17.

**3**    Expand the invoice if necessary to view all items including the Net Due of $9,040.00, which matches the aging balance.

**4**    Click the **right arrow** button in the lower left-hand corner of the invoice in the box labeled Vendor Balance on Mar 18, 2011. A customer ledger appears for part of the month of March.

| Remit to: | Thomasville Cabinets 401 East Main Street Thomasville, NC 27360 | | | | | | | | |
|---|---|---|---|---|---|---|---|---|---|

**Figure 5.17**

Purchase/Receipt from Thomasville Cabinets

Ship to: Century Kitchens, 1836 55th Street Southwest, Address Line 2, Naples, FL 34116, US

Date: Mar 18, 2011
Invoice No.: TC14899
☐ Drop ship
☐ Waiting on bill
View related transactions

UNPAID

| Customer SO No. | Customer invoice No. | Terms | Ship via | A/P account |
|---|---|---|---|---|
| | | Net 30 Days | UPS Ground | 2000 |

Apply to Purchase Order No.: 9     Apply to Purchases: 0.00

| Item | Remaining | Received | Description | GL Account | Unit Price | Amount | Job |
|---|---|---|---|---|---|---|---|
| 1002 | 5.00 | 5.00 | Base Single Door | 1300 | 400.00 | 2,000.00 | |
| 1003 | 3.00 | 3.00 | Base Double Door Double Drawer | 1300 | 480.00 | 1,440.00 | |
| 1004 | 1.00 | 1.00 | Base Double Door with Tray | 1300 | 440.00 | 440.00 | |
| 1005 | 1.00 | 1.00 | Base Oven Cabinet | 1300 | 240.00 | 240.00 | |
| 1007 | 2.00 | 2.00 | Pantry | 1300 | 520.00 | 1,040.00 | |
| 1009 | 1.00 | 1.00 | Easy Reach Corner | 1300 | 600.00 | 600.00 | |
| 1010 | 1.00 | 1.00 | Wall MV Cabinet | 1300 | 480.00 | 480.00 | |
| 1011 | 1.00 | 1.00 | Wall Refrigerator | 1300 | 240.00 | 240.00 | |
| 1012 | 4.00 | 4.00 | Wall Double Door | 1300 | 320.00 | 1,280.00 | |
| 1015 | 2.00 | 2.00 | Wall Blind Corner | 1300 | 640.00 | 1,280.00 | |

Other payments and credits: 0.00     9,040.00 Invoice total
Amount paid at purchase: 0.00     9,040.00 Net due

Vendor balance on Mar 18, 2011   16,660.00

**5** Click **Options** from the button bar, change the range by changing the To: date to **Mar 31, 2011**, and the From: date to **Jan 1, 2011**, and then click **OK**. A revised vendor ledger for Thomasville Cabinets appears as shown in Figure 5.18.

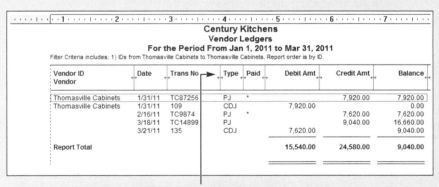

**Figure 5.18**

Thomasville Cabinets Vendor Ledger for the Period January 1, 2011, to March 31, 2011

**Century Kitchens**
**Vendor Ledgers**
**For the Period From Jan 1, 2011 to Mar 31, 2011**
Filter Criteria includes: 1) IDs from Thomasville Cabinets to Thomasville Cabinets. Report order is by ID.

| Vendor ID Vendor | Date | Trans No | Type | Paid | Debit Amt | Credit Amt | Balance |
|---|---|---|---|---|---|---|---|
| Thomasville Cabinets | 1/31/11 | TC87256 | PJ | * | | 7,920.00 | 7,920.00 |
| Thomasville Cabinets | 1/31/11 | 109 | CDJ | | 7,920.00 | | 0.00 |
| | 2/16/11 | TC9874 | PJ | * | | 7,620.00 | 7,620.00 |
| | 3/18/11 | TC14899 | PJ | | | 9,040.00 | 16,660.00 |
| | 3/21/11 | 135 | CDJ | | 7,620.00 | | 9,040.00 |
| **Report Total** | | | | | **15,540.00** | **24,580.00** | **9,040.00** |

The types here are PJ (purchases journal)
and CDJ (cash disbursements journal)

**6** Note that the ending payables balance due is $9,040.00, which is made up of three invoices and two payments on account.

**7** Close all open windows.

Scott has copied down the information Juan requested. He is now ready to fulfill Juan's other request for a summary report for all payables.

## To create and print a summary aged payables report:

1  Click **Reports & Forms** and then click **Accounts Payable**.

2  Double-click **Aged Payables 1** from the Report List. (This, of course, is the report you just created and saved.)

3  Click **Options** from the button bar and then check the **Summarize report** check box.

4  Click **OK** to reveal the newly modified aged payables report as shown in Figure 5.19.

**Figure 5.19**

Summary Aged Payables Report

Note that in Summary Format, no invoices are shown

Century Kitchens
Aged Payables
As of Mar 31, 2011
Filter Criteria includes: 1) Includes Drop Shipments. Report order is by ID. Report is printed in Summary Format.

| Vendor | 0 - 30 | 31 - 60 | 61 - 90 | Over 90 days | Amount Due |
|---|---|---|---|---|---|
| Ameron Industries Inc. | 3,850.00 | | | | 3,850.00 |
| Dupont Surfaces | 2,280.00 | | | | 2,280.00 |
| Kraft Maid | 12,100.00 | | | | 12,100.00 |
| Thomasville Cabinets | 9,040.00 | | | | 9,040.00 |
| | 27,270.00 | | | | 27,270.00 |

5  Click **Save** on the button bar, type **Aged Payables 2** as the name of this report, and then click the **Save** button.

6  Close all windows.

## End Note

As you gather the reports and set out to deliver them, you are struck by how easily and quickly Scott has been able to respond to the managers' requests. Within a short time, Peachtree has generated accurate, up-to-the-minute financial information to help Scott and his staff make important business decisions. The many preset reports—summaries, details, and supporting documentation—anticipate the information that owners often need to make sound business decisions.

## Chapter 5 Questions

**1** What does the Business Status Center display?

**2** What does the blue text indicate in the Business Status Center?

**3** What happens to the information displayed in the Business Status Center when you change the system date and/or accounting period?

**4** What is the default order for the Customers Who Owe Money section?

**5** How do you sort the Customers Who Owe Money section by amount due in ascending or descending order?

**6** What three ways can you access an aged receivables report?

**7** From an invoice to a customer, how do you access that particular customer's ledger?

**8** What happens if you don't uncheck the box Include items with no quantity on hand in the Options section of the inventory valuation report?

**9** What's the difference between an aged payables report in detail vs. summary format?

**10** What do PJ and CDJ stand for in the Type column of the vendor ledger?

## Chapter 5 Assignments

**1** *Set the system date to 1/31/11 and the accounting period to* **Period 1 – 01/01/11–01/31/11.** *Then use the Business Status Center to answer the following questions:*

a. What is the balance in accounts receivable?

b. How much did I Bowen owe as of 1/31/11, and when was it due?

c. What was the cost of sales?

d. How much does the company owe Dupont by 4/17/11?

e. How much of the company's receivables are 31 to 60 days overdue?

f. How much of the company's payables are 31 to 60 days overdue?

**2** *Set the system date to 2/28/11 and the accounting period to* **Period 2 – 02/01/11–02/28/11.** *Prepare and print the following reports (using the same parameters used in the chapter) using the Century Kitchens Peachtree files. (Place your name in the footer of each report. To do so, scroll to the bottom of any report in Design mode, double-click the* **Text – Footer** *and then type your name. This will help you locate your report as opposed to any other student's report when using computer labs.)*

a. Create and print a summary aged receivables report as of 2/28/11.

b. Create and print a detailed aged receivables report as of 2/28/11.

c. Create and print a summary aged payables report as of 2/28/11.

    d.    Create and print a detailed aged payables report as of 2/28/11.

    e.    Create and print an inventory valuation report (using the same filters you used in the chapter) as of 2/28/11.

**3**    *Set the system date to 3/31/11 and the accounting period to* **Period 3 – 03/01/11–03/31/11.** *Answer the following questions:*

    a.    What is the amount of the largest customer receivable, and what is the customer's name? What invoice(s) support that receivable?

    b.    What is the largest past due invoice? When is it due? Which customer owes that amount?

    c.    Which vendor is owed the largest total amount, and what is that total? What invoice(s) support that payable?

    d.    How much do we owe Ameron? What are the invoice number(s) which correspond to that balance?

    e.    What is the largest dollar value inventory item in stock as of 3/31/11? How much did we pay for it?

## Chapter 5 Cases

### Chapter 5 Case Problem 1

# KELLY JENNINGS ADVERTISING

**1**    *Set the system date to 1/31/08 and the accounting period to* **Period 1 – 01/01/08–01/31/08.** *Then use the Business Status Center to answer the following questions:*

    a.    What was the balance in accounts receivable?

    b.    How much did Paulson's Nursery owe, and what is the due date?

    c.    What were the total expenses for the period?

    d.    How much did the company owe KCOY that was due 1/10/08?

    e.    How much of the company's receivables were 31 to 60 days overdue?

    f.    How much of the company's payables were 0 to 30 days overdue?

**2**    *Set the system date to 2/29/08 and the accounting period to* **Period 2 – 02/01/08–02/29/08.** *Prepare, print, and save (just add 1 to the standard name of each report modified like you did in the chapter) the following reports (do not show the ID, Contact, or Telephone 1 fields) using the Kelly Jennings Advertising Peachtree files. (Place your name in the footer of each report. To do so, scroll to the bottom of any report in Design mode, double-click the* Text – Footer, *and then type your name. This will help you locate your report as opposed to any other student's report when using computer labs.)*

a. A summary aged receivables report as of 2/29/08.

b. A summary aged payables report as of 2/29/08.

c. An inventory valuation report as of 2/29/08.

**3** *Answer the following questions as of 2/29/08:*

a. What is the amount of the second largest customer receivable, and what is the customer's name? What invoice(s) support that receivable?

b. What is the second largest past due invoice? When is it due? Which customer owes that amount?

c. What is the amount of the smallest vendor payable, and what is the vendor's name? What invoice(s) support that payable?

d. What is the second largest past due payable? When is it due? Which vendor is owed?

e. What is the largest total dollar value inventory item in stock? How much was paid for it?

## Chapter 5 Case Problem 2
# SIERRA MARINA

**1** *Set the system date to 7/31/10 and the accounting period to* **Period 1 – 07/01/10–07/31/10.** *Then use the Business Status Center to answer the following questions:*

a. What was the balance in accounts receivable?

b. How much did Microsoft owe, and what is the due date?

c. What were the total expenses for the period?

d. How much did the company owe Exxon/Mobil and what is the due date?

e. How much of the company's receivables were 31 to 60 days overdue?

f. How much of the company's payables were 31 to 60 days overdue?

**2** *Set the system date to 8/31/10 and the accounting period to* **Period 2 – 08/01/10–08/31/10.** *Prepare, print, and save (just add 1 to the standard name of each report modified like you did in the chapter) the following reports (do not show the ID, Contact, or Telephone 1 fields). (Place your name in the footer of each report. To do so, scroll to the bottom of any report in Design mode, double-click the* **Text – Footer,** *and then type your name. This will help you locate your report as opposed to any other student's report when using computer labs.)*

a. A summary aged receivables report as of 8/31/10.

b. A summary aged payables report as of 8/31/10.

**3**   *Answer the following questions by exploring the reports you created in 2 above.*

   a.   How many days did Yahoo rent the 10 Passenger Pontoon Boat?

   b.   What was the invoice number for Microsoft dated 7/15/10?

   c.   What GL Account was used to categorize the bill from the Fresno Bee on 7/26/10?

   d.   What invoice number was used by Southern CA Edison to bill the company on 7/30/10?

### Chapter 5 Case Problem 3

## JASON GALAS, ATTORNEY AT LAW, PC

**1**   *Set the system date to 1/31/12 and the accounting period to* **Period 1 – 01/01/12–01/31/12.** *Then use the Business Status Center to answer the following questions:*

   a.   What was the balance in accounts receivable?

   b.   How much did Epic Medical Services owe, and what is the due date?

   c.   What were the total expenses for the period?

   d.   How much did the company owe Randol Leasing and what is the due date?

   e.   How much of the company's receivables were 31 to 60 days overdue?

   f.   How much of the company's payables were 31 to 60 days overdue?

**2**   *Set the system date to 2/29/12 and the accounting period to* **Period 2 – 02/01/12–02/29/12.** *Prepare, print, and save (just add 1 to the standard name of each report modified like you did in the chapter) the following reports (do not show the ID, Contact, or Telephone 1 fields).*

   a.   An aged receivables report as of 2/29/12.

   b.   A summary aged payables report as of 2/29/12.

**3**   *Answer the following questions by exploring the reports you created in 2 above.*

   a.   How many hours were billed for tax consulting services on invoice 568?

   b.   What was the invoice number for Woot Inc. dated 2/7/12?

   c.   What GL Account was used to categorize the bill from TXU Energy on 2/29/12?

   d.   What invoice number was used by Al Mar Maintenance Group to bill the company on 2/29/12?

# Creating a Peachtree File to Record and Analyze Business Events

*part*

2

*In this Part, you will:*

- **Set up your business's accounting system.**
- **Enter cash-oriented business activities.**
- **Enter additional business activities.**
- **Enter adjusting entries.**
- **Perform budgeting activities.**
- **Generate reports of business activities.**

**P**art 2 is designed to teach you how to use Peachtree and the accounting methods and concepts you've learned in your introductory accounting course. This part is divided into six chapters, each with its own set of questions, assignments, and case problems. You'll follow the adventures of Donna and Karen at Wild Water Sports who have hired you to help them set up their business in Peachtree, capture various business transactions, make adjusting entries, set up and use budgets, and generate key business reports. You'll utilize Peachtree to establish accounts, customers, vendors, items, and employees and then record business transactions using key source documents like sales receipts, invoices, bills, deposit forms, and checks. You will learn how to create journal entries in Peachtree to accrue revenues and expenses, adjust deferred assets and liabilities, and record depreciation of long-lived assets. Finally, you'll learn how Peachtree's budgeting and reporting process can help Wild Water Sports plan and control its business activities.

# Setting Up Your Accounting System

## *Case:* Wild Water Sports, Inc.

Donna Chandler and her best friend Karen Wilson have been water sports enthusiasts since they were six years old. They would spend a good portion of each summer vacation wake boarding and skiing the lakes and reservoirs of central Florida. After high school, each went her separate way. Donna went off to a four-year college and then began a career in real estate, while Karen attended a local community college and started her career in small business accounting.

At their ten-year high school reunion, they became reacquainted and reminisced about their fun-filled weekends and summers with boats and boys. They pondered how they could combine their careers and their love of boating into a business. They vowed to keep in touch. Later that year, Donna called with a plan. She had run into a business investor, Ernesto Martinez, who had opened a retail boat dealership in Orlando, Florida, but didn't have the time to mind the details. Donna felt she could handle the marketing and sales if Karen could handle the day-to-day business operations. From that plan, Wild Water Sports, Inc., was born. The company had some existing cash, receivables, inventory, equipment, and liabilities. Karen and Donna have decided to make an investment by purchasing common stock in the existing company; each will gain a one-third interest in the corporation, and the remaining one-third will belong to Ernesto.

Karen knows she will need some help with the daily accounting records and has chosen Peachtree as her accounting program to replace the manual accounting system that currently exists. When she contacted an employment agency to find a part-time accountant, you answered her call. Since you are a student who can use some spending money and have completed a basic accounting course, you were hired the same day.

Your job will be to work with Karen and establish and maintain accounting records for Wild Water Sports using Peachtree. The company will open its doors for business under new ownership in January but needs to set up accounts, items, customers, vendors, employees, etc. The company rents its showroom and service bays from a former auto dealership. It plans to offer top-of-the-line ski boats, personal watercraft, accessories, skis, and boats. It also plans to service boats and equipment and offer training. The company has leased a reservoir that will be used as a training site and also be available for rent to groups.

You agree to meet with Karen the next day to get started.

## Creating a New Company File

When you return to Karen's office, she's already purchased a new computer, the Peachtree software, Microsoft's Office suite, and supplies. The software is loaded and ready to go. Karen explains that you have two choices to begin setting up your company. Peachtree has a built-in Setup Guide, which can guide you through the company setup process, or you can skip the guide and set up the company yourself. Since this is your first time setting up a company in Peachtree, you opt for the Setup Guide.

"Starting with the Setup Guide is probably a good idea," Karen says. "Besides, no matter which method you start with, you can always change the decisions you make during setup later."

Karen explains that this process will accomplish various tasks. First, you will provide company information like an address, phone number, name, etc. Then you'll be asked to establish a chart of accounts (standard accounts and numbers to store your business event information). You'll want to use the accrual vs. cash method of accounting and the standard calendar months for reporting your financial information. Since this company has existing transactions and account balances, you will need to eventually establish those beginning balances and enter new transactions beginning in January 2013, the first month of business under new ownership.

### To create a new company file:

1    Start Peachtree and close any previously created company files.

2    Click **New Company** from the File menu or click **Create a new company** from the Peachtree window that appears. The Create a New Company – Introduction window should appear as shown in Figure 6.1.

**Figure 6.1**

The New Company Setup Window

**3** Click **Next** and then enter the information as specified in Figure 6.2.

**Figure 6.2**

Company Information

**4** Click **Next**. A window appears asking you to select a method to create your company.

**5** Choose the first option to use a sample business type and then click **Next**.

**6** Select **Retail Company** from the list of simplified business types. This will establish your basic chart of accounts as shown in Figure 6.3.

### Figure 6.3

Selecting a Business Type

**7**   Click **Next** and then select **Accrual accounting**.

**8**   Click **Next** and then select **Real Time** as your posting method.

**9**   Click **Next** and then select **12 monthly accounting periods** as your period structure.

**10**   Click **Next** and then select your starting month as **January 2013**.

**11**   Click **Next** and then click **Finish** to complete your new company setup.

**12**   After a few minutes of setup, Peachtree will reveal the Setup Guide as shown in Figure 6.4. If the Setup Guide does not appear, click **Setup Guide** from the File menu. Close this window, click **File**, and then click **Close Company**. Click **OK** if any Peachtree Solutions windows appear.

### Figure 6.4

Peachtree's Setup Guide

Donna has met with Ernesto and determined his business did have some outstanding balances from a few customers and owed some vendors for purchases made in the previous months. His business has an existing bank account and a MasterCard business credit card account. It also owned some equipment and had a related note payable.

Karen has also decided to use Peachtree's job tracking feature to follow service-related efforts for customers. The firm plans to market its service program to existing customers and will need to track costs for each job as well as bill customers based on hours worked and materials used for each job. You decide to begin with setting up the customer information.

## Set Up Customers

*Video Demonstration*

*Demo 6A - Setting up new customers*

The customer setup process includes creating existing customers, establishing beginning balances, creating default conditions for all customers, determining sales tax issues, and establishing defaults for statements and invoices.

"We will run credit checks on all new customers before giving them credit," Karen explains. "Our default credit amount will be $65,000 and net 30 days with no discount."

"How do you indicate whether customers are subject to sales tax or not?" you ask.

"First things first," Karen answers. "Before we can specify a sales tax condition for a customer, we must first establish a sales tax authority and establish a sales tax code. The company is located in Orange County, Florida, which collects ½% surtax in addition to the state sales tax rate of 6%. We'll set that up after we establish customers and their beginning balances and then go back to each customer to specify each as being subject to this sales tax."

---

**To set up customers:**

1  Open the Wild Water Sports, Inc., file by clicking **File**, click **Open Previous Company**, and then select **Wild Water Sports, Inc**. Note that the Setup Guide should open automatically. If not, click **Company** from the Navigation bar. From the Company Center, click the **Setup Guide** button. Alternatively, click the **File** menu and then click **Setup Guide**.

2  Move the Setup Guide window down slightly so that you can access the System Date and Accounting Period buttons.

3  Change the system date to **12/31/12** and the accounting period to **Period 1 – 01/01/13–01/31/13**.

4  Click **Customers** from the Setup Guide. (*Note:* If the Setup Guide is hidden by the Peachtree window, click Setup Guide from the File menu.)

5  The Peachtree Setup Guide – Customers window opens as shown in Figure 6.5. Note that in this section you will enter customers, then beginning balances, defaults, sales tax, and statement and invoice defaults.

6  Select the **Yes, I want to enter customers now** option and then click **Next**.

**Figure 6.5**

Setting Up Customers

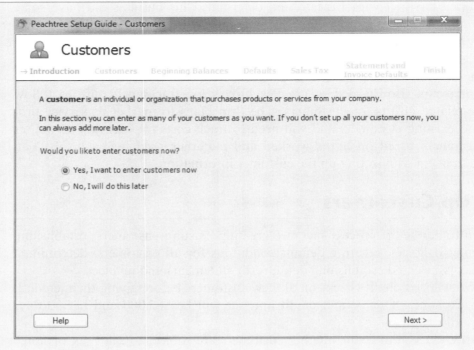

7    Click the **Add New Customer** button.

8    Type **50001** as the Customer ID and then type **Orlando Water Sports** as the customer name.

9    Click the **History** tab and then click the **Customer Beginning Balances** button and then click **Yes** to save this customer.

10   Type the information specified in Figure 6.6 to establish $48,300, the beginning balance owed by Orlando Water Sports.

**Figure 6.6**

Sales to Orlando Water Sports

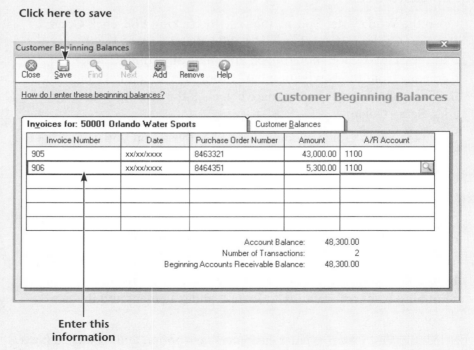

**11** Click **Save** to save the customer beginning balance and then click **Close** to close the window.

**12** Click the **General** tab and then click **New** and then enter two additional customers (**50002** and **50003**) and their related beginning balances as shown below.

| Customer ID | Customer Name | Invoice Number | Date | Purchase Order | Amount |
|---|---|---|---|---|---|
| 50002 | Buena Vista Water Sports | 910 | 12/10/12 | P23423 | $30,000 |
| 50002 | Buena Vista Water Sports | 915 | 12/15/12 | P23435 | $ 3,000 |
| 50003 | Walking on Water | 920 | 12/28/12 | WW5258 | $15,000 |

**13** To close the Maintain Customers/Prospects screen, click **Close** after you have entered the above information and saved the new customers and balances.

**14** Click **Next** and then select **Yes, but I already entered balances or I want to skip this for now** since you already entered beginning balances.

**15** Click **Next** to view the default payment, credit, and finance charge terms.

**16** Click the **Change Customer Defaults** button.

**17** Change the Credit Limit to **65,000.00** so that your window looks like Figure 6.7.

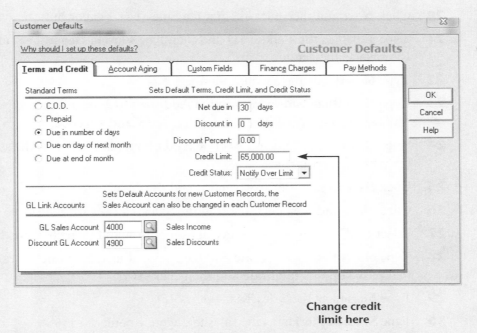

**Figure 6.7**

Changing Customer Defaults

Change credit limit here

**18** Click **OK** to close the Customer Defaults window and then click **OK** to save your changes. Your Setup Guide window should look like Figure 6.8.

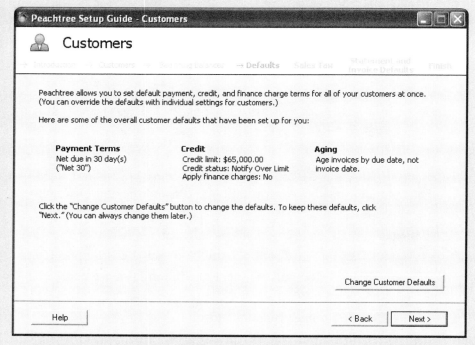

**19** Click **Next** and then select **Yes, I collect sales tax from my customers**.

**20** Click **Next** and then click the **Set Up Sales Tax Vendor** button.

**21** Type **12000** as the Vendor ID and then type **Florida Department of Revenue** as the vendor name.

**22** Type **6854102** as the account number.

**23** Type **1379 Blountstown Hwy** in the Address text box and then type **Tallahassee FL 32304-2716** as the city, state, and zip code.

**24** Select **2310** in the Expense Acct: text edit box. (*Note:* This is the sales tax payable account.)

**25** Click **Save** to save this new vendor and then click **Close**.

**26** Click **Next** and then click the **Run the Sales Tax wizard** button.

**27** Select the **Set up a new sales tax** option button and then click **Next**.

**28** Type **6.5** as the total tax rate and then select **1** as the number of rates that make up this total rate and then click **Next**.

**29** Type **Florida** as the Sales Tax Agency ID.

**30** Type **State of Florida** as the sales tax agency name.

**31** Select **12000** as the vendor you send taxes to.

**32** Select **by single rate** when asked how sales taxes are calculated.

**33** Type **6.5** as the rate.

**34** Select **2310** as the account to track sales taxes. Your window should look like Figure 6.9.

**Figure 6.9**

Adding a Sales Tax Agency

**35** Click **Next** to continue.

**36** Type **01** as the Sales Tax ID.

**37** Type **Florida Sales Tax** as the sales tax name.

**38** Select **No** when asked if you charge sales taxes on freight. Your screen should look like Figure 6.10.

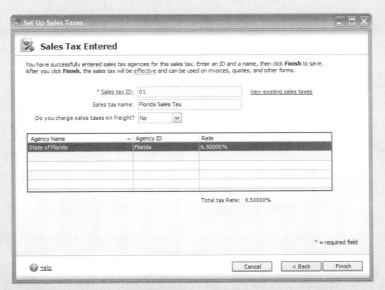

**Figure 6.10**

Entering a Sales Tax

**39**  Click **Finish** to exit this window.

**40**  Select **Close the sales tax wizard** and then click **Finish**.

**41**  Click **Next** in the Customer Setup Guide.

**42**  Click the **Assign Sales Tax to Customer** button.

**43**  Select **50001** from the Customer ID drop-down text box.

**44**  Select **01** from the Sales Tax drop-down text box. Your screen should look like Figure 6.11.

**Figure 6.11**

Assigning a Sales Tax Code to a Customer

**45**  Click the **right arrow** next to the Customer ID text box to move to the next customer. Click **Yes** to save the changes you made to Orlando Water Sports.

**46**  Change the Sales Tax text box to **01** for all remaining customers.

**47**  Close the Maintain Customer/Prospects window.

**48**  Click **Next** two times in the Customer Setup Guide.

**49**  Select the **Return to the main Setup Guide screen** option button and then click **Next**.

**50**  Close the Setup Guide window. (Place a check in the **Don't show this screen at startup** check box and then click **Close**, and then click **OK** to exit the Setup Guide.) Click **Reports & Forms** from the menu and then click **Accounts Receivable**.

**51**  Double-click **Customer Ledgers**.

**52**  Click **Print** and then click **OK** to print the Customer Ledgers report for January. Your printed report should look like Figure 6.12. (*Note:* Yours will have a date, time, and page number in the header.)

**Wild Water Sports, Inc.**
**Customer Ledgers**
**For the Period From Jan 1, 2013 to Jan 31, 2013**
Filter Criteria includes: Report order is by ID. Report is printed in Detail Format.

| Customer ID Customer | Date | Trans No | Type | Debit Amt | Credit Amt | Balance |
|---|---|---|---|---|---|---|
| 50001 Orlando Water Sports | 1/1/13 | Balance Fwd | | | | 48,300.00 |
| 50002 Buena Vista Water Sport | 1/1/13 | Balance Fwd | | | | 33,000.00 |
| 50003 Walking on Water | 1/1/13 | Balance Fwd | | | | 15,000.00 |
| Report Total | | | | | | 96,300.00 |

**Figure 6.12**

Printed Customer Ledgers

**53** Click **Close** to close the Customer Ledgers window.

**54** Double-click **Customer List** from the Select a Report or Form window. You may have to resize the columns so that the whole customer name appears on your report.

**55** Click the **Print** button and then click **OK** to print. Your printed document should look like Figure 6.13.

**Wild Water Sports, Inc.**
**Customer List**

Filter Criteria includes: 1) Customers only. Report order is by ID.

| Customer ID | Customer | Bill To Contact | Telephone 1 | Resale No |
|---|---|---|---|---|
| 50001 | Orlando Water Sports | | | |
| 50002 | Buena Vista Water Sports | | | |
| 50003 | Walking on Water | | | |

**Figure 6.13**

Customer List

**56** Click **Close** to close the Customer List window and then click **Close** to close the Select a Report or Form window.

**57** Close the Accounts Receivable reports window as well.

"Why did we print a customer list and a customer ledger?" you ask. "What's the difference?"

"In its default form, the customer list displays the customer's ID, name, contact information, phone number, type, and balance only," Karen responds. "The customer ledger lists detailed transaction information as well as outstanding balances per customer. I wanted to show you both because, depending on the situation, you may need to print one or both."

You've decided since you have no current jobs pending, you will create new jobs as they occur. Thus, the next step in the Setup Guide is to set up vendors.

# Set Up Vendors

Now that Karen's customers are established, you'll need to set up vendors, which includes setting up vendor defaults, creating vendors, and inputting beginning balances. Most of your vendors will be supplying inventory for you to

*Video Demonstration*

*Demo 6B - Setting up new vendors*

sell and will give you 30 days' credit with no discount available and $150,000 in credit.

"When do we establish accounts payable in the general ledger?" you ask.

"You will later," Karen responds. "However, the general ledger only reflects the balance owed, not to whom you owe it! The following process will establish the two vendors we owe at the beginning of the period and specifically identify the amounts and invoices relating to the overall accounts payable balances, which we'll input into the general ledger later."

## To set up vendors:

**1** Click **Setup Guide** from the File menu to reopen the Setup Guide.

**2** Click **Vendors**.
*Trouble?* If you close the Peachtree accounting program and then return at a later time, the system date of the computer, and thus the system date for Peachtree, reverts to the date you are working with the information (i.e., today's date). You will need to reset the system date to **12/31/12**.

**3** Select **Yes, I want to enter vendors now** and then click **Next**.

**4** Click the **Add New Vendor** button.

**5** Type **10000** as the Vendor ID and then type **Malibu Boats** as the vendor name.

**6** Type **1200** as the expense account. (Actually it is the inventory account, not an expense account.)

**7** Click **Save**.

**8** Click the **History** tab and then click the **Vendor Beginning Balances** button.

**9** Type the information specified in Figure 6.14 to establish $76,000, the beginning balance owed to Malibu Boats.

**Figure 6.14**

Purchases from Malibu Boats

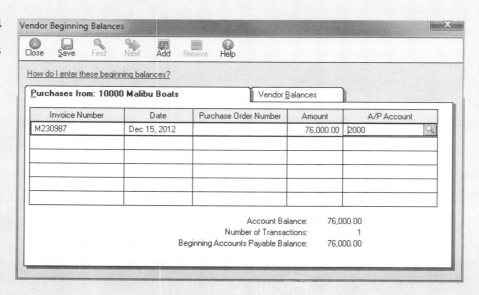

**10**  Click **Save** to save the vendor beginning balance and then click **Close** to close the window.

**11**  Click the **General** tab and then click **New** to enter a new vendor for your credit card.

**12**  Type **11000** as the Vendor ID and **MasterCard** as the vendor name.

**13**  Type **6450** as the expense account most often charged when the credit card is used.

**14**  Click the **History** tab and then click **Save** to save this vendor information.

**15**  Click the **Vendor Beginning Balances** button and enter invoice **MC0909238** on **12/12/12** for **$1,000** in the Vendor Beginning Balances window, click **Save**, and then click **Close**. Click **Close** again to close the Maintain Vendor window and then close the two Setup Guide windows.

**16**  Click the **Reports & Forms** menu item and then click **Accounts Payable**.

**17**  Double-click **Vendor Ledgers** from the Select a Report or Form window.

**18**  Click the **Print** button and then click **OK** to print. Your printed document should look like Figure 6.15.

**Figure 6.15**

Vendor Ledgers

**Wild Water Sports, Inc.**
**Vendor Ledgers**
**For the Period From Jan 1, 2013 to Jan 31, 2013**

Filter Criteria includes: Report order is by ID.

| Vendor ID / Vendor | Date | Trans No | Type | Paid | Debit Amt | Credit Amt | Balance |
|---|---|---|---|---|---|---|---|
| 10000 Malibu Boats | 1/1/13 | Balance Fwd | | | | | 76,000.00 |
| 11000 MasterCard | 1/1/13 | Balance Fwd | | | | | 1,000.00 |
| 12000 Florida Department of Re | | | | | | | 0.00 |
| **Report Total** | | | | | | | 77,000.00 |

**19**  Close the Vendor Ledger window.

**20**  Double-click **Vendor List** from the Select a Report window.

**21**  Click the **Print** button and then click **OK** to print. Your printed document should look like Figure 6.16.

**Figure 6.16**

Vendor List

**Wild Water Sports, Inc.**
**Vendor List**

Filter Criteria includes: Report order is by ID.

| Vendor ID | Vendor | Contact | Telephone 1 | Tax Id No |
|---|---|---|---|---|
| 10000 | Malibu Boats | | | |
| 11000 | MasterCard | | | |
| 12000 | Florida Department of Revenue | | | |

**22**  Close the Vendor List window and then click **Close** to close the Select a Report or Form window.

"That was painless," you admit.

"True, but we have much more work to do so let's keep going," Karen suggests.

## Set Up Inventory and Service Items

*Video Demonstration*

***Demo 6C - Setting up new inventory and service items***

"Now it's time to establish information about our inventory in Peachtree," Karen says. "Peachtree has some very nice inventory features that will help us track inventory cost and quantities."

She suggests that you set up some new activity items and inventory part items. Items show up on a company's invoice as a description of work performed or product delivered. For Wild Water Sports, activity items would be things like changing engine oil and filter, engine tune-ups, and 20-hour service checks, for example. Inventory part items would include boats, accessories, and parts for repairs.

To set up items, Karen and Donna had to agree on prices for common service items, hourly service rates for nonstandard repairs, and pricing for products to be sold. They also had to set up item names and descriptions. They agreed to charge customers for actual hours worked by their employees at a predetermined rate per hour as opposed to a flat amount for certain types of work. As a result, they'll be setting up activity items, not service items. There is a big difference in Peachtree. Again, service items would charge a flat amount for work, whereas activity items involve an employee charging a job for hours worked for a specific activity. Stock items, on the other hand, are inventory items that the company purchases for resale. In this company's case, that would include the various boats it purchases from the manufacturer for resale to the consumer. Karen provides you the pertinent information and suggests you establish activity items and stock items now.

### To set up activity items:

**1** Select **Inventory and Service Items** from the Setup Guide to begin. (You will need to reopen the Setup Guide as previously instructed.)

**2** Select **Yes, I want to enter inventory items or service items now** and then click **Next**.

**3** Click the **Add New Item or Service** button.

**4** Type **101** in the Item ID text box and type **Engine Service** in the Description text box.

**5** Select **Activity item** as the Item Class from the drop-down edit list.

**6** Type **Labor for changing engine oil and filter** in the Description edit box.

**7** Type **125** in the Billing Rate #1 edit box.

**8** Click the **magnifying glass** icon next to the GL Income Account edit box to view a list of accounts from which to choose.

**9** Click **New** to add a new account.

**10**   Type **4010** as the new Account ID, type **Service Income** as the Description, and then choose **Income** as the account type from the Account Type drop-down edit list. (This final step is critical to the proper placement and treatment of transactions in this account.)

**11**   Click **Save** and then click **Close**.

**12**   Make sure **4010** is selected as the GL Income Acct and then select **1** in the Item Tax Type edit box. Click **Save**. Your completed inventory item should look like Figure 6.17.

**Figure 6.17**

Adding a New Inventory Activity Item

**13**   Continue this process for the remaining activity items listed below by clicking the **New** button and saving your changes.

| Item ID | Description | General Description | Item Class | Billing Rate 1 | Item Tax Type | GL Income Acct |
|---------|-------------|---------------------|------------|----------------|---------------|----------------|
| 102 | Engine Tune-up | Labor for engine tune-up | Activity item | $250.00 | 1 | 4010 Service Income |
| 103 | 20-Hour Service | Labor for 20-hour service check | Activity item | $175.00 | 1 | 4010 Service Income |
| 104 | Service | Hourly service rate | Activity item | $ 85.00 | 1 | 4010 Service Income |

**14**   Now, on the same screen (Maintain Inventory Items), enter the following inventory part item by clicking **New** and then typing **201** in the Item ID text box and then typing **Malibu Sunsetter LXi** in both Description text boxes.

**15**   Select **Stock item** as the Item Class.

**16**   Type **60000** in the Price Level 1 edit box.

**17**   Type **48000** in the Last Unit Cost box. (*Note:* All merchandise is marked up 25% of cost; thus, all merchandise cost is 80% of the sales price.)

**18** Select **Average** as the Cost Method.

**19** Accept **4000** as the GL Sales Acct, **1200** as the GL Inventory Acct, **5000** as the GL Cost of Sales Acct, and **1** as the Item Tax Type.

**20** Click **Save** to save your work. Your window should look like Figure 6.18.

**Figure 6.18**

Item ID 201

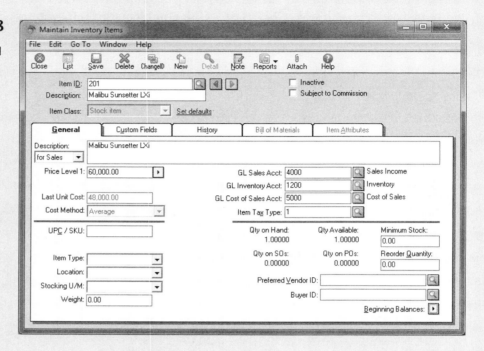

**21** Click the **Beginning Balances arrow** in the lower right-hand corner of the Maintain Inventory Items window.

**22** Choose the **201** Item ID and then type **1** as the Quantity and **48000** as the Unit Cost. Press [Enter]. The Inventory Beginning Balances window should look like Figure 6.19.

**Figure 6.19**

Entering Beginning Inventory Balances

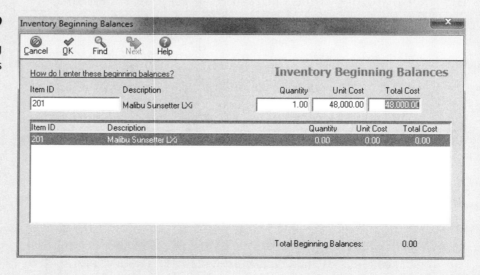

**23**  Click **OK** in the Inventory Beginning Balances window to save your work.

**24**  Click **New** to add a new stock item.

**25**  Continue this process for the remaining inventory part items listed below. Remember, all of these items are Item Class: Stock item, Item Tax Type 1, use the average cost method, and are recorded to the 4000 Sales Income account.

| Item ID | Description | Price Level 1 | Unit Cost | Qty |
|---------|-------------|---------------|-----------|-----|
| 202 | Malibu Sportster LX | $52,000 | $41,600 | 1 |
| 203 | Malibu Sunscape LSV | $65,000 | $52,000 | 2 |
| 204 | Malibu Vride | $48,000 | $38,400 | 2 |
| 205 | Malibu WakeSetter VLX | $57,000 | $45,600 | 1 |
| 206 | Malibu WakeSetter XTI | $70,000 | $56,000 | 1 |

**26**  Close the **Maintain Inventory Items** window and the two **Setup Guide** windows.

**27**  Click the **Reports & Forms** menu and then click **Inventory**.

**28**  Double-click **Item List** from the Select a Report or Form window.

**29**  Click the **Print** button and then click **OK** to print. Your printed document should look like Figure 6.20.

**Figure 6.20**

Item List

| | Wild Water Sports, Inc. | | | | | |
|---|---|---|---|---|---|---|
| | Item List | | | | | |
| Filter Criteria includes: Report order is by ID. | | | | | | |
| Item ID | Item Description | Item Class | Active? | Item Type | Qty on Hand | |
| 101 | Engine Service | Activity item | Active | | | |
| 102 | Engine Tune Up | Activity item | Active | | | |
| 103 | 20 Hour Service | Activity item | Active | | | |
| 104 | Service | Activity item | Active | | | |
| 201 | Malibu Sunsetter LXi | Stock item | Active | | 1.00 | |
| 202 | Malibu Sportster LX | Stock item | Active | | 1.00 | |
| 203 | Malibu Sunscape LSV | Stock item | Active | | 2.00 | |
| 204 | Malibu Vride | Stock item | Active | | 2.00 | |
| 205 | Malibu WakeSetter VLX | Stock item | Active | | 1.00 | |
| 206 | Malibu WakeSetter XTI | Stock item | Active | | 1.00 | |

**30**  Close the **Item List**.

**31**  Double-click **Inventory Valuation Report** from the Select a Report or Form window.

**32**  Click the **Options** button.

**33**  Click **Columns** in the other Options section.

**34**  Uncheck the Show check box for the **Stocking U/M** field and then click **OK**.

**35**  Click the **Print** button and then click **OK** to print. Your printed document should look like Figure 6.21.

**36**  Close the Inventory Valuation Report and the Select a Report or Form window.

**Figure 6.21**

Inventory Valuation Report

**Wild Water Sports, Inc.**
**Inventory Valuation Report**
**As of Jan 31, 2013**

Filter Criteria includes: 1) Stock/Assembly. Report order is by ID. Report is printed with shortened descriptions.

| Item ID<br>Item Class | Item Descriptio | Cost Method | Qty on Han | Item Value | Avg Cos | % of Inv Valu |
|---|---|---|---|---|---|---|
| 201<br>Stock item | Malibu Sunsetter | Average | 1.00 | 48,000.00 | 48000.00 | 12.90 |
| 202<br>Stock item | Malibu Sportster | Average | 1.00 | 41,600.00 | 41600.00 | 11.18 |
| 203<br>Stock item | Malibu Sunscape | Average | 2.00 | 104,000.00 | 52000.00 | 27.96 |
| 204<br>Stock item | Malibu Vride | Average | 2.00 | 76,800.00 | 38400.00 | 20.65 |
| 205<br>Stock item | Malibu WakeSett | Average | 1.00 | 45,600.00 | 45600.00 | 12.26 |
| 206<br>Stock item | Malibu WakeSett | Average | 1.00 | 56,000.00 | 56000.00 | 15.05 |
| | | | | 372,000.00 | | 100.00 |

Karen reminds you that you're just in the setup mode and are not actually entering any business transactions for the current period. Next up is payroll setup.

## Set Up Payroll

*Video Demonstration*

*Demo 6D - Setting up payroll*

"Now it's time to establish information about our employees in Peachtree," Karen says. "Peachtree has some very nice payroll features that will help us track employee information, prepare payroll tax reports, and account for our employee cost."

"Will it calculate payroll withholding for federal and state taxes?" you ask.

"It will if we purchase a payroll tax table service," Karen answers, "but we haven't decided whether we want to pay for that or not. We'll decide later. For the time being, we'll do our payroll in house and maintain our own payroll tax tables."

The company employs five people: Donna and Karen as managers, and Raul, Peggy, and Ryder as sales staff and service technicians. For each employee, you'll need to add personal address, contact, and tax information. In doing so, Karen points out that you will also be setting up payroll tax items like salary and hourly as well as identifying how often your employees are paid (monthly in this case). You'll also be identifying each employee's salary or hourly rate, taxes to be withheld, state worked, filing status, tax rates (like unemployment), and tax payees (like the Florida Department of Revenue) to whom state taxes are paid. Karen then explains the actual process of entering employees into Peachtree for Wild Water Sports by using Donna as an example, but first she must set up employee defaults for payroll.

**To set up payroll:**

**1**  Select **Employees** from the Setup Guide to begin.

**2**  Click **In-house payroll, where I do everything myself** and then click **Next**.

**3**  Click the **Run Payroll Setup Wizard** button and then click **Next**.

**4**  Click the **Do It Yourself In-House** option button and then click **Next**.

**5**  Click the **Do It Yourself** option button again and then click **Next** two times. Type **2.7** as the Unemployment Percent for Your Company and accept the remaining default accounts as shown in Figure 6.22.

**Figure 6.22**

Initial Payroll Setup

**6**  Click **Next** and then click **Next** again to accept the pay types and GL Account Numbers provided. (All pay types for this business will be recorded as wages expense.)

**7**  Click **Next** leaving all check boxes unchecked since the company does not provide payment for vacation, sick time, insurance plans, retirement plans, or flexible spending accounts.

**8**  Accept the default payroll tax liability and expense accounts by clicking **Next** again and then click **Finish** to end the payroll setup process.

**9**  Continue with the Setup Guide for employees by clicking **Next**.

**10**  Select **Yes, I want to enter employees now** and then click **Next**.

**11**  Click the **Add New Employee or Sales Rep** button.

**1**   Type **001** as Donna's employee number.

**2**   Then fill in the blank spaces on the General tab using the information in Figure 6.23. Then click **Save**.

**Figure 6.23**

Adding Information for a New
Employee in the General Tab

**Click this tab to enter more employee information**

**Enter this information**

**3**   Select the **Pay Info** tab.

**4**   Select **Salary** from the Pay Method drop-down edit box, select **Monthly** from the Frequency drop-down edit box, and then type **4166.67** as her monthly salary rate and then press [**Enter**]. Your screen should look like Figure 6.24.

**Figure 6.24**

Pay Info Tab Information

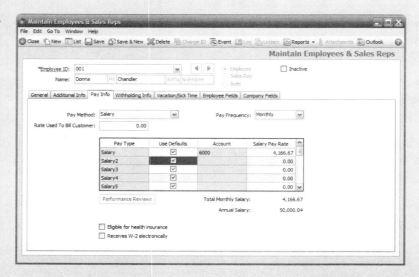

**5** Select the **Withholding Info** tab.

**6** Select **Married** as Donna's Filing Status for the Federal, State, and Local boxes, and leave her Allowances (Allow) at 0. Then click **Save**.

**7** Select the **Employee Fields** tab, noting the various fields and accounts where payroll transactions will be allocated as shown in Figure 6.25.

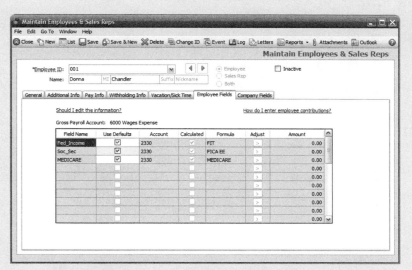

**Figure 6.25**

Employee Fields

**8** Select the **Company Fields** tab, noting the various fields and accounts where payroll transactions will be allocated as shown in Figure 6.26.

**Figure 6.26**

Employer Fields

**9** Click **Save** to save this employee but don't close this window.

You note that Donna Chandler is now set up as an employee for the company, but you still have more employees to go. Karen suggests you add one employee for now, perhaps Ryder Zacovic, an hourly employee. You respond that you're up to the task.

### To enter Ryder as an employee into Peachtree:

**1** Click **New** in the Maintain Employees & Sales Reps window.

**2** Be certain that the General tab is selected. Then fill in the form with the following information:
Employee ID: 003
Name: Ryder Zacovic
Social Security number: 556-74-6585
Address: 1554 Rose Avenue Apt. #4, Orlando, FL 32804
Country: USA

**3** Select the appropriate tabs to enter the following additional information:
Pay Method: Hourly – Time Ticket Hours
Frequency: Monthly
Hourly Rate: 15
Filing Status: Single
Allowances (Allow): 0

**4** Click **Save** and then click **Close**.

You have now entered two employees into Peachtree's payroll system and decide to enter the remaining employees later. If you were starting Peachtree midyear, it would be appropriate to enter beginning balances for withholding and payroll taxes now. Since you are starting to use Peachtree at the beginning of the fiscal/calendar year, this is not necessary.

### To finish the employee setup process:

**1** Click **Next** and then select **No** when asked if you have any employees that you need to enter salary history for.
Click **Next**.

**2** Click the **Change Employee Defaults** button.

**3** Click the **Employee Fields** tab.

**4** Uncheck all of the Calc check boxes as shown in Figure 6.27.

**Uncheck all boxes in this column**

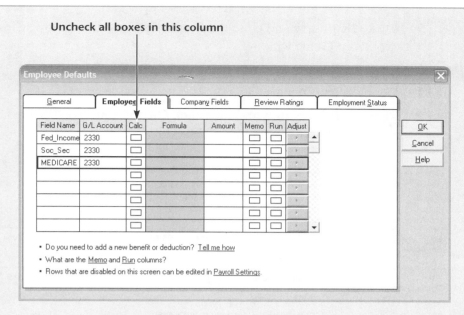

**Figure 6.27**

Turning Off Automatic Calculation of Payroll Taxes for the Employee

**5** Click the **Company Fields** tab.

**6** Type **2340** as the default liability account for Fed_Unemp_C.

**7** Type **2360** as the default liability account for St_Unemp_C.

**8** Uncheck all of the Calc check boxes as shown in Figure 6.28.

**Uncheck all boxes in this column**

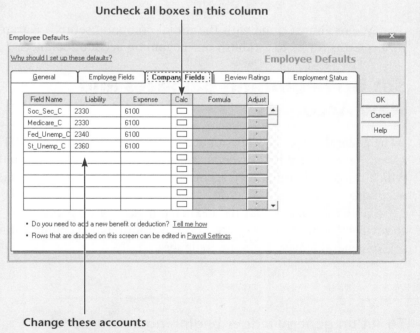

**Change these accounts**

**Figure 6.28**

Turning Off Automatic Calculation of Payroll Taxes for the Employer

9 Click **OK** to save and close the Employee Defaults window. Close the two Setup Guide windows.

10 Click the **Reports & Forms** menu and then click **Payroll**.

11 Double-click **Employee List**.

12 Click the **Print** button and then click **OK** to print. Your printed document should look like Figure 6.29.

**Figure 6.29**

Employee List

**Wild Water Sports, Inc.**
**Employee List**

Filter Criteria includes: Report order is by ID.

| Employee ID Employee | Address line 1 Address line 2 City ST ZIP | Masked SS No | Fed Filing Status | Pay Type |
|---|---|---|---|---|
| 001 Donna Chandler | 12 Ridgeway Lane  Orlando, FL  32807 | XXX-XX-4714 | Married | Salaried |
| 003 Ryder Zacovic | 1554 Rose Avenue Apt. #4  Orlando, FL  32804 USA | XXX-XX-6585 | Single | Hourly |

13 Close the Employee List and Select a Report or Form window.

"We're almost done with the initial company setup," Karen explains. "All that is left is for us to establish our beginning account balances."

## Set Up Beginning Balances and New Accounts

*Video Demonstration*

*Demo 6E - Setting up beginning balances and new accounts*

"The general ledger is where all accounts reside," says Karen. "This includes all asset, liability, equity, revenue, and expense accounts. Each business event which impacts a company's accounting records will affect at least two of these accounts."

She then explains that the next step in setting up a company in Peachtree is to review the chart of accounts, add any additional accounts you want, and then set up general ledger beginning balances.

**To set up general ledger beginning balances:**

1 Click **Chart of Accounts** from the Setup Guide.

2 Click **Next** and then click the **Add New Accounts** button.

3 Enter the information from Figure 6.30 to create a new account.

Enter this information

**Figure 6.30**

Adding a New Account

4 Click **Save** and then click **Close** to close the Maintain Chart of Accounts window.

5 Click **Next** in the Setup Guide, choose **Yes** to the question **Do any of your accounts have balances?** and then click **Next**.

6 Click the **Enter Account Beginning Balances** button.

7 Scroll down the window, select **From 12/1/12 through 12/31/12**, and then click **OK**.

8 Enter the following balances for each account:

| Account | Description | Assets, Expenses | Liabilities, Equity, Income |
|---------|-------------|------------------|------------------------------|
| 1020 | Checking Account | 25,000 | |
| 1100 | Accounts Receivable | 96,300 | |
| 1200 | Inventory | 372,000 | |
| 1500 | Property and Equipment | 75,000 | |
| 1900 | Accumulated Depreciation | | 7,500 |
| 2000 | Accounts Payable | | 77,000 |
| 2700 | Long-Term Debt—Noncurrent | | 383,800 |
| 3930 | Common Stock | | 100,000 |

**9**  After entering the above information, your screen should look like Figure 6.31.

**Figure 6.31**

Chart of Accounts Beginning Balances

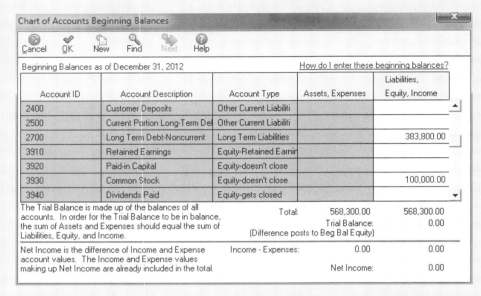

**10**  Make sure that the total of your Assets, Expenses column equals the total of your Liabilities, Equity, Income column. If they are equal, click the **OK** button to indicate you've entered all the beginning balances. If not, recheck your entries.

**11**  Click **Next** two more times. Click **Return to main Setup Guide screen**, click **Next**, and then close the Setup Guide window. If presented, click **No, I will set up later. . .** option.

**12**  Click the **Reports & Forms** menu, click **General Ledger**, and then double-click **Chart of Accounts**.

**13**  Click **Print** and then click **OK** to print. The first part of your printed document should look like Figure 6.32.

**Figure 6.32**

Partial View of the Printed Chart of Accounts

**Wild Water Sports, Inc.**
**Chart of Accounts**
**As of Jan 31, 2013**

Filter Criteria includes: Report order is by ID. Report is printed with Accounts having Zero Amounts and in Detail Format.

| Account ID | Account Description | Active? | Account Type |
|---|---|---|---|
| 1010 | Cash on Hand | Yes | Cash |
| 1020 | Checking Account | Yes | Cash |
| 1100 | Accounts Receivable | Yes | Accounts Receivable |
| 1150 | Allowance for Doubtful Acc | Yes | Accounts Receivable |
| 1200 | Inventory | Yes | Inventory |
| 1230 | Inventory Parts | Yes | Inventory |
| 1400 | Prepaid Expenses | Yes | Other Current Assets |
| 1500 | Property and Equipment | Yes | Fixed Assets |
| 1900 | Accum. Depreciation - Pro | Yes | Accumulated Depreciation |
| 2000 | Accounts Payable | Yes | Accounts Payable |

**14**    Click **Close** to close the Chart of Accounts window.

**15**    Close the Select a Report or Form window.

You have now entered your beginning balances and have set up the subsidiary ledgers for accounts payable, accounts receivable, and inventory, which identify vendors, customers, and inventory items that support those balances. Now you will need to verify that the details you established for each of these accounts are the same as those for the general ledger accounts you just established. Karen explains that this is a critical step in setting up the company.

**To verify that accounts payable, accounts receivable, and inventory details match your general ledger balances:**

**1**    Click **General Ledger** from the **Reports & Forms** menu.

**2**    Double-click **General Ledger Trial Balance** to view the trial balance at 1/31/13 as shown in Figure 6.33.

**Wild Water Sports, Inc.**
**General Ledger Trial Balance**
**As of Jan 31, 2013**

Filter Criteria includes: Report order is by ID. Report is printed in Detail Format.

| Account ID | Account Description | Debit Amt | Credit Amt |
|---|---|---|---|
| 1020 | Checking Account | 25,000.00 | |
| 1100 | Accounts Receivable | 96,300.00 | |
| 1200 | Inventory | 372,000.00 | |
| 1500 | Property and Equipment | 75,000.00 | |
| 1900 | Accum. Depreciation - Pro | | 7,500.00 |
| 2000 | Accounts Payable | | 77,000.00 |
| 2700 | Long Term Debt-Noncurren | | 383,800.00 |
| 3930 | Common Stock | | 100,000.00 |
| | Total: | 568,300.00 | 568,300.00 |

**Figure 6.33**

General Ledger Trial Balance at 1/31/13

**3**    Click **Print** and then click **OK** to print.

**4**    Gather up the Customer Ledgers, Vendor Ledgers, and Inventory Valuation report you previously printed.

**5**    Compare the report total in the Customer Ledgers report and make sure it equals the Accounts Receivable balance of $96,300.00. If it doesn't, go back and figure out what you did wrong.

**6**    Compare the report total in the Vendor Ledgers report and make sure it equals the Accounts Payable balance of $77,000.00. If it doesn't, go back and figure out what you did wrong.

**7** Compare the report total in the Inventory Valuation report and make sure it equals the Inventory balance of $372,000.00. If it doesn't, go back and figure out what you did wrong.

**8** Close the Select a Report or Form window.

You are both relieved that the detail amounts you entered in the subsidiary ledgers for customers, vendors, and inventory items equal the general ledger balances you entered as of the beginning of the year.

Karen then enlightens you as to the arrangement that she and Donna have with Ernesto. The three agreed that the opening balance equity (assets less liabilities) was $100,000 as was shown previously in the trial balance. Donna and Karen will each be purchasing stock in the company for $100,000 on 1/1/13. This will give the company a total value of $300,000 and thereby give each stockholder (Ernesto, Donna, and Karen) a one-third interest in the company.

"We are well on our way to getting this company set up," Karen remarks.

"Should we save our work?" you ask.

"Funny you should mention that," Karen responds. "Peachtree automatically saves every event you record. In fact, Peachtree doesn't even have a Save or Save As feature like most other software."

"Shouldn't we at least make a copy of the file in case something happens to this one?" you inquire.

"Good point," Karen says. "Once we're set up, we can use Peachtree's backup procedure to save a copy."

Your final task is to back up your data file for safekeeping.

## Backing Up Your Company File

"It is very important to keep a backup of your company file just in case your computer hard drive crashes or your data file gets corrupted or destroyed," Karen explains. She goes on to explain that most business users save their files to USB drives or online storage centers often referred to as cloud drives.

Karen suggests that the two of you try it out using a USB drive.

**To back up and restore a file using Peachtree's backup procedure to an external disk:**

**1** Open the Wild Water Sports file if by chance you closed it after the last lesson.

**2** Connect your USB drive.

**3** Click **Back Up** from the File menu.

**4** Click the check box to indicate you want to include the company name in the backup file name.

**5** Click the **Backup** button.

**6**   Choose a location you'd like to back your file up to. In Figure 6.34, we chose to back the file up to an external disk located in Drive F in a folder we called Peachtree. Choose a location from the **Save in** drop-down list.

**Figure 6.34**

Backing Up to an External Drive

**7**   Click **Save** to begin the backup process.

**8**   Click **OK** when Peachtree informs you of the size of the file to be backed up and then click **OK** again to begin. When the backup is finished, you'll be returned to the main Peachtree window.

**9**   To restore that same file from the external drive to your hard drive, choose **Restore** from the Peachtree file menu.

**10**   Click **Browse** to identify the location of your backup file as shown in Figure 6.35. (Once again, your location and file name may be different from that shown.)

**Figure 6.35**

Restoring a Peachtree File

11  Click **Next** and then select **A New Company** to restore your backup file to a new company folder.

12  Click **Next** two more times to accept the default information.

13  Click **Finish** to execute the backup. Your backup has now been restored.

14  Once the file has been restored, be sure to change the system date to **1/31/13**.

"Why did you restore your files to a new company folder?" you ask.

"Good question," Karen answers. "I do that to start fresh and to have a full-version backup on my computer. It's not really necessary as long as we continue to make backups on a regular basis."

"What about the User Security section of the Setup Guide?" you ask. "We didn't complete that section."

"You only need to set up user names and passwords if more than one user will use Peachtree at the same time or if you need to restrict the information some users can access," Karen answers. "Since we only have the one computer with Peachtree and we don't desire any restricted access, we can skip that part."

## End Note

Karen thanks you for your patience in helping create a Peachtree file for Wild Water Sports. You've created a new company by setting up company preferences, company items, customers, vendors, accounts, and employees. Next up, you'll begin recording business transactions.

## Business Events Summary

| Business Event | Process Steps | Page |
|---|---|---|
| Create customer | Use Customers from the Setup Guide | 115 |
| Set up sales taxes | Use Customers from the Setup Guide | 118 |
| Create vendor | Use Vendors from the Setup Guide | 122 |
| Create inventory item | Use Inventory and Service Items from the Setup Guide | 124 |
| Create service item | Use Inventory and Service Items from the Setup Guide | 124 |
| Set up payroll | Use Employees from the Setup Guide | 129 |
| Create employee | Use Employees from the Setup Guide | 129 |
| Create account | Use Chart of Accounts from the Setup Guide | 134 |
| Set up beginning balances | Use Chart of Accounts from the Setup Guide and then use Account Beginning Balances | 135 |
| Back up company file | Use Backup from the File menu | 138 |
| Print customer ledger | Select Accounts Receivable from the Reports & Forms menu | 120 |
| Print customer list | Select Accounts Receivable from the Reports & Forms menu | 121 |
| Print vendor ledger | Select Accounts Payable from the Reports & Forms menu | 123 |
| Print vendor list | Select Accounts Payable from the Reports & Forms menu | 123 |
| Print item list | Select Inventory from the Reports & Forms menu | 127 |
| Print inventory valuation report | Select Inventory from the Reports & Forms menu | 127 |
| Print employee list | Select Payroll from the Reports & Forms menu | 134 |
| Print chart of accounts | Select General Ledger from the Reports & Forms menu | 136 |
| Print general ledger trial balance | Select General Ledger from the Reports & Forms menu | 137 |

## Chapter 6 Questions

**1**   What information should you have handy when setting up a new company using the New Company Wizard?

**2**   What key parts of the Setup Guide were illustrated in this text for Wild Water Sports, Inc.?

**3**   What does the customer setup process involve?

**4**   What does the vendor setup process involve?

**5**   What does the inventory and service item setup process involve?

**6**   What does the employee setup process involve?

**7**   What does the chart of accounts setup process involve?

**8**   What is the difference between an activity item, a service item, and a stock item?

**9**   Does the act of entering beginning balances for customers, vendors, and inventory items create balances in the general ledger?

**10**   Why is it important to back up your company information?

## Chapter 6 Exercises

### Chapter 6 Exercise 1

### CREATE A NEW COMPANY

Having just completed your second year of college studying business and accounting, you are looking for summer employment when you run across an ad from a Jessica Gil, a local CPA, who is in need of part-time help. After an hour interview you get the job and are anxious to apply your newfound knowledge in accounting to help a business gain success. Jessica has just taken on a new client, Boston Catering, a catering firm located in Cambridge, Massachusetts, that provides catering services to businesses in the Cambridge and Boston area. So far Boston Catering has been manually keeping its accounting records, but it wishes to convert to Peachtree starting July 1, the beginning of their fiscal year. Jessica would like you to spearhead this effort by creating a Peachtree file containing the company's existing customers, vendors, and employees and then entering its business events in July.

The company's federal employer ID is 99-2158715 and its state employer ID and state unemployment ID is 4513-41. It is located at 305 Hampshire Street, Cambridge, MA 02139 with a phone number of 617-555-2806. The company is organized as a corporation using the accrual accounting method posting in real time in 12 monthly accounting periods per year and sells both services and products. It decides to build its own chart of accounts (see below) and will starting using Peachtree 7/1/2010. The company does not sell products online. It does charge sales tax of 5% (Sales tax ID = ST, Sales tax name = Sales Tax) on all items which is paid to the Massachusetts Dept of Revenue (ID MDR). It does not create estimates and does not use sales receipts because all products and services are invoiced. Statements and progress billings are not used but the company wishes to use Peachtree to manage the bills it owes. The company does not print checks but does keep track of inventory (change standard inventory account to food inventory) and does accept credit cards. Customers of this catering business are billed a fixed fee but the company wants to keep track of hourly employees' hours so it has chosen to track time in Peachtree. The company is not subject to the Mass. Workforce Training Tax and no employees have modified their allowances.

The company's existing bank account is with Bank of America in Cambridge. The 6/30/2010 statement reveals an ending balance of $8,345. You decide to use the following accounts:

| Account ID | Description | Account Type | Beginning Balance |
|---|---|---|---|
| 100 | Cash | Cash | 8,345 |
| 110 | Accounts Receivable | Accounts Receivable | 24,000 |
| 120 | Prepaid Insurance | Other Current Assets | 3,000 |
| 130 | Inventory | Inventory | 2,625 |
| 140 | Furniture & Equipment | Fixed Assets | 62,030 |
| 145 | Accumulated Depreciation | Accumulated Depreciation | 2,030 |
| 200 | Accounts Payable | Accounts Payable | 9,000 |
| 205 | Payroll Liabilities | Other Current Liabilities | - |
| 206 | Sales Tax Payable | Other Current Liabilities | - |
| 210 | Note Payable | Long Term Liabilities | 50,000 |
| 300 | Common Stock | Equity-doesn't close | 23,970 |
| 310 | Retained Earnings | Equity-Retained Earnings | 15,000 |
| 410 | Bar Sales | Income | |
| 420 | Catering Sales | Income | |
| 501 | Bar Purchases | Cost of Sales | |
| 502 | Food Purchases | Cost of Sales | |
| 503 | Restaurant Supplies | Cost of Sales | |
| 510 | Advertising | Expenses | |
| 515 | Bank Charges | Expenses | |
| 520 | Depreciation | Expenses | |
| 525 | Insurance | Expenses | |
| 530 | Other | Expenses | |
| 535 | Payroll | Expenses | |
| 540 | Professional Fees | Expenses | |
| 545 | Rent | Expenses | |
| 550 | Telephone | Expenses | |
| 555 | Uniforms | Expenses | |
| 560 | Utilities | Expenses | |

Create a new company using Peachtree Setup Guide. Use Boston Catering Ch 6 Ex 1 as the Company Name.

Print an Account Listing report (Click the **Lists** menu and then click **Chart of Accounts**) and then create a backup file with the name Boston Catering Ch 6 Ex 1 (Backup).

## Chapter 6 Exercise 2
# ADD CUSTOMERS

You must have completed Exercise 1 in this chapter to complete this exercise.

Restore the backup file you created in Exercise 1. Change the company name to Boston Catering Ch 6 Ex 2. Return to the Setup Guide and then add the following customers to your file.

| | MA General Hospital | Fidelity Investments | John Hancock |
|---|---|---|---|
| Customer ID | MAGH | FI | JH |
| Address | 55 Fruit St. | 1 Devonshire St. | 601 Congress St. |
| City | Boston | Boston | Boston |
| State | MA | MA | MA |
| Zip | 02114 | 02109 | 02210 |
| Phone | 617-555-2000 | 617-555-1000 | 617-555-3000 |
| Beginning Balance | $7,000 | $8,000 | $9,000 |
| Balance from invoice/date | 928 6/15/10 | 927 6/3/10 | 929 6/23/10 |
| Terms | Net 30 | Net 30 | Net 30 |
| Credit Limit | $10,000 | $10,000 | $10,000 |
| GL sales account | 420 | 420 | 420 |
| Sales Tax Item | Sales Tax 5% | Sales Tax 5% | Sales Tax 5% |

Print a Customer Ledgers report as of 6/30/10. (*Note:* Not all of the above items are the default values so you'll need to be sure all fields for all customers match the above.)

## Chapter 6 Exercise 3
# ADD VENDORS

You must have completed Exercise 1 in this chapter to complete this exercise.

Restore the backup file you created in Exercise 1. Change the company name to Boston Catering Ch 6 Ex 3. Add the following vendors to your file.

| | Sanford Winery | Fiddlehead Cellars | US Food Service |
|---|---|---|---|
| Vendor ID | SAN | FID | US |
| Address | 5010 Santa Rosa Rd. | 1597 East Chestnut Ave. | One Technology Dr. |
| City | Lompoc | Lompoc | Peabody |
| State | CA | CA | MA |
| Zip | 93436 | 93436 | 01960 |
| Account | 130 | 130 | 130 |
| Phone | 805-555-5900 | 805-555-0204 | 978-555-5100 |
| Beginning | $2,000 | $3,000 | $4,000 |
| Balance from invoice/date | 1577 6/12/10 | 32  6/13/10 | A54  6/27/10 |
| Terms | Net 30 | Net 30 | Net 30 |

Print a Vendor Ledger report as of 6/30/10.

## Chapter 6 Exercise 4
# ADD ITEMS

You must have completed Exercise 1 in this chapter to complete this exercise.

Restore the backup file you created in Exercise 1. Change the company name to Boston Catering Ch 6 Ex 4. Add the following items to your file. The GL Salary/Wages Acct is 535 for all items. The GL Cost of Sales Acct is 502 for all catering items and 501 for all bar items. The GL Inventory Acct is 130. The company uses the average cost method and all items are item tax type 1.

| # | Item Class | Description | Vendor | Last Unit Cost | Price Level 1 | GL Sales Acct | Quantity |
|---|---|---|---|---|---|---|---|
| A100 | Service | Appetizers Heavy | - | - | $18 | 420 | - |
| A200 | Service | Appetizers Light | - | - | $12 | 420 | - |
| S100 | Service | Spring Supper | - | - | $35 | 420 | - |
| S200 | Service | Summer Supper | - | - | $40 | 420 | - |
| S300 | Service | Fall Supper | - | - | $65 | 420 | - |
| S400 | Service | Winter Supper | - | - | $50 | 420 | - |
| D100 | Service | Desserts | - | - | $ 6 | 420 | - |
| P100 | Service | Pastries | - | - | $ 5 | 420 | - |
| W100 | Stock item | Sanford Chardonnay | Sanford Winery* | $45 | $60 | 410 | 25 |
| W200 | Stock item | Fiddlehead Pinot Noir | Fiddlehead Cellars* | $50 | $65 | 410 | 30 |

*You will need to add these vendors to complete this assignment.

Print an Item List report by clicking the **List** menu item, and then clicking **Inventory & Services** twice.

## Chapter 6 Exercise 5
## ADD EMPLOYEES

You must have completed Exercise 1 in this chapter to complete this exercise.

Restore the backup file you created in Exercise 1. Change the company name to Boston Catering Ch 6 Ex 5. Complete the Payroll Setup Wizard using the payroll expense account (535) for both hourly and salary employees. Set up for manual payroll where you will compute all items as per the chapter. Payroll is paid monthly at the end of the month and all payroll tax liabilities should use a new account (207) called Payroll Tax Payable, another current liabilities account type, and all payroll tax expenses should be recorded in the normal payroll expense account (535). All employees are subject to Medicare, Social Security, and Federal Unemployment federal taxes and state unemployment taxes. Hourly employees use time tickets to report hours to be paid. Make sure you set up your company file to use manual calculations and then add the following employees (note Employee ID in parentheses next to each name):

| | Nathan Chambers (NC) | Kyle Hain (KH) | Amy Casey (AC) |
|---|---|---|---|
| Address | One Leighton St. | 101 Canal St. #9 | 1449 Main St. #30 |
| City | Cambridge | Boston | Waltham |
| State | MA | MA | MA |
| Zip | 02141 | 02114 | 02451 |
| Phone | 617-555-9822 | 617-555-0905 | 617-555-1234 |
| SS# | 154-74-8745 | 541-84-7312 | 641-87-9825 |
| Earnings | $50,000/year | $16/hour | $18/hour |
| Filing Status | Single | Single | Married |

Print an Employee List report by clicking the **List** menu item, and then clicking **Employees & Payroll**, and then clicking **Employees**.

# Chapter 6 Assignments

## Chapter 6 Assignment 1

## ADDING MORE INFORMATION: WILD WATER SPORTS

Restore the Wild Water Sports, Inc. 6A file found on the text CD or download it from the text Website. Use the Setup Guide to add additional accounts, items, customers, vendors, and employees.

*corporation*

*merchandising*

a.  Create a new account with Account ID = 4030, Description = Parts Income, Account Type = Income.

b.  Add the following *activity items:*

| Item ID | Description | Item Class | General Description | Billing Rate 1 | GL Income Acct | Item Tax Type |
|---------|-------------|------------|---------------------|----------------|----------------|----------------|
| 105 | Cleaning | Activity item | Labor for cleaning boats | 75.00 | 4010 | 1 |
| 106 | Painting & Body Repairs | Activity item | Labor for painting and body repairs | 80.00 | 4010 | 1 |

c.  Add the following inventory items (all use the average cost method, are item class stock items, and are item tax type 1) and use GL Sales Acct = 4030, GL Inventory Acct = 1230, and GL Cost of Sales Acct = 5000.

| Item ID | Description/ General Description | Price Level 1 | Last Unit Cost | Quantity on Hand |
|---------|----------------------------------|---------------|----------------|------------------|
| 901 | Engine Oil | 5.00 | 4.00 | 0 |
| 902 | Oil Filter | 15.00 | 12.00 | 0 |
| 903 | Tune-up Parts | 250.00 | 200.00 | 0 |
| 904 | Air Filter | 35.00 | 28.00 | 0 |

d.  Add the following customers (all with sales tax code 1):

| Customer ID | Customer Name | Balance Due |
|-------------|---------------|-------------|
| 50004 | Freebirds | $0 |
| 50005 | Florida Sports Camp | $0 |

e.  Add the following vendors:

| Vendor ID | Vendor Name | Address | Phone | Expense Account | Balance Owed |
|-----------|-------------|---------|-------|-----------------|--------------|
| 10100 | MB Sports | 280 Air Park Road, Atwater, CA 95301 | 209-357-4153 | 1200 | $0 |
| 10200 | Tige Boats | 6803 US Hwy 83 N., Abilene, TX 79601 | 325-676-7777 | 1200 | $0 |

f.   Add the following employees:

| Employee Name | Karen Wilson | Pat Ng |
|---|---|---|
| Employee ID | 002 | 004 |
| Address | 16 Ocean Dr., Orlando, FL 32807 | 432 West Hwy 3, Orlando, FL 32807 |
| Social Security number | 654-85-7844 | 125-95-4123 |
| Salary | $4,166.67 per month | n/a |
| Hourly wage | n/a | $18 per hour using time tickets |
| Filing status | Single | Single |
| Filing state | Florida | Florida |
| Pay frequency | Monthly | Monthly |
| Allowances | 0 | 0 |

g.   Print the following for January 2013 (similar to what you did in the chapter):

1   Customer Ledgers report

2   Customer List

3   Vendor Ledgers report

4   Vendor List

5   Employee List

6   Item List

7   Inventory Valuation report

### Chapter 6 Assignment 2

## CREATING A NEW COMPANY: CENTRAL COAST CELLULAR

Van Morrison would like to use Peachtree for his new company, Central Coast Cellular. (Use company name: Central Coast Cellular Ch 6.) The company's address is 950 Higuera St., San Luis Obispo, CA 93401. The company's phone number is 805-555-9874. It uses the accrual method of accounting, posts in real time, and uses 12 monthly accounting periods. The company's main business is cellular phone sales and rentals, but it also earns revenue by consulting with customers on alternative cellular phone plans. Choose a retail company chart of accounts for this case. Central Coast Cellular's fiscal and tax year begins January 1, 2009. The company's federal employer ID is 77-9418745 and its state employer ID is 65-8588. Payroll is done manually. Federal taxes are accrued to the federal payroll taxes payable account. State taxes are accrued to the state payroll taxes payable account. California collects a training tax (CA_Train) from employers as a percentage of employee income. The company collects an 8% sales tax payable to the State Board of Equalization (SBOE). Create a sales tax ID = 01 and a sales tax name = Sales Tax. There is no sales tax on freight.

Change the following defaults in Peachtree. Default terms for customers are net 30 with no discount and a credit limit of $10,000. Default terms for vendors are net 30 with no discount and a credit limit of $15,000 and a standard expense account 1200 (Inventory). Employee withholding and employer payroll taxes will be manually calculated. The company uses the average inventory costing method. Set up the following vendors, customers, employees, and inventory items. Each ID is noted within the ( ).

Set up the following vendors:

- Verizon Communications (VZ), 1255 Corporate Drive, Irving, TX 75038, 972-507-5000, Terms: Net 30, Contact: Francisco Rojas

- Nokia Mobile Phones (NK), 23621 Park Sorrento Road, Suite 101, Calabasas, CA 91302, 818-876-6000, Terms: Net 30, Contact: Brandy Parker

- Ericsson, Inc. (EK), 740 East Campbell Road, Richardson, TX 75081, 972-583-0000, Terms: Net 30, Contact: Monty Python

- State Board of Equalization (SBOE)

Set up the following customers:

- Tribune (T), 3825 S. Higuera St., San Luis Obispo, CA 93401, 805-781-7800, Terms: Net 30, Contact: Sara Miles, Sales Tax Code: 01

- City of San Luis Obispo (SLO), 990 Palm Street, San Luis Obispo, CA 93401, 805-781-7100, Terms: Net 30, Contact: Robert Preston, Sales Tax Code: 01

- Sterling Hotels Corporation (ST), 4115 Broad Street, Suite B-1, San Luis Obispo, CA 93401, 805-546-9388, Terms: Net 30, Contact: Monica Flowers, Sales Tax Code: 01

Set up the following employees. All employees are paid semimonthly and are subject to Social Security, FUTA, Medicare, SUI (State Unemployment Insurance used instead of SUTA at 1.2%), SDI, and California's Employment Training taxes. Federal taxes are payable to the U.S. Treasury. State taxes are payable to the Employment Development Department (EDD).

- Name: Mr. Jay Bruner (JB), Address: 552 Olive St., San Luis Obispo, CA 93401, Phone: 805-555-7894, SS#: 578-94-3154, Start date: 1/1/09, Salary: $1,500 paid semimonthly, single

- Name: Mr. Alex Rodriguez (AR), Address: 1480 Monterey St., San Luis Obispo, CA 93401, Phone: 805-555-1579, SS#: 487-98-1374, Start date: 1/1/09, Salary: $2,000 paid semimonthly, married

- Name: Ms. Megan Paulson (MP), Address: 400 Beach St., San Luis Obispo, CA 93401, Phone: 805-555-4489, SS#: 547-31-5974, Start date: 1/1/09, Hourly: $12 per hour, married

Set up the following inventory items:

- Consulting Services (CON) Item Class: Service, Rate: $95, Taxable, and using income account: Consulting (a new income account that must be set up)

- Nokia 8290 (N8290) Item Class: Stock item, Last Unit Cost: $150, Preferred vendor: Nokia, Price Level 1: $225

- Nokia 8890 (N8890) Item Class: Stock item, Last Unit Cost: $175, Preferred vendor: Nokia, Price Level 1: $250

- Nokia 3285 (N3285) Item Class: Stock item, Last Unit Cost: $200, Preferred vendor: Nokia, Price Level 1: $300

- Ericsson LX588 (ELX588) Item Class: Stock item, Last Unit Cost: $50, Preferred vendor: Ericsson, Price Level 1: $85

- Ericsson T19LX (ET19LX) Item Class: Stock item, Last Unit Cost: $75, Preferred vendor: Ericsson, Price Level 1: $100

After you have printed the following reports, create a backup of this file and store it on some type of external medium (flash drive, Internet site, CD, disk, etc.).

a.   Customer List

b.   Vendor List

c.   Employee List

d.   Item List

## *Chapter 6 Assignment 3*
## CREATING A NEW COMPANY: SANTA BARBARA SAILING

Rob Dutton, an old friend from your high school days, has just purchased Santa Barbara Sailing and is getting ready to start business July 1, 2012. He purchased the corporation from its previous owner for $50,000 and assumption of the company's existing long-term debt. In return, he now owns 100% of the outstanding capital stock. The company owns several sailboats, which it charters and rents to the public and businesses in town. There is an existing company bank account at Coast Hills Federal Credit Union, and there are existing customer accounts receivable balances and vendor accounts payable balances, which are expected to be collected/paid in the near future. Rob has asked you to help him set up Peachtree to account and report for his business activities to the bank on an accrual basis with real-time processing.

The company's federal tax ID is 99-9851206 and its state tax ID is 387-1801-1. It is located at 133 Harbor Way, Santa Barbara, CA 93109, and its phone number is 805-962-2826. (Use company name: Santa Barbara Sailing Ch 6.) Its primary source of revenue will be the rental of boats upon which it will collect sales tax of 8%, which will then be paid to the Board of Equalization quarterly. Three is no sales tax on freight. Rob suggests that you let Peachtree create accounts for you assuming a Service Company. The company will use a calendar year (1/1–12/31) but will start entering business events and beginning balances as of 6/30/12. It will not use Peachtree's job tracking feature but will use the in-house payroll system. The state unemployment tax rate is 3.4%. (*Hint:* Be sure to follow the process shown in the text to set up a new company. Set the system date to 7/31/12 and the period to Period 7 and then set up the following accounts/balances).

| Account ID | Description | Account Type | Beg. Balance |
|---|---|---|---|
| 1020 | Checking Account | Cash | 10,000 |
| 1100 | Accounts Receivable | Accounts Receivable | 9,950 |
| 1500 | Property & Equipment | Fixed Asset | 302,450 |
| 2000 | Accounts Payable | Accounts Payable | 7,500 |
| 2700 | Long-Term Debt– Noncurrent | Long Term Liabilities | 264,900 |
| 3930 | Common Stock | Equity | 50,000 |
| 4010* | Rental Income | Income | 0 |

*New account. All others exist but you need to set up beginning balances.

Set up the following customers with beginning balances:

| Customer ID | Name | Address | Phone | Contact | Invoice | Date | Amount |
|---|---|---|---|---|---|---|---|
| 100 | Santa Barbara Medical | 470 South Patterson, Santa Barbara, CA 93111 | 805-555-9841 | Sam Smith | 6995 | 6/23/12 | 1,485 |
| 101 | Raytheon | 7418 Hollister Ave., Goleta, CA 93117 | 805-555-1247 | Rosa Parks | 6999 | 6/25/12 | 8,465 |

Set up the following vendors with beginning balances:

| Vendor ID | Name | Address | Phone | Expense Account | Invoice | Date | Amount |
|---|---|---|---|---|---|---|---|
| 200 | Catalina Yachts | 21200 Victory Blvd., Woodland, CA 91367 | 310-555-9814 | 1500 | 23098 | 6/15/12 | 7,500 |
| 201 | Board of Equalization | | | 2310 | | | |

Set up the following inventory items, which are all taxable, Item class: Service, and use the 4010 Rental Income GL Sales Account:

| Item ID | Description | Price Level 1 |
|---|---|---|
| CAT 28 | Catalina 28 Daily Rental | 220 |
| CAT 32 | Catalina 32 Daily Rental | 275 |
| CAT 42 | Catalina 42 Daily Rental | 465 |
| CAT 50 | Catalina 50 Daily Rental | 560 |

Set up the following employees. (All employees are paid semimonthly. Tax amounts are calculated manually. *Hint:* Be sure you set the employee defaults so that taxes are not automatically calculated.)

| Employee ID | Name | Address | Phone | Social Security Number | Pay | Filing Status |
|---|---|---|---|---|---|---|
| RD | Rob Dutton | 1044 Padre St., Santa Barbara, CA 93105 | 805-555-9714 | 239-09-7466 | Salary 2,708.33 | Single |
| JW | Jeanne Wine | 4678 Berkeley Rd., Goleta, CA 93117 | 805-555-1247 | 222-32-0298 | Hourly 18.00 | Married |

Print the following as of 7/1/12. (*Hint:* Set the system date to 7/1/12 and the accounting period to Period 7.)

a. Customer Ledgers

b. Customer List

c. Vendor Ledgers

d. Vendor List

e. Employee List

f. Item List

g. Chart of Accounts

h. General Ledger Trial Balance

## Chapter 6 Cases

### Chapter 6 Case Problem 1

## FOREVER YOUNG

Sebastian Young played quarterback for the Los Angeles Raiders for the 12 years of his professional football career. As a team leader, Sebastian guided his team to three Super Bowl victories and earned the respect of his teammates, the coaching staff, the press, and fans across the country. Now retired, Sebastian is a guest commentator for a variety of sports talk shows on radio and television. He recently formed a sole proprietorship, called Forever Young, to promote himself as a motivational speaker to large corporations and organizations. He uses the accrual method of accounting, posts in real time, and uses 12 monthly accounting periods. He has hired Cory Walsh to promote and coordinate his appearances and Anne Sunshine to manage the office. He has contacted some vendors and customers and is about to embark on a new business adventure. He has asked you to set up an accounting system for the business. The business's tax ID is 94-9723900, and it is located at 100 Westwood Blvd., Los Angeles, CA 90024. The phone number is 310-555-2324. (Use company name: Forever Young Ch 6.) The company is in the business of providing professional consulting and is organized as a sole proprietorship starting business 1/1/08. You decide to build your own chart of accounts rather than have Peachtree suggest accounts. You choose not to track jobs, and the company is not responsible for collecting sales tax. You further decide to calculate the company's semi-monthly payroll manually. When asked, set the state unemployment rate to 0% as the actual unemployment amount will be provided when you pay employees.

When you are done, you are to back up your new company with the file name Forever Young Ch 6. Be sure to keep this file in a safe place because it will be used as a starting file for this case in the next chapter. Be sure to set the system date to 1/1/08 and the accounting period to Period 1: 01/01/08 to 01/31/08.

Set up the following new accounts for which there are no beginning balances. (*Note:* In this case, the company only needs to create one additional payroll tax liability account.)

| Account ID | Description | Type |
|---|---|---|
| 1010 | Checking | Cash |
| 1100 | Accounts Receivable | Accounts Receivable |
| 1500 | Furniture & Equipment | Fixed Assets |
| 2000 | Accounts Payable | Accounts Payable |
| 2100 | Payroll Liabilities | Other Current Liabilities |
| 3050 | Owner's Equity | Equity-doesn't close |
| 3060 | Net Income* | Equity—Retained Earnings |
| 4000 | Consulting Income | Income |
| 6000 | Payroll Expenses | Expenses |
| 6100 | Professional Fees | Expenses |

*Note: All Peachtree files require a retained earnings type of account to fold net income into. A sole proprietorship doesn't have this account so this account is used instead.

Set up the following customers with no beginning balances using Consulting Income as the GL Sales Account:

| Customer ID | Name | Address |
|---|---|---|
| 100001 | Levi Strauss | 100 Market St., San Francisco, CA 94099 |
| 100002 | Boeing Aerospace | 139 Boeing Park Dr., El Segundo, CA 90233 |

Set up the following vendors with no beginning balances using Professional Fees as the Expense Account:

| Vendor ID | Name | Address |
|---|---|---|
| 200001 | Fleet Promotions | 3099 Wilshire Blvd. #300, Los Angeles, CA 90024 |
| 200002 | Galas & Associates | 37321 Santa Monica Blvd. #100, Los Angeles, CA 90024 |

Set up the following items, which are not taxable, and use the Consulting Income as the GL Sales Acct. and Payroll Expenses as both the GL Salary/Wages Acct and the GL Cost of Sales Acct. (use Service as the Item Class):

| Item ID | Description | Price Level 1 |
|---|---|---|
| 001 | Full-Day Seminar | 10,000 |
| 002 | Half-Day Seminar | 6,000 |
| 003 | One-Hour Presentation | 2,000 |

Set up the following employees who are all single, have no allowances, and are paid semimonthly (use Payroll Expenses as the expense account for all employees and be sure you set the employee defaults so that taxes are not automatically calculated):

| Employee ID | Name | Address | Method of Payment |
|---|---|---|---|
| 501 | Cory Walsh | 399 Sunset Blvd., Bel Air, CA 90033 | Salary $3,333.33/period |
| 502 | Anne Sunshine | 2983 Olympic Blvd., Los Angeles, CA 90032 | Hourly $20/hour |

Create and print the following as of 1/1/08:

a. Chart of Accounts

b. Customer List

c. Vendor List

d. Item List

e. Employee List

Make a backup of this file and name the backup file Forever Young Ch 6. Store this in a safe location as you will use this in the next chapter.

## Chapter 6 Case Problem 2

# OCEAN VIEW FLOWERS

Ocean View Flowers, a wholesale flower distributor, is located at 100 Ocean Ave., Lompoc, CA 93436. Since the company sells to retailers, it does not collect sales tax. Select Detailed type: Distributor as the business type when selecting a chart of accounts, using accrual accounting, with real-time posting and with a 12-month accounting period. Ocean View started business January 1, 2008, and the owners would like you to use Peachtree to keep track of their business transactions. Ocean View is a calendar year company (for both fiscal and tax purposes) and will need to use the inventory and manual payroll features of Peachtree. In addition, the company filed for federal (91-3492370) and state (23-432) employer ID numbers. All employees are single and paid semi-monthly but do not earn sick or vacation pay. Hourly employee payroll is charged to general ledger account 77500, while salaried employee payroll is charged to general ledger account 77000. All state payroll taxes are paid to the Employment Development Department and are accrued to a state payroll tax payable account, while all federal payroll taxes are paid to the U.S. Treasury and are accrued to a federal payroll tax payable account. All payroll tax amounts will be hand calculated without the use of Peachtree's built-in tables. Default credit terms for customers should be net 30 and a credit limit of $12,000. Default credit terms for vendors should be net 30 and a credit limit of $20,000 and a default expense account = inventory. The company has elected to track inventory cost using the average method. Be sure to set the system date to 1/1/08 and the accounting period to Period 1 – 01/01/08 – 01/31/08. The company's expected customers and vendors are shown below.

| Customer ID | Name | Address | Contact |
| --- | --- | --- | --- |
| VF | Valley Florists | 101 Main St., Los Angeles, CA 90113 | Sam Davies |
| FTD | FTD | 2033 Lakewood Dr., Chicago, IL 60601 | Beverly Rose |
| CB | California Beauties | 239 Hyde Street, San Francisco, CA 95114 | Farrah Faucet |
| ES | Eastern Scents | 938 42nd Street, New York, NY 10054 | Nick Giovanni |
| LL | Latin Ladies | 209 Zona Rosa, Mexico City, DF 06600 Mexico | Juan Valdez |

| Vendor ID | Name | Address | Contact |
| --- | --- | --- | --- |
| HF | Hawaiian Farms | 2893 1st Street, Honolulu, HI 05412 | Mahalo Baise |
| BB | Brophy Bros. Farms | 90 East Hwy 246, Santa Barbara, CA 93101 | Tim Beach |
| PF | Princess Flowers | 92 West Way, Medford, OR 39282 | Bonnie Sobieski |
| KP | Keenan's Pride | 10 East Betteravia, Santa Maria, CA 93454 | Kelly Keenan |
| VF | Vordale Farms | 62383 Lido Isle, Newport, CA 90247 | Donna Vordale |

Ocean View Flowers employees were hired on 1/4/08 and are subject to federal and state taxes and withholding, state unemployment, state disability, and state employee training taxes. When asked, set the state unemployment rate to 0% as the actual unemployment amount will be provided when you pay employees. All other tax fields are a part of Peachtree's default setup. A list of employees is shown below. Be sure to set up each employee's GL account properly (i.e., account 77500—Wages Expense for hourly employees and 77000—Salaries Expense for salaried employees).

| Employee ID | Name | Address | Social Security Number | Compensation |
| --- | --- | --- | --- | --- |
| MC | Margie Conner | 2322 Courtney, Buellton, CA 93246 | 654-85-1254 | $12/hour |
| KG | Kelly Gusland | 203 B St., Lompoc, CA 93436 | 567-78-1334 | $15/hour |
| SC | Stan Comstock | 383 Lemon St., Lompoc, CA 93436 | 126-85-7843 | $2,083.34/ period |
| MM | Marie McAninch | 1299 College Ave., Santa Maria, CA 93454 | 668-41-9578 | $2,500/ period |
| ET | Edward Thomas | 1234 St. Andrews Way, Lompoc, CA 93436 | 556-98-4125 | $2,916.67/ period |

This is a continuous case in that the next chapter will use the work you've accomplished here as the basis for recording additional business events. After you've printed the following reports, create a backup of this file and store it on some type of external medium (flash drive, Internet site, CD, disk, etc.). The backup file should be named Ocean View Flowers Ch 6 for easy identification later. You'll be restoring this file in the next chapter.

Create and print the following:

a.   Customer List

b.   Vendor List

c.   Employee List

## *Chapter 6 Case Problem 3*
# ALOHA PROPERTY MANAGEMENT

Aloha Property Management, Inc., a property manager, is located at 4-356 Kuhio Highway, Suite A-1, Kapaa Kauai, HI 96746. (Use company name: Aloha Property Management Ch 6.) The phone number is 808-823-8375. The company specializes in Hawaii Vacation Rentals. The federal tax ID number is 72-6914707, and it plans to start using Peachtree as its accounting program on January 1, 2008. The firm has been in business for two years using a manual accounting system but wishes to have you help it migrate to Peachtree. It is a property management corporation filing Form 1120 each year and collecting a 4% general excise tax (Tax ID: HI Tax, description: HI Sales Tax) on all rental income that must be paid to the State of Hawaii Department of Taxation (DOT) located at P.O. Box 1425, Honolulu, HI 96806-1425. The company chose to use 23100 (Sales Tax Payable) as the default account. Create a sales tax code with ID = Tax, Description = Excise Tax, which is made up of one tax authority ID = HI Tax. Choose Detailed type: Property Management Company as the business type for this case.

Aloha plans to use Peachtree's sales receipts to record cash sales. It also plans to use Peachtree's payroll features but will plan to calculate payroll manually as it currently has only two W-2 employees. Aloha doesn't prepare estimates or track employee time or segments. It does, however, plan to enter bills as received and then enter payments later. It uses the accrual method of accounting, posts in real time, and uses 12 monthly accounting periods. Reports are to be accrual based, and Aloha plans to use the income and expense accounts created in Peachtree for a property management company and will be providing services only, no products. Most revenue comes from renting properties located on the island of Kauai to individual and corporate accounts. The company's policy is to collect a 50% deposit upon reservation, with the balance due upon arrival. Some customers (those that have prior credit approval) are invoiced upon arrival, and the remaining payment is due 30 days thereafter. Deposits are recorded as prepayments on account even though revenue is not recorded until customers arrive. Other customers (those that don't have prior credit approval) must pay upon arrival, at which time a sales receipt is generated and the remaining payment is collected. Default payment terms for customers are due on receipt (i.e., net due in 0 days) with no discounts available. Default payment terms for vendors are net due in 30 days with a credit limit of $5,000. Service items are used, but no inventory is maintained. Existing service items, customers, vendors, and employee information is provided below. (*Note:* Deposits for rentals not yet provided are shown as negative numbers.) The default sales account is 40000 and the default cost of sales account is 57000. All customers are subject to the excise tax. Be sure to set the system date to 1/1/08 and the accounting period to Period 1 – 01/01/08 – 01/31/08.

| Item ID | Service Item Name | Description | Price Level 1 |
|---|---|---|---|
| M1 | Moana Unit #1 | Weekly rent for Moana Unit #1 | $ 2,000 |
| M2 | Moana Unit #2 | Weekly rent for Moana Unit #2 | $ 2,500 |
| M3 | Moana Unit #3 | Weekly rent for Moana Unit #3 | $ 4,000 |
| M4 | Moana Unit #4 | Weekly rent for Moana Unit #4 | $12,000 |
| V1 | Villa Kailani Unit #1 | Weekly rent for Villa Unit #1 | $ 3,000 |
| V2 | Villa Kailani Unit #2 | Weekly rent for Villa Unit #2 | $ 4,500 |
| V3 | Villa Kailani Unit #3 | Weekly rent for Villa Unit #3 | $ 4,200 |
| V4 | Villa Kailani Unit #4 | Weekly rent for Villa Unit #4 | $ 6,000 |

| Customer ID | Customer Name | Balance Due (Deposits) | Invoice Number | Invoice Date |
|---|---|---|---|---|
| B | Boeing | $ 10,000 | 7505 | 12/31/07 |
| GM | General Motors | $ 75,000 | 7506 | 12/31/07 |
| BM | Brice Montoya | ($3,000) | 999 | 12/31/07 |
| SR | Sara Rice | ($6,000) | 999 | 12/31/07 |
| AC | Apple Computer | $ 25,000 | 7507 | 12/31/07 |

| Vendor ID | Vendor Name | Balance Owed | Invoice Number | Invoice Date | Expense Account |
|---|---|---|---|---|---|
| RC | Reilly Custodial | $4,500 | 65431 | 12/31/07 | 70000 |
| BS | Blue Sky Pools | $1,800 | 791 | 12/31/07 | 70000 |
| UST | United States Treasury | | 0 | n/a | 23400 |
| HI DOT | State of Hawaii Department of Taxation | | 0 | n/a | 23100 |

| Employee Name | Fran Aki | Danièle Castillo |
|---|---|---|
| Employee ID | FA | DC |
| Social Security number | 128-85-7413 | 984-74-1235 |
| Salary | $75,000 per year | n/a |
| Hourly wage | n/a | $20 per hour |
| Filing status | Married | Single |
| Taxes | Subject to Medicare, Social Security, FUTA, and all applicable state taxes | Subject to Medicare, Social Security, FUTA, and all applicable state taxes |
| Filing state | Hawaii | Hawaii |

The company owns two buildings: Moana Lani Kai located in Princeville and Villa Kailani located in Poipu. It owes $3,875,000 (a 25-year note payable) on the two properties for which it paid $2,000,000 and $3,000,000, respectively, several years ago. Accumulated depreciation on the two assets as of 12/31/07 was $500,000 and $700,000, respectively. The land on which the buildings sit is leased from the state of Hawaii for 100 years at a nominal amount per year.

The company has one checking account with the Bank of Hawaii, which had a balance of $15,000 as of 12/31/07. The Hawaii withholding, unemployment, and disability identification number is 84325184. The unemployment tax rate is 2.4%, and the disability tax rate is 0.01%. Federal taxes are paid to the U.S. Treasury (use Vendor ID UST) and state taxes are paid to the State of Hawaii Department of Taxation (use Vendor ID HI DOT). All employees are paid monthly. Use the default accounts provided by Peachtree for in-house payroll setup. The company does not offer a 401(k) plan and does not track vacation. The company will manually calculate payroll taxes rather than have Peachtree calculate them. You will need to set up two additional payroll tax fields: HI_ET_ER as an employer field and SDI as an employee field. Both this and the SUI_ER payroll tax fields accrue to Payroll Tax Expenses (account 72000) and to State Payroll Taxes Payable (account 23600). On the employee side, be sure to change the G/L account for state withholding and SDI to State Payroll Taxes Payable (account 23600).

Use the information provided above to create a new Peachtree file for Aloha. (*Hint:* Read the entire case before you begin, establish the new company files, accepting the default name provided, and modify preferences like you did in the main chapter.) Enter all beginning asset, liability, and equity account balances as of 12/31/07. Your trial balance at 12/31/07 should look like this:

| Account ID | Account Description | Debit Amt | Credit Amt |
|---|---|---|---|
| 10200 | Regular Checking Account | 15,000.00 | |
| 11000 | Accounts Receivable | 101,000.00 | |
| 15500 | Building | 5,000,000.00 | |
| 17500 | Accum Depreciation—Building | | 1,200,000.00 |
| 20000 | Accounts Payable | | 6,300.00 |
| 27000 | Notes Payable—Noncurrent | | 3,875,000.00 |
| 39003 | Common Stock | | 10,000.00 |
| 39005 | Retained Earnings | | 24,700.00 |
| | Total: | 5,116,000.00 | 5,116,000.00 |

This is a continuous case in that the next chapter will use the work you've accomplished here as the basis for recording additional business events. After you've printed the following reports, create a backup of this file and store it on some type of external medium (flash drive, Internet site, CD, disk, etc.). The backup file should be named Aloha Property Management Ch 6 for easy identification later. You'll be restoring this file in the next chapter.

Create and print the following:

a. Customer Ledgers

b. Vendor Ledgers

c. Employee List

d. Item List

e. General Ledger Trial Balance

# Cash-Oriented Business Activities

*In this Chapter, you will:*

- Record cash-oriented business transactions classified as financing activities, such as owner contributions.
- Record cash-oriented business transactions classified as investing activities, such as equipment purchases.
- Record cash-oriented business transactions classified as operating activities, such as sales orders, inventory purchases, sales invoicing, expense disbursements, and payroll.
- Evaluate a firm's performance and financial position.

## *Case:* **Wild Water Sports, Inc.**

You and Karen completed the initial setup of the Peachtree program at the beginning of January and are ready to begin recording business transactions for the month. The new company has completed its first month of business, and Ernesto is pleased with the new business relationship he established with Karen and Donna. However, no one knows the extent of their profitability or financial position since none of the accounting events has yet been recorded into Peachtree. You had to start the spring semester, and Karen has been busy just keeping the business going.

"I'm brand new to Peachtree," you explain. "I know a little about financial accounting and I'm taking a managerial class right now, but I haven't had a course in Peachtree or any other computerized accounting program for that matter."

"No problem," Karen says, trying to reassure you. "Peachtree is very easy for first-time users to learn, and you'll be pleased with how much it will help the company understand its performance and financial position."

The two of you agree to meet today to review the business transactions that took place in January. Karen agrees to explain the nature of each transaction and how it should be recorded in Peachtree. She suggests that the best way to accomplish this is to view each transaction by the three fundamental business activities: financing, investing, and operating.

"I remember studying those concepts in my first accounting course," you comment. "If I remember correctly, financing activities are initiated when money or other resources are obtained from short-term nontrade creditors, long-term creditors, and/or owners. Financing activities are completed when amounts owed are repaid to or otherwise settled with these same creditors and/or owners. Investing activities are initiated when the money obtained from financing activities is applied to nonoperating uses, such as buying investment securities and/or productive assets like equipment, buildings, land, or furniture and fixtures. Investing activities are completed when the investment securities and/or productive assets are sold. Finally, operating activities occur when the money obtained from financing activities and the productive assets obtained from investing activities are applied to either purchase or produce goods and services for sale. These operating activities are substantially completed when goods are delivered or when services are performed."

"Wow, they taught you well!" Karen exclaims. "Let's begin with a few cash-oriented financing activities."

## Recording Cash-Oriented Financing Activities

You begin with two financing activities. The first occurred on January 3 when the company received $200,000 from Karen and Donna ($100,000 each) as their purchase of stock in the company. The second deposit was made on January 4 when the company borrowed $250,000 from its bank (Bank of Florida) at 5% payable in five years. Karen reminds you to make sure the system date is set to **1/1/13** and the Period is set to **Period 1**.

*[handwritten note in margin: Debit Cash Cr - liab. acct]*

---

### To record the cash received from the sale of stock and borrowing:

1 Start the Peachtree program.

2 Restore the **Wild Water Sports, Inc. 7** file from your Data Files CD or download it from the Internet. See "Restoring Peachtree Backup Files from Your CD" in Chapter 1 if you need more information. If the Setup Guide window appears, click the **Don't show this screen at startup** check box and then close the Setup Guide window.

3 Set the system date to **1/1/13** and the accounting period to **Period 1**.

4 Click **Tasks** from the menu and then click **General Journal Entry**.

5 Enter the information for Karen and Donna's stock purchase as shown in Figure 7.1. Be sure to enter the correct date.

Type 1 as the journal entry number as a reference

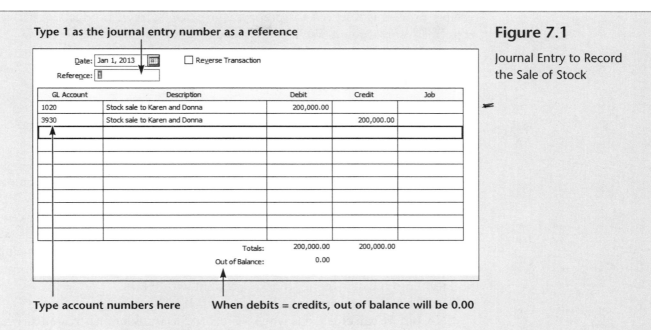

**Figure 7.1**

Journal Entry to Record
the Sale of Stock

| GL Account | Description | Debit | Credit | Job |
|---|---|---|---|---|
| 1020 | Stock sale to Karen and Donna | 200,000.00 | | |
| 3930 | Stock sale to Karen and Donna | | 200,000.00 | |
| | | | | |

Totals: 200,000.00 200,000.00

Out of Balance: 0.00

Type account numbers here    When debits = credits, out of balance will be 0.00

**6** Click **Save** to record the journal entry.

**7** Enter the information for borrowing as shown in Figure 7.2.

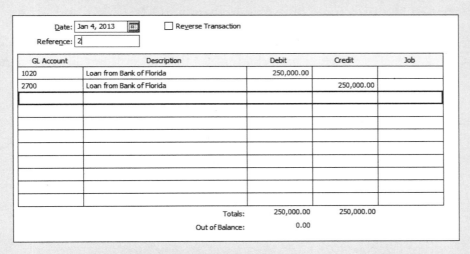

**Figure 7.2**

Journal Entry to Record
the Borrowing of Funds

| GL Account | Description | Debit | Credit | Job |
|---|---|---|---|---|
| 1020 | Loan from Bank of Florida | 250,000.00 | | |
| 2700 | Loan from Bank of Florida | | 250,000.00 | |
| | | | | |

Totals: 250,000.00 250,000.00

Out of Balance: 0.00

**8** Click **Save** to record the journal entry.

**9** Click **Close** to close the General Journal Entry window.

"Do we always record transactions with journal entries like I did in college?" you ask.

"Actually, no," Karen answers. "We usually use source documents like receipts but those transactions affect revenues or accounts receivable. Peachtree's receipts process is reserved for prepayments, cash sales of products or services, or payments on account. We'll get to those types of transactions shortly."

You have now recorded two different cash-oriented financing activities: the sale of stock to investors and the borrowing of funds on a long-term basis. Now it's time to look at recording cash-oriented investing activities.

# Recording Cash-Oriented Investing Activities

After recording the cash received from investors and creditors, the company decided to temporarily invest those funds in a money market account with its bank. By transferring those funds from its checking to a money market account, the company expected to generate some interest revenue until the funds were needed. To accomplish this transfer, Karen wrote check number 1001 on January 8 from the company's checking account with Bank of Florida and deposited the check into the new money market account with ETrade.

"Do we have a general ledger account for this?" you ask.

"No, but we can create one while we record this transaction," Karen answers.

**To create a new general ledger account, add a new vendor, and record the purchase of money market funds:**

1 Open the Banking center from the Navigation bar.

2 Click the **Write Checks** button and then select **New Check** from the pop-up menu.

3 Select **Checking Account** from the drop-down list of accounts and then click **OK**.

4 Click the magnifying glass icon in the Vendor ID text box and then click **New** to go to the Maintain Vendors window.

5 Type **11100** in the Vendor ID text box and then press **[Tab]**.

6 Type **ETrade** in the Name text box.

7 Click the drop-down arrow in the Expense Account text box and then click **New**.

8 Type **1030** in the Account ID text box and then press **[Tab]**.

9 Type **Short-Term Investments** in the Description text box.

10 Select **Cash** as the Account Type. Your Maintain Chart of Accounts window should look like Figure 7.3.

11 Click **Save** and then click **Close**. Click the drop-down arrow in the Expense Account text box and select **1030**. Your Maintain Vendors window should look like Figure 7.4.

**Click Save to save your new account**

**Figure 7.3**

Creating a New Account

**Be sure to select the proper account type when creating a new account. The default account type is Cash and students often forget to change this when creating new accounts!**

**Click Save to save this new vendor**

**Click this drop-down arrow to view a list of existing accounts or to create a new account**

**Figure 7.4**

Creating a New Vendor

**Type 1030 (your new Short-Term Investments account) even though it's not an "expense" account**

**12** Click **Save** and then click **Close**.

**13** Type **11100** in the Vendor ID box.

**14** Type **1001** as the check number.

**15** Type **01/08/13** as the date.

**16** Type **300000** as the check amount.

**17** Be sure that **1020** is selected as the Cash Account.

**18** Type **1030** (it actually should already be there) in the Expense Account text box.

*Trouble?* The Expense Account title is somewhat misleading because you can type or select any account to appear here, including assets.

**19** Your Write Checks window should look like Figure 7.5.

**Figure 7.5**

Creating a New Check

Click this magnifying glass to view a list of existing vendors or to create a new vendor

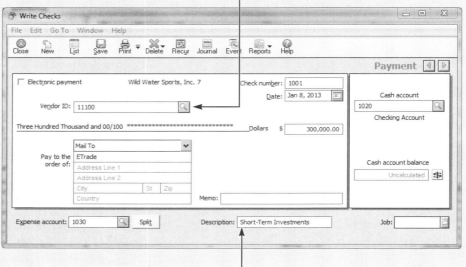

Once you type an account in the Expense Acct text box, that account's description appears here

**20** Click **Save** to record this transaction. Do not close this window.

Wild Water also had other cash-oriented investment activity in January. On January 10, it purchased new office furniture for the sales, marketing, and service staff from the local Staples store and new equipment for the service bays from AJ Marine Equipment.

"How should we classify the purchase of furniture and fixtures since the only fixed asset account we have is Property and Equipment?" you ask.

"Since we won't have much invested in fixed assets, we'll just lump everything together into the existing account," Karen responds. "Peachtree now has a tracking system we could use to monitor the location of our various fixed assets, but since we won't have that many individual assets, we won't worry about tracking them at this point."

## To record the purchase of furniture and equipment:

**1** Type **1002** as the check number (if it is not already there).
*Trouble?* If you previously closed the Write Checks window, open it again by clicking the **Write Checks** icon from the Banking center.

**2** Type **01/11/13** as the date of purchase in the Write Checks window.

**3** Click the magnifying glass icon in the Vendor ID text box and then click **New**.

**4** Type **11200** in the Vendor ID text box and then press **[Tab]**.

**5** Type **Staples** in the Name text box.

**6** Type **1500** in the Expense Account text box.

**7** Click **Save** and then click **Close**.

**8** Type **11200** in the Vendor ID text box.

**9** Type **70000** as the check amount and then press **[Tab]**. Your new check should look like Figure 7.6.

Click Save to save the current check and create a new check

**Figure 7.6**

Check to Purchase New Furniture

**10** Click **Save** to enter another purchase.

**11** Type **1003** as the check number (again, it should already be there).

| | |
|---|---|
| **12** | Type **01/11/13** as the date of purchase in the Write Checks window. |
| **13** | Click the magnifying glass icon in the Vendor ID text box and then click **New**. |
| **14** | Type **11300** in the Vendor ID text box and then press **[Tab]**. |
| **15** | Type **AJ Marine Equipment** in the Name text box. |
| **16** | Type **1500** in the Expense Account text box. |
| **17** | Click **Save** and then click **Close**. |
| **18** | Type **11300** in the Vendor ID text box. |
| **19** | Type **100000** as the check amount. |
| **20** | Click **Save** and then click **Close**. |

"When is depreciation recorded on fixed assets?" you ask.

"Not until the end of the accounting period, before we create financial statements," Karen responds. "But we have lots to do before that."

# Recording Cash-Oriented Operating Activities

"There are many cash-oriented operating activities," Karen comments. "These kinds of activities include receiving and recording orders from customers, invoicing those orders when products or services are delivered, and collecting cash from customers. They also include ordering products from vendors, receiving those products and recording bills, paying for those bills or other expenses as they become due, and, of course, recording payroll activities."

Karen explains that Wild Water uses both sales and purchase orders to help manage its business activities. She remarks that, typically, neither sales orders nor purchase orders have an impact on financial statements, but they do play an important role as a control feature in Peachtree. So she plans on using them.

*Video Demonstration*

*Demo 7A - Using sales orders*

## Sales Orders

For example," she says, "in January, we had two customers order boats. One was a special order, and one was for a boat we didn't have in stock. We sold Florida Sports Camp a customized Item 206 Malibu WakeSetter XTI for $70,000 plus tax. It gave its address as 78 Hwy 150, Orlando, FL 31310. We also sold Performance Rentals (a new customer whose address is 15 Hwy 22, Orlando, FL 32807) a Tige 22v (a new item with Item ID = 301 and a cost of $63,000) for $78,750 plus tax. Both of these boats were sold on a cash-only basis so both customers' credit terms need to reflect that fact. We recorded sales orders 101 and 102 for those sales, respectively." Karen reminds you that sales orders are internal documents and do not constitute sales for accounting purposes. Karen decides first to show you the sales orders recorded when the customers placed their orders. Then she'll show you how the two deposits on sales were accounted for and the purchase orders generated to order boats from the vendors.

### To update a customer's information, create a new customer, and create a sales order:

**1**  Open the Customers & Sales center from the Navigation bar.

**2**  Click **Customers** and then select **View and Edit Customers**.

**3**  Double-click Customer ID **50005**.

**4**  Update this existing customer's record by entering the business address **78 Hwy 150, Orlando, FL 31310**.

**5**  Click the **Payment & Credit** tab.

**6**  Select **Customize terms for this customer** from the Terms and Credit drop-down text box and change the terms to Net due in **0** days and credit information to **0** Credit Limit as shown in Figure 7.7.

Uncheck here to modify this customer's credit terms

Set credit limit to 0.00          Set net due in 0 days

**Figure 7.7**

Updating Terms and Credit

**7**  Click **Save** and then click **Close**.

**8**  Click **New** to add a new customer.

**9**    Type **50006** in the Customer ID text box and then press **[Tab]**.

**10**    Type **Performance Rentals** in the Name text box.

**11**    Type **15 Hwy 22, Orlando, FL 32807** as the customer's address. Your new customer window should look like Figure 7.8.

**Figure 7.8**

Add a New Customer

**12**    Click the **Payment & Credit** tab.

**13**    Change the terms and credit information to due in 0 days and $0 credit limit as you did for Florida Sports Camp above.

**14**    Click **Save** and then click **Close** to add this new customer.

**15**    Close the Customer List.

**16**    Click **Sales Orders** and then select **New Sales Order**.

**17**    Select Customer ID **50005**.

**18**    Type **1/12/13** as the date.

**19**    Type **1/29/13** as the Ship By date.

**20**    Type **101** as the SO No. (Sales Order Number).

**21**    Select **Cust. Pickup** in the Ship Via text box.

**22**    Type **1** in the Quantity text box.

**23**    Type **206** in the Item text box.

**24**    Select **01** in the Sales Tax Code text box. Your new sales order should look like Figure 7.9.

**Type Item ID here**        **Type sales order number in this text box**

**Figure 7.9**

Sales Order 101

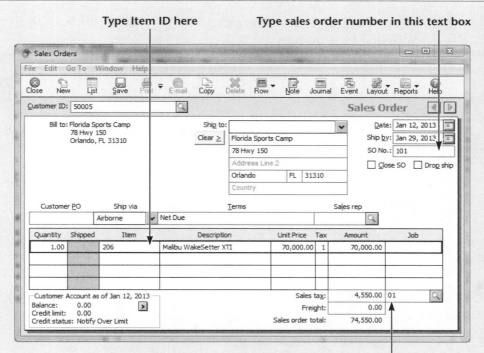

Be sure to set sales tax code to 01 as shown here

**25** Click **Save**. This sales order is saved, and a new blank sales order is revealed.

**26** Select Customer ID **50006**.

**27** Type **1/13/13** as the date.

**28** Type **1/29/13** as the Ship By date.

**29** Accept **102** as the SO No. (Sales Order Number).

**30** Select **Cust. Pickup** in the Ship Via text box.

**31** Type **1** in the Quantity text box.

**32** Click the magnifying glass icon in the Item text box and then click **New**.

**33** Type **301** as the Item ID.

**34** Type **Tige 22v** as the Description.

**35** Select **Stock item** as the Item Class.

**36** Type **Tige 22v** as the General Description. (Note that the text may appear red, indicating a misspelled word.)

**37** If so, press the **F7** key or select **Check spelling** from the Edit menu and then select **Add** to add this word to the global dictionary.

**38** Click **Add** again to add 22v to the dictionary and then click **OK** to close this window.

*Trouble?* Adding these words to the global dictionary works fine if you're using Peachtree at home or at work since that dictionary will be available to you all the time. However, if you are working in a lab environment on different computers or if those computers are reset nightly to their original settings, chances are the next time you access this or other documents where these words appear they will once again be read. This is because the dictionary is global to Peachtree, not to your individual file. Thus, you can either ignore the misspellings or re-add the words to the dictionary.

**39** Type **78750** as Price Level 1.

**40** Type **63000** as the Last Unit Cost.

**41** Select **Average** as the Cost Method.

**42** Leave **4000** as the GL Sales Acct.

**43** Leave **1200** as the GL Inventory Acct.

**44** Leave **5000** as the GL Cost of Sales Acct.

**45** Leave **1** as the Item Tax Type.

**46** Select **10200** as the Preferred Vendor ID. Your Maintain Inventory Items window should look like Figure 7.10.

**Figure 7.10**

Adding a New Inventory Item

**47** Click **Save** and then click **Close**.

**48** Type **301** in the Item ID box again if it doesn't automatically appear.

**49** Select **01** in the Sales Tax Code text box.

**50** Click **Save** and then click **Close**.

## Deposits on Future Sales

*Video Demonstration*

In both transactions, the customer was required to pay a 25% deposit upon order ($17,500.00 and $19,687.50, respectively).

"How do you account for the amounts received?" you ask.

"We treat them just like payments received from customers, but since there is no invoice to allocate them to, we just leave them as credit balances in customers' accounts," Karen answers. "Accounting would normally require you to treat these as unearned revenue and record them as liabilities; however, we only make adjustments for credit balances in accounts if, prior to preparing financial statements, we still have remaining credits in customer accounts."

*Demo 7B - Recording cash deposits on future sales*

Remember, in both cases, customers remitted cash to Wild Water, but a sale could not be recorded because the products had not been delivered and thus the earnings process was not complete.

### To record the receipt of deposits on future sales:

**1** Open the Customers & Sales center from the Navigation bar.

**2** Click **Receive Money** and then select **Receive Money from Customer**.

**3** Select **Checking Account** and then click **OK**.

**4** Click on the magnifying glass icon across from the Customer ID text box. From the drop-down menu, select **50005 Florida Sports Camp** as the customer from which the first cash payment was received.

**5** Type **8755** in the Reference text box as the customer's check number.

**6** Type **SR0001** in the Receipt Number text box.

**7** Type the date **1/12/13**.

**8** Select **Check** as the payment method.

**9** Check the **Prepayment** check box (above the Job column near the bottom of the screen) since this is not a cash sale or payment on account.

**10** Type **Deposit on boat order** in the Description text box.

**11** Type **17500** in the Amount text box and then press **[Tab]**. Your Receipts window should look like Figure 7.11.

**Figure 7.11**

Receipt of Deposit from
Florida Sports Camp

Leave this box blank as we'll deposit this amount later

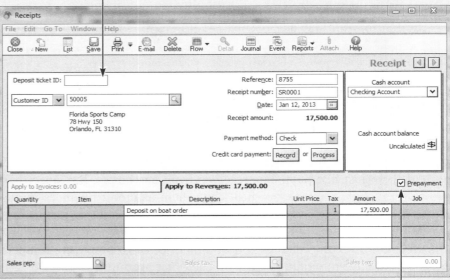

Place a check here to indicate this is a customer prepayment

**12**  Click **Save** to record the receipt and get ready for another. Click the magnifying glass icon in the Customer ID text box.

**13**  Select **50006 Performance Rentals** as the customer from which the second deposit was received.

**14**  Type **987452** in the Reference text box as the credit card receipt number.

**15**  Accept **SR0002** in the Receipt Number text box.

**16**  Type the date as **1/13/13**.

**17**  Select **MasterCard** as the payment method.

**18**  Check the **Prepayment** check box since this is not a cash sale or payment on account.

**19**  Type **Deposit on boat order** in the Description text box.

**20**  Type **19687.50** in the Amount text box.

**21**  Click **Save** and then click **Close**.

*Video Demonstration*

*Demo 7C - Recording purchase orders*

## Purchase Orders

"We then had to order those boats from the manufacturers using purchase orders 4001 and 4002. Let me show you how purchase orders are used in Peachtree."

"Are all purchase orders related to customers?" you ask.

"Not necessarily," Karen responds. "Sometimes we order for inventory to have in our showroom, but in these two cases we were ordering boats for specific customers."

## To create a purchase order:

**1**  Open the Vendors & Purchases center from the Navigation bar.

**2**  Click **Purchase Orders** and select **New Purchase Order**.

**3**  Select **10000** from the Vendor ID drop-down list.

**4**  Type **1/11/13** as the date.

**5**  Type **4001** as the purchase order number.

**6**  Type **1** as the quantity.

**7**  Type **206** as the item (Malibu WakeSetter XTI).

**8**  Select **Best Way** in the Ship Via text box and then press **[Tab]**. Your purchase order should now look like Figure 7.12.

**Click here to save this purchase order**

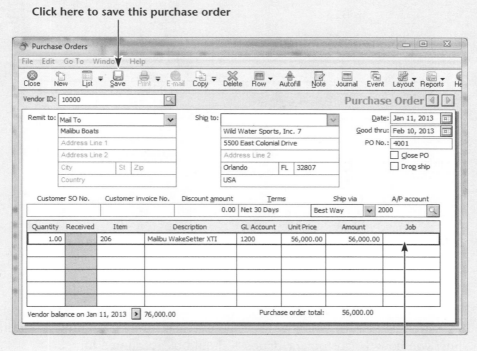

**Figure 7.12**

Purchase Order 4001

**Even though this purchase order is related to a specic customer order, Peachtree will not allow stock items to be assigned to jobs**

**9**  Click **Save** to save this purchase order and open a new one.

**10**  Select **10200 Tige Boats** from the Vendor ID drop-down list.

**11**  Type **1/11/13** as the date (if it's not already there).

**12** Accept **4002** as the purchase order number.

**13** Type **1** as the quantity.

**14** Type **301** as the item.

**15** Select **Best Way** in the Ship Via text box and then press **[Tab]**. Your purchase order should look like Figure 7.13.

**Figure 7.13**

Purchase Order 4002

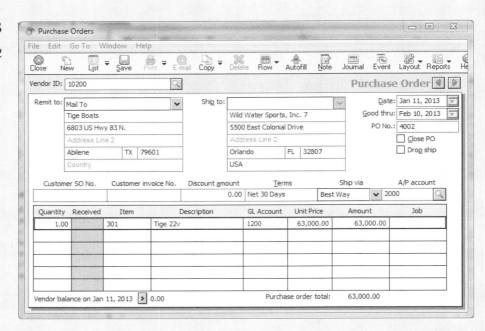

**16** Click **Save** and then click **Close** to add this new purchase order.

Karen has shown you how to create purchase orders and now would like to show you how the customers' deposits should be accounted for.

## Cash Collected on Account

"Typically, we collect cash from sales on account, such as sales made to customers where we gave them credit terms like net 30," Karen comments. "If you recall when we set up our accounting system on January 1, 2013, we had some customers who owed us money from previous sales. The balances owed were reflected in accounts receivable."

"Do you record those cash collections like we just recorded the previous cash receipts?" you ask.

"Yes, plus we had some cash sales during January, which I'll show you as well," Karen answers. "We had one cash boat sale and one cash boat service during the month, both from new customers."

## To record cash collected on account:

**1**  Click **Receive Money** from the Customers & Sales center and then select **Receive Money from Customer**.

**2**  Select **50002 Buena Vista Water Sports** from the Customer ID drop-down list.

**3**  Type **65454** in the Reference text box as the customer's check number.

**4**  Type **SR0003** in the Receipts text box.

**5**  Type **1/15/13** as the date received.

**6**  Select **Check** as the payment method.

**7**  Place a check in the **Pay** check box on the Invoice 910 row shown in the Apply to Invoices tab. Your screen should look like Figure 7.14.

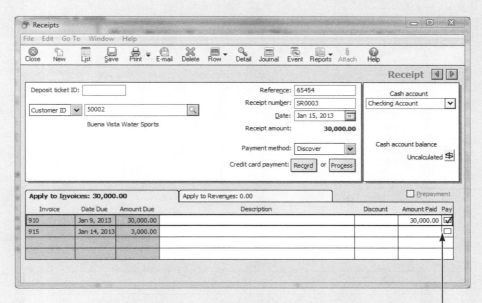

**Figure 7.14**

Receipt of Cash on Account

Place a check in this box to indicate what this customer is paying for

**8**  Click **Save** but don't close this window.

## To record cash sales to a new customer:

**1**  Click the magnifying glass icon in the Customer ID text box and then click **New**.

**2**  Type **50007** in the Customer ID text box and then press **[Tab]**.

3    Type **Seth Blackman** in the Name text box.

4    Type **140 Fir Ave., Miami, FL 33109** as the customer's billing address.

5    Click **Save** and then click **Close**.

6    Select **50007** from the Customer ID text box.

7    Type **161** in the Reference text box as the customer's check number.

8    Type **SR0004** as the Receipt Number.

9    Type **1/18/13** as the date of sale.

10    Select **Check** as the Payment Method.

11    Type **1** as the Quantity sold.

12    Select **202** from the drop-down list of items.

13    Type **01** as the Sales Tax Code. Your screen should look like Figure 7.15.

**Figure 7.15**

Recording a Cash Sale

Type 202 as the item sold for cash

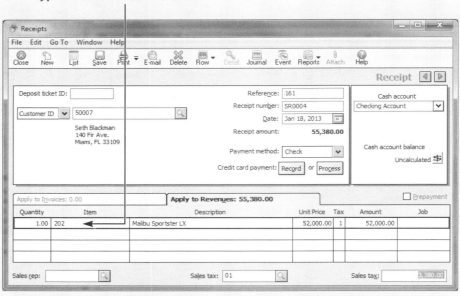

14    Click **Save** and then click **Close**.

"Have all of these cash receipt transactions been recorded in our checking account?" you ask.

"Peachtree treats all cash receipts (payments on account, advance payments, etc.) as undeposited amounts unless we place a deposit ticket number in the Receipts window. This is because bank deposits are often made at a different time than cash is actually received," Karen answers. "We've made those deposits now, so let me show you how we record them in Peachtree."

## To record cash deposits made to banks:

**1** Click the **Bank Deposits** in the Customers & Sales center and then click **New Bank Deposit**.

**2** Click in the **Deposit** check box on the first two rows presented.

**3** Type **1/13/13** as the date of deposit.

**4** Type **1** in the Deposit Ticket ID text box.

**5** Be sure **1020** is the Account ID to which you are depositing these funds. Your window should look like Figure 7.16.

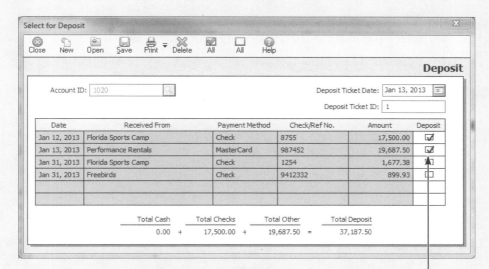

**Figure 7.16**

Selecting Receipts for Deposit

Place checks in these boxes to indicate which receipts are to be deposited

**6** Click **Save**.

**7** Click in the **Deposit** check box on the remaining two rows.

**8** Type **1/18/13** as the date of deposit.

**9** Type **2** in the Deposit Ticket ID text box.

**10** Click **Save** and then click **Close**.

## Receipt and Payment of Inventory

You have now accounted for the payments received from customers and the bank deposits that reflect amounts deposited into the checking account. Karen explains that the next item on your list is to record the inventory received from Purchase Order 1001 and the related payment to the vendor.

"When inventory received is related to a purchase order, it's important to do more than just record the check that paid for the inventory," Karen points out. "We also have to close out the purchase order and properly record the receipt of inventory. In this case, we received the two boats ordered under

*Video Demonstration*

*Demo 7E - Receiving inventory*

Purchase Orders 4001 and 4002. Both of these were cash-only purchases in that the vendor did not extend us credit and thus payment was due on receipt. Therefore, we have to receive inventory first, creating an asset (inventory) and a liability (accounts payable). Then we'll have to write a check to pay the liability."

## To record the receipt of inventory:

**1**  Open the Inventory & Services center.

**2**  Click **Receive Inventory** and then select **Receive Inventory** from the pop-up menu.

**3**  Select **10000** from the Vendor ID drop-down list.

**4**  Type **1/29/13** as the date.

**5**  Type **MB20397** as Malibu's Invoice No.

**6**  Select **4001** from the Apply to Purchase Order No. drop-down list.

**7**  Type **1** in the Received text box. Your window should look like Figure 7.17.

**Figure 7.17**

Recording the Receipt of Inventory and Bill

Select Purchase Order here

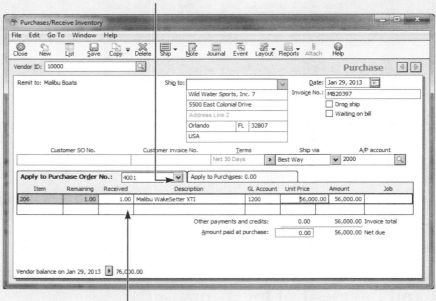

Type number of units received here

**8**  Click **Save** to record receipt of this inventory.

**9**  Select **10200** from the Vendor ID drop-down list.

**10**  Accept **1/29/13** as the date.

**11**   Type **T2309443** as Tige's Invoice No.

**12**   Select **4002** from the Apply to Purchase Order No. drop-down list.

**13**   Type **1** in the Received text box. Your window should look like Figure 7.18.

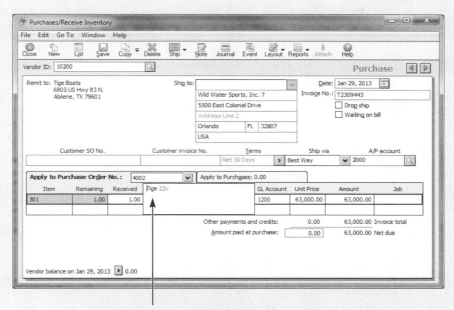

**Figure 7.18**

Recording the Receipt of Additional Inventory and Bill

Type number of units received here

**14**   Click **Save** to record receipt of this inventory and then click **Close**.

## To record the payment of inventory:

**1**   Open the Vendors & Purchases center, click **Pay Bills**, and then select **Pay Bill**.

**2**   Select **10000** as the Vendor ID.

**3**   Type **1004** as the check number if it is not already present.

**4**   Type **1/29/13** as the check date.

**5**   Click in the **Pay** check box on the row containing the 56,000.00 amount. *Note:* The date due indicates that this invoice isn't due until 2/28 and that an earlier invoice was actually due 1/14. Malibu shipped the company this product on a pay-on-receipt basis even though the Peachtree system showed Wild Water Sports as having 30 days' credit. Karen makes a note to follow up with Malibu on the credit terms. See Figure 7.19.

**Figure 7.19**

Payment of Malibu Bill

Clicking in this Pay check box places the 56,000.00 amount in both the Amount Paid text box and the payment amounts sections of the check

6 Click **Save**.

7 Select **10200** as the Vendor ID.

8 Type **1005** as the check number if it is not already present.

9 Accept **1/29/13** as the check date.

10 Click in the **Pay** check box on the row containing the 63,000.00 amount. See Figure 7.20.

**Figure 7.20**

Payment of Tige Bill

Select Vendor ID by clicking here to reveal a list of vendors

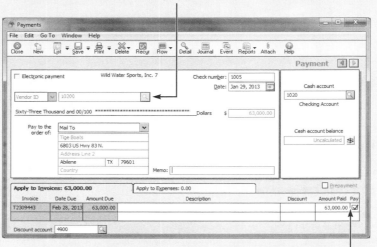

Place a check here to indicate payment of this invoice

11 Click **Save** and then click **Close**.

Karen explains that, as a result of paying these vendors for boats received under purchase orders, cash has decreased and inventory has increased. Both customers, for whom these boats were ordered, were contacted, and they picked up their boats on January 30.

## Inventory Sales

"I'll show you how we record the sales of these boats via the invoice process," Karen says. "Remember that both of these customers remitted their deposits when we placed the orders, and thus we only need to collect the remaining 75% balances owed."

"How do we account for the deposits already received?" you ask.

"Recall that, when we received these deposits earlier in January, we credited each of these customer's accounts receivable balances," she answers. "Because of that, we need to use the invoicing process to record the sales first, apply the existing credits, and then record the receipt of the balance due on the sale. Florida Sports Camp remitted $57,050 as the balance due on its purchase, while Performance Rentals remitted $64,181.25."

**To record sales, the application of advanced deposits received, and the receipt of payment for the balance due:**

1   Open the Customers & Sales center, click **Sales Invoices**, and then select **New Sales Invoice**.

2   Select **50005 Florida Sports Camp** from the Customer ID drop-down list.

3   Type **1/29/13** as the invoice date and **10001** as the Invoice No.

4   Select **101** in the Apply to Sales Order No. text box. (This links this invoice with the previously recorded sales order for this customer.)

5   Type **1** in the Shipped text box.

6   Click the button next to the words **Amount Paid at Sale**.

7   Type **4532** in the Reference text box (this is Florida Sports Camp's check number).

8   Type **57050** in the Receipt Amount text box.

9   Select **Check** as the Payment Method. Your Receive Payment window should look like Figure 7.21.

10   Click **OK**.

11   Click **Save** to save this invoice and then click the Invoice left arrow button (in the upper-right corner of the invoice screen) to return to Invoice 10001 as shown in Figure 7.22.

**Figure 7.21**

Time of Sale Receipt

Leave this blank as you'll deposit this to the bank later

**Figure 7.22**

Invoice 10001

Choose 101 as the Sales Order to which this invoice applies

Click here to see the previous invoice

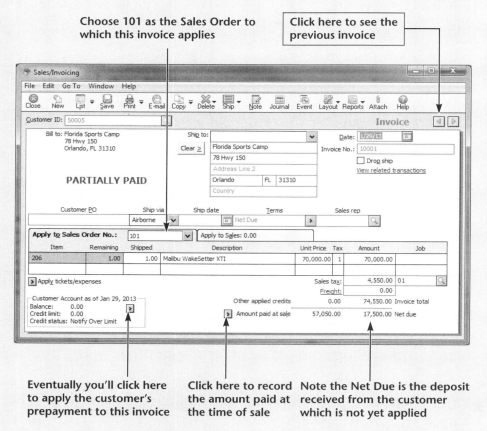

Eventually you'll click here to apply the customer's prepayment to this invoice

Click here to record the amount paid at the time of sale

Note the Net Due is the deposit received from the customer which is not yet applied

**12** Note that the invoice indicates a net amount due of $17,500.00 but that the balance reflected in the lower left-hand corner of the invoice indicates a balance of 0. Click the arrow button located next to the 0 amount to reveal the Customer Ledger shown in Figure 7.23.

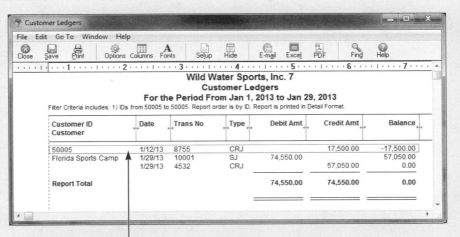

**Figure 7.23**

Florida Sports Camp Customer Ledger

Double-click on this row to view the original cash receipt accounted for as a prepayment

**13** Double-click the row containing the **17,500.00** amount.

**14** Uncheck the **Prepayment** check box.

**15** Click the **Apply to Invoices** tab.

**16** Check the **Pay** check box to apply this previously recorded prepayment to Invoice 10001 just recorded as shown in Figure 7.24.

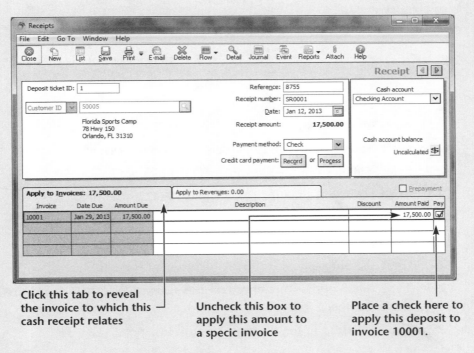

**Figure 7.24**

Applying a Prepayment

Click this tab to reveal the invoice to which this cash receipt relates

Uncheck this box to apply this amount to a specic invoice

Place a check here to apply this deposit to invoice 10001.

**17** Click **Save** to save your changes and then click **Close** to close the Receipts window.

**18** Close the Customer Ledger and Sales/Invoicing windows.

**19** Click **Sales Invoices** from the Customers & Sales navigation bar and then select **View and Edit Sales Invoices**.

**20** Double-click Invoice No. **10001** to reveal the paid-in-full invoice with a Net Due of 0.00 as shown in Figure 7.25.

**Figure 7.25**

Paid-in-Full Invoice

This invoice is now shown as paid in full once we applied the prepayment

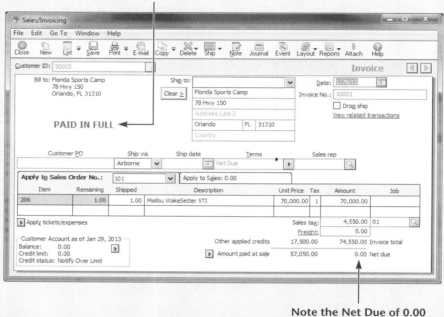

Note the Net Due of 0.00

**21** Click **Close** to close Invoice No. 10001 and click **Close** to close the Sales Invoice List.

**22** Click **Sales Invoices** and then select **New Sales Invoice**.

**23** Select **50006** from the Customer ID drop-down list.

**24** Type **1/30/13** as the invoice date and **10002** as the Invoice No.

**25** Select **102** in the Apply to Sales Order No. text box.

**26** Type **1** in the Shipped text box.

**27** Click the button next to the words **Amount Paid at Sale**.

**28** Type **10885** in the Reference text box (this is Performance Rentals check number).

**29** Type **64181.25** in the Receipt Amount text box.

**30** Select **Check** as the Payment Method.

**31** Click **OK**.

**32**  Click **Save** to save this invoice and then click the Invoice left arrow button to return to the partially paid invoice.

**33**  Click the arrow button located next to the 0.00 amount in the lower-left box.

**34**  Double-click the row containing the **19,687.50** amount.

**35**  Uncheck the **Prepayment** check box.

**36**  Click the **Apply to Invoices** tab.

**37**  Check the **Pay** check box to apply this previously recorded prepayment to Invoice No. 10002 just recorded.

**38**  Click **Save** to save your changes and then click **Close** to close the Receipts window.

**39**  Click **Close** to close the Customer Ledger window.

**40**  Click **Close** to close the Sales/Invoicing window.

Karen comments that in the examples shown, the prepayment could be applied to an invoice in total. In other words, there was no leftover prepayment. If, however, a prepayment was for an amount larger than the invoice to which it was being applied, the same steps shown are taken, but, in addition, a new prepayment must be recorded for the difference. Let's take, for example, the Florida Sports Camp sale. If the prepayment had been $20,000.00 instead of $19,687.50, the difference ($312.50) would have been recorded as another prepayment and the $19,687.50 would have been applied to the sales invoice. The result would have been a credit balance of $312.50, and the sales invoice would have been recorded as paid in full.

Now that the invoices are recorded, sales and accounts receivable have been increased, cost of goods sold has been increased, and inventory has been decreased. Wild Water has also recorded the receipt of full payment from the customers, but it hasn't recorded the related deposit to its bank account.

**To record the deposit of funds from boat sales:**

**1**  Click **Bank Deposits** from the Banking center and then select **New Bank Deposit**.

**2**  Type **1/30/13** as the Deposit Ticket Date.

**3**  Accept **3** as the Deposit Ticket ID.

**4**  Click in both check boxes under the Deposit title to record a total deposit of 121,231.25.

**5**  Click **Save** and then click **Close**.

*Video Demonstration*

*Demo 7F - Paying expenses*

## Payment for Monthly Expenses, Inventory, and Bills

"Next," Karen comments, "I'd like to show you how Wild Water will pay for monthly expenses and bills. Currently, most of our vendors want us to pay on receipt of their bills, so we've been recording expenses only when we pay the bills. In a couple of months, we will be in a position to ask for credit terms from most of our vendors. In the meantime, we write checks at the end of the month to pay for expenses."

One of the payments was for insurance for the year, which will be treated as prepaid insurance and adjusted prior to preparing financial statements. A second payment represents inventory parts received (oil, air filters, and oil filters used in servicing boats). Still another represents an amount due to Malibu Boats, which was established as a liability when the company was first set up. This payment requires the use of Peachtree's bill payment process. The balance of Wild Water's payments this month relates to expenses already incurred.

"Let's first look at how we pay for expenses and then how we pay for inventory parts received," Karen suggests.

### To record checks written for expenses:

1   Click **Write Checks** in the Banking center and then select **New Check**.

2   Type **1006** as the check number if it is not already there.

3   Type **1/29/13** as the check date.

4   Click the magnifying glass in the Vendor ID text box and then click **New** to create a new vendor.

5   Type **11400** as the new Vendor ID.

6   Type **Manchester Insurance** in the Name text box.

7   Type the vendor's address as **234 Wilshire Blvd., Los Angeles, CA 91335**.

8   Select **1400 Prepaid Expenses** in the Expense Account text box.

9   Click the **Purchases Info** tab.

10  Select **Customize terms for this Vendor** from the Terms and Credit text box.

11  Select the **Due in Number of Days** button, and then Type **0** in the Net due in text box and **0** in the Credit limit box.

12  Click **Save** and then click **Close**.

13  Select **11400** as the Vendor ID.

14  Type **22000** as the check amount and then press **[Tab]**. Your Write Checks window should look like Figure 7.26.

**Figure 7.26**

Check 1006 to Manchester Insurance

**15**  Click **Save**.

**16**  Type **1007** as the check number if it is not already there.

**17**  Type **1/29/13** as the check date if it is not already there.

**18**  Click the magnifying glass in the Vendor ID text box and then click **New** to create a new vendor.

**19**  Type **11600** as the new Vendor ID.

**20**  Type **Central Florida Gas & Electric** in the Name text box.

**21**  Select **6400 Utilities Expense** in the Expense Account text box.

**22**  Click the **Purchases Info** tab.

**23**  Select **Customize terms for this vendor** from the Terms and Credit text box.

**24**  Type **0** in the Net due in text box and **0** in the Credit limit box.

**25**  Click **Save** and then click **Close**.

**26**  Select **11600** as the Vendor ID.

**27**  Type **1/29/13** as the check date if it is not already there.

**28**  Type **890** as the amount.

**29**  Click **Save**.

**30**  Click the magnifying glass in the Vendor ID text box and then click **New** to create a new vendor.

**31**  Type **11700** as the new Vendor ID.

**32**  Type **Verizon** in the Name text box.

**33**  Select **6500 Telephone Expenses** in the Expense Account text box.

**34**  Click the **Purchases Info** tab.

35    Select **Customize terms for this vendor** from the Terms and Credit text box.

36    Type **0** in the Net due in text box and **0** in the Credit limit box.

37    Click **Save** and then click **Close**.

38    Select **11700** as the Vendor ID.

39    Type **1008** as the check number if it is not already there.

40    Type **1/29/13** as the check date if it is not already there.

41    Type **1700** as the amount.

42    Click **Save** and then click **Close**.

## To record inventory parts received and paid for:

1    Open the Inventory & Services center, click **Receive Inventory**, and then select **Receive Inventory**.

2    Click the magnifying glass in the Vendor ID text box and then click **New** to create a new vendor.

3    Type **11500** as the new Vendor ID.

4    Type **Chevron** in the Name text box.

5    Type the vendor's address as **2389 Peachtree Blvd., Atlanta, GA 30311**.

6    Select **1230 Inventory Parts** in the Expense Account text box.

7    Click the **Purchases Info** tab.

8    Select **Customize terms for this vendor** from the Terms and Credit text box.

9    Type **0** in the Net due in text box and **0** in the Credit limit box.

10    Click **Save** and then click **Close**.

11    Select **11500** as the Vendor ID.

12    Type **1/29/13** as the date and then type **EM239879978** as the Invoice No.

13    Type **25** as the Quantity on the first row of the Apply to Purchases tab.

14    Select **904** from the Item drop-down list.

15    Type **150** as the Quantity on the second row.

16    Select **901** from the Item drop-down list.

17    Type **25** as the Quantity on the third row.

**18** Select **902** from the Item drop-down list. Your screen should look like Figure 7.27.

*Trouble?* If there are not enough rows on your inventory receipt, simply enlarge the Purchases/Receive Inventory window and more rows will appear.

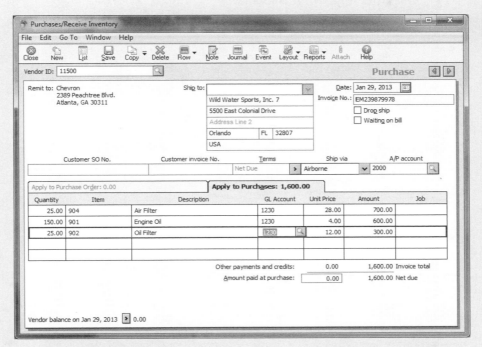

**Figure 7.27**

Receiving Inventory Parts

**19** Click **Save** and then click **Close**.

"Let's now look at how we pay for bills already established in accounts payable," Karen suggests.

## To record checks written to pay bills:

**1** Click **Pay Bills** in the Vendors & Purchases center and then select **Pay Bill**.

**2** Select **11500** from the Vendor ID text box.

**3** Type **1009** in the Check Number text box.

**4** Type **1/29/13** as the date.

**5** Click the **Apply to Invoices** tab.

**6** Check the **Pay** box in the row containing Invoice EM239879978.

**7**   Click **Save**.

**8**   Select **10000** from the Vendor ID text box.

**9**   Type **1010** in the Check Number text box.

**10**   Type **1/29/13** as the date.

**11**   Click the **Apply to Invoices** tab.

**12**   Check the Pay box in the row containing Invoice M230987 as shown in Figure 7.28.

**Figure 7.28**

Payment of Bills

**13**   Click **Save** and then click **Close**.

# Payroll

Now it's time to calculate payroll. Karen explains that entering information about payroll is a little tricky since Wild Water has decided not to use Peachtree's payroll service. To participate at any level would have required a monthly or annual fee, and, since Wild Water Sports has so few employees, the company has decided to manually compute payroll.

"Is that why we previously set up Wild Water to calculate payroll manually?" you ask.

"Exactly," Karen answers. "That was a part of the Peachtree setup process. Now we are going to enter payroll information for the month of January."

"Wouldn't it be faster to use the payroll service?" you ask.

"Well, yes," Karen responds, "but, as you'll see, entering payroll withholding and tax information manually isn't that difficult."

"Peachtree has a nice timesheet capability, which is how we'll track Ryder's and Pat's time," Karen explains. "It also has a job cost tracking feature so that, when either Ryder or Pat works on a specific boat, their time can be automatically charged to a customer and a specific job for that customer. Timesheets are typically used when a company is trying to keep track of hours worked on specific jobs. They are not required. Many companies who don't track job costs will only enter the hours for each employee right before processing the payroll. However, in this company's situation, timesheets are very helpful. Before we can enter the employees' time, we must make sure that a customer/job entry is set up. Later we'll do this during the month as each job is started, but for now we'll enter them after the fact. Two jobs were started in the last couple days of January—one for Florida Sports Camp and one for Freebirds. Let me show you how to create those jobs entries, both of which are for customers we've already created in Peachtree."

### To create new jobs for existing customers:

1  Open the Customers & Sales center, click **Jobs**, and then select **New Job** from the pop-up menu.

2  Type **3001** in the Job ID text box.

3  Click on the drop-down box in the For Customer text box and then click **New**.

4  Type **50008** as the Customer ID and **Alisa Hay** as the Customer Name.

5  Enter this customer's address as **2999 Dover Blvd., Daytona Beach, FL 32114** and select sales tax code **01**.

6  Click the **Payment & Credit** tab and then select **Customize terms for this customer** from the Terms and Credit drop-down text box. Set the terms to net due in **0** days with a **0.00** credit limit.

7  Click **Save** and then click **Close**.

8  Select **50008** from the list of customers provided in the For Customer text box. Your Maintain Jobs window should look like Figure 7.29.

9  Click **Save** to save this new job.

10  Click **New** to add a new job.

11  Add a new Job ID **3002** with no description for customer **50005**; then add a new Job ID **3003** with no description for customer **50004**.

12  Be sure to save both jobs after creating them and then close the Maintain Jobs window.

**Figure 7.29**

Adding a New Job

With the new jobs added, Karen explains that you can now enter the hours worked into Peachtree's time records. These can either be entered using time-sheets which create time tickets, or by creating time tickets directly. Karen offers to show you both methods.

*Video Demonstration*

*Demo 7G - Recording payroll timesheets*

## To complete weekly timesheets or time tickets for January:

**1** Open the Employees & Payroll Center.

**2** Click **Time and Expense Tickets**, and then select **New Weekly Time-sheet**.

**3** Select **003** from the drop-down list of employees.

**4** Type **1/7/13** in the Week including text box.

**5** Select **Administrative** from the drop-down arrow in the first row of the Customer/Job/Administrative column.

**6** Click in the Activity Item ID column, click the drop-down arrow, and then click **New** to add a Activity Item ID. (*Note:* All timesheet entries for employees require an Activity Item ID.)

**7** Create a new activity by typing **801** as the Item ID, select **Activity item** as the Item Class, and type **Office Work** in the Description text box.

**8** Click **Save** and then click **Close** to close the Maintain Inventory Items window.

**9** Select **801** as the Activity Item as shown in Figure 7.30.

**Select Administrative from this list of alternatives**

**Click here to view a drop-down list of employees**

**Figure 7.30**

Entering Time Ticket Information

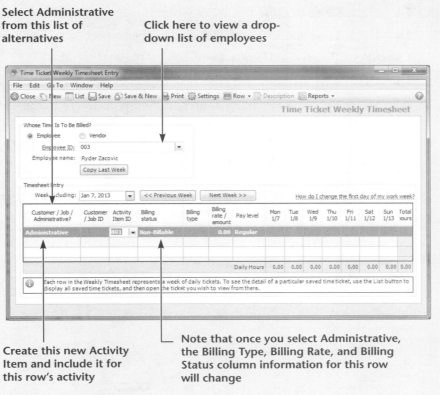

**Create this new Activity Item and include it for this row's activity**

**Note that once you select Administrative, the Billing Type, Billing Rate, and Billing Status column information for this row will change**

**10** Type **6** as the hours worked on Mon 1/7 and then press **[Tab]** to move to the next date.

**11** Type **4** as the hours worked on Tue 1/8 and then press **[Tab]**. The Weekly Timesheet should look like Figure 7.31.

**Enter hours here**

**Figure 7.31**

Entering Hours into the Weekly Timesheet for Ryder Zacovic (ID 003)

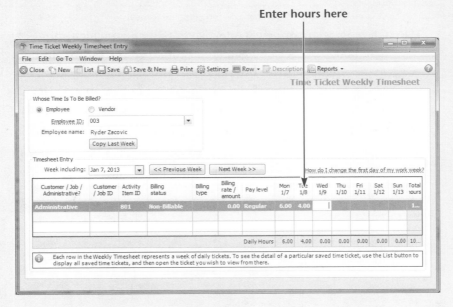

**12** Click **Save** to save this weekly timesheet. (Entering time on a weekly timesheet also automatically creates daily time tickets.)

**13** Click **Close** to close this weekly timesheet.

**14** Click **Time and Expense Tickets** and then select New Time Ticket.

**15** Select Employee ID **004**.

**16** Choose **As an Administrative task** from the To be applied text box.

**17** Select **801** as the Activity Item and then type **1/7/13** in the Ticket date: text box.

**18** Type **4** in the Duration text box and then select **Non-Billable** from the Billing status: text box. Your screen should look like Figure 7.32.

**Figure 7.32**

Entering Hours into the Time Ticket Window for Pat Ng (ID 004)

**19** Click **Save** and a new Time Ticket will open, which should be numbered 000004. Select **004** as the Employee ID, **801** as the Activity Item, **As an Administrative task** as the To be applied text, and **Non-Billable** as the Billing status. Then type **6** as the Duration and **1/8/13** as the Ticket date.

**20** Click **Save** and then click **Close** to close Time Ticket 000004.

**21** Click **Time and Expense Tickets** and then click **View and Edit Time Tickets**. Your window should look like Figure 7.33.

**Figure 7.33**

Time Tickets List

**22**  Enter time tickets 5 through 16 shown below in Figure 7.34 using either the timesheet or time ticket method previously demonstrated.

| Ticket No | Date | Employee/Vendor | Activity Item | Customer/Job | Billing Status | Invoiced? | Duration | Billing Amount |
|---|---|---|---|---|---|---|---|---|
| 000001 | 1/7/2013 | 003 | 801 | | Non-Billable | No | 6.00 | $0.00 |
| 000002 | 1/8/2013 | 003 | 801 | | Non-Billable | No | 4.00 | $0.00 |
| 000003 | 1/7/2013 | 004 | 801 | | Non-Billable | No | 4.00 | $0.00 |
| 000004 | 1/8/2013 | 004 | 801 | | Non-Billable | No | 6.00 | $0.00 |
| 000005 | 1/10/2013 | 003 | 801 | | Non-Billable | No | 8.00 | $0.00 |
| 000006 | 1/11/2013 | 003 | 801 | | Non-Billable | No | 6.00 | $0.00 |
| 000007 | 1/14/2013 | 003 | 801 | | Non-Billable | No | 4.00 | $0.00 |
| 000008 | 1/10/2013 | 004 | 801 | | Non-Billable | No | 2.00 | $0.00 |
| 000009 | 1/11/2013 | 004 | 801 | | Non-Billable | No | 4.00 | $0.00 |
| 000010 | 1/14/2013 | 004 | 801 | | Non-Billable | No | 6.00 | $0.00 |
| 000011 | 1/21/2013 | 003 | 801 | | Non-Billable | No | 8.00 | $0.00 |
| 000012 | 1/23/2013 | 003 | 801 | | Non-Billable | No | 8.00 | $0.00 |
| 000013 | 1/25/2013 | 003 | 801 | | Non-Billable | No | 7.00 | $0.00 |
| 000014 | 1/21/2013 | 004 | 801 | | Non-Billable | No | 8.00 | $0.00 |
| 000015 | 1/23/2013 | 004 | 801 | | Non-Billable | No | 8.00 | $0.00 |
| 000016 | 1/25/2013 | 004 | 801 | | Non-Billable | No | 8.00 | $0.00 |

**Figure 7.34**

Time Tickets to Be Entered

**23**  Create Ticket Number 000017 using the information provided in Figure 7.35.

**Figure 7.35**

Time Ticket 00017 to Record Billable Time

**24**  Enter time tickets 18 through 23 shown below in Figures 7.36 using either the timesheet or time ticket method previously demonstrated.

| Ticket No. | Date | Employee/Vendor | Activity Item | Customer/Job ID | Billing Status | Invoiced? | Duration | Billing Amount |
|---|---|---|---|---|---|---|---|---|
| 000018 | 1/29/2013 | 003 | 103 | 3003 | Billable | No | 3.00 | $525.00 |
| 000019 | 1/29/2013 | 003 | 106 | 3003 | Billable | No | 4.00 | $320.00 |
| 000020 | 1/29/2013 | 003 | 801 | | Non-Billable | No | 1.00 | $0.00 |
| 000021 | 1/30/2013 | 004 | 102 | 3002 | Billable | No | 6.00 | $1,500.00 |
| 000022 | 1/30/2013 | 004 | 105 | 3002 | Billable | No | 1.00 | $75.00 |
| 000023 | 1/30/2013 | 004 | 801 | | Non-Billable | No | 1.00 | $0.00 |

**Figure 7.36**

Additional Time Tickets to Be Entered

"That takes care of January's hourly timesheets, but now we have to manually process payroll for those timesheets and for our two salaried employees," Karen explains. "Processing payroll for salaried employees simply requires us to enter the end-of-period date, in this case a month end of 1/31, and specify the taxes to be withheld and the employer's tax expenses. The same is basically true for our hourly employees at Wild Water Sports since both of our hourly employees' payrolls are based on time ticket hours."

*Video Demonstration*

*Demo 7H - Processing payroll*

### To process payroll for January:

1   From the Employees & Payroll center, click **Pay Employees** and then select **Enter Payroll For One Employee**.

2   Click **Cancel** to close the Peachtree Payroll Solution advertisement (if it appears) and then click in the check box **Do not display this message again** and then click **OK**.

3   Choose **Checking Account** as the cash account used for this transaction and then click **OK**.

4   Type **1011** as the Check Number.

5   Type **1/31/13** in the Date text box.

6   Type **1/31/13** in the Pay Period Ends text box.

7   Select Employee ID **001**.

8   Enter information for Donna Chandler's paycheck from Figure 7.37. Be sure to put employee tax amounts as negative numbers and company amounts as positive numbers.

**Figure 7.37**

Donna Chandler's Paycheck for the Pay Period Ending 1/31/13

The salary amount comes from our original employee setup

Make sure your net check equals this amount

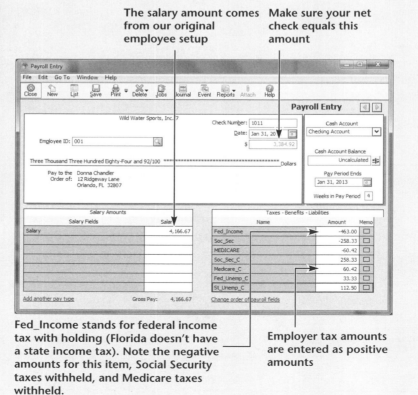

Fed_Income stands for federal income tax with holding (Florida doesn't have a state income tax). Note the negative amounts for this item, Social Security taxes withheld, and Medicare taxes withheld.

Employer tax amounts are entered as positive amounts

**9**   Click **Save**.

**10**   Select Employee ID **003**.

**11**   Type **1012** as the Check Number.

**12**   Since you have already entered Ryder's hours via timesheets, the 60 hours should show up in the lower left-hand corner of your check.

   *Trouble?* If no hours are showing, you may not have the correct pay period selected. Be sure your Pay Period Ends text box shows Jan 31, 2013. The text (Employee uses Time Ticket hours) should also appear under the Employee ID. If it doesn't, go back to the setup for this employee and make sure the setup specifies that this employee uses time ticket hours.

**13**   Enter information for Ryder Zacovic's paycheck from Figure 7.38. Once again, be sure to put employee tax amounts as negative numbers and company amounts as positive numbers.

**Figure 7.38**

Ryder Zacovic's Paycheck for the Pay Period Ending 1/31/13

Make sure this text is present for this employee

Make sure your net check equals this amount

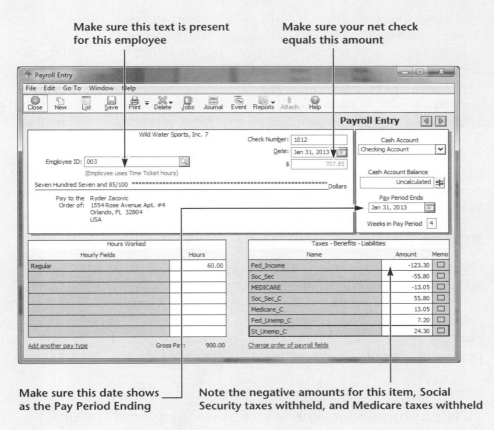

Make sure this date shows as the Pay Period Ending

Note the negative amounts for this item, Social Security taxes withheld, and Medicare taxes withheld

**14**   Click **Save**.

**15** Continue the payroll process based on the following payroll information:

| Item | Employee | |
|---|---|---|
| | Wilson | Ng |
| Check Number | 1013 | 1014 |
| Salary/Hours Worked | 4,166.67 | 54 |
| Fed_Income | −710.00 | −133.16 |
| Soc_Sec | −258.33 | −60.26 |
| Medicare | −60.42 | −14.09 |
| Soc_Sec_ER | 258.33 | 60.26 |
| Medicare_ER | 60.42 | 14.09 |
| FUTA_ER | 33.33 | 7.78 |
| SUI_ER | 112.50 | 26.24 |
| Net check amount | 3,137.92 | 764.49 |

**16** Click **Close** to close the Payroll Entry window.

"How did you determine the withholding amounts and the other tax items?" you ask.

"Withholding amounts came from the payroll tax withholding tables I downloaded from the Internal Revenue Service Website at http://www.irs.gov," says Karen. "The others were provided by our local CPA, as follows: Social Security is 6.2% of earnings, Medicare is 1.45% of earnings, and federal unemployment is 0.8% of earnings up to $7,000, while state unemployment is 2.7% of earnings up to $7,000." (See Appendix 1—"Payroll Taxes.")

Karen further explains that, since the hourly employees' time was recorded on timesheets, she did not have to enter hours on each employee's paycheck. If, however, the company didn't use timesheets, it would be necessary to enter hours worked by hourly employees in each Payroll Entry window.

## Billing Customers for Time

*Video Demonstration*

*Demo 71 - Billing customers for time and materials*

"What about the customer jobs we charged for Ryder's and Pat's time?" you ask. "Don't we have to bill the customers for the time charged?"

Yes," Karen answers. "You are quite perceptive. As it turns out, these jobs were completed and the boats were picked up by the customers. If they were not complete, we would wait to bill them until they were complete. Let me show you the process for generating an invoice based on time recorded via the payroll system."

### To bill customers for time recorded via the payroll system:

**1** Open the Customers & Sales center, click **Sales Invoices**, and then select **New Sales Invoice**.

**2** Select Customer ID **50008**.

**3** Type **1/30/13** as the date.

**4** Type **10003** as the Invoice No.

**5** Click the arrow button next to **Apply Tickets/Expenses**.

**6**   Place a check in the **Use** column, select **No Consolidation** in the Consolidate By drop-down list, and then select the option button **Use Item Description for Invoicing** as shown in Figure 7.39.

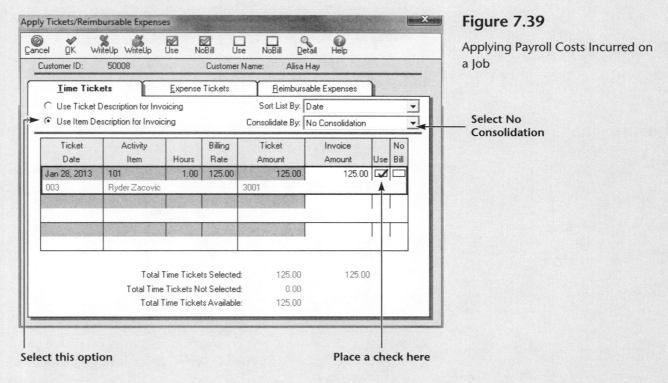

**Figure 7.39**

Applying Payroll Costs Incurred on a Job

Select this option

Place a check here

**7**   Click **OK**.

**8**   Add 5 quarts of engine oil and 1 oil filter to the invoice, specify job **3001** for both, and specify sales tax code **01**. Your invoice should look like Figure 7.40.

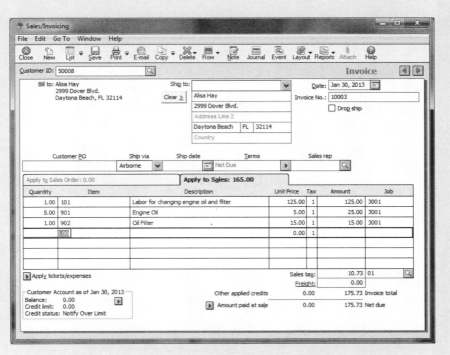

**Figure 7.40**

Invoice 10003

9   Click the arrow button next to the text **Amount Paid at Sale**.

10  Type **4** as the Deposit Ticket ID since this amount was then directly deposited into the company's checking account.

11  Type **9845** in the Reference text box of the Receive Payment window and select check as the payment method.

12  Type **175.73** as the Receipt Amount and then click **OK**.

13  Your new invoice should now indicate a 0.00 Net Due.

14  Click **Save** and then click **Close**.

15  Click **50004** from the Customers list in the Customers & Sales center to edit Freebirds data.

16  Type **1000 Boomer St., Tallahassee FL 32303** as its address, click **Save**, and then click **Close**.

17  Click **Sales Invoices** and select **New Sales Invoice** from the Customers & Sales center.

18  Select Customer ID **50004**.

19  Type **1/31/13** as the date.

20  Type **10004** as the Invoice No.

21  Click the arrow button next to **Apply Tickets/Expenses**.

22  Place a check in the **Use** column for both rows presented and select the option button **Use Item Description for Invoicing** as shown in Figure 7.41.

**Figure 7.41**

Applying Payroll Costs Incurred on a Job

Select this option          Place a check here

23  Click **OK**.

24  Select **01** as the sales tax code.

**25**  Click the arrow button next to the text **Amount Paid at Sale**.

**26**  Type **9412332** in the Reference text box of the Receive Payment window.

**27**  Type **899.93** as the Receipt Amount and select **Check** as the Payment method. (Do not enter a Deposit Ticket ID.) And then click **OK**.

**28**  Your new invoice should now indicate a 0.00 Net Due as shown in Figure 7.42.

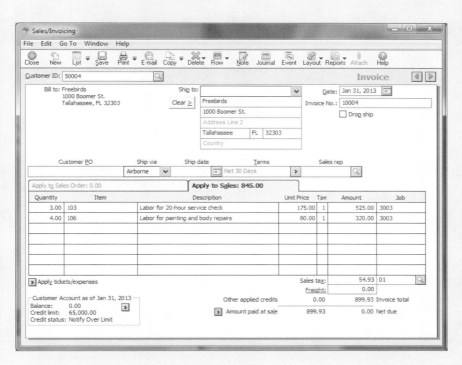

**Figure 7.42**

Invoice 10004

**29**  Click **Save**.

**30**  Select Customer ID **50005**.

**31**  Accept **1/31/13** as the date.

**32**  Accept **10005** as the Invoice No.

**33**  Click the arrow button next to **Apply Tickets/Expenses**.

**34**  Place a check in the **Use** column for both rows presented, select the option button **Use Item Description for Invoicing**, and then click **OK**.

**35**  Select **01** as the sales tax code.

**36**  Click the arrow button next to the text **Amount Paid at Sale**.

**37**  Type **1254** in the Reference text box of the Receive Payment window.

**38**   Type **1677.38** as the Receipt Amount and select **Check** as the
Payment method. (Do not enter a Deposit Ticket ID.) And then
click **OK**.

**39**   Your new invoice should now indicate a 0.00 Net Due as shown
in Figure 7.43.

**Figure 7.43**

Invoice 10005

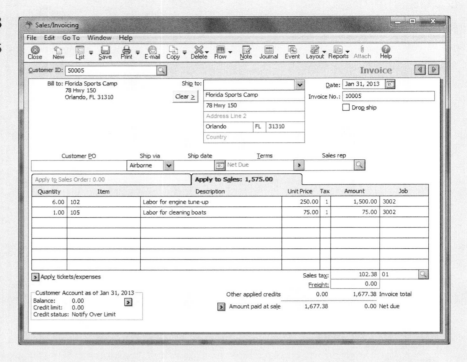

**40**   Click **Save** and then click **Close** in the Sales/Invoicing window.

"Did we deposit funds collected from those last two transactions?" you ask.
"No," Karen answers. "We won't deposit them until the next month."

You've now recorded many operating activities, including cash sales, purchase orders, writing checks, and processing payroll, and you'd like to know
how the business did for the month.

## Evaluate a Firm's Performance and Financial Position

The best way to evaluate a firm's performance and financial position at this
point is to generate an income statement and a balance sheet as of January 31,
2013. Karen suggests that you apply what you have learned from past experiences with Peachtree to create and print a standard income statement and a standard balance sheet for January.

## To prepare a standard income statement and a balance sheet for January:

**1** Set the system date to **1/31/13**.

**2** Click **Reports & Forms** and then click **Financial Statements**.

**3** Double-click <**Standard**> **Income Stmnt** from the Select a Report or Form window.

**4** Uncheck the **Print Page Numbers** and **Show Zero Amounts** check boxes.

**5** Click **OK** to view the income statement for January as shown in Figure 7.44.

| | | | | | |
|---|---|---|---|---|---|
| Wild Water Sports, Inc. 7 | | | | | |
| Income Statement | | | | | |
| For the One Month Ending January 31, 2013 | | | | | |
| | Current Month | | | Year to Date | |
| **Revenues** | | | | | |
| Sales Income | $ 200,750.00 | 98.73 | $ | 200,750.00 | 98.73 |
| Service Income | 2,545.00 | 1.25 | | 2,545.00 | 1.25 |
| Parts Income | 40.00 | 0.02 | | 40.00 | 0.02 |
| Total Revenues | 203,335.00 | 100.00 | | 203,335.00 | 100.00 |
| **Cost of Sales** | | | | | |
| Cost of Sales | 160,632.00 | 79.00 | | 160,632.00 | 79.00 |
| Total Cost of Sales | 160,632.00 | 79.00 | | 160,632.00 | 79.00 |
| Gross Profit | 42,703.00 | 21.00 | | 42,703.00 | 21.00 |
| **Expenses** | | | | | |
| Wages Expense | 10,205.34 | 5.02 | | 10,205.34 | 5.02 |
| Payroll Tax Expense | 1,137.88 | 0.56 | | 1,137.88 | 0.56 |
| Utilities Expense | 890.00 | 0.44 | | 890.00 | 0.44 |
| Telephone Expense | 1,700.00 | 0.84 | | 1,700.00 | 0.84 |
| Total Expenses | 13,933.22 | 6.85 | | 13,933.22 | 6.85 |
| Net Income | $ 28,769.78 | 14.15 | $ | 28,769.78 | 14.15 |

**Figure 7.44**

Income Statement for January 2013

**6** Click **Print** from the button bar and then click **OK** to print this statement.

**7** Click **Close**.

**8** Double-click <**Standard**> **Balance Sheet** from the Select a Report or Form window.

**9** Make sure the **Print Page Numbers** and **Show Zero Amounts** check boxes are unchecked.

**10** Click **OK** to view the balance sheet for January as shown in Figures 7.45 and 7.46.

**Figure 7.45**

Asset Section of the Balance Sheet as of January 31, 2013

Wild Water Sports, Inc. 7
Balance Sheet
January 31, 2013

ASSETS

| | | |
|---|---:|---:|
| **Current Assets** | | |
| Checking Account | $ 22,366.61 | |
| Short-Term Investments | 300,000.00 | |
| Accounts Receivable | 66,300.00 | |
| Inventory | 330,400.00 | |
| Inventory Parts | 1,568.00 | |
| Prepaid Expenses | 22,000.00 | |
| | | |
| Total Current Assets | | 742,634.61 |
| | | |
| **Property and Equipment** | | |
| Property and Equipment | 245,000.00 | |
| Accum. Depreciation-Prop&Eqt | (7,500.00) | |
| | | |
| Total Property and Equipment | | 237,500.00 |
| | | |
| **Other Assets** | | |
| | | |
| Total Other Assets | | 0.00 |
| | | |
| Total Assets | $ | 980,134.61 |

**Figure 7.46**

Liabilities and Capital Section of the Balance Sheet as of January 31, 2013

Wild Water Sports, Inc. 7
Balance Sheet
January 31, 2013

LIABILITIES AND CAPITAL

| | | |
|---|---:|---:|
| **Current Liabilities** | | |
| Accounts Payable | $ 1,000.00 | |
| Sales Tax Payable | 13,216.79 | |
| Federal Payroll Taxes Payable | 2,990.86 | |
| FUTA Payable | 81.64 | |
| State Payroll Taxes Payable | 275.54 | |
| | | |
| Total Current Liabilities | | 17,564.83 |
| | | |
| **Long-Term Liabilities** | | |
| Long-Term Debt-Noncurrent | 633,800.00 | |
| | | |
| Total Long-Term Liabilities | | 633,800.00 |
| | | |
| Total Liabilities | | 651,364.83 |
| | | |
| **Capital** | | |
| Common Stock | 300,000.00 | |
| Net Income | 28,769.78 | |
| | | |
| Total Capital | | 328,769.78 |
| | | |
| Total Liabilities & Capital | $ | 980,134.61 |

**11**  Click **Print** from the button bar and then click **OK** to print this statement.

**12**  Click **Close**.

"Is there a way for us to see what transactions made up these balances?" you ask.

"Yes," Karen responds. "We'll print a Find Transactions report, which will show us every transaction recorded in chronological order. It will include the type of transaction, the date it was recorded, a number reference (like check number, invoice number, etc.), the name of the entity (vendor name, customer name, employee name, etc.), the balance sheet account affected (checking, accounts receivable, undeposited funds, etc.), other accounts affected (inventory, revenue, expenses, etc.), and the amount. Let me show you how to create this report."

## To prepare a transaction list by date report for January:

**1**  Click **Company Reports** from the Select a Report or Form window.

**2**  Double-click **Find Transactions Report**.

**3**  If your system date is still set at 1/31/13, the report you get will only show you transactions recorded on 1/31/13. To change the report to reflect all transactions recorded in January 2013, click the **Options** button on the report button bar.

**4**  Change the From date to **1/1/13** and then click **OK**.

**5**  Click **Print** from the report button bar and then click **OK** to print. The report shown in Figure 7.47 should appear.
*Trouble?* On occasion, you might accidentally enter the wrong date for a transaction (for example, accepting the default date, which might be before January 2013 or after January 2013). This might occur if you forgot to set the system date to some date in January 2013. If you're pretty sure you entered a transaction but don't see it on your transactions list, dates are likely your problem. To verify this, try entering 1/1/08 as the From date and 12/31/15 as the To date. If your missing transaction appears, double-click it to correct the date, and you'll be good to go!

**6**  Click **Save**.

**7**  Type **Find Transactions Report 1/13** as the new name of the report and then click **Save**.

**8**  Close the Find Transactions Report 1/13 report and then close the Select a Report or Form window.

### Figure 7.47

Find Transactions Report

**Wild Water Sports, Inc. 7**
**Find Transactions Report**
**For the Period From Jan 1, 2013 to Jan 31, 2013**

Filter Criteria includes: 1) All Transaction Types. Report order is by Date.

| Date | Type | Reference | ID | Name | Amount |
|------|------|-----------|----|------|--------|
| 1/1/13 | General Journal Entry | 1 | | | 200,000.00 |
| 1/4/13 | General Journal Entry | 2 | | | 250,000.00 |
| 1/7/13 | Time Ticket | 000001 | 003 | Ryder Zacovic | |
| 1/7/13 | Time Ticket | 000003 | 004 | Pat Ng | |
| 1/8/13 | Payment | 1001 | 11100 | ETrade | 300,000.00 |
| 1/8/13 | Time Ticket | 000002 | 003 | Ryder Zacovic | |
| 1/8/13 | Time Ticket | 000004 | 004 | Pat Ng | |
| 1/10/13 | Time Ticket | 000005 | 003 | Ryder Zacovic | |
| 1/10/13 | Time Ticket | 000008 | 004 | Pat Ng | |
| 1/11/13 | Payment | 1002 | 11200 | Staples | 70,000.00 |
| 1/11/13 | Payment | 1003 | 11300 | AJ Marine Equipment | 100,000.00 |
| 1/11/13 | Purchase Order | 4001 | 10000 | Malibu Boats | 56,000.00 |
| 1/11/13 | Purchase Order | 4002 | 10200 | Tige Boats | 63,000.00 |
| 1/11/13 | Time Ticket | 000006 | 003 | Ryder Zacovic | |
| 1/11/13 | Time Ticket | 000009 | 004 | Pat Ng | |
| 1/12/13 | Receipt | 8755 | 50005 | Florida Sports Camp | 17,500.00 |
| 1/12/13 | Sales Order | 101 | 50005 | Florida Sports Camp | 74,550.00 |
| 1/13/13 | Receipt | 987452 | 50006 | Performance Rentals | 19,687.50 |
| 1/13/13 | Sales Order | 102 | 50006 | Performance Rentals | 83,868.75 |
| 1/14/13 | Time Ticket | 000007 | 003 | Ryder Zacovic | |
| 1/14/13 | Time Ticket | 000010 | 004 | Pat Ng | |
| 1/15/13 | Receipt | 65454 | 50002 | Buena Vista Water Sports | 30,000.00 |
| 1/18/13 | Receipt | 161 | 50007 | Seth Blackman | 55,380.00 |
| 1/21/13 | Time Ticket | 000011 | 003 | Ryder Zacovic | |
| 1/21/13 | Time Ticket | 000014 | 004 | Pat Ng | |
| 1/23/13 | Time Ticket | 000012 | 003 | Ryder Zacovic | |
| 1/23/13 | Time Ticket | 000015 | 004 | Pat Ng | |
| 1/25/13 | Time Ticket | 000013 | 003 | Ryder Zacovic | |
| 1/25/13 | Time Ticket | 000016 | 004 | Pat Ng | |
| 1/28/13 | Time Ticket | 000017 | 003 | Ryder Zacovic | 125.00 |
| 1/29/13 | Payment | 1004 | 10000 | Malibu Boats | 56,000.00 |
| 1/29/13 | Payment | 1005 | 10200 | Tige Boats | 63,000.00 |

"Not bad for our first month," Karen comments. "But we need to pay off some of the debt acquired with the company acquisition. Plus, we can't forget that some costs such as interest and depreciation expenses have not been accrued or paid, so this information is not complete."

**Wild Water Sports, Inc. 7**
**Find Transactions Report**
**For the Period From Jan 1, 2013 to Jan 31, 2013**
Filter Criteria includes: 1) All Transaction Types. Report order is by Date.

| Date | Type | Reference | ID | Name | Amount |
|------|------|-----------|-----|------|--------|
| 1/29/13 | Payment | 1006 | 11400 | Manchester Insurance | 22,000.00 |
| 1/29/13 | Payment | 1007 | 11600 | Central Florida Gas & Electric | 890.00 |
| 1/29/13 | Payment | 1008 | 11700 | Verizon | 1,700.00 |
| 1/29/13 | Payment | 1009 | 11500 | Chevron | 1,600.00 |
| 1/29/13 | Payment | 1010 | 10000 | Malibu Boats | 76,000.00 |
| 1/29/13 | Purchase | EM23987997 | 11500 | Chevron | 1,600.00 |
| 1/29/13 | Purchase | MB20397 | 10000 | Malibu Boats | 56,000.00 |
| 1/29/13 | Purchase | T2309443 | 10200 | Tige Boats | 63,000.00 |
| 1/29/13 | Receipt | 4532 | 50005 | Florida Sports Camp | 57,050.00 |
| 1/29/13 | Sale/Invoice | 10001 | 50005 | Florida Sports Camp | 74,550.00 |
| 1/29/13 | Time Ticket | 000018 | 003 | Ryder Zacovic | 525.00 |
| 1/29/13 | Time Ticket | 000019 | 003 | Ryder Zacovic | 320.00 |
| 1/29/13 | Time Ticket | 000020 | 003 | Ryder Zacovic | |
| 1/30/13 | Receipt | 10885 | 50006 | Performance Rentals | 64,181.25 |
| 1/30/13 | Receipt | 9845 | 50008 | Alisa Hay | 175.73 |
| 1/30/13 | Sale/Invoice | 10002 | 50006 | Performance Rentals | 83,868.75 |
| 1/30/13 | Sale/Invoice | 10003 | 50008 | Alisa Hay | 175.73 |
| 1/30/13 | Time Ticket | 000021 | 004 | Pat Ng | 1,500.00 |
| 1/30/13 | Time Ticket | 000022 | 004 | Pat Ng | 75.00 |
| 1/30/13 | Time Ticket | 000023 | 004 | Pat Ng | |
| 1/31/13 | Payroll Entry | 1011 | 001 | Donna Chandler | 3,384.92 |
| 1/31/13 | Payroll Entry | 1012 | 003 | Ryder Zacovic | 707.85 |
| 1/31/13 | Payroll Entry | 1013 | 002 | Karen Wilson | 3,137.92 |
| 1/31/13 | Payroll Entry | 1014 | 004 | Pat Ng | 764.49 |
| 1/31/13 | Receipt | 1254 | 50005 | Florida Sports Camp | 1,677.38 |
| 1/31/13 | Receipt | 9412332 | 50004 | Freebirds | 899.93 |
| 1/31/13 | Sale/Invoice | 10004 | 50004 | Freebirds | 899.93 |
| 1/31/13 | Sale/Invoice | 10005 | 50005 | Florida Sports Camp | 1,677.38 |

**Report Total:** 1,957,472.5

**Number of Transactions:** 60

**Figure 7.47**

Continued

# End Note

The two of you decide to quit for the day because you've accomplished quite a lot. You've recorded the firm's financing, investing, and operating activities for the month of January, which included processing purchase orders, receiving inventory, paying for inventory and other bills, recognizing cash sales, and writing checks, including some for payroll. Next up are February transactions and a few noncash activities.

## Business Events Summary

| Business Event | Process Steps | Page |
| --- | --- | --- |
| Receive cash from the sale of stock | Use a general journal entry to record a debit to the checking account and a credit to the common stock from the Company center | 160 |
| Receive cash from borrowings | Use a general journal entry to record a debit to the checking account and a credit to a liability account from the Company center | 160 |
| Invest funds | Use Write Checks from the Banking center | 162 |
| Purchase land, furniture, buildings, or equipment | Use Write Checks from the Banking center | 165 |
| Receive order from customer | Use Sales Order from the Customers & Sales center | 167 |
| Receive cash deposits on future sales | Use Receive Money from the Customers & Sales center | 171 |
| Order inventory | Use Purchase Orders from the Vendors & Purchases center | 173 |
| Receive cash payment on account | Use Receive Money from the Customers & Sales center | 175 |
| Receive cash payment from a cash sale | Use Receive Money from the Customers & Sales center | 175 |
| Deposit cash to bank | Use Bank Deposits from the Banking center | 177 |
| Receive inventory | Use Receive Inventory from the Inventory & Services center | 178 |
| Pay for inventory and/or bills due | Use Pay Bills from the Vendors & Purchases center | 179 |
| Sales on account | Use Sales Invoices from the Customers & Sales center | 181 |
| Apply cash deposits received to sales | Access Customer Ledgers from the sales invoice | 181 |
| Receive cash payment at time of sale | Use Amount Paid at Sale on the sales invoice | 181 |
| Pay expenses | Use Write Checks from the Banking center | 186 |
| Create new jobs | Use Jobs from the Customers & Sales center | 191 |
| Enter employee hours | Use Time and Expense Tickets from the Employees & Payroll center | 192 |
| Process payroll and pay employees | Use Pay Employees from the Employees & Payroll center | 196 |
| Bill customers for billable hours | Use Sales Invoices from the Customers & Sales center and then use the Apply Tickets/Expenses option on the sales invoice | 198 |
| Evaluate a firm's performance and financial position | Use the View All Financial Statements option from the Company center | 202 |

## Chapter 7 Questions

**1** Compare and contrast operating, investing, and financing activities.

**2** Describe some of the financing activities you recorded for Wild Water in January.

**3** Describe some of the investing activities you recorded for Wild Water in January.

**4** Describe some of the operating activities you recorded for Wild Water in January.

**5** How should you account for advanced deposits received on customer orders?

**6** Do sales orders increase revenue? If not, why not?

**7** How are cash sales of products on hand recorded?

**8** What steps are involved when a company receives inventory ordered from a vendor that requires immediate payment?

**9** When is it appropriate to use timesheets for payroll?

**10** What is involved in the processing of payroll for Wild Water Sports?

## Chapter 7 Exercises

### Chapter 7 Exercise 1

## CASH-ORIENTED FINANCING ACTIVITIES

Restore the file Boston Catering Ch 7 found on the text CD or download it from the text Website. Set the system date to **7/1/10**. Add the following transactions and then print a standard balance sheet as of 7/31/10.

a. On 7/6/10 the company sold 1,000 shares of common stock to a new private investor (Broad Investments) for $50,000. Funds were deposited directly into the company's checking account on the same date on its check 23413.

b. On 7/8/10 the company borrowed $25,000 from Bank of America at 8% due in 4 years. Bank of America's check 823908 was deposited directly into the company's checking account on the same date after the company signed the long-term note payable.

### Chapter 7 Exercise 2

## CASH-ORIENTED INVESTING ACTIVITIES

Restore the file Boston Catering Ch 7 found on the text CD or download it from the text Website. Do not use the file created in Exercise 1 above. Set the system date to **7/1/10**. Add the following transactions and then print a standard balance sheet as of 7/31/10.

a. On 7/13/10 the company purchased new equipment for $3,000 using check 1501 from Outlet Tool Supply (ID: OUT), a new vendor.

b. On 7/15/10 the company invested $5,000 on a short-term basis with an investment firm named North Eastern Investments (ID: NEI) using check 1502. Create a new cash type account 101 called Short-Term Investments.

## Chapter 7 Exercise 3

## CASH-ORIENTED OPERATING ACTIVITIES—SALES

Restore the file Boston Catering Ch 7 found on the text CD or download it from the text Website. Do not use the file created in Exercise 1 or 2 above. Set the system date to **7/1/10**. Add the following transactions and then print a standard balance sheet as of 7/31/10 and a standard income statement for the month ended 7/31/10.

a. On 7/14/10 the company received check 25141 from MA General Hospital in the amount of $7,000 as payment on account. Amount was deposited to the bank the same day using Deposit ticket ID: 390 and Receipt number R001.

b. On 7/16/10 the company recorded sales receipt R002 for a new customer MIT (Customer ID: MIT), terms due on receipt, sales tax applicable, for 50 item A100 and 50 item A200, delivered. On the same date it received check 523420 from MIT in the amount of $1,575 as payment in full. Amount was deposited to the bank the same day using Deposit ticket ID: 391.

## Chapter 7 Exercise 4

## CASH-ORIENTED OPERATING ACTIVITIES— PURCHASES

Restore the file Boston Catering Ch 7 (Backup) found on the text CD or download it from the text Website. Do not use the file created in the exercises above. Set the system date to **7/1/10**. Add the following transactions and then print a standard balance sheet as of 7/31/10 and an item list report.

a. On 7/5/10 the company ordered 24 bottles of item W100 from the Sanford Winery on purchase order 101.

b. On 7/7/10 the company ordered 48 bottles of a new item W201 (Fiddlehead Syrah, Last Unit Cost $25, Price Level 1 $40, Average Cost Method) on purchase order 102.

c. On 7/28/10 the company ordered 12 bottles of a new item W300 (Foley Pinot Noir, Last Unit Cost $50, Price Level 1 $70, Average Cost Method) from a new vendor, Foley Estates (Vendor ID: FOL 6121 Hwy. 246, Lompoc, CA 93436), on purchase order 103 with terms net 15.

d. On 7/22/10 the company received the 24 bottles of item W100 from Sanford Winery, which had been ordered using purchase order 101 along with invoice 230987 due in 30 days.

e. On 7/29/10 the company received the 48 bottles of item W201 from Fiddlehead Winery, which had been ordered using purchase order 102 along with invoice F232 due in 30 days.

*Chapter 7 Exercise 5*

## CASH-ORIENTED OPERATING ACTIVITIES—EXPENSES

Restore the file Boston Catering Ch 7 (Backup) found on the text CD or download it from the text Website. Do not use the file created in the exercises above. Set the system date to **7/1/10**. Add the following transactions and then print a standard balance sheet as of 7/31/10 and a standard income statement for the month ended 7/31/10.

a. On 7/15/10 the company paid rent to New England Property Management (a new vendor with Vendor ID: NE) on check 1503 for $3,000.

b. On 7/29/10 the company paid a bill due Sanford Winery for $2,000 on check 1504.

c. During the month of July, Kyle Hain worked 8 hours a day from the 19th through the 23rd, all of which was unbilled time. He also worked 6 hours of billable time on Saturday, July 24th, during the John Hancock summer supper catered event. Create a new activity item (X100, Wait Staff, Rate $25, Account: Catering Sales, Tax Code: Non taxable) and use it for both billable and unbilled time. Amy Casey also worked 8 hours a day from the 19th through the 23rd, all of which was unbilled time. She also worked 8 hours of billable time on Saturday, July 24th, during the John Hancock summer supper catered event. Payroll checks are issued starting with check #1505 on July 31. Paycheck information is shown below:

| Pay/Tax/Withholding | Chambers | Hain | Casey |
|---|---|---|---|
| Hours | n/a | 46 | 48 |
| Rate | $50,000 | $ 16.00 | $ 18.00 |
| Regular pay | 4,166.67 | 736.00 | 864.00 |
| Federal withholding | 570.83 | 100.83 | 118.37 |
| Social Security employee | 258.33 | 45.63 | 53.57 |
| Medicare employee | 60.42 | 10.67 | 12.53 |
| MA withholding | 283.99 | 23.26 | 32.99 |
| MA disability insurance employer | 0.42 | 0.07 | 0.09 |
| Social Security employer | 258.33 | 45.63 | 53.57 |
| Medicare company | 60.42 | 10.67 | 12.53 |
| Federal unemployment | 33.33 | 5.89 | 6.91 |
| MA unemployment | 125.00 | 22.08 | 25.92 |
| Check amount | 2,993.10 | 555.61 | 646.54 |

d. On 7/31/10 the company recorded sales invoice 931 for John Hancock, terms due on receipt, sales tax applicable, for 175 item S200 and 30 W200 delivered, and 14 hours of wait staff time. On the same date, it received check 12311 from the customer in the amount of $9,747.50 as payment in full. Amount was deposited to the bank the same day using Deposit Ticket ID: 39.

e. On 7/31/10 the company paid $2,000 to the US Food Service for food purchased and consumed for the various events in July using check 1508. (*Note:* This is not a payment on account. It is a payment for food consumed and thus is recorded as food purchases.)

## Chapter 7 Assignments

*Chapter 7 Assignment 1*

## ADDING MORE INFORMATION: WILD WATER SPORTS

Restore the file **Wild Water Sports, Inc. 7A** found on the text CD or down-loaded from the text Website and then add the following business events in chronological order. Be sure to set the system date to **2/1/13** and the accounting period to **Period 2 – 02/01/13–02/28/13**.

| Event # | Date | Business Event |
|---|---|---|
| 1 | 2/1/13 | Received five sets of tune-up parts (Item 903) from Delco (new vendor with ID = 11800 with terms net due in zero days with a zero credit limit and default expense account inventory parts) on its Invoice 9874564. Wrote Check No. 1015 for $1,000 as payment for those parts. (*Hint:* Use Pay Bill process.) |
| 2 | 2/1/13 | Accepted a new job (3004) to tune up a boat owned by Orlando Water Sports. |
| 3 | 2/1/13 | Paid $24,000 to Coe Marketing (new vendor with ID = 11850) for new advertising campaign, which will last one year, with Check No. 1016. (*Hint:* All prepaid balances are recorded to the prepaid expense account.) |
| 4 | 2/1/13 | Deposited funds received 1/31 of $2,577.31 into the checking account using Deposit Ticket ID 5. |
| 5 | 2/2/13 | Created Purchase Order No. 4003 to MB Sports (ID = 10100) to order an MB B52 V23 Team Edition (a new Item ID = 401) on behalf of our customer, Performance Rentals. Last Unit Cost: $60,000, Price Level 1: $75,000. Credit terms due on receipt, Ship Via Best Way. (Use Average Cost method.) |
| 6 | 2/2/13 | Collected $18,750 as an advance payment from Performance Rentals (its Check No. 2001), which was equal to the 25% down payment required on all boat orders. (Use Receipt Number SR0005.) |
| 7 | 2/2/13 | Recorded Sales Order 103 from Performance Rentals for one Item 401 for customer pickup by 2/28, including sales tax. |
| 8 | 2/2/13 | Pat Ng worked four hours on Job No. 3004, tuning up a boat owned by Orlando Water Sports, using billing type Activity Rate. (*Hint:* Record on a time ticket now!) |
| 9 | 2/3/13 | Recorded journal entry 3 for receipt of $100,000 from a new investor, Sam Ski, in exchange for common stock representing a 25% interest in the company. |
| 10 | 2/3/13 | Recorded Invoice 10006 to Orlando Water Sports for Job No. 3004 based on work performed by Pat Ng and one set of tune-up parts (Item ID = 903). $1,331.25 was collected at the time of sale with Check No. 9774. |
| 11 | 2/5/13 | Deposited the advance payment received from Performance Rentals and the check received from Orlando Water Sports using Deposit Ticket ID 6. |
| 12 | 2/5/13 | Received Check No. 390 for $3,000 as payment on invoice 915 from Buena Vista Water Sports using Receipt Number SR0006. |
| 13 | 2/5/13 | Recorded journal entry 4 for receipt of a $50,000 check, No. 188774, from CitiBank (new Vendor ID = 11050) as the proceeds from a three-year 6% loan negotiated by Sam Ski. The company plans to use these funds in the future to pay down some older, more expensive debt. (Record this debt to account 2700.) |

| Event # | Date | Business Event |
|---|---|---|
| 14 | 2/6/13 | Wrote Check No. 1017 in the amount of $75,000 to ETrade as a short-term investment. |
| 15 | 2/6/13 | Deposited a $3,000 check received on 2/5 using Deposit Ticket ID 7. |
| 16 | 2/6/13 | Created Purchase Order No. 4004 to Malibu Boats to order a Malibu Sunscape LSV (Item ID = 203) and a Malibu Vride (Item ID = 204) on behalf of a new customer, Fantasy Sports. |
| 17 | 2/6/13 | Recorded Sales Order 104 to Fantasy Sports (ID = 50009, located at 345 Sunset Rd., Orlando, FL 31312). Specify sales tax code 01 for the new customer, C.O.D. as terms, and Cust. Pickup as the Ship Via option. for customer pickup by 3/31/13 for one Item 203 and one Item 204, both of which were ordered from Malibu on Purchase Order No. 4004. |
| 18 | 2/6/13 | Collected $28,250 as an advance payment from Fantasy Sports (its Check No. 1005), which was equal to the 25% down payment required on all boat orders, using Receipt Number SR0007. |
| 19 | 2/8/13 | Received Check No. 1988 for $43,000 as payment on account from Orlando Water Sports using Receipt Number SR0008. |
| 20 | 2/8/13 | Sold a Malibu WakeSetter VLX (Item ID = 205) from inventory to Walking on Water for $57,000 plus tax of $3,705 and recorded the sale with Receipt Number SR0009. Received the customer's Check No. 232 as payment in full. Updated the customer's address as 874 Nightingale Dr., Kissimmee, FL 34743. |
| 21 | 2/8/13 | Accepted a new job (ID = 3005) to paint a boat owned by Alisa Hay. |
| 22 | 2/9/13 | Made a deposit of $131,955 from checks received on 2/6 and 2/8 using Deposit Ticket ID 8. |
| 23 | 2/9/13 | Ryder Zacovic worked five hours on Job No. 3005, painting a boat owned by Alisa Hay. (Be sure to use the Activity rate as the Billing Type and record this using ticket number 000025.) |
| 24 | 2/10/13 | Recorded Invoice 10007 to Alisa Hay under Job No. 3005 based on work performed by Ryder Zacovic. Check No. 741 collected $426. (*Note:* If a notice of going over the credit limit appears, you can ignore it since this is a cash sale.) |
| 25 | 2/12/13 | Deposited $426 from Alisa Hay using Deposit Ticket ID 9. |
| 26 | 2/15/13 | Wrote Check No. 1018 to Sunset Auto (new Vendor ID = 11550) for $45,000 to purchase a truck for the business. (Record as Property and Equipment.) |
| 27 | 2/19/13 | Recorded receipt of the MB B52 V23 Team Edition ordered on behalf of Performance Rentals on Purchase Order No. 4003. Wrote Check No. 1019 to MB Sports for $60,000 as payment for this purchase based on its Invoice 230987. |
| 28 | 2/20/13 | Created Invoice 10009 to Performance Rentals for sale of MB B51 V23 based on Sales Order 103. Recorded receipt of payment made at the time of sale from Performance Rentals of $61,125 with its Check No. 23098. Applied the deposit received when this boat was ordered. (Make sure you save the invoice first, then go back to the receipt to apply the deposit.) |
| 29 | 2/21/13 | Deposited Performance Rentals' check received 2/20 using Deposit Ticket ID 10. |
| 30 | 2/26/13 | Wrote Check No. 1020 to pay MasterCard bill of $1,000. (*Hint:* Use the Pay Bills function to record this transaction just like in the text.) |
| 31 | 2/26/13 | Wrote Check No. 1021 to Central Florida Gas & Electric for $930 for utilities expense (GL Account 6400). |
| 32 | 2/26/13 | Wrote Check No. 1022 to Verizon for $1,820 for telephone expense (GL Account 6500). |

| Event # | Date | Business Event |
|---|---|---|
| 33 | 2/26/13 | Wrote Check No. 1023 to Brian Szulczewski (new Vendor ID = 11825) for $2,700 for advertising expense (GL Account 6600). |
| 34 | 2/26/13 | Wrote Check No. 1024 to Staples for $4,500 for other office expenses (GL Account 6550). |
| 35 | 2/28/13 | Record time ticket information provided in Table 7.1 either by individual time ticket or timesheet, your choice. (*Note:* Some of these hours are related to jobs for which time had already been recorded. Those hours are designated in Table 7.1 with an *. All other hours not designated with an * are for administrative office work activities.) |
| 36 | 2/28/13 | Process payroll per the information provided in Table 7.2, starting with Check No. 1025. |

### Table 7.1

TimeSheet Information

| Date | Zacovic | Date | Ng |
|---|---|---|---|
| 2/1 | 8 hrs. | 2/2 | 4 hrs.* |
| 2/6 | 5 hrs. | 2/5 | 8 hrs. |
| 2/8 | 5 hrs. | 2/7 | 8 hrs. |
| 2/9 | 5 hrs.* | 2/12 | 8 hrs. |
| 2/13 | 8 hrs. | 2/14 | 8 hrs. |
| 2/15 | 8 hrs. | 2/19 | 8 hrs. |
| 2/20 | 8 hrs. | 2/21 | 8 hrs. |
| 2/22 | 8 hrs. | 2/26 | 8 hrs. |
| 2/28 | 8 hrs. | 2/27 | 8 hrs. |
| Total | 63 hrs. | | 68 hrs. |

### Table 7.2

Payroll Information for Wild Water Sports

| Item | Chandler/001 | Wilson/002 | Zacovic/003 | Ng/004 |
|---|---|---|---|---|
| | | Employee/Employee ID | | |
| Check Number | 1025 | 1026 | 1027 | 1028 |
| Earnings/Hours | 4,166.67 | 4,166.67 | 63 | 68 |
| Federal Withholding | −463.00 | −710.00 | −129.47 | −167.69 |
| Social Security Employee | −258.33 | −258.33 | −58.59 | −75.89 |
| Medicare Employee | −60.42 | −60.42 | −13.70 | −17.75 |
| Social Security Company | 258.33 | 258.33 | 58.59 | 75.89 |
| Medicare Company | 60.42 | 60.42 | 13.70 | 17.75 |
| Federal Unemployment | 33.33 | 33.33 | 7.56 | 9.79 |
| State Unemployment | 112.50 | 112.50 | 25.51 | 33.05 |
| Check Amount | 3,384.92 | 3,137.92 | 743.24 | 962.67 |

Print the following with no page numbers and no zero amounts and with the accounting period set to Period 2:

a.  Standard income statement

b.  Standard balance sheet

c.  Find transactions report for the period February 1 through February 28, 2013.

## *Chapter 7 Assignment 2*

# ADDING MORE INFORMATION: CENTRAL COAST CELLULAR

Restore the file **Central Coast Cellular Ch 7** found on the text CD or download it from the text Website. Change the system date to **1/1/09** and the accounting period to **Period 1 – 01/01/09–01/31/09**. Add the following business events:

*sole proprietorship*

*merchandising*

| Event # | Date | Business Event |
|---|---|---|
| 1 | 1/2/09 | Mr. Van Morrison deposited $200,000 of his personal funds into the company checking account and received 25,000 shares of common stock. |
| 2 | 1/2/09 | The company signed a lease with Central Coast Leasing (Vendor ID CCL, 2830 McMillan Ave #7, San Luis Obispo, CA 93401, 805-544-2875) to rent retail space at $3,000 a month for five years. Payment is due on the 13th of the month. The default expense account for this vendor is account 6300. |
| 3 | 1/6/09 | The company temporarily invested $75,000 by writing Check No. 3001 to Schwab Investments (Vendor ID SI, 1194 Pacific Street, San Luis Obispo, CA 93401, 805-788-0502). (*Hint:* You will need to create a new other current assets account type named Short-Term Investments, Account ID = 1300. This will be the default expense account for this vendor.) |
| 4 | 1/7/09 | The company borrowed and then deposited $125,000 from Wells Fargo Bank (Vendor ID WF, 665 Marsh St., San Luis Obispo, CA 93401, 805-541-0143) due in five years with annual interest of 8% and payments made monthly. The default expense account for this vendor is account 2700. |
| 5 | 1/8/09 | The company purchased office furniture by writing Check No. 3002 for $20,000 to Russco (Vendor ID R, 3046 S. Higuera St. #A, San Luis Obispo, CA 93401, 805-547-8440). The default expense account for this vendor is account 1500. |
| 6 | 1/9/09 | Using Purchase Order No. 101, the company ordered 40 ELX588 and 60 ET19LX phones from Ericsson. Using Purchase Order No. 102, the company ordered 25 N3285, 50 N8290, and 15 N8890 phones from Nokia. |
| 7 | 1/9/09 | The company purchased supplies from Russco for $3,000 using Check No. 3003. These supplies are expected to last over the next year. You'll need to add another current assets type of account 1410 called Supplies. |
| 8 | 1/13/09 | The company wrote Check No. 3004 to Central Coast Leasing for $6,000 ($3,000 for January's rent and $3,000 as a prepaid expense). |
| 9 | 1/14/09 | The company received and deposited an advance payment of $10,000 from the City of San Luis Obispo (a customer) as part of a consulting contract to be started in February using Deposit Ticket ID 001 to deposit its Check No. 2034978. |

| Event # | Date | Business Event |
|---------|------|----------------|
| 10 | 1/15/09 | The company received a shipment of phones from Ericsson on Purchase Order No. 101. Items were received and a bill recorded due in 30 days. All items ordered were received. Ericsson's Invoice A3908 was included with the shipment. |
| 11 | 1/16/09 | The company created sales receipt 501 to record 50 hours of consulting services and the sale of 25 Ericsson LX588 phones to Sterling Hotels Corporation. A check (number 6514) was received and deposited for $7,425 using Deposit Ticket ID 002. |
| 12 | 1/16/09 | On January 16, 2009, the company paid semimonthly payroll using the regular checking account starting with Check No. 3005 for the period January 4 to January 16, 2003. Megan Paulson worked 80 hours during the period. (*Hint:* Be sure Megan was set up with a Pay Method = Hourly – Hours per Pay Period.) Payroll tax information is shown in Table 7.3. |

### Table 7.3

Payroll Information for Central Coast Cellular

|  | Employee | | |
|--|----------|--|--|
| **Tax or Withholding** | **Rodriguez** | **Bruner** | **Paulson** |
| Check Number | 3005 | 3006 | 3007 |
| Gross Pay | $2,000.00 | $1,500.00 | $ 960.00 |
| Federal Withholding | −300.00 | −225.00 | −144.00 |
| Social Security Employee | −124.00 | −93.00 | −59.52 |
| Medicare Employee | −29.00 | −21.75 | −13.92 |
| State Withholding | −100.00 | −75.00 | −48.00 |
| SDI | −10.00 | −7.50 | −4.80 |
| Social Security Company | 124.00 | 93.00 | 59.52 |
| Medicare Company | 29.00 | 21.75 | 13.92 |
| FUTA | 6.40 | 4.80 | 3.07 |
| SUTA | 24.00 | 18.00 | 11.52 |
| California Employee Training Tax | 2.00 | 1.50 | 0.96 |
| Check Amount | 1,437.00 | 1,077.75 | 689.76 |

Print the following with no page numbers and no zero amounts:

a.   Standard income statement for the one month ending January 31, 2009.

b.   Standard balance sheet as of January 31, 2009.

c.   Find transactions report for the period January 1 through January 16, 2009.

## Chapter 7 Assignment 3

## ADDING MORE INFORMATION: SANTA BARBARA SAILING

*merchandising*

Restore the file **Santa Barbara Sailing Ch 7** found on the text CD or download it from the text Website, and then add the following business events after you set the system date to **7/1/12** and change the accounting period to **Period 7**.

| Event # | Date | Business Event |
|---------|------|----------------|
| 1 | 7/02/12 | Rob Dutton contributed an additional $100,000 to the company in exchange for common stock, which was then immediately deposited into the company's checking account. |
| 2 | 7/04/12 | Rented the CAT 50 to Raytheon for seven days using Sales Receipt No. 10001 and collected Check No. 983 for $4,233.60, which will be deposited later. |
| 3 | 7/04/12 | Rented the CAT 42 to a new customer, Deckers (Customer ID: 102, Address: 495-A South Fairview Ave., Goleta, CA 93117, Terms: COD) for seven days using Sales Receipt No. 10002 and collected Visa payment (ref: 7524) for $3,515.40. |
| 4 | 7/07/12 | Purchased a new J-24 sailboat (to rent to customers) for $42,000 with Check No. 101 from a new vendor, J-Boats, (Vendor ID: 202, Address: P.O. Box 90, Newport, RI 02840, Phone: 401-846-8410, Terms: COD, Expense Account: 1500). |
| 5 | 7/07/12 | Created a new service item with Item ID: J-24, Description: J-24 Daily Rental, Price Level: $160 per day, GL Sales Acct: 4010 Rental Income. |
| 6 | 7/08/12 | Deposited checks from Raytheon and Deckers received on 7/04/12 into checking account using Deposit Ticket ID 1. |
| 7 | 7/09/12 | Paid existing bill from Catalina of $7,500 using Check No. 102. |
| 8 | 7/09/12 | Hired a new hourly employee, Nathan Snyder (Employee ID: NS, SS#: 390-09-2877, single male, earning $8 per hour, paid semimonthly, and subject to all normal state and federal taxes). |
| 9 | 7/10/12 | Received full payment on account from Raytheon of $8,465 (its Check No. 39892). |
| 10 | 7/11/12 | Received advance payment of $1,000 (Check No. 974565) from a new customer, Montecito Bank & Trust (Customer ID: 103, Address: P.O. Box 2460, Santa Barbara, CA 93120, Phone: 805-963-7511, Terms: COD). |
| 11 | 7/11/12 | Deposited checks totaling $9,465 from Raytheon and Montecito Bank & Trust on Deposit Ticket ID 2. |
| 12 | 7/14/12 | Wrote Check No. 103 for $24,000 to Levy Property Management (new vendor with Vendor ID: 203) for rent of harbor facilities and docks for one year. (Classify all of this payment as Prepaid Expenses (Account ID: 1400), which will be adjusted monthly.) |
| 13 | 7/14/12 | Rented the CAT 50 to Montecito Bank & Trust for 14 days using Invoice 7001. Applied the advance deposit received 7/11/12 to this invoice and collected the balance owed of $7,467.20 with Check No. 974637. |
| 14 | 7/14/12 | Rented the CAT 42 to Santa Barbara Medical using Sales Receipt No. 10003 for 14 days and received a MasterCard payment for $7,030.80 with reference 8741. |
| 15 | 7/15/12 | Rented the J-24 and CAT 28 to Deckers using Sales Receipt No. 10004 for 14 days and received a Visa payment for $5,745.60 with reference 0574. |
| 16 | 7/16/12 | Paid employees on check numbers 104, 105, and 106 for the period 7/1/12–7/15/12. Wine and Snyder worked 38 and 20 hours, respectively, during that period. Change the description of account 2330 from Federal Payroll Taxes Payable to Payroll Taxes Payable. Payroll tax information is shown in Table 7.4. |

| **Table 7.4** | Item | Employee | | |
|---|---|---|---|---|
| | | **Dutton** | **Wine** | **Snyder** |
| Payroll and Earnings Information for Santa Barbara Sailing | Gross Pay | $2,708.33 | $ 684.00 | $ 160.00 |
| | Federal Withholding | −514.58 | −129.96 | −30.40 |
| | Social Security Employee | −167.92 | −42.41 | −9.92 |
| | Medicare Employee | −39.27 | −9.92 | −2.32 |
| | CA – Income tax | −216.67 | −54.72 | −12.80 |
| | CA – Disability | −16.25 | −4.10 | −0.96 |
| | Check Amount | 1,753.64 | 442.89 | 103.60 |
| | CA Employment Training Tax | 2.71 | 0.68 | 0.16 |
| | Social Security Employer | 167.92 | 42.41 | 9.92 |
| | Medicare Employer | 39.27 | 9.92 | 2.32 |
| | Federal Unemployment | 21.67 | 5.47 | 1.28 |
| | CA – Unemployment | 92.08 | 23.26 | 5.44 |

Print the following as of 7/31/12 with no page numbers and no zero amounts:

a.  Standard income statement

b.  Standard balance sheet

c.  Standard statement of cash flows

d.  Find transactions report for the period 7/1/12 through 7/31/12

## Chapter 7 Cases

### Chapter 7 Case Problem 1

## FOREVER YOUNG

*sole proprietorship*

*service*

Restore the backup you made for **Forever Young** in Chapter 6 into a new company folder. (Do not restore this backup into an existing folder. See the Preface to this book for more detailed instructions on how to do this.) Change the company name to include Ch 7 at the end so that the new company name is **Forever Young Ch 7**. Change the system date to **1/1/08** and the accounting period to **Period 1 – 01/01/08–01/31/08**. Add the following business events:

| Event # | Date | Business Event |
|---|---|---|
| 1 | 1/2/08 | Sebastian deposited $20,000 into his new company's checking account as his initial investment. |
| 2 | 1/3/08 | Paid Galas $6,000 in legal fees for setting up contracts with future customers (classify as Professional Fees) using Check No. 1. |
| 3 | 1/3/08 | Signed a contract with Panasonic (new customer, ID 100003, with terms due on receipt) to speak at its sales convention (Item 002— half-day seminar) on 1/5/08 using Sales Order No. 1001. Collected a 50% deposit of $3,000 (Check No. 9873) and immediately deposited it into the checking account using Deposit Ticket ID 001 and Sales Receipt SR1. |
| 4 | 1/4/08 | Paid Office Depot (a new vendor, ID 200003) $4,000 for furniture using Check No. 2. |

| Event # | Date | Business Event |
|---|---|---|
| 5 | 1/4/08 | Paid Classic Leasing (a new vendor, ID 200004) $8,000 rent on office space using Check No. 3. (Half of payment represents January rent and half represents a security deposit.) (*Hint:* Create a new expense type of account ID 6200 Rent and a new other asset type of account ID 1900 Security Deposit.) |
| 6 | 1/5/08 | Spoke at the Panasonic sales convention, received remaining amount owed of $3,000 on Check No. 9923, provided Invoice 501 to customer, billing them for services rendered, and applied previous credit. |
| 7 | 1/7/08 | Deposited Panasonic check for $3,000 into checking account using Deposit Ticket ID 002. |
| 8 | 1/9/08 | Signed a contract with Gateway (new customer, ID 100004, with terms due on receipt) to speak at its sales convention (Item 001—full-day seminar) on 1/12/08 using Sales Order No. 1002. Collected a 50% deposit of $5,000 (Check No. 15487) and immediately deposited it into the checking account using Deposit Ticket ID 003 and Sales Receipt SR2. |
| 9 | 1/10/08 | Purchased supplies from Office Depot for $1,500 using Check No. 4, which will be used over the next six months. (*Hint:* Create a new other current asset type of account ID 1200 Supplies.) |
| 10 | 1/11/08 | Signed a contract with Adobe (new customer, ID 100005, with terms due on receipt) to speak at its officers' retreat (Item 001—full-day seminar) on 1/19/08 using Sales Order No. 1003. Collected a 50% deposit of $5,000 (Check No. 698747) and immediately deposited it into the checking account using Deposit Ticket ID 004 and Sales Receipt SR3. |
| 11 | 1/12/08 | Spoke at the Gateway sales convention, received remaining amount owed on Check No. 15623, provided Invoice 502 to customer, billing them for services rendered, and applied previous credit. |
| 13 | 1/15/08 | Paid semimonthly payroll starting with Check No. 5 for the period 1/1/08 to 1/15/08. Payroll tax information is shown in Table 7.5. Anne worked 23 hours during this period. |

| | Employee | | **Table 7.5** |
|---|---|---|---|
| Item | Walsh | Sunshine | Payroll and Earnings Information for Forever Young |
| Check Number | 5 | 6 | |
| Gross Pay | $3,333.33 | $ 460.00 | |
| Federal Withholding | −633.33 | −87.40 | |
| Social Security Employee | −206.67 | −28.52 | |
| Medicare Employee | −48.33 | −6.67 | |
| CA – Income Tax | −266.67 | −36.80 | |
| CA – Disability | −20.00 | −2.76 | |
| Check Amount | 2,158.33 | 297.85 | |
| Social Security Employer | 206.67 | 28.52 | |
| Medicare Employer | 48.33 | 6.67 | |
| Federal Unemployment | 26.67 | 3.68 | |
| CA – Unemployment | 113.33 | 15.64 | |
| CA Employment Training Tax | 3.33 | 0.46 | |

Print the following as of 1/31/08 with no page numbers and no zero amounts:

a.  Standard income statement

b.  Standard balance sheet

c.  Standard statement of cash flows

d.  Find transactions report for the period 1/1/08 through 1/31/08

## Chapter 7 Case Problem 2

# OCEAN VIEW FLOWERS

Restore the backup you made for Ocean View Flowers in Chapter 6 into a new company folder. (Do not restore this backup into an existing folder.) (See the Preface to this book for more detailed instructions on how to do this.) Change the company name to include Ch 7 at the end so that the new company name is **Ocean View Flowers Ch 7**. Change the system date to **1/1/08** and the accounting period to **Period 1 – 01/01/08–01/31/08**. Add the following business events:

| Event # | Date | Business Event |
|---|---|---|
| 1 | 1/4/08 | The company sold common stock to Scott Wilson (add as a vendor with ID = SW), an investor, for $100,000 cash. The company deposited the check into the regular checking account. (Remember to use a general journal entry for this type of transaction.) |
| 2 | 1/7/08 | The company borrowed $50,000 from Santa Barbara Bank & Trust (add as a new vendor with ID = SBBT). The long-term note payable is due in three years with interest due annually at 10%. The company deposited the check into the regular checking account. (Remember to use a general journal entry for this type of transaction.) |
| 3 | 1/8/08 | The company temporarily invested $25,000 in a certificate of deposit due in three months, which will earn 7% per annum. Check No. 101, drawn on the regular checking account, was made payable to Prudent Investments (PI), 100 Main Street, San Francisco, CA 95154. |
| 4 | 1/11/08 | The company purchased furniture from Stateside Office Supplies (SOS), 324 G St., Lompoc, CA 93436, for $20,000 with Check No. 102. |
| 5 | 1/14/08 | The company purchased computer equipment from Gateway Computers (GC), 100 Cowabunga Blvd., Sioux City, IA 23442, for $15,000 with Check No. 103. |
| 6 | 1/14/08 | The company created Purchase Order No. 01 to order the following new items from Brophy Bros. Farms, which specializes in daylilies. It ordered 1,000 Almond Puff Daylilies (AP) at a cost of $12 per unit, 2,000 Calistoga Sun Daylilies (CS) at a cost of $8 per unit, and 500 Caribbean Pink Sands Daylilies (CPS) at a cost of $13 per unit. All daylilies are sold at a 100% markup (2 times cost) and are recorded to GL Sales account 40000. (Rename this account to Daylilies Sales.) Cost of goods sold is recorded to GL Cost of Goods Sold account 50000. (Rename this account to Cost of Sales – Flowers.) (Also, be sure to use Average Cost for these inventory items. Remember, if you use a different costing method by accident, you'll need to delete this item and then re-create it!) |

| Event # | Date | Business Event |
|---------|------|----------------|
| 7 | 1/15/08 | The company paid payroll. All employees worked the entire period. Kelly Gusland worked 60 hours and Margie Conner 75 hours. Checks were written using the regular checking account. Payroll taxes and withholding for employees during the period 1/1/08 through 1/15/08 are shown in Table 7.6. (Be sure you have correctly established the hourly rate in the employee's file located in the Pay Info tab across from the Account.) |
| 8 | 1/18/08 | The company received its order in full from Brophy Bros. Farms (Purchase Order No. 01) along with its Invoice BB34908. |
| 9 | 1/21/08 | The company paid Stateside Office Supplies for purchase of supplies expected to last over the next six months using Check No. 109 for $1,500. Record this in a new other current assets type of account 14300 called Supplies. |
| 10 | 1/22/08 | The company recorded its first cash sale (Sales Receipt No. 1000) to Valley Florists in which it sold 100 Almond Puffs, 100 Calistoga Suns, and 100 Caribbean Pink Sands. The $6,600 (Check No. 0809) was deposited directly into the regular checking account using Deposit Ticket ID 5001. (Note that there is no sales tax for Ocean View because it is a wholesaler.) |
| 11 | 1/25/08 | The company recorded its second cash sale (Sales Receipt No. 1001) to Eastern Scents in which it sold 600 Almond Puffs and 300 Caribbean Pink Sands. The $22,200 VISA charge (20349802) was deposited directly into the regular checking account using Deposit Ticket ID 5002. (Note that there is no sales tax for Ocean View because it is a wholesaler.) |
| 12 | 1/28/08 | The company received an advance payment on account (Sales Receipt No. 1002) from FTD with Check No. 92384 in the amount of $5,000, which was deposited into the regular checking account using Deposit Ticket ID 5003. |
| 13 | 1/29/08 | Paid the Brophy Bros. bill with Check No. 110 in the amount of $34,500. |
| 14 | 1/30/08 | The company wrote Check No. 111 to Hawaiian Farms for $3,000 to pay rent expense, Check No. 112 to Edison, Inc. (E) for $500 to pay utilities expense, and Check No. 113 to General Telephone & Electric (GTE) for $400 to pay telephone expense (a new expense type of account 77100). (Be sure to modify the expense account for Hawaiian Farms for this expenditure.) |
| 15 | 1/31/08 | The company paid payroll for the period ended January 31, 2008. All employees worked the entire period. Kelly Gusland worked 65 hours, and Margie Conner worked 70 hours. Payroll taxes and withholding for employees during the period 1/16/08 through 1/31/08 are shown in Table 7.7. |

### Table 7.6

Earnings Information for
Ocean View Flowers 1/1/08
through 1/15/08

| Tax or Withholding | Employee | | | | |
| --- | --- | --- | --- | --- | --- |
| | Thomas | Gusland | Conner | McAninch | Comstock |
| Check Number | 104 | 105 | 106 | 107 | 108 |
| Hours/Salary | 2,916.67 | 60 | 75 | 2,500.00 | 2,083.34 |
| Federal Income | −667.00 | −118.00 | −118.00 | −402.00 | −286.00 |
| Social Security | −180.83 | −55.80 | −55.80 | −155.00 | −129.17 |
| Medicare | −42.29 | −13.05 | −13.05 | −36.25 | −30.21 |
| State | −192.30 | −19.32 | −9.32 | −153.55 | −61.86 |
| SDI | −14.58 | −4.50 | −4.50 | −12.50 | −10.42 |
| Social Security Company | 180.83 | 55.80 | 55.80 | 155.00 | 129.17 |
| Medicare Company | 42.29 | 13.05 | 13.05 | 36.25 | 30.21 |
| FUTA | 23.33 | 7.20 | 7.20 | 20.00 | 16.67 |
| SUI | 1.46 | 0.45 | 0.45 | 1.25 | 1.04 |
| California Training Tax | 2.92 | 0.90 | 0.90 | 2.50 | 2.08 |
| Check Amount | 1,819.67 | 689.33 | 699.33 | 1,740.70 | 1,565.68 |

### Table 7.7

Earnings Information for
Ocean View Flowers 1/16/08
through 1/31/08

| Tax or Withholding | Employee | | | | |
| --- | --- | --- | --- | --- | --- |
| | Thomas | Gusland | Conner | McAninch | Comstock |
| Check Number | 114 | 115 | 116 | 117 | 118 |
| Hours/Salary | 2,916.67 | 65 | 70 | 2,500.00 | 2,083.34 |
| Federal Income | −667.00 | −130.00 | −109.00 | −402.00 | −286.00 |
| Social Security | −180.83 | −60.45 | −52.08 | −155.00 | −129.17 |
| Medicare | −42.29 | −14.14 | −12.18 | −36.25 | −30.21 |
| State | −192.30 | −23.63 | −8.12 | −153.55 | −61.86 |
| SDI | −14.58 | −4.88 | −4.20 | −12.50 | −10.42 |
| Social Security Company | 180.83 | 60.45 | 52.08 | 155.00 | 129.17 |
| Medicare Company | 42.29 | 14.14 | 12.18 | 36.25 | 30.21 |
| FUTA | 23.33 | 7.80 | 6.72 | 20.00 | 16.67 |
| SUI | 1.46 | 0.49 | 0.42 | 1.25 | 1.04 |
| California Training Tax | 2.92 | 0.98 | 0.84 | 2.50 | 2.08 |
| Check Amount | 1,819.67 | 741.90 | 654.42 | 1,740.70 | 1,565.68 |

This is a continuous case in that the next chapter will use the work you've accomplished here as the basis for recording additional business events. After you've printed the following reports, create a backup of this file and store it on some type of external medium (flash drive, Internet site, CD, disk, etc.). The backup file should be named **Ocean View Flowers Ch 7** for easy identification later. You'll be restoring this file in the next chapter. Print the following with no page numbers and no zero amounts:

a. Standard balance sheet

b. Standard income statement

c. Statement of cash flows

d. Find transactions report for the period 1/1/08 through 1/31/08

*Chapter 7 Case Problem 3*

# ALOHA PROPERTY MANAGEMENT

Restore the backup you made for Aloha in Chapter 6 into a new company folder. (Do not restore this backup into an existing folder.) (See the Preface to this book for more detailed instructions on how to do this.) Change the company name to include Ch 7 at the end so that the new company name is **Aloha Property Management Ch 7**. Change the system date to **1/1/08** and the accounting period to **Period 1 – 01/01/08–01/31/08**. Add the following business events:

service

corporation

| Event # | Date | Business Event |
|---------|------|----------------|
| 1 | 1/3/08 | Adventure Travel purchased common stock from Aloha in exchange for $50,000 cash, which was deposited into the company's regular checking account. |
| 2 | 1/4/08 | Received payment on account from General Motors (GM) in the amount of $75,000 on its Check No. 6874. Use Deposit Ticket ID 001. |
| 3 | 1/7/08 | Wrote Check No. 984 for $40,000 to World Investments (WI) as a short-term investment. (*Hint:* Create a new other current asset type of account called Short-Term Investments – Account Number 10700.) |
| 4 | 1/8/08 | Wrote Check No. 985 for $24,000 to GEICO Insurance (GEICO) as payment for a one-year insurance policy with coverage provided from January 1, 2008 through December 31, 2008, and recorded this transaction as Prepaid Expenses – Account Number 14000. |
| 5 | 1/11/08 | Collected two checks from a new customer, Pixar Studios (PX). The two checks, a $14,000 check (Check No. 2348907) and a $10,000 check (Check No. 2348908), were for two different deposits on future rentals. Record these as two different receipts. No receipt numbers are used. |
| 6 | 1/11/08 | Deposited the checks received from Pixar into the Bank of Hawaii using Deposit Ticket ID 002. |
| 7 | 1/11/08 | Recorded Sales Receipt No. 5115 for rent of Villa Unit 1 for one week. Collected MasterCard payment (reference 234098) in full of $3,120 from a new customer, Coast Union Bank (CU). (*Hint:* Select MasterCard as the Payment Method.) |
| 8 | 1/11/08 | Recorded Invoice 7508 for rental of Moana Unit 4 for one week to Sara Rice. Recorded receipt of balance owed of $6,480 with Check No. 654. |
| 9 | 1/11/08 | Recorded Sales Receipt No. 5116 for rent of Villa Unit 2 for one week. Collected MasterCard payment (reference 942813) in full of $4,680 from a new customer, Berkshire Hathaway (BH). |
| 10 | 1/12/08 | Deposited checks and MasterCard payments of $14,280 to the regular checking account using Deposit Ticket ID 003. |
| 11 | 1/14/08 | Wrote Check No. 986 for $23,000 to Furniture King (FK) as payment for new furniture. Recorded this to account 15000. |
| 12 | 1/15/08 | Wrote Check No. 987 for $4,500 as payment on account to Reilly Custodial. (*Hint:* Use Vendors/Pay Bills.) |
| 13 | 1/18/08 | Recorded Sales Receipt No. 5117 for rent of Moana Unit 3 and Villa Unit 3 for one week each. Collected American Express (AMEX) payment in full (reference 8741321654) of $8,528 from a new customer, Bridgette Hacker (BRH). |
| 14 | 1/18/08 | Recorded Sales Receipt No. 5118 for rent of Moana Unit 4 for one week. Collected Check No. 909 as payment in full of $12,480 from a new customer, Lockheed Martin (LM). |

| Event # | Date | Business Event |
|---------|------|----------------|
| 15 | 1/18/08 | Recorded Invoice 7509 for rental of Villa Units 1 and 2 for one week to Boeing, terms net 30. The company chose to ignore the over credit limit message. |
| 16 | 1/21/08 | Deposited $21,008 of undeposited funds to the regular checking account with Deposit Ticket ID 004. |
| 17 | 1/23/08 | Paid Reilly Custodial $3,000 on Check No. 988 for maintenance expenses. (Use account 70000.) |
| 18 | 1/24/08 | Collected a $5,125 deposit from a new customer, Exxon Mobil (EM) (its Check No. 30035). No receipt numbers are used. |
| 19 | 1/25/08 | Recorded Invoice 7510 for rental of Villa Unit 4 for one week to Brice Montoya. Recorded receipt of balance owed of $3,240 with Check No. 1874. |
| 20 | 1/28/08 | Deposited $8,365 of undeposited funds to regular checking account with Deposit Ticket ID 005. |
| 21 | 1/30/08 | Wrote Check No. 989 for $12,000 to Pacific Electric (PE) to account 78000 Utilities Expenses. |
| 22 | 1/30/08 | Wrote Check No. 990 for $3,700 to AT&T (ATT) to account 76000 Telephone Expenses. |
| 23 | 1/30/08 | Wrote Check No. 991 for $15,000 to Sunset Media (SM) to account 60100 Advertising Expenses. |
| 24 | 1/31/08 | Process payroll per the information provided in Table 7.8. Use Regular Checking account. |

**Table 7.8**

Earnings Information for Aloha Property Management

| Pay/Tax/Withholding | Employee | |
|---------------------|----------|----------|
|                     | Aki | Castillo |
| Check Number | 992 | 993 |
| Hours | n/a | 150 |
| Rate | n/a | $20.00 |
| Gross Pay | 6,250.00 | 3,000.00 |
| Federal Withholding | −856.25 | −411.00 |
| Social Security Employee | −387.50 | −186.00 |
| Medicare Employee | −90.63 | −43.50 |
| State Withholding | −442.33 | −195.33 |
| SDI (State Disability Insurance) | −1.25 | −0.60 |
| Social Security Employer | 387.50 | 186.00 |
| Medicare Company | 90.63 | 43.50 |
| Federal Unemployment | 50.00 | 24.00 |
| SUI (State Unemployment) | 187.50 | 90.00 |
| HI E&T | 0.63 | 0.30 |
| Check Amount | 4,472.04 | 2,163.57 |

*Requirements*

This is a continuous case in that the next chapter will use the work you've accomplished here as the basis for recording additional business events. After you've printed the following reports create a backup of this file and store it on some type of external medium (flash drive, Internet site, CD, disk, etc.). The backup file should be named **Aloha Property Management Ch 7** for easy identification later. You'll be restoring this file in the next chapter. Print the following with no page numbers and no zero amounts:

a. Standard balance sheet

b. Standard income statement

c. Statement of cash flows

d. Find transactions report for the period 1/1/08 through 1/31/08

## Comprehensive Problems

## Comprehensive Problem 1: SARAH DUNCAN, CPA

*job costing*

Sarah Duncan, CPA, is starting her new practice as a corporation at One Constellation Road, Vandenberg Village, CA 93436. She'll start effective 9/1/09 and use a 12-month calendar year (January 1–December 31) for financial and tax purposes under the accrual accounting method on a real-time basis. She'll be using Peachtree's manual payroll calculations feature to account for herself and her one employee. Her federal tax ID number, EIN, and California EDD number is 574-85-4125. (Be sure to set payroll to manual calculations and perform payroll setup before entering the transactions below.) Sarah lives at 259 St. Andrews Way, Vandenberg Village, CA 93436. Her Social Security number is 574-85-4125 and her employee ID = SD. She's married and earns $72,000 per year and has an hourly billing rate of $150. Bob Humphrey, her other employee, lives at 453 Sirius, Vandenberg Village, CA 93436. His Social Security number is 632-78-1245 and his employee ID = BH. He's single and earns $20 per hour and has an hourly billing rate of $100. Her business, of course, is in the Accounting Services area as a certified public accountant, and thus she uses the "Accounting Agency" chart of accounts. She does not collect sales tax for her services, nor does she use sales receipts because she invoices her clients for services provided and gives them 15-day credit terms and a standard $10,000 credit limit. She does accept credit card payments and tracks time spent on each client's services for billing purposes. She will have two payroll items: salary and hourly. All payroll costs (salary, wages, and employee and employer payroll taxes) are recorded to a new account called Payroll Expenses (Account ID 77100). In addition to normal payroll taxes, California charges employers a training tax. All state taxes, employee and employer, accrue to G/L account 23600 (State Payroll Taxes Payable), while all federal taxes, employee and employer, accrue to G/L account 23400 (Federal Payroll Taxes Payable). She will perform accounting, tax, and consulting services. Sarah and her employee are paid monthly, but file weekly timesheets on Friday of each week. Clients are also invoiced on Fridays of each week once timesheets have been processed. Her vendors usually give her 30-day credit terms. Add the following transactions. (*Note:* Be sure to enter these business events in the proper date period.)

*service*

*sole proprietorship*

| Event # | Date | Business Event |
|---------|------|----------------|
| 1 | 9/1/09 | Opened a business checking account with a $50,000 deposit as her investment in the business in exchange for common stock. |
| 2 | 9/1/09 | Purchased a $15,000 copier (Equipment) from Xerox Corporation, completely financed with a note payable for three years with monthly payments of $463.16 due starting 10/1/09. |

| Event # | Date | Business Event |
|---|---|---|
| 3 | 9/1/09 | Signed an engagement letter to perform tax services for Valley Medical Group (ID = VMG), a new client located at 234 Third St., Lompoc, CA 93436. |
| 4 | 9/4/09 | Purchased furniture and fixtures from Sam Snead (ID = SS), a prior tenant in her rented office space, for $4,000 using Check No. 1001. |
| 5 | 9/4/09 | Sarah worked five hours each day on 9/2, 9/3, and 9/4 on the Valley Medical tax job and three hours more on each of those days that were not billable related to administrative work. Bob worked six hours each day on 9/3 and 9/4 on the Valley Medical tax job and two more hours on each of those days that were not billable related to staff training. (*Hint:* You'll need to create three activity items: Tax services (ID = TAX), Administrative (ID = AD), and Staff Training (ID = ST).) |
| 6 | 9/4/09 | Created Invoice 5001 to Valley Medical based on time costs incurred using terms net 15. |
| 7 | 9/7/09 | Wrote Check No. 1002 for $15,000 to Dean Witter (ID = DW) to purchase an investment. Create a new other current assets type of account 14300 called Short-Term Investment. |
| 8 | 9/7/09 | Wrote Check No. 1003 to Wiser Realty (ID = WR) as payment for rent ($3,000) and deposit ($6,000). |
| 9 | 9/8/09 | Signed an engagement letter to perform accounting services for Pactuco (ID = P), a new client located at 345 Central Ave., Lompoc, CA 93436. |
| 10 | 9/9/09 | Signed an engagement letter to perform consulting services for Celite Corporation (ID = C), a new client located at 20 Central Ave., Lompoc, CA 93436. |
| 11 | 9/9/09 | Received a pre-payment in the amount of $5,000 from Celite Corporation (its Check No. 86546) as an advance on services to be rendered. Sarah anticipates completing services for this client by the end of the month. She then deposited the check into the regular checking account using Deposit Ticket ID 300. |
| 12 | 9/11/09 | Sarah worked five hours each day on 9/7, 9/8, and 9/9 on the Valley Medical job and three more hours on each of those days, which were not billable administrative. She also worked eight hours on 9/10 on the Pactuco job performing accounting services and eight hours on 9/11 on the Celite job performing consulting services. Bob worked five hours each day on 9/7, 9/8, and 9/9 on the Valley Medical tax job and three more hours on each of those days, which were not billable administrative. He also worked eight hours on 9/10 on the Pactuco job performing accounting services and eight hours on 9/11 on the Celite job performing consulting services. Create two new activities: Accounting Services (ID = A) and Consulting Services (ID = C). |
| 13 | 9/11/09 | Created Invoices 5002, 5003, and 5004 to Valley Medical, Pactuco, and Celite based on time costs incurred using terms net 15. Apply credits available for Celite. |
| 14 | 9/14/09 | Signed an engagement letter to perform consulting services for Lompoc Hospital (ID = LH), a new client located at 233 D St., Lompoc, CA 93436. |
| 15 | 9/15/09 | Sold the short-term investments for $16,500 with the proceeds from the sale remaining in the short-term investment account. (Record the gain of $1,500 as other income and the related increase in the short-term investment account via a journal entry.) |
| 16 | 9/16/09 | Received a payment of $7,200 from Valley Medical Group on its Check No. 2340987 as payment on account and deposited it to the regular checking account using Deposit Ticket ID 301. |

| Event # | Date | Business Event |
|---|---|---|
| 17 | 9/18/09 | Sarah worked four hours each day from 9/14 to 9/18 on the Pactuco job performing accounting services and two hours on 9/14 and 9/15 on the Celite job performing consulting services. She also worked five hours each on 9/17 and 9/18 on the Lompoc Hospital job performing consulting services. Bob worked eight hours 9/14 on the Valley Medical tax job, eight hours on 9/15 on the Pactuco job performing accounting services, and eight hours each day on 9/16 and 9/17 on the Celite job performing consulting services. On 9/18, he attended four hours of staff training at a local university. |
| 18 | 9/18/09 | Created Invoices 5005, 5006, 5007, and 5008 to Valley Medical, Pactuco, Celite, and Lompoc Hospital, respectively, based on time costs incurred using terms net 15. |
| 19 | 9/25/09 | Sarah worked six hours each day from 9/21 through 9/24 on the Pactuco accounting engagement and two hours each of those days as nonbillable hours doing administrative work. Bob worked six hours each day from 9/21 through 9/24 and seven hours on 9/25 on the Lompoc Hospital job performing consulting services. |
| 20 | 9/25/09 | Created Invoices 5009 and 5010 to Pactuco and Lompoc Hospital based on time costs incurred using terms net 15. |
| 21 | 9/29/09 | Wrote Check No. 1004 to Pacific Gas & Electric (ID = PGE) for $400 in utilities expenses. |
| 22 | 9/29/09 | Wrote Check No. 1005 to Mark Jackson Insurance (ID = MJ) for $8,000 in liability insurance for the year 9/1/09 through 8/31/10. (Record as a prepaid expense!) |
| 23 | 9/29/09 | Wrote Check No. 1006 to Allan Hancock College (ID = AHC) for $300 in professional development expense for Bob's training. |
| 24 | 9/29/09 | Received Invoice 20938 from Verizon Wireless (ID = VW) in the amount of $525 for telephone expenses for September. Terms are net 30. (*Hint:* Use Enter Bills tool in Vendors & Purchases tasks.) |
| 25 | 9/29/09 | Received Invoice 123897 from Staples (ID = S) in the amount of $1,500 for supplies (create a new other current assets account 14600). Terms are net 30. |
| 26 | 9/30/09 | Paid herself her $6,000 monthly salary and her assistant Bob Humphrey for 123 hours of work at $20 per hour as shown in Table 7.9. |

| | Employee | |
|---|---|---|
| Pay/Tax/Withholding | Duncan | Humphrey |
| Hours | n/a | 123 |
| Rate | n/a | 20.00 |
| Check Number | 1008 | 1009 |
| Gross Pay | 6,000.00 | 2,460.00 |
| Federal Withholding | −770.50 | −305.05 |
| Social Security Employee | −372.00 | −152.52 |
| Medicare Employee | −87.00 | −35.67 |
| CA Withholding | −231.40 | −77.98 |
| CA Disability | −4.80 | −1.97 |
| Social Security Employer | 372.00 | 152.52 |
| Medicare Company | 87.00 | 35.67 |
| Federal Unemployment | 48.00 | 19.68 |
| CA Unemployment | 204.00 | 83.64 |
| CA Training Tax | 6.00 | 2.46 |
| Check Amount | 4,534.30 | 1,886.81 |

**Table 7.9**

Earnings Information for Sarah Duncan, CPA

*Requirements*

Create a Peachtree file for Sarah Duncan, CPA. Modify the company name to include Ch 7 at the end so that the company name is Sarah Duncan, CPA Ch 7. Change the system date to **9/1/09**. Add vendors, inventory items, customers, and employees first and then record business transactions in chronological order (remember that dates are in the month of September 2009). After you've printed the following reports (with no page numbers and no zero amounts), create a backup of this file and store it on some type of external medium (flash drive, Internet site, CD, disk, etc.). The backup file should be named Sarah Duncan, CPA Ch 7 for easy identification later.

a.   Customer ledgers

b.   Vendor ledgers

c.   Employee list

d.   Item list

e.   Standard balance sheet

f.   Standard income statement

g.   Statement of cash flows

h.   Find transactions report

## Comprehensive Problem 2: PACIFIC BREW INC.

Pacific Brew Inc. was incorporated January 1, 2008, upon the issuance of 50,000 shares of $1 par value common stock for $50,000 worth of net assets (originally belonging to Michael Patrick as a sole proprietor). Thus, beginning assets, liabilities, and equity are:

| Account | Description | Debits | Credits |
|---|---|---|---|
| 1020 | Checking Account | 47,500 | |
| 1100 | Accounts Receivable | 250 | |
| 1200 | Inventory | 2,750 | |
| 2000 | Accounts Payable | | 500 |
| 3930 | Common Stock | | 50,000 |

The company is located at 500 West Ocean, Arcata, CA 95521. Michael Patrick, as president, oversees this beer distributor's operations (use the simplified chart of accounts for a distribution company). The company will use a calendar year using 12-month periods, has a federal employer ID number of 77-1357465, and plans to use Peachtree's inventory (average costing method), purchase orders, and manual payroll features on a real-time basis using the accrual method of accounting. The company does not collect sales taxes. Customers are given a $10,000 credit limit and 30-day terms. Vendors typically give the company 30-day terms as well and a $30,000 credit limit.

In addition to distributing beer, Pacific Brew provides consulting services to customers on bar operations, menu plans, and beverage selection. These services are billed to customers at the rate of $85 per hour and are recorded in an income account called sales income. (*Hint:* Create a new item ID = C, description = Consulting, class = Service.)

Pacific has two other employees as shown below. Federal withholding, unemployment, Social Security, and Medicare are paid to the U.S. Treasury, while California withholding, unemployment, employee disability, and employee training tax are paid to the EDD (Employment Development Department). Payroll is paid semimonthly with gross pay recorded to a new account 6090 (Salaries & Wages Expense). State taxes accrue to account 2350 (State Payroll Taxes Payable), and federal payroll taxes accrue to account 2330 (Federal Payroll Taxes Payable). All payroll taxes are calculated manually. Vendors, inventory items, customers, and employees are listed below.

## Vendors

| Name | Mad River | Lost Coast | JD Salinger (landlord) | Humboldt |
|---|---|---|---|---|
| Vendor ID | MR | LC | JD | H |
| Address | 195 Taylor Way | 123 West Third St. | 101 Market St. | 865 10th St. |
| City | Blue Lake | Eureka | San Francisco | Arcata |
| State | CA | CA | CA | CA |
| Zip | 95525 | 95501 | 94102 | 95521 |
| Phone | 707-555-4151 | 707-555-4484 | 415-555-6141 | 707-555-2739 |
| Beginning Balance | $500 (MR2800) | $0 | $0 | $0 |

## Inventory

| Item ID | Description | Cost | Price | Beginning Quantity |
|---|---|---|---|---|
| 302 | Mad River Pale Ale | 5.00 | 6.00 | 100 |
| 303 | Mad River Stout | 6.00 | 7.00 | 125 |
| 304 | Mad River Amber Ale | 4.00 | 5.00 | 100 |
| 305 | Mad River Porter | 5.50 | 6.50 | 200 |
| 402 | Lost Coast Pale Ale | 5.25 | 6.25 | 0 |
| 403 | Lost Coast Stout | 6.25 | 7.25 | 0 |
| 404 | Lost Coast Amber Ale | 4.25 | 5.25 | 0 |
| 502 | Humboldt Pale Ale | 5.50 | 6.50 | 0 |
| 506 | Humboldt IPA | 6.50 | 7.50 | 0 |
| 507 | Humboldt Red Nectar | 7.00 | 8.00 | 0 |

## Customers

| Name | Avalon Bistro | Hole in the Wall | Ocean Grove |
|---|---|---|---|
| ID | AB | HW | OG |
| Address | 1080 3rd St. | 590 G St. | 570 Ewing St. |
| City | Arcata | Arcata | Trinidad |
| State | CA | CA | CA |
| Zip | 95521 | 95521 | 95570 |
| Phone | 707-555-0500 | 707-555-7407 | 707-555-5431 |
| Invoice | 1400 | | |
| Beginning Balance | $250 | $0 | $0 |

|  | River House | Michael's Brew House | Bon Jovi's |
|---|---|---|---|
|  | RH | MB | BJ |
|  | 222 Weller St. | 2198 Union St. | 4257 Petaluma Hill |
|  | Petaluma | San Francisco | Santa Rosa |
|  | CA | CA | CA |
|  | 95404 | 94123 | 95404 |
|  | 707-555-0123 | 415-555-9874 | 707-555-5634 |
|  | $0 | $0 | $0 |

## *Employees*

| Name | Michael Patrick | Shawn Lopez | Emilio Duarte |
|---|---|---|---|
| ID | MP | SL | ED |
| Address | 333 Spring Rd. | 234 University Dr. | 23 Palm Dr. #23 |
| City | Arcata | Arcata | Arcata |
| State | CA | CA | CA |
| Zip | 95521 | 95521 | 95521 |
| Phone | 707-555-9847 | 707-555-1297 | 707-555-6655 |
| SS# | 655-85-1253 | 702-54-8746 | 012-58-4654 |
| Earnings | Salary – $2083.33 | Wages – $12/hour | Wages – $11/hour |
| Filing Status | Married | Single | Single |

## *Chronological List of Business Events*

| Event # | Date | Business Event |
|---|---|---|
| 1 | 12/31/07 | Be sure you've recorded beginning balances as per above. |
| 2 | 1/4/08 | Using Purchase Order No. 1001, ordered 500 each of Items 302, 303, 304, and 305 from Mad River for immediate delivery. Terms: due on receipt. (Change terms for this vendor.) |
| 3 | 1/4/08 | Using Purchase Order No. 1002, ordered 400 each of Items 502, 506, and 507 from Humboldt for immediate delivery. Terms: due on receipt. |
| 4 | 1/4/08 | Using Purchase Order No. 1003, ordered 300 each of Items 402, 403, and 404 from Lost Coast for immediate delivery on net 30-day terms. |
| 5 | 1/7/08 | Rented a warehouse from JD Salinger, landlord, for $2,500 per month by paying first and last month's rent with Check No. 101 for $5,000. |
| 6 | 1/7/08 | Purchased furniture and office equipment from JD Salinger for $8,000 with Check No. 102 (record to Property & Equipment Account 1500). |
| 7 | 1/9/08 | Borrowed $40,000 from Wells Fargo Bank (ID = WF) as a long-term note payable due in three years. |
| 8 | 1/10/08 | Invested $30,000 in a Wells Fargo Bank certificate of deposit for 60 days with Check No. 103. (Create a new cash type of account, ID = 1050, description = Certificates of Deposit.) |
| 9 | 1/10/08 | Purchased several computer systems and printers (classified as Property & Equipment). Check No. 104 was written for $10,200 to West Coast Computer Supply (ID = WCCS) to purchase the equipment. |
| 10 | 1/11/08 | Received all items ordered on Purchase Order No. 1001 to Mad River. The full amount ($10,250) was paid at purchase based on Invoice MR2987, reference Check No. 105. |
| 11 | 1/11/08 | Provided 50 hours of consulting services on Sales Receipt 5001 to Michael's Brew House. A check (#230897) in the amount of $4,250 was deposited into the checking account with Deposit Ticket ID A4001 that same day. |

| Event # | Date | Business Event |
|---|---|---|
| 12 | 1/14/08 | Received all items ordered on Purchase Order No. 1002 to Humboldt. The full amount ($7,600) was paid at purchase based on Invoice H2098, reference Check No. 106. |
| 13 | 1/14/08 | Received and shipped an order (Sales Receipt 5002) to Bon Jovi's for 25 units of Item 305, 30 units of Item 506, and 50 units of Item 507. Check payment (#9234897) of $787.50 was deposited into the checking account that same day with Deposit Ticket ID A4002. |
| 14 | 1/15/08 | Provided 60 hours of consulting services (Sales Receipt 5003) to River House. Check 209 as payment of $5,100 was deposited into the checking account that same day with Deposit Ticket ID A4003. |
| 15 | 1/16/08 | Received and shipped an order (Sales Receipt 5004) to Ocean Grove for 30 units of Item 304, 40 units of Item 302, and 50 units of Item 502. VISA credit card payment (#32090823409) of $715 was deposited into the checking account that same day with Deposit Ticket ID A4004. |
| 16 | 1/16/08 | Received and shipped an order (Sales Receipt 5005) to Avalon Bistro for 40 units of Item 302, 50 units of Item 507, and 35 units of Item 506. Check (#3897612) payment of $902.50 was deposited into the checking account that same day with Deposit Ticket ID A4005. |
| 17 | 1/16/08 | Received and shipped an order (Sales Receipt 5006) to Michael's Brew House for 100 each of Items 302, 305, and 506. MasterCard payment (#238987098) of $2,000 was deposited into the checking account that same day with Deposit Ticket ID A4006. |
| 18 | 1/16/08 | Paid employees for the period ended 1/16/08. See tax information in Table 7.10. |

| | Employee | | |
|---|---|---|---|
| Pay/Tax/Withholding | Duarte | Lopez | Patrick |
| Check | 107 | 108 | 109 |
| Hours Worked | 80 | 75 | n/a |
| Gross Pay | 880.00 | 900.00 | 2,083.33 |
| Federal Withholding | −120.56 | −123.30 | −285.42 |
| Social Security Employee | −54.56 | −55.80 | −129.17 |
| Medicare Employee | −12.76 | −13.05 | −30.21 |
| CA – Withholding | −48.40 | −49.50 | −114.58 |
| CA – Disability | −4.40 | −4.50 | −10.42 |
| Social Security Company | 54.56 | 55.80 | 129.17 |
| Medicare Company | 12.76 | 13.05 | 30.21 |
| Federal Unemployment | 7.04 | 7.20 | 16.67 |
| CA – Unemployment Company | 26.40 | 27.00 | 62.50 |
| CA – Employment Training Tax | 0.88 | 0.90 | 2.08 |
| Check Amount | 639.32 | 653.85 | 1,513.53 |

**Table 7.10**

Earnings Information for Pacific Brew Inc.

### Requirements

Create a Peachtree file for Pacific Brew. Modify the company name to include Ch 7 at the end so that the company name is **Pacific Brew Ch 7**. Change the system date to **1/1/08**. Add vendors, inventory items, customers, and employees first and then record business transactions in chronological order (remember that dates are in the month of January 2008). After you've printed the following reports (with no page numbers and no zero amounts), create a backup of this file and store it on some type of external medium (flash drive, Internet site, CD, disk, etc.). The backup file should be named **Pacific Brew Ch 7** for easy identification later. You'll be restoring this file in Chapter 11.

a.   Customer ledgers

b.   Vendor ledgers

c.   Employee list

d.   Item list

e.   Standard balance sheet

f.   Standard income statement

g.   Statement of cash flows

h.   Find transactions report

## Comprehensive Problem 3: SUNSET SPAS INC.

corporation

merchandising

service

Sunset Spas Inc. was incorporated January 1, 2007, upon the issuance of 10,000 shares of $2 par value common stock for $100,000. The company is located at 300 West Street, Del Mar, CA 92014. Bryan Christopher, president, will oversee this spa retailer's operation (use Retail Company listed under the Detailed types heading as the chart of accounts). The company will follow accrual accounting, use real-time posting, have 12 monthly accounting periods, and have a federal employer ID number of 77-9851247 and a California EDD number of 012-3435-8. It plans to use Peachtree's inventory, purchase orders, and payroll features. The following tables list the suppliers it purchases from, the items it intends to carry in inventory, and the customers it has lined up. The customers' billing and shipping addresses are the same. The company collects 7.75% sales tax (Sales Tax Code = TAX, description = CA Sales Tax), which is remitted to one tax authority (ID = SBE, description = Sales Tax) on all spa sales that are credited to account 23100 (Sales Tax Payable). Payments are made quarterly to the California State Board of Equalization (ID = CSBE). No sales tax is collected on installation services.

In addition to selling spas, Sunset Spas also provides consulting and installation services to customers. Consulting services are billed to customers at the rate of $80 per hour, while installation services are billed to customers at the rate of $75 per hour, and both are recorded in an income account 40200 called Sales: Services. Spa sales are recorded in an income account 40000 titled Sales: Merchandise. The company uses the average inventory cost method. All customers currently have credit terms of "due on receipt." Vendors typically require payment on delivery.

Sunset also employs two other people, as shown below. Federal withholding, federal unemployment (FUTA), Social Security, and Medicare are paid to the U.S. Treasury (ID = UST), while California withholding, state unemployment (SUTA), employee disability, and employee training tax (Emp_Train) are paid to the Employment Development Department (ID = EDD). Payroll is paid semimonthly with employees paid a salary recorded to account 77000 and employees paid hourly wages recorded to account 77500. State taxes accrue to account 23600 (State Payroll Taxes Payable), and federal payroll taxes accrue to account 23400 (Federal Payroll Taxes Payable). All payroll taxes are calculated manually.

## Vendors

| Name | Sundance Spas | Cal Spas |
|------|---------------|----------|
| ID | SS | CS |
| Address | 14525 Monte Vista Ave. | 1462 East Ninth Street |
| City | Chino | Pomona |
| State | CA | CA |
| Zip | 91710 | 91766 |
| Phone | 909-614-0679 | 909-623-8781 |

## Customers

| Name | J's Landscaping | Marriott Hotels | Pam's Designs |
|------|-----------------|-----------------|---------------|
| ID | J | MH | PD |
| Address | 12 Bones Way | 97444 Miramar | 5144 Union |
| City | San Diego | San Diego | San Diego |
| State | CA | CA | CA |
| Zip | 92354 | 92145 | 92129 |
| Phone | 858-555-1348 | 858-555-7407 | 707-555-5748 |

## Employees

| Name | Bryan Christopher | Loriel Sanchez | Sharon Lee |
|------|-------------------|----------------|------------|
| ID | BC | LS | SL |
| Address | 12 Mesa Way | 2342 Court | 323 Ridgefield Pl. |
| City | Del Mar | Del Mar | Del Mar |
| State | CA | CA | CA |
| Zip | 92014 | 92014 | 92014 |
| Phone | 858-555-1264 | 858-555-3365 | 858-555-9874 |
| SS# | 556-95-4789 | 475-54-8746 | 125-58-8452 |
| Earnings | Salary – $2,500 | Wages – $13/hour | Wages – $12/hour |
| Filing Status | Married (one income) | Single | Single |

## Inventory Items

| ID | Description | Vendor | Cost | Price |
|----|-------------|--------|------|-------|
| 201 | Maxus | Sundance | $5,000 | $7,000 |
| 202 | Optima | Sundance | $6,000 | $8,000 |
| 203 | Cameo | Sundance | $7,000 | $9,000 |
| 301 | Galaxy | Cal Spas | $4,500 | $6,500 |
| 302 | Ultimate | Cal Spas | $5,500 | $7,500 |
| 303 | Aqua | Cal Spas | $7,500 | $9,500 |
| C | Consulting | | | $80/hour |
| I | Installation | | | $75/hour |

## Chronological List of Business Events

| Event # | Date | Business Event |
|---------|------|----------------|
| 1 | 1/3/07 | Sold 10,000 shares of no-par common stock for $100,000 cash to various shareholders. Deposited these funds into the regular checking account. |
| 2 | 1/4/07 | Borrowed $200,000 from Hacienda Bank as a long-term note payable due in three years. The money was deposited into the company's regular checking account. |
| 3 | 1/5/07 | Using Purchase Order No. 5001, ordered 10 each of Items 201, 202, and 203 from Sundance Spas for immediate delivery. Terms: Net due. |
| 4 | 1/5/07 | Using Purchase Order No. 5002, ordered five each of Items 301, 302, and 303 from Cal Spas for immediate delivery. Terms: Net due. |
| 5 | 1/8/07 | Rented a retail store front from K Realty (ID = K), landlord, for $3,000 per month by paying first month's rent and a deposit with Check No. 101 for $6,000. This is a long-term lease for five years. |
| 6 | 1/8/07 | Purchased shelving, desks, and office equipment from Office Max (ID = OM) for $8,000 with Check No. 102. (furniture and fixtures = $4,500, equipment = $3,500.) |
| 7 | 1/9/07 | Invested $30,000 in a short-term investment with Poole Investments (ID = PI) with Check No. 103. Create a new other current assets account 14800 called Short-Term Investments. |
| 8 | 1/10/07 | Purchased several computer systems and printers (classified as equipment). Check No. 104 was written for $8,900 to Coast Computer Supply (ID = CCS) to purchase the equipment. |
| 9 | 1/11/07 | Received all items ordered on Purchase No. Order 5001 from Sundance Spas. Received and paid Invoice 98789 with Check No. 105 for $180,000. |
| 10 | 1/11/07 | Provided 10 hours of consulting to J's Landscape on Sales Receipt 7001. Consulting services are taxable. Check (#2098) for $862 was deposited into the bank that same day with Deposit Ticket ID 901. (*Hint:* Be sure consulting was already set up as a service item (ID = C) that is billed at $80 per hour, is taxable, and is recorded into an income account 40200 Sales: Services.) |
| 11 | 1/12/07 | Received all items ordered on Purchase Order No. 5002 from Cal Spas. Received and paid Invoice A9892 with Check No. 106 for $87,500. |
| 12 | 1/15/07 | Received an order and delivered three each of Item 301, one each of Item 202, and one each of Item 303 to Pam's Design on Sales Receipt 7002. Check (#230980) for $39,867.50 was deposited into the checking account with Deposit Ticket ID 902. |
| 13 | 1/15/07 | Provided eight hours of consulting services on Sales Receipt 7003 to Marriott. Check (#90189) for $689.60 was deposited into the checking account that same day with Deposit Ticket ID 903. |
| 14 | 1/16/07 | Received an order and delivered three each of Item 201 and two each of Item 203 to J's Landscape on Sales Receipt 7004. Check(#622) for $42,022.50 was deposited into the checking account that same day with Deposit Ticket ID 904. |
| 15 | 1/16/07 | Received a deposit from Marriott Hotels for future consulting services of $5,000, which was deposited into the checking account that same day with Deposit Ticket ID 905. Reference its Check No. 3098. |
| 16 | 1/16/07 | Paid employees. Sanchez worked 75 hours and Lee worked 83 hours during the period ended 1/16/07. See tax information in Table 7.11. |

| Pay/Tax/Withholding | Employee | | |
| --- | --- | --- | --- |
| | Christopher | Sanchez | Lee |
| Check | 107 | 108 | 109 |
| Hours | n/a | 75 | 83 |
| Rate | n/a | 13.00 | 12.00 |
| Gross Pay | 2,500.00 | 975.00 | 996.00 |
| Federal Withholding | −342.50 | −133.58 | −136.45 |
| Social Security Employee | −155.00 | −60.45 | −61.75 |
| Medicare Employee | −36.25 | −14.14 | −14.44 |
| CA – Withholding | −137.50 | −53.63 | −54.78 |
| CA – Disability | −12.50 | −4.88 | −4.98 |
| Social Security Employer | 155.00 | 60.45 | 61.75 |
| Medicare Company | 36.25 | 14.14 | 14.44 |
| Federal Unemployment | 20.00 | 7.80 | 7.97 |
| CA – Unemployment | 6.25 | 2.44 | 2.49 |
| CA – Employment Training Tax | 2.50 | 0.98 | 1.00 |
| Check Amount | 1,816.25 | 708.32 | 723.60 |

**Table 7.11**

Earnings Information for Sunset Spas

### Requirements

Create a Peachtree file for Sunset Spas. Modify the company name to include Ch 7 at the end so that the company name is **Sunset Spas Ch 7**. Change the system date to **1/1/07**. Add vendors, inventory items, customers, and employees first and then record business transactions in chronological order (remember that dates are in the month of January 2007). After you've printed the following reports (with no page numbers and no zero amounts), create a backup of this file and store it on some type of external medium (flash drive, Internet site, CD, disk, etc.). The backup file should be named **Sunset Spas Ch 7** for easy identification later. You'll be restoring this file in Chapter 11.

a. Customer ledgers

b. Vendor ledgers

c. Employee list

d. Item list

e. Standard balance sheet

f. Standard income statement

g. Statement of cash flows

h. Find transactions report

## Comprehensive Problem 4: BRIDGETTE SWEET PHOTOGRAPHY

Bridgette Sweet has asked you to help her use Peachtree for her photography business. She's been in business since January 2010 but wants to start using Peachtree effective January 2013, which is the beginning of her fiscal year. She's been using a spreadsheet to keep track of her business transactions but is certain that Peachtree will help her get organized. You begin your work creating her Peachtree file.

Her company name is Bridgette Sweet Photography, with a legal title of Bridgette Sweet Photography, Inc., with a federal employer ID of 77-6412488. Her studio is located at 828 S. Wabash Ave., Chicago, IL 60605. Her main focus is photographing weddings and corporate events and selling prints and frames resulting from her work. The company does keep an inventory of frames using the average cost method, so Bridgette wants to use Peachtree inventory and purchase order features. She will also sell prints and albums at her cost but does not stock these items. She has a checking account that had a balance of $9,000 at 12/31/12. As a service company (photographer) she will use a chart of accounts appropriate to her business. Her standard payment terms are net 30 and credit limit is $15,000.

Bridgette does not plan to use Peachtree payroll or payroll tax service and thus will be calculating payroll manually. She employs two individuals as photography assistants and wants to track time using Peachtree. Employees are all subject to Illinois taxes and are paid monthly. The company's SUTA rate is 5.4% and federal and state taxes are paid and filed quarterly. The company's Dept. of Employment Security Acct No. is 3383710-8 and its Dept. of Revenue FEIN and SEQ No. is 32-2930766 102. All other taxes are paid quarterly. (Set up payroll just like you did in the previous chapter except that all payroll tax liabilities are recorded to one account 23400 (Payroll Tax Payable), being sure to uncheck tax calculations. However, for this problem record all payroll tax liabilities to account 23400 and change the name of that account to Payroll Taxes Payable.) Hourly employee payroll is tracked to account 77500 (wages expense) and salaried employee payroll is tracked to account 77000 (salaries expense). All employees use time tickets to record their time. All billing is done at the employee rate for Kyle and Nick and at the activity rate for Bridgette.

The state of Illinois imposes a 9.75% sales tax on all services and merchandise, which the company must collect and remit quarterly to the Illinois Dept. of Revenue. Use ST as the sales tax ID and Sales Tax the sales tax name. All customers located in Illinois must be charged this state sales tax.

As of 12/31/12 the company owned $10,000 in Furniture and $5,000 in Equipment, had $2,000 and $1,000 in Accumulated Depreciation related to each and owed $12,000 on a note payable due in three years. Common stock and retained earnings were $15,000 and $19,000, respectively, as of 12/31/12. Details of accounts receivable ($26,000), inventory–frames and mats ($3,000)– and accounts payable ($4,000) balances are shown below.

## Vendors

| ID | US | PF | GP | ILR |
|---|---|---|---|---|
| Name | US Photo | Peterson Framing | GP Leasing | Illinois Dept. of Revenue |
| Address | 140 S. Dearborn St. | 2420 W. Belmont | 4045 North Rockwell St. | |
| City | Chicago | Chicago | Chicago | Springfield |
| State | Illinois | Illinois | Illinois | Illinois |
| Zip | 60603 | 60618 | 60618 | 62726 |
| A/P Balance | $1,000 | $500 | $2,500 | $0 |
| Expense Account | 50000 | 12000 | 74500 | 23100 |
| Invoice Number | 974 | 187633 | 5101 | n/a |
| Date | 12/15/12 | 11/24/12 | 12/3/12 | n/a |

## Customers

| ID | Hain | Foster | Yelp |
|---|---|---|---|
| Name | Hain Wedding | Foster Corporation | Yelp Corporation |
| Address | 4011 W. 63rd | 2139 S. Laramie Ave. | 1640 W. Fulton St. |
| City | Chicago | Chicago | Chicago |
| State | Illinois | Illinois | Illinois |
| Zip | 60629 | 60804 | 60605 |
| Sales Tax | ST | ST | ST |
| A/R Balance | $8,000 | $3,000 | $15,000 |
| Invoice number | 3512 | 3515 | 3521 |
| Invoice date | 12/5/12 | 11/15/12 | 10/31/12 |

## Items

| Item ID | On Hand | Item Class | Description | Last Unit Cost | Price Level 1 | Sales Acct | Cost of Sales Acct |
|---|---|---|---|---|---|---|---|
| 1000 | n/a | Activity | Weddings | | $200 | 40200 | n/a |
| 1010 | n/a | Activity | Corporate Events | | $250 | 40300 x | n/a |
| 1020 | 20 | Stock item | Frames | $150 | $350 | 40800 | 51500 |
| 1030 | 0 | Non-stock | Prints | $ 20 | | 40000 | 50000 |
| 2000 | 0 | Activity | Administrative | | | 40000 | 50000 |

x New income type account 40300 Corporate Income

## Employees

| Employee ID | BS | KG | NP |
|---|---|---|---|
| Name | Bridgette Sweet | Kyle Garrett | Nick Pease |
| Address | 323 Lakeshore Dr. | 893 West 34th St. | 100 Park Ave. #2 |
| City | Chicago | Chicago | Chicago |
| State | Illinois | Illinois | Illinois |
| Zip | 60000 | 60001 | 60602 |
| Hire Date | 1/1/10 | 3/1/10 | 7/1/10 |
| Social Security # | 215-85-9874 | 312-54-7125 | 556-84-7124 |
| Earnings | $5,000/month | $25/hour | $20/hour |
| Filing Status | Married | Single | Single |
| Billing Rate | n/a | $75/hour | $60/hour |

*Chronological List of Business Events*

| Event # | Date | Business Event |
|---|---|---|
| 1 | 1/02/13 | Created two new jobs: Job ID: 432, Description: Photo Shoot, for Yelp Corporation, and Job ID: 433, Description: Photo Shoot, for a new Customer ID Dutton, Name Dutton Wedding. |
| 2 | 1/03/13 | Received $15,000 on check #4230980 from Yelp Corporation as payment on account and deposited it to the checking account on Deposit ticket ID: 323. |
| 3 | 1/04/13 | Bridgette, Kyle, and Nick all worked 6 hours on a photo shoot for Yelp Corporation. Remember all billing is done at the employee rate for Kyle and Nick and at the activity rate for Bridgette. |
| 4 | 1/07/13 | Created two new purchase orders: 6411 to Peterson Framing for 50 frames for inventory and 6412 to US Photo for 100 prints to be billed to Yelp Corporation on job 432. |
| 5 | 1/10/13 | Received all 50 frames ordered on purchase order 6411 with an invoice #8746 from Peterson Framing. Received all 100 prints ordered on purchase order 6412 with an invoice #10413 from US Photo. |
| 6 | 1/11/13 | Invoiced Yelp Corporation $14,333.35 on invoice 10207 for time and prints incurred on job 432 and for 25 frames with Net 30 terms. (*Note:* Consolidate time by Activity Item and ship via UPS Ground.) |
| 7 | 1/14/13 | Purchased $5,600 of additional equipment (account 15100) from new vendor ID: CC, Name: Costco using check 9843. |
| 8 | 1/19/13 | Bridgette, Kyle, and Nick all worked 7, 3, and 2 hours, respectively, on job 433 the Dutton Wedding. |
| 9 | 1/21/13 | Created purchase order 6413 to US Photo for 30 prints to be billed to Dutton Wedding job 433. |
| 10 | 1/22/13 | Paid rent to GP Leasing in the amount of $1,750 using check 9844. |
| 11 | 1/24/13 | Received all 30 prints ordered on purchase order 6413 with an invoice #10489 from US Photo. |
| 12 | 1/25/13 | Invoiced Dutton Wedding $12,845 on invoice 10208 for time and prints incurred on job 433 and for 30 frames with Net 30 terms. (*Note:* Consolidate time by Activity Item and ship via UPS Ground.) |
| 13 | 1/28/13 | Bridgette, Kyle, and Nick all worked 4, 3, and 2 hours, respectively, on a new job 434 (Photo Shoot) for a new Customer ID: BW, Name: Benson Wedding. |
| 14 | 1/29/13 | Created purchase order 6414 to US Photo for 35 prints (cost $24 each) and 3 albums (a new non-stock item with Item ID:1040, Description: Albums, Last Unit Cost $75) to be billed to Benson Wedding job 434). |
| 15 | 1/30/13 | Received and deposited check number 12533 for $8,000 on Deposit ID: 324 as prepayment from a new Customer ID: KW, Name: Krenwinkle Wedding job 435, a photo shoot. |
| 16 | 1/30/13 | Received all 35 prints ordered on purchase order 6414 with invoice #10598 from US Photo and all 3 albums ordered on purchase order 6414 with invoice #10599 from US Photo. (*Hint:* record as two separate receipts.) |

| Event # | Date | Business Event |
|---------|------|----------------|
| 17 | 1/31/13 | Invoiced Benson Wedding $4346.10 on invoice 10209 for time and costs incurred on job 434 and for 5 frames with Net 30 terms. (*Note:* Consolidate time by Activity Item and ship via UPS Ground.) |
| 18 | Various | In addition to the billable hours described above, employees worked additional administrative hours. A listing of all hours worked is shown below. |
| 19 | 1/31/13 | Pay bills due by 1/31/13. Total payment $4,000 using checks 9845-9847. |
| 20 | 1/31/13 | Pay employees as per the schedule below using checks 9848-9850 from the regular checking account. |

| Date | Customer/Job ID | Activity | Billing Status | Sweet | Garrett | Pease |
|------|-----------------|----------|----------------|-------|---------|-------|
| 1/03 | Administrative | 2000 | Non-Billable | 3 | 2 | 2 |
| 1/04 | Yelp/432 | 1010 | Billable | 6 | 6 | 6 |
| 1/15 | Administrative | 2000 | Non-Billable | - | 8 | 8 |
| 1/17 | Administrative | 2000 | Non-Billable | - | 8 | 8 |
| 1/19 | Dutton/433 | 1000 | Billable | 7 | 3 | 2 |
| 1/22 | Administrative | 2000 | Non-Billable | - | 8 | 8 |
| 1/28 | Benson/434 | 1000 | Billable | 4 | 3 | 2 |
| 1/30 | Administrative | 2000 | Non-Billable | - | 8 | 8 |
| Total | | | | 20 | 46 | 44 |

| Pay/Tax/Withholding | Sweet | Garrett | Pease |
|---------------------|-------|---------|-------|
| Hours | n/a | 46 | 44 |
| Annual salary/ hourly rate | $60,000 | $ 25.00 | $ 20.00 |
| Gross pay | 5,000.00 | 1,150.00 | 880.00 |
| Federal withholding | 685.00 | 157.55 | 120.56 |
| Social Security employee | 310.00 | 71.30 | 54.56 |
| Medicare employee | 72.50 | 16.68 | 12.76 |
| State withholding | 347.33 | 54.73 | 34.21 |
| Social Security employer | 310.00 | 71.30 | 54.56 |
| Medicare company | 72.50 | 16.68 | 12.76 |
| Federal unemployment | 40.00 | 9.20 | 7.04 |
| State unemployment | 150.00 | 34.50 | 26.40 |
| Check amount | 3,585.17 | 849.74 | 657.91 |

## *Requirements*

Create a Peachtree file for Bridgette Sweet Photography. Modify the company name to include Ch 7 at the end so that the company name is Bridgette Sweet Photography Ch 7. Change the system date to 1/1/13 and the accounting period to Period 1. Add vendors, inventory items, customers, and employees first and then record business transactions in chronological order (remember that dates are in the month of January 2013). After you've printed the following reports (for the month of January 2013, with no page numbers and no zero amounts), create a backup of this file and store it on some type of external medium (flash drive, Internet site, CD, disk, etc.). The backup file should be named Bridgette

Sweet Photography Ch 7 for easy identification later. You'll be restoring this file in Chapter 11.

a.   General ledger trial balance

b.   Customer ledger

c.   Vendor ledger

d.   Employee list

e.   Item list

f.   Standard balance sheet

g.   Standard income statement

h.   Statement of cash flows

i.   Find transactions report

## Comprehensive Problem 5: CRYSTAL CLEAR POOL SERVICE

Sharon Calhoun, a college friend of yours, has been asked by her parents to help them computerize the accounting in their sole proprietorship. Her parents own Crystal Clear Pool Service. They have been in business for over a year and Sharon concurs with their desire to automate their accounting system. However, she's a marketing student and does not know the first thing about computerized accounting. You have agreed to help them out. The plan is to start using the computerized accounting system October 1, 2012.

The company has a federal employer ID of 76-9421357. The business is located at 160 Portal Lane, Sedona, AZ 86336 and its phone number is 928-555-2900. The company will use a fiscal year (10/1 to 9/30) and will start entering business events and beginning balances as of 10/1/12. It will use the In-House payroll system. The state unemployment rate for Crystal is 6%. The company does keep an inventory of pool supplies such as chlorine and muriatic acid and will be using the average cost method, so you decided to use Peachtree's inventory and purchase order features. You have chosen to create your own chart of accounts appropriate to the business (see below). Standard payment terms are net 30 and credit limit is $15,000.

The company employs two individuals as assistants but will not track time using Peachtree. Employees are all subject to Arizona taxes and are paid monthly. All taxes are paid and filed quarterly. The company's state employer ID is 1254871-8 and its state unemployment ID is 21-8741399111. (*Hint:* Set up payroll just like you did in the chapter, being sure to uncheck tax calculations.) Hourly employee payroll is tracked to account 660 (wages expense). All billing is done at the beginning of each month of service.

The state of Arizona imposes a 6% sales tax on all services and merchandise, which the company must collect and remit quarterly to the Arizona Dept. of Revenue. Use ST as the sales tax ID and Sales Tax the sales tax name. All customers located in Arizona must be charged this state sales tax.

## Chart of Accounts

| Account ID | Description | Type | Balance at 9/30/12 |
|---|---|---|---|
| 101 | Checking | Cash | 8,000 |
| 120 | Accounts Receivable | Accounts Receivable | 15,000 |
| 130 | Inventory | Inventory | 5,000 |
| 140 | Prepaid Expenses | Other Current Assets | 3,000 |
| 150 | Equipment | Fixed Assets | 22,000 |
| 160 | Accumulated Depreciation | Accumulated Depreciation | 2,000 |
| 200 | Accounts Payable | Accounts Payable | 6,500 |
| 210 | Payroll Tax Payable | Other Current Liabilities | 0 |
| 220 | Sales Tax Payable | Other Current Liabilities | 0 |
| 250 | Notes Payable | Long-Term Liabilities | 20,000 |
| 300 | Owner's Capital | Equity-doesn't close | 18,000 |
| 310 | Withdrawals | Equity-gets closed | 0 |
| 320 | Retained Earnings | Equity Retained Earnings | 6,500 |
| 400 | Pool Services Revenue | Income | |
| 410 | Pool Supplies Revenue | Income | |
| 420 | Parts Revenue | Income | |
| 500 | Cost of Supplies/Parts Sold | Cost of Sales | |
| 600 | Advertising Expense | Expenses | |
| 610 | Depreciation Expense | Expenses | |
| 620 | Payroll Tax Expense | Expenses | |
| 630 | Rent Expense | Expenses | |
| 640 | Supplies Expense | Expenses | |
| 650 | Utilities Expense | Expenses | |
| 660 | Wages Expense | Expenses | |

## Vendors

| ID | 201 | 202 | 203 |
|---|---|---|---|
| Name | Cactus Pool Supply | Sun Systems | Arizona Dept. of Revenue |
| Address | 1070 East Ray Road | 2030 Pinnacle Peak | 1600 West Monroe Street |
| City | Chandler | Phoenix | Phoenix |
| State | AZ | AZ | AZ |
| Zip | 85225 | 85027 | 85007 |
| A/P Balance | $4,500 | $2,000 | $0 |
| Expense Account | 130 | 130 | 220/210 |
| Invoice Number | 87413516 | 584731 | n/a |
| Date | 8/25/12 | 9/14/12 | n/a |

## Customers

| ID | 100 | 101 | 102 | 103 |
|---|---|---|---|---|
| Name | Wyndham Sedona | Hilton Resort | Poco Diablo | Adobe Grand |
| Address | 1500 Kestrel Cir | 90 Ridge Trail Drive | 1752 Highway 179 | 35 Hozoni Drive |
| City | Sedona | Sedona | Sedona | Sedona |
| State | AZ | AZ | AZ | AZ |
| Zip | 86336 | 86336 | 86336 | 86336 |
| A/R balance | $6,000 | $4,000 | $0 | $5,000 |
| Invoice number | 10123 | 10124 | n/a | 10128 |
| Invoice date | 9/1/12 | 9/1/12 | n/a | 9/1/12 |
| Sales account | 400 | 400 | 400 | 400 |
| Sales tax | ST | ST | ST | ST |

*Items*

| Item ID | On Hand | Item Class | Description | Last Unit Cost | Price Level 1 | Sales Acct | Cost of Sales Acct |
|---------|---------|------------|-------------|----------------|---------------|------------|--------------------|
| 1000 | n/a | Activity | Pool Service | | $125 | 400 | n/a |
| 1010 | n/a | Activity | Pool Repairs | | $125 | 400 | n/a |
| 2000 | 200 | Stock item | Chlorine | $ 5 | $ 8 | 410 | 500 |
| 2100 | 125 | Stock item | Pool Shock | $12 | $ 18 | 410 | 500 |
| 2200 | 250 | Stock item | Pool Algaecide | $10 | $ 14 | 410 | 500 |
| 2300 | 0 | Non-stock item | Parts | - | - | 420 | 500 |

*Employees*

| Employee ID | 501 | 502 |
|-------------|-----|-----|
| Name | Danielle Patrick | Jeev M Singh |
| Address | 613 Desert Sage Ln | 60 Cactus Dr |
| City | Sedona | Sedona |
| State | AZ | AZ |
| Zip | 86336 | 86336 |
| Hire Date | 10/1/11 | 10/1/11 |
| Social Security # | 841-85-1478 | 351-78-9413 |
| Hourly Rate | $18 | $20 |
| Filing Status | Single | Single |

*Chronological List of Business Events*

| Event # | Date | Business Event |
|---------|------|----------------|
| 1 | 10/1/12 | Invoiced customers 100–103 40 hours each for pool services to be rendered in October using invoice numbers 10130–10133 with sales tax. |
| 2 | 10/5/12 | Received following payments from customers on account and deposited amounts using Deposit ticket ID 89: check 8432 from customer 100 for $6,000, check 123458 from customer 101 for $2,000, VISA payment 6541384 from customer 103 for $5,000. |
| 3 | 10/8/12 | Created purchase order 44 to Sun Systems (Vendor ID 202) for the purchase of $3,200 in parts needed for repair work being completed for Poco Diablo (Customer ID: 102) on a new job ID 261 Pool repairs. |
| 4 | 10/10/12 | Received parts ordered on purchase order 44 from Sun Systems on its invoice 584922. |
| 5 | 10/12/12 | Completed job 261 for Poco Diablo and invoiced it on invoice number 10134 for 18 hours in pool repairs and for parts reimbursement for a total of $5,777. |
| 6 | 10/22/12 | Purchased equipment from Cactus Pool Supply using check 289 for $2,500. |
| 7 | 10/25/12 | Paid rent expense to Century 21 Leasing (a new vendor ID: 204) using check 290 for $1,789. |
| 8 | 10/30/12 | Invoiced customers 100–103 for pool supplies used in October using invoice numbers 10135–10138 with sales tax. Customer 100–25 units of chlorine, 10 units of pool shock, and 5 units of pool algaecide. Customer 101–20 units of chlorine, 8 units of pool shock, and 4 units of pool algaecide. Customer 102–15 units of chlorine, 5 units of pool shock, and 2 units of pool algaecide. Customer 103–30 units of chlorine, 12 units of pool shock, and 7 units of pool algaecide. |

| Event # | Date | Business Event |
|---------|------|----------------|
| 9 | 10/31/12 | Paid all bills with a due date before 10/31/12 using checks 291 and 292. |
| 10 | 10/31/12 | Paid employees with checks 293 and 294 (see below for detail). |

| Pay/Tax/Withholding | Patrick | Singh |
|---------------------|---------|-------|
| Hours | 160 | 150 |
| Rate | $   18.00 | $   20.00 |
| Gross pay | 2,880.00 | 3,000.00 |
| Federal withholding | 394.56 | 411.00 |
| Social Security employee | 178.56 | 186.00 |
| Medicare employee | 41.76 | 43.50 |
| State withholding | 115.20 | 120.00 |
| Social Security employer | 178.56 | 186.00 |
| Medicare company | 41.76 | 43.50 |
| Federal unemployment | 23.04 | 24.00 |
| State unemployment | 115.20 | 120.00 |
| Check amount | 2,149.92 | 2,239.50 |

## Requirements

Create a Peachtree file for Crystal Clear Pool Service. Modify the company name to include Ch 7 at the end so that the company name is **Crystal Clear Pool Service Ch 7**. Change the system date to **10/1/12** and the accounting period to **Period 1**. Add vendors, inventory items, customers, and employees first and then record business transactions in chronological order (remember that dates are in the month of October 2012). After you've printed the following reports (for the month of October 2012, with no page numbers and no zero amounts), create a backup of this file and store it on some type of external medium (flash drive, Internet site, CD, disk, etc.). The backup file should be named **Crystal Clear Pool Service Ch 7** for easy identification later. You'll be restoring this file in Chapter 11.

a.   General ledger trial balance

b.   Customer ledger

c.   Vendor ledger

d.   Employee list

e.   Item list

f.   Standard balance sheet

g.   Standard income statement

h.   Statement of cash flows

i.   Find transactions report

# Additional Business Activities

8

## Learning Objectives

*In this Chapter, you will:*

- Record additional business transactions classified as financing activities, such as repayment of loans.
- Record additional business transactions classified as investing activities, such as selling short-term investments for a gain or loss.
- Record additional business transactions classified as operating activities, such as purchasing and selling inventory on account.
- Record business transactions classified as noncash investing and financing activities, such as the purchase of equipment with long-term debt.

## *Case:* Wild Water Sports, Inc.

You and Karen have finished entering business events that took place during the months of January and February and are ready to begin recording transactions for March. Karen explains that so far the transactions entered have involved cash-related financing activities such as owner contributions; cash-related investing activities such as equipment purchases; and cash-related operating activities such as creating purchase orders, receipt of customer payments, cash sales, making deposits, receiving inventory, payment of purchases, invoicing time and costs, payment of expenses, accounting for employees' time, and payment of payroll.

In March and April, the company had similar business events to record in addition to some new ones. During these months, the company entered into some additional cash-related financing activities such as the payment of loans, additional cash-related investing activities such as the sale of short-term investments, and additional cash-related operating activities such as the purchase and sale of inventory on account and the related payment and receipt of those transactions. Further, the company entered into some noncash investing and financing activities when it purchased some equipment with long-term debt.

Karen suggests that you work through these transactions for March, paying particular attention to those you haven't encountered yet.

# Recording Additional Financing Activities

*Video Demonstration*

*Demo 8A - Recording the payment of a loan*

You recall that as of December 31, 2012, the company had a long-term liability of $383,800. Then, in January, the company borrowed an additional $250,000 from the Bank of Florida, which was due in five years and carried a 5% interest cost.

"When do we make payments on those loans?" you ask.

"Our agreement on the $250,000 loan with the Bank of Florida called for monthly payments of $4,717.81 beginning February 4," Karen answers. "I was so busy with Peachtree and the business that I completely forgot! I wrote two checks yesterday to cover our first two payments, and the bank has been kind enough to waive the late payment fee."

The company also borrowed an additional $50,000 from CitiBank on February 5. Payments on that loan are due annually. The loan payable of $383,800 has payments due July 1 of every year.

**To record the checks written to make payment on the Bank of Florida loan:**

1  Start the Peachtree program.

2  Restore the **Wild Water Sports, Inc. 8** file from your Data Files CD or download it from the Internet. See "Restoring Peachtree Backup Files from Your CD" in Chapter 1 if you need more information.

3  Set the system date to **3/1/13** and the accounting period to **Period 3**.

4  Click **Write Checks** from the Banking center and then select **New Check**. The Write Checks window appears with your current system date.

5  Type **1029** as the Check Number. The bank had provided a loan amortization schedule as shown in Figure 8.1.

**Figure 8.1**

Loan Amortization Schedule

| Month | Payment | Interest | Principal | Balance |
|---|---|---|---|---|
| | | | | $250,000.00 |
| 1 | $4,717.81 | $1,041.67 | $3,676.14 | $246,323.86 |
| 2 | $4,717.81 | $1,026.35 | $3,691.46 | $242,632.40 |
| 3 | $4,717.81 | $1,010.97 | $3,706.84 | $238,925.56 |
| 4 | $4,717.81 | $ 995.52 | $3,722.29 | $235,203.27 |
| 5 | $4,717.81 | $ 980.01 | $3,737.79 | $231,465.48 |
| 6 | $4,717.81 | $ 964.44 | $3,753.37 | $227,712.11 |
| 7 | $4,717.81 | $ 948.80 | $3,769.01 | $223,943.10 |
| 8 | $4,717.81 | $ 933.10 | $3,784.71 | $220,158.39 |
| 9 | $4,717.81 | $ 917.33 | $3,800.48 | $216,357.91 |
| 10 | $4,717.81 | $ 901.49 | $3,816.32 | $212,541.59 |
| 11 | $4,717.81 | $ 885.59 | $3,832.22 | $208,709.37 |
| 12 | $4,717.81 | $ 869.62 | $3,848.19 | $204,861.19 |

**6**   Click the magnifying glass in the Vendor ID text box and then click **New**.

**7**   Type **11025** as the new Vendor ID, **Bank of Florida** as the Name and **2700**—Long-Term Debt—Noncurrent as the Expense Account. Click **Save** and then click **Close**.

**8**   Select **11025** as the Vendor ID in the Write Checks window for your Check No. 1029.

**9**   Type **4717.81** as the check amount.

**10**   Click the **Split** button in the lower left-hand corner of the check.

**11**   Accept **2700** as the Account No. and then press **[Tab]** two times.

**12**   Type **3676.14** as the new amount for this row.

**13**   Press **[Tab]** two times again to move to the beginning of the next row and the Account No. column.

**14**   Click the magnifying glass in this text box and then click **New** to open the Maintain Chart of Accounts window.

**15**   Type **6725** as the new Account ID and type **Interest Expense** as the Description.

**16**   Select **Expenses** from the Account Type drop-down list.

**17**   Click **Save** and then click **Close** to close the Maintain Chart of Accounts window.

**18**   Press **[Tab]** two times. Your Split Transaction window should look like Figure 8.2.

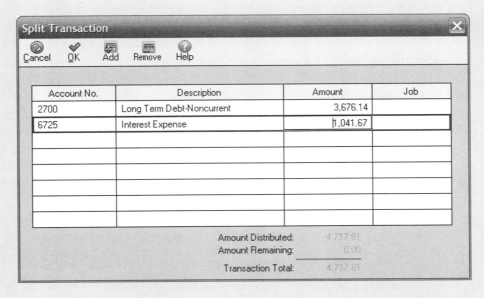

**Figure 8.2**

Splitting Transactions between Accounts

**19**   Click **OK** to close the Split Transaction window. Your check should look like Figure 8.3.

**Figure 8.3**

Check to Pay Installment on
Long-Term Debt

If your check affects multiple accounts you would click this
Split button to reveal the Split Transactions window

**20**  Click **Save** to record the check.

**21**  Using the amortization schedule in Figure 8.1, enter information for
Check No. 1030, on the same date, to record the second payment
using the interest expense and principal information provided. (*Note:*
This transaction will have the same check amount but different interest expense and debt reduction.)

**22**  Click **Save** and then **Close** to record the check.

With the addition of a new owner, and the related funds received from the
new owner's investment, the company decided to pay down the older, higher interest 10% debt with the Bank of Orlando. It made a payment of $387,690.58,
which accounted for interest at 10% for 37 days ($3,890.58), and paid the princi-
pal balance due of $383,800. Before the company made this payment, it decided
to transfer $300,000 from its short-term investment account with ETrade to its
Bank of Florida checking account. Karen suggests you try recording this transfer made with ETrade Check No. 101 and the loan payment that was made on
3/6 with Check No. 1031.

**To record the electronic transfer of funds and record payment
on a loan:**

**1**  Click **Write Checks** from the Banking center and then select **New
Check**. The Write Checks window appears with your current system
date. Note that the default Cash Account is 1020 (Checking Account).

**2**  Click the magnifying glass in the Cash Account text box and select **1030 Short-Term Investments**.

**3**  Type **101** as the Check Number and **3/6/13** as the date.

**4**  Select **11025** – Bank of Florida as the Vendor ID.

**5**  Type **300000** as the check amount.

**6**  Select **1020** as the Expense Account. (In reality, this is not an expense account but the account we want to record this transaction to.) Your check should look like Figure 8.4.

**Figure 8.4**

Check to Transfer Funds from Short-Term Investments to Checking

**7**  Click **Save**.

**8**  Click the magnifying glass in the Cash Account text box and select **1020 Checking Account**.

**9**  Type **1031** as the Check Number and **3/6/13** as the date.

**10**  Create a new vendor with ID 11030, Bank of Orlando, default Expense Account 2700.

**11**  Select **11030** – Bank of Orlando as the Vendor ID.

**12**  Type **387690.58** as the check amount.

**13**  Click the **Split** button in the lower left-hand corner of the check.

**14**  Type **2700** as the Account No. and then press **[Tab]** two times.

**15**  Type **383800** as the new amount for this row.

**16**  Press **[Tab]** two times again to move to the beginning of the next row and the Account No. column.

**17**  Type **6725** as the Account No. and then press **[Tab]** two times.

**18**   **3890.58** should appear as the new amount for this row. Your Split Transaction window should look like Figure 8.5.

**Figure 8.5**

Split of Bank of Orlando Debt Repayment

Select Account No. here

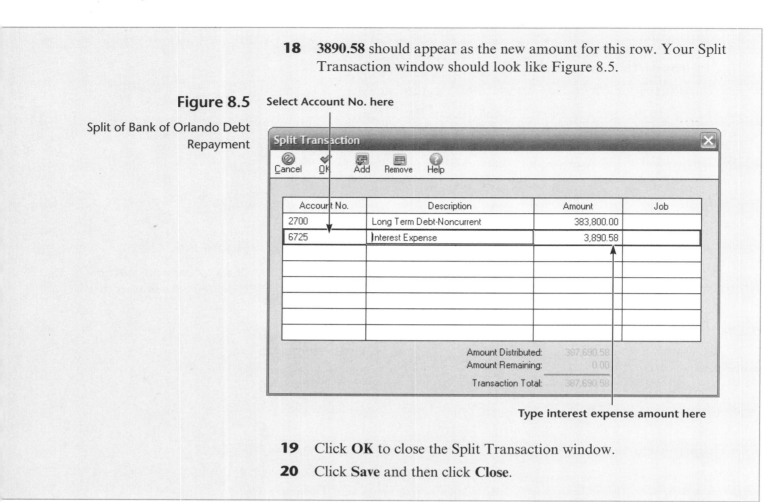

Type interest expense amount here

**19**   Click **OK** to close the Split Transaction window.

**20**   Click **Save** and then click **Close**.

You have now recorded payments of long-term debt. Now it's time to look at some additional investing activities.

## Recording Additional Investing Activities

You may recall from your accounting courses that investing activities generally result in the acquisition of noncurrent assets from buying or selling investment securities or productive equipment. Wild Water Sports engaged in several investing activities that you and Karen need to record in March. The company made some additional short-term investments, and it sold previously purchased investment securities for a profit.

In February, Wild Water Sports made an investment with ETrade for $75,000. On March 7, it sold that investment for a profit of $3,000. All funds were retained with ETrade. In addition, it used $35,000 of those money market funds to purchase stock in Apple Computer, again as a short-term investment.

"These types of transactions are best recorded with a general journal entry," Karen says. "Although the $3,000 gain is a receipt of cash, Peachtree's receipts process is reserved for prepayments, cash sales of products or services, or payments on account."

"So is this just like the recording of loan or stock sale proceeds?" you ask.

"Exactly," Karen answers.

*Video Demonstration*

*Demo 8B - Recording the sale of short-term investments*

---

## To record short-term investment activity:

**1**  Click **General Journal Entry** from the **Tasks** menu.

**2**  Type **3/7/13** as the date and type **5** as the Reference.

**3**  Select **1030** as the first GL Account, type **Sale of investments for a gain** as the Description, and then type **3000** as the Debit amount.

**4**  Select **7100** as the second GL Account, leave **Sale of investments for a gain** in the Description, and then type **3000** as the Credit amount.

**5**  Click **Save** and then click **Close**.

**6**  Click **Account Register** from the Banking center.

**7**  Change the Cash Account to **1030 Short-Term Investments**.

**8**  Note that the transaction you just recorded may not be shown. That transaction was recorded on 3/7/13, but your system date is 3/1/13. Thus, Peachtree may not show you any transactions after that date.

**9**  Select **This Year** from the drop-down text box labeled Show transactions for: Your window should look like Figure 8.6.

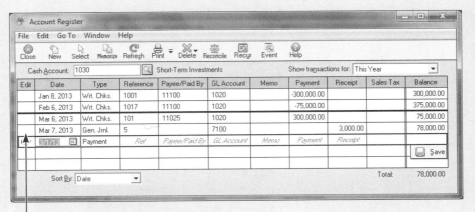

**Figure 8.6**

Account Register

All transactions for the year should now be shown

**10**  Close the Account Register window.

"Why didn't we record the Apple Computer stock purchase in our records?" you ask.

"Well, remember that the funds used to purchase this stock were already in our short-term investment account," Karen answers. "Thus, this is just a reallocation of our short-term investment from a money market category to a stock category. We, as shareholders, consider both the money market funds and the stock investment to be short-term investments; thus, we don't differentiate them in the accounting records."

# Recording Additional Operating Activities

Donna has been working hard establishing credit with the company's suppliers. Recently, she's convinced Malibu, MB Sports, and Tige to give Wild Water 15-day credit terms with a credit limit of $70,000. Several purchase orders have been created to acquire more inventory for the company's showroom and to purchase inventory ordered by some new customers.

"Now that we have some credit with our suppliers, we'll be able to offer credit to some of our better customers," Karen points out. Now that the company has secured a 15-day credit line with Malibu, MB, and Tige, vendor information in Peachtree needs to be updated. Karen demonstrates the process of modifying vendor information for terms.

**To update vendor records for changes in terms:**

**1**    Click the **Vendors** button in the Vendors & Purchases center and then click **View and Edit Vendors**.

**2**    Double-click **Malibu Boats** to open the Edit Vendor window.

**3**    Click the **Purchase Info** tab.

**4**    Click the **Terms & Credit** arrow and select **Customize terms for this vendor**.

**5**    Type **15** in the Net due in text box and then type **70000** as the credit limit. See Figure 8.7.

**Figure 8.7**

Adjusting Vendor Terms

Click here to change terms

Terms and Credit

Customize terms for this vendor

○ C.O.D.
○ Prepaid
◉ Due in number of days
○ Due on day of next month
○ Due at end of month

☐ Use discounts

Discount in    0    days
Discount Percent:    0.00

Net due in    15    days

Credit Limit:    70,000.00

**Type 15 here**                            **Type 70,000 here**

**6** Click **Save** to save this vendor's updated information and then click Close to close the Malibu Boats Maintain Vendors window.

**7** Perform this same process for MB Sports and Tige.

**8** Close all open windows.

Karen suggests that you now input the purchase orders created in March and the related bills received from suppliers.

**To record purchase orders for the month of March:**

**1** Click the **Vendors** button in the Vendors & Purchases center and then click **View and Edit Vendors**.

**2** Double-click **Malibu Boats** to open the Maintain Vendor window.

**3** Type **1 Malibu Ct., Merced, CA 95340** as this vendor's address and then click **Save**.

**4** Close the Maintain Vendors and Vendor List windows.

**5** Click **Purchase Orders** from the Vendors & Purchases center and then select **New Purchase Order**.

**6** Enter purchase order information as shown in Figure 8.8.

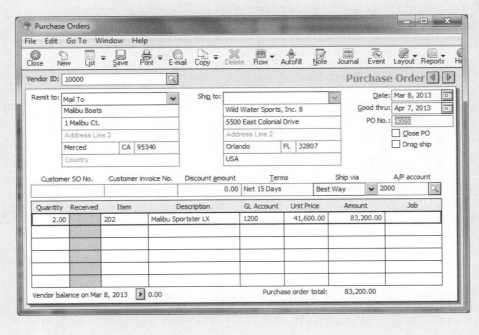

**Figure 8.8**

Malibu Purchase Order No. 4005

**7** Click **Save**.

8    Create and save Purchase Order No. 4006 to Tige Boats on 3/12/13 ordering one Tige 22v (Item 301) and one Tige 24v (a new stock item with ID 302, a Last Unit Cost of $70,000, and a Price Level 1 of $87,500 using the average cost method and cost of goods sold and income accounts as for all other boats).

9    Create and save Purchase Order No. 4007 to MB Sports on 3/12/13 ordering 1 MB 220V (a new stock item with ID 402, a Last Unit Cost of $52,000, and a Price Level 1 of $65,000 using the same cost method and a cost of goods sold and income accounts as all other boats) for a new customer (ID 50010, Spirit Adventures, 500 Butterfly Lake Rd., Fort Lauderdale, FL 33308, using the standard terms and credit). Create this new customer and sales order 105 assuming the customer will pick up the boat when it arrives. This customer is subject to normal Florida sales taxes.

10   Close all windows.

Some of the boats ordered on the purchase orders entered above were received in the month of March. Since these were all ordered on account, Peachtree requires that you record the receipt of inventory at the same time you record the receipt of the bill invoicing the company for payment. In addition, boats ordered with Purchase Order No. 4004 issued in February were received in March.

### ✈ To record receipt of inventory and bill:

1    Click **Receive Inventory** from the Inventory & Services center and then select **Receive Inventory**.

2    Select **10000** as the Vendor ID.

3    Select Purchase Order No. **4004** from the Apply to Purchase Order No. drop-down list.

4    Type **3/6/13** as the date.

5    Type **MB23987** as the Invoice No.

6    Type **1** in the Received column for both boats ordered.

7    Select **Best Way** from the Ship Via drop-down list and then click **Save**.

8    Select **10000** as the Vendor ID.

9    Select Purchase Order No. **4005** from the Apply to Purchase Order No. drop-down list.

10   Type **3/15/13** as the date.

11   Type **MB24002** as the Invoice No.

12   Type **2** in the Received column.

13   Select **Best Way** from the Ship Via drop-down list and then click **Save**.

14   Select **10200** as the Vendor ID.

**15**   Select Purchase Order No. **4006** from the Apply to Purchase Order No. drop-down list.

**16**   Type **3/28/13** as the date.

**17**   Type **T02398** as the Invoice No.

**18**   Type **1** in the Received column for both boats ordered.

**19**   Select **Best Way** from the Ship Via drop-down list, click **Save**, and then click **Close**.

Two service-related jobs (3006 and 3007) were started and completed in the month of March. Both were to customers who were invoiced for the work and given 15-day credit terms. Karen explains that in both of these cases, jobs need to be created, time recorded, and invoices generated. First off, she suggests that you update credit terms for two existing customers.

## To update customer terms and address:

**1**   Click **Customers & Sales**, click **Customers**, and then select **View and Edit Customers**.

**2**   Double-click **Buena Vista Water Sports**.

**3**   Type **100 Disney Way, Orlando, FL 31310** as the customer's address.

**4**   Click the **Payment & Credit** tab.

**5**   Select **Customize terms for this customer** from the Terms & Credit drop-down box and then change the Terms to Net due in **15** days, click **Save**, and then click **Close**.

**6**   Change the Terms to Net due in **15** days for Performance Rentals as well. Then change its credit limit to **$10,000**.

**7**   Click **Save** and then click **Close**.

**8**   Close the Customer List as well.

Next, you need to create the jobs (for tracking purposes) and assign jobs to customers.

## To create new jobs:

**1**   Click **Customers & Sales**, click **Jobs**, and then select **New Job**.

**2**   Type **3006** as the Job ID and then type or select **50002** in the For Customer text box.

**3** Click **Save**.

**4** Create a second new job 3007 for customer 50006.

**5** Close the Maintain Jobs window.

Karen explains that as employees work on various jobs, time must be entered and assigned to a job or customer, and an activity must always be specified.

### To enter employee time on jobs:

**1** Open the Employees & Payroll center, click **Time and Expense Tickets**, and then select **New Weekly Timesheet**.

**2** Select **003** Ryder Zacovic as the Employee ID.

**3** Type **3/11/13** in the Week Including text box.

**4** Enter the information shown in Figure 8.9.

**Figure 8.9**

Ryder Zacovic Time Tickets for the Week Including 3/11/13

Select Employee 003

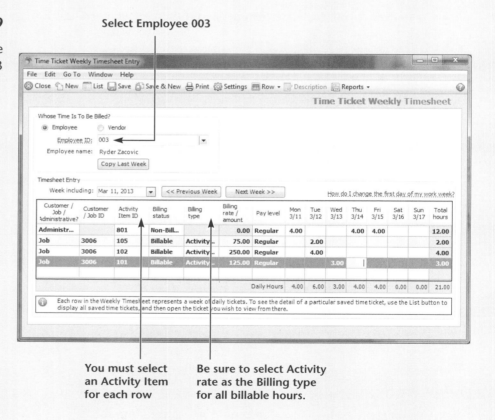

You must select an Activity Item for each row

Be sure to select Activity rate as the Billing type for all billable hours.

**5**  Click **Save & New**.

**6**  Enter the information shown in Figure 8.10.

Select Employee 003

**Figure 8.10**

Ryder Zacovic Time Tickets for the Week Including 3/18/13

You must select an Activity Item for each row

Be sure to select Activity rate as the Billing type or all billable hours.

**7**  Click **Save** and then **Close**.

"Now that the jobs are complete and time has been charged to a job, it's time to bill the customer for work performed and parts used," Karen explains.

"Do we use sales orders for service activities?" you ask.

"I guess we can," Karen responds. "But for now I just use sales orders to record customer orders for boats to be delivered in the future."

---

## To invoice customers for job-related work:

**1**  Open the Customers & Sales center.

**2**  Click **Sales Invoices** and then select **New Sales Invoice**.

**3**  Select **50002** Buena Vista Water Sports from the Customer ID list.

**4**  Type **3/19/13** as the invoice date.

**5**  Type **10010** as the Invoice No.

**6**  Click the **Apply Tickets/Expenses** button.

**7** Check the **Use** check box for all items presented, select **No Consolidation** from the Consolidate By drop-down text box, and then select the **Use Item Description for Invoicing** option button as shown in Figure 8.11.

### Figure 8.11

Applying Tickets to an Invoice

Select the Use check boxes here

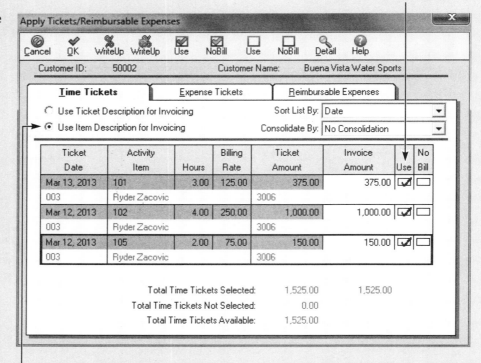

Click in this option button

**8** Click **OK** to close the window and apply information to the invoice.

**9** Add the Ship Via information and tune-up parts, engine oil, air filter, and oil filter to the invoice as shown in Figure 8.12.
*Trouble?* You may have to increase the window size to view all of the line items for this invoice.

**10** Click **Save**.

**11** Select **50006** Performance Rentals from the Customer ID list.

**12** Type **3/26/13** as the invoice date.

**13** Type **10008** as the Invoice No.

**14** Click the **Apply Tickets/Expenses** button.

**15** Check the **Use** check box for all four items presented and then select **Activity Item** from the Consolidate By list as shown in Figure 8.13.

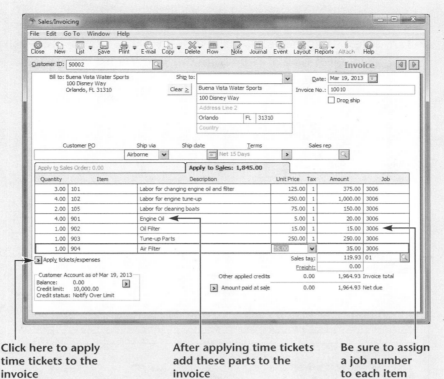

**Figure 8.12**

Invoice for Service and Parts

**Click here to apply time tickets to the invoice**

**After applying time tickets add these parts to the invoice**

**Be sure to assign a job number to each item**

**Select Activity Item as the Consolidate By option**

**Figure 8.13**

Apply Time Tickets

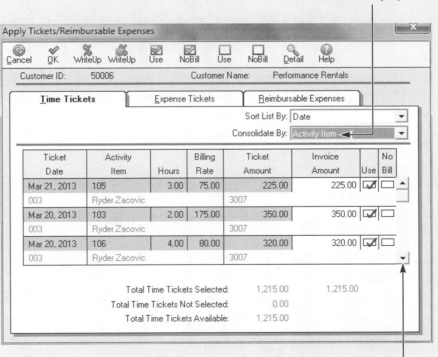

**Be sure to select all four time tickets for this employee that apply to this job. Scroll down the window to see 1 additional time ticket not shown here.**

**16** Click **OK** to accept this time ticket application.

**17** Select **01** as the Sales Tax code, and 3007 as the Job for each item, and then select **Cust. Pickup** from the Ship Via list. Your invoice should look like Figure 8.14.

**Figure 8.14**

Performance Rentals
Invoice 10008

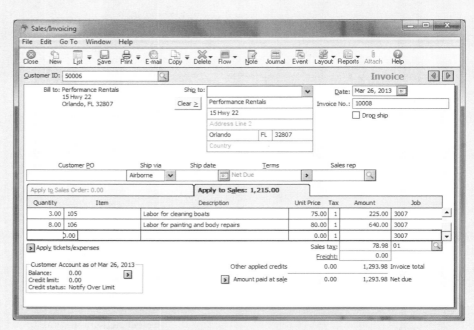

**18** Click **Save** and then click **Close**. (Click **Yes** to allow customer to go over its credit limit.)

There was one cash boat purchase during the month to a new customer, Sonia Garcia. She purchased a Malibu Vride off the showroom floor on March 12 for $51,120 using Check No. 8593, including sales tax.

## To record a cash sale and deposit cash received:

**1** Click **Receive Money** from the Customers & Sales center and then select **Receive Money from Customer**.

**2** Type **11** as the Deposit Ticket ID since this amount was deposited at the same time as the product was sold.

**3** Create a new customer: 50011 Sonia Garcia with cash terms, i.e., no credit (check the **C.O.D.** option and put a **0** in the Credit Limit box).

**4** Select **50011** as the Customer ID for this cash receipt.

**5** Type **8593** in the Reference text box as the customer's check number.

**6** Type **SR0010** in the Receipts text box.

**7** Type **3/12/13** as the date received.

**8** Select **Check** as the payment method.

**9** Click on the **Apply to Revenues** tab.

**10** Type **1** as the Quantity sold.

**11** Select **204** from the drop-down list of items.

**12** Type **01** as the Sales Tax code. Your screen should look like Figure 8.15.

**Figure 8.15**

Cash Sale to Sonia Garcia

**13** Click **Save** and then click **Close**.

Three invoices were generated in the month of March for boat sales. One, to Fantasy Sports (Sales Order 104), was invoiced with Invoice 10011 and represented an order received during the month for which Fantasy had already paid a deposit. Upon Fantasy's request, Donna approved net 30 credit terms on the balance owed and the temporary increase in credit. The other two were sales from the showroom floor: on account on Invoices 10012 and 10013, respectively.

"How do we know when to accept an over-the-credit-limit situation?" you ask.

## To record invoices from the sale of boats on account and apply deposits received:

**1** Click **Sales Invoices** from the Customers & Sales center and then click **New Sales Invoice**.

**2** Select **50009** Fantasy Sports from the Customer ID list.

**3** Type **3/7/13** as the invoice date.

*Video Demonstration*

*Demo 8C - Recording invoices and applying payments*

**4**   Type **10011** as the Invoice No.

**5**   Select **104** from the Apply to Sales Order No. list.

**6**   Type **1** in the Shipped column for both Items 203 and 204.

**7**   Click **Save** to save this invoice. Click **Yes** to allow the sale to be recorded, even though it exceeds the customer's credit limit. (*Note:* This is a temporary increase as future sales will still be limited to the standard $65,000 credit limit.)

**8**   Click the **back arrow** in the Sales/Invoicing window until you see the Invoice 10011 you just created.

**9**   Click on the **arrow** button next to the Customer Account section in the lower-left corner of the invoice.

**10**  Click the **Options** button in the button bar, change the range of dates for the Customer Ledger that appears to **1/1/13 to 3/31/13**, and then click **OK**.

**11**  Double-click the transaction reported on **2/6/13** to bring up the receipt you recorded in February when Fantasy Sports paid its $28,250 deposit.

**12**  Uncheck the **Prepayment** check box.

**13**  Click the **Apply to Invoices** tab and then type **28250** in the Amount Paid column, and then press **[Tab]** as shown in Figure 8.16.

**Figure 8.16**

Applying a Deposit to an Invoice

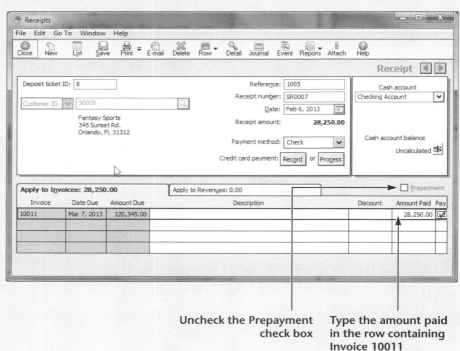

Uncheck the Prepayment check box

Type the amount paid in the row containing Invoice 10011

**14**  Click **Save** and then click **Yes** when asked if it is okay to record a transaction in a different period. Then click **Close**.

**15** Click **Close** again to close the customer ledger.

**16** Click the **back arrow** in the Sales/Invoicing window and then click the **forward arrow** until you see the Invoice 10011 you just adjusted. It should look like Figure 8.17. (Note the Other Applied Credits amount of 28,250 shown at the bottom of the invoice indicating the deposit has been applied to this invoice.)

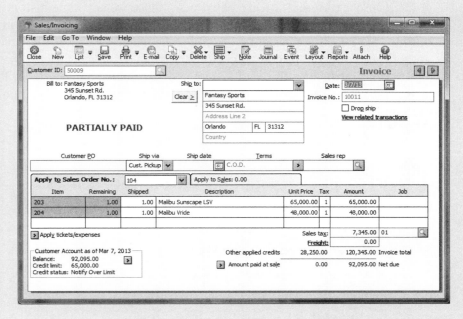

**Figure 8.17**

Modified Invoice after Applying Deposit

**17** Click **New**.

**18** Select **50004** Freebirds from the Customer ID list.

**19** Type **3/23/13** as the invoice date.

**20** Type **10012** as the Invoice No.

**21** Select **Cust. Pickup** from the Ship Via list.

**22** Type **2** in the Quantity column and select **203** as the Item.

**23** Select **01** as the Sales Tax code and then click **Save** to save this invoice. Note that in this case no sales order was created since the boats were on hand and did not need to be ordered from the supplier.

**24** Click **Yes** to accept the over-the-credit-limit notification.

**25** Change the terms for customer 50005 Florida Sports Camp to the default terms of net **30** and **$65,000** credit limit.

**26** Return to the Sales/Invoicing window and select **50005** Florida Sports Camp from the Customer ID list.

**27** Type **3/23/13** as the invoice date.

**28** Type **10013** as the Invoice No.

**29** Select **Cust. Pickup** from the Ship Via list.

**30** Type **1** in the Quantity column and select **301** as the Item.

**31**   Select **01** as the Sales Tax code and then click **Save** to save this invoice.

**32**   Click **Yes** to accept the over-the-credit-limit notification.

**33**   Click **Close**.

"Each case is different," Karen answers. "Once we get some history of good payment from a customer, we will permanently change its credit limit. In the meantime, the Peachtree system will remind us when we exceed the credit limit we established for each individual customer."

At the end of the month, Wild Water Sports received a check from Performance Rentals for $10,000 as a deposit toward the purchase of a boat on its showroom floor.

### To record receipt of deposit from Performance Rentals:

**1**   Open the Customers & Sales center, click **Receive Money**, and then select **Receive Money from Customer**.

**2**   Type **12** as the Deposit Ticket ID.

**3**   Type **8774** as the check number received in the Reference text box.

**4**   Select **50006** Performance Rentals from the Customer ID list.

**5**   Type **SR0011** in the Receipt Number text box.

**6**   Type **3/31/13** as the date.

**7**   Check the **Prepayment** check box.

**8**   Type **10000** as the amount. Your receipt should look like Figure 8.18.

**Figure 8.18**

Deposit on Sale

**9**   Click **Save** and then click **Close**.

"When do we get around to paying the bills and collecting cash from these invoices?" you ask.

"It's important to pay bills on a timely basis to keep your suppliers happy and keep our good credit," Karen answers. "First off, we can view what bills are outstanding and when they are due and then choose which to pay and when."

## To choose which bills to pay and pay bills.

**Video Demonstration**

*Demo 8D - Paying bills*

**1**   Set the system date to **3/31/13**.

**2**   Click **Analysis** from the menu and then select **Payment Manager**.

**3**   Click the **Bracket** button from the button bar.

**4**   Select **Total** from the Days Past Due drop-down list. See Figure 8.19.

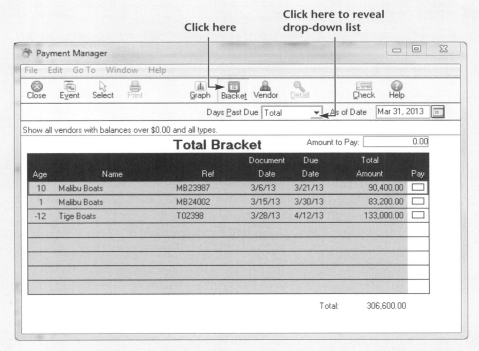

**Figure 8.19**

Payment Manager

**5**   Note that the oldest bill you have is to Malibu Boats for $90,400. You decide to pay this bill only. Close the Payment Manager window.

**6**   Open the Vendors & Purchases center, click **Pay Bills**, and then select **Pay Bill**.

**7**   Type **1032** as the check number.

**8**   Type **3/22/13** as the payment date.

**9**   Select Vendor ID **10000** Malibu Boats.

**10**  Place a check in the **Pay** column on the row containing the $90,400 amount. Your screen should look like Figure 8.20.

**Figure 8.20**

Payment to Malibu Boats

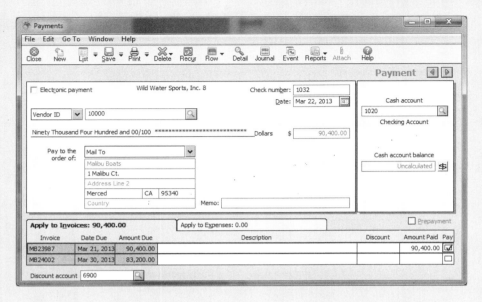

**11**  Click **Save** and then click **Close**.

Karen explains that by using the Payment Manager, you could have selected more bills to be paid and actually printed and recorded the checks right there. However, you are currently hand-writing checks so you used the Payment Manager just to see what bills were due, hand-wrote the check, and then used the Pay Bills feature to record the check written.

"We also collected two payments from customers on account in March," Karen says. "Orlando Water Sports paid us $5,300.00 on 3/21, and Buena Vista paid us $1,964.93 on 3/29."

### To record cash collections on account and related deposits:

**1**  Open the Customers & Sales center, click **Receive Money**, and then select **Receive Money from Customer**.

**2**  Select **50001** Orlando Water Sports as the Customer ID.

**3**  Type **9152** as the Reference and **SR0012** as the Receipt Number.

**4**  Type **3/22/13** as the date received.

**5**  Select **Check** as the Payment Method.

**6**  Place a check in the **Pay** column of the row containing Invoice 906 for $5,300. Your screen should look like Figure 8.21.

**Figure 8.21**

Receipt from Orlando Water Sports

**7**  Click **Save**.

**8**  Select **50002** Buena Vista Water Sports as the Customer ID.

**9**  Type **741** as the Reference and **SR0013** as the Receipt Number.

**10**  Type **3/29/13** as the date received.

**11**  Select **Check** as the Payment Method.

**12**  Place a check in the **Pay** column of the row containing Invoice 10010 for $1,964.93.

**13**  Click **Save** and then click **Close**.

**14**  Click **Bank Deposits** from the Customers & Sales center and then select **New Bank Deposit**.

**15**  Select the two deposits shown in the Select for Deposit window.

**16**  Type **3/29/13** as the deposit date.

**17**  Confirm **13** as the Deposit Ticket ID.

**18**  Click **Save** and then click **Close** to record the deposit and close the window.

"In addition to paying bills from vendors for merchandise purchased, the company also has to pay its sales tax and payroll tax obligations," Karen reminds you. "Before we can do that and pay the rest of our end-of-the-month bills and payroll, we'll need to transfer some funds from our short-term investment account at ETrade to our checking account."

Karen offers to make the electronic transfer of $40,000 from ETrade to the Bank of Florida, and you agree to record the accounting effect of that transfer and record checks to pay the sales tax and payroll tax obligations.

## To record the transfer of funds:

**1** From the Tasks menu, click **General Journal Entry**.

**2** Create the journal entry shown in Figure 8.22.

**Figure 8.22**

Journal Entry to Transfer Funds from ETrade

| Date: Mar 29, 2013 | ☐ Reverse Transaction | | | | |
|---|---|---|---|---|---|
| Reference: 6 | | | | | |
| GL Account | Description | Debit | Credit | Job | |
| 1020 | To record the transfer of funds from ETrade | 40,000.00 | | | |
| 1030 | To record the transfer of funds from ETrade | | 40,000.00 | | |
| | | | | | |
| | | | | | |
| | | | | | |
| | | | | | |
| | | | | | |
| | | | | | |
| | | | | | |
| | | | | | |
| | Totals: | 40,000.00 | 40,000.00 | | |
| | Out of Balance: | 0.00 | | | |

**3** Click **Save** and then click **Close**.

"How do we know how much to pay in sales and payroll taxes?" you ask.

"Peachtree doesn't have a quick way to determine that," Karen answers, "but we plan on paying the sales and payroll tax obligations with monthly deposits based on reports available in Peachtree. In March, we will pay amounts owing for the two months ended in February, but in April we will pay amounts owing from March, etc. For sales taxes, we'll use the Taxable/Exempt Sales report to identify the amount of sales taxes collected and owed. For payroll taxes, we'll use the Payroll Register report to identify the amount of taxes withheld from employees and the amount of taxes we owe as an employer."

**Video Demonstration**

**Demo 8E - Paying sales and payroll tax liabilities**

## To pay sales tax and payroll tax obligations owed as of 2/28/13:

**1** Click **Reports & Forms** and then click **Accounts Receivable**.

**2** Scroll down the list of reports and double-click **Taxable/Exempt Sales**.

**3** Click the **Options** button, type **1/1/13** as the From date, type **2/28/13** as the To date, and then click **OK**. See Figure 8.23.

**Wild Water Sports, Inc. 8**
**Taxable / Exempt Sales**
**For the Period From Jan 1, 2013 to Feb 28, 2013**

Filter Criteria includes: Report is printed in Summary Format.

| Sales Tax Agency | Sales Tax Agency Name | Tax Rate | Taxable Sale | Tax Amount | Exempt Sales | Total Sales |
|---|---|---|---|---|---|---|
| Florida | State of Florida | 6.50000 | 336,985.00 | 21,904.04 | | 336,985.00 |
| Florida | Total State of Florida | | 336,985.00 | 21,904.04 | | 336,985.00 |

**Figure 8.23**

Sales Tax Liability

**4**  Click **Print** and then click **OK** to print the report. Note the liability amount of $21,904.04 as we'll write that check in a minute.

**5**  Click **Close** to close the report.

**6**  From the Select a Report or Form window (which should still be open), click **Payroll**, and then double-click **Payroll Register**.

**7**  Click the **Options** button, type **1/1/13** as the From date, type **2/28/13** as the To date, and then click **OK**.

**8**  Scroll to the bottom of the report to see the summary total as shown in Figure 8.24.

**This is the Fed_Unemp_C (Federal Unemployment Taxes for the Employer)**

**Figure 8.24**

Payroll Register 1/1/13 to 2/28/13

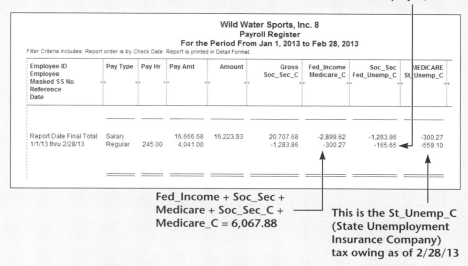

**Wild Water Sports, Inc. 8**
**Payroll Register**
**For the Period From Jan 1, 2013 to Feb 28, 2013**

Filter Criteria includes: Report order is by Check Date. Report is printed in Detail Format.

| Employee ID Employee Masked SS No Reference Date | Pay Type | Pay Hr | Pay Amt | Amount | Gross Soc_Sec_C | Fed_Income Medicare_C | Soc_Sec Fed_Unemp_C | MEDICARE St_Unemp_C |
|---|---|---|---|---|---|---|---|---|
| Report Date Final Total 1/1/13 thru 2/28/13 | Salary Regular | 245.00 | 16,666.68 4,041.00 | 16,223.93 | 20,707.68 -1,283.86 | -2,899.62 -300.27 | -1,283.86 -165.65 | -300.27 -559.10 |

**Fed_Income + Soc_Sec + Medicare + Soc_Sec_C + Medicare_C = 6,067.88**

**This is the St_Unemp_C (State Unemployment Insurance Company) tax owing as of 2/28/13**

**9**  Click **Print** and then click **OK** to print the report. Note the liability amount as we'll also write that check in a minute.

**10**  Click **Close** to close the report.

**11**  Close the Select a Report or Form window as well.

**12**  From the Banking center, click **Write Checks**, and then select **New Check**.

**13**  Type **1033** as the Check Number.

**14**  Type **3/29/13** as the date.

**15**  Type **12000** as the Vendor ID.

16 Type **21904.04** as the amount.

17 Type **2310** Sales Tax Payable (it should already be there) as the Expense Account (even though this is not an expense account).

18 Click **Save**.

19 Type **1034** as the Check Number (it should already be there).

20 Type **3/29/13** as the date.

21 Type **12000** as the Vendor ID.

22 Type **559.10** as the amount. (*Note:* This amount came from the Payroll Register in Figure 8.24.)

23 Type **2360** SUTA Payable as the Expense Account.

24 Click **Save**.

25 Type **1035** as the Check Number (it should already be there).

26 Type **3/29/13** as the date.

27 Add U.S. Treasury as a new vendor with Vendor ID = 12100 and default expense account = 2330 Federal Payroll Taxes Payable.

28 Type **12100** as the Vendor ID.

29 Type **6233.53** as the amount.

30 Click the **Split** button to split the distribution of this check amount into two accounts. Type the accounts and amounts as shown in Figure 8.25. Note the amounts come from Figure 8.24.

**Figure 8.25**

Split Transaction Detail

31 Click **OK**, click **Save**, and then click **Close** to close the Write Checks window.

"How can we be sure the correct amounts were paid?" you ask.

"Well, we can verify ending balances by looking in the general ledger," Karen answers. "Let's take a look."

## To verify sales tax and payroll tax amounts have been recorded:

**1** Click **Reports & Forms**, and then click **General Ledger**.

**2** Double-click **General Ledger** from the list of reports available.

**3** Click the **Options** button, and then select **Period Range** from the Time Frame drop-down list.

**4** Select **Period 1 (1/1/13)** in the From drop-down list and **Period 3 (3/31/13)** in the To drop-down list.

**5** Click **OK**.

**6** Scroll down to account 2310 Sales Tax Payable as shown in Figure 8.26.

Ending balance for February

**Figure 8.26**

Account 2310 from the General Ledger

**Wild Water Sports, Inc. 8**
**General Ledger**
**For the Period From Jan 1, 2013 to Mar 31, 2013**
Filter Criteria includes: Report order is by ID. Report is printed with shortened descriptions and in Detail Format.

| Account ID Account Description | Date | Reference | Jrnl | Trans Description | Debit Amt | Credit Amt | Balance |
|---|---|---|---|---|---|---|---|
| 2310 | 1/1/13 | | | Beginning Balance | | | |
| Sales Tax Payable | 1/18/13 | 161 | CRJ | Seth Blackman - St | | 3,380.00 | |
| | 1/29/13 | 10001 | SJ | Florida Sports Ca | | 4,550.00 | |
| | 1/30/13 | 10002 | SJ | Performance Rent | | 5,118.75 | |
| | 1/30/13 | 10003 | SJ | Alisa Hay - State of | | 10.73 | |
| | 1/31/13 | 10004 | SJ | Freebirds - State of | | 54.93 | |
| | 1/31/13 | 10005 | SJ | Florida Sports Ca | | 102.38 | |
| | | | | Current Period Ch | | 13,216.79 | -13,216.79 |
| | 2/1/13 | | | Beginning Balance | | | -13,216.79 |
| | 2/3/13 | 10006 | SJ | Orlando Water Spo | | 81.25 | |
| | 2/8/13 | 232 | CRJ | Walking on Water - | | 3,705.00 | |
| | 2/10/13 | 10007 | SJ | Alisa Hay - State of | | 26.00 | |
| | 2/20/13 | 10009 | SJ | Performance Rent | | 4,875.00 | |
| | | | | Current Period Ch | | 8,687.25 | -8,687.25 |
| | 3/1/13 | | | Beginning Balance | | | -21,904.04 |
| | 3/7/13 | 10011 | SJ | Fantasy Sports - St | | 7,345.00 | |
| | 3/12/13 | 8593 | CRJ | Sonia Garcia - Stat | | 3,120.00 | |
| | 3/19/13 | 10010 | SJ | Buena Vista Water | | 119.93 | |
| | 3/23/13 | 10012 | SJ | Freebirds - State of | | 8,450.00 | |
| | 3/23/13 | 10013 | SJ | Florida Sports Ca | | 5,118.75 | |
| | 3/26/13 | 10008 | SJ | Performance Rent | | 78.98 | |
| | 3/29/13 | 1033 | CDJ | Florida Departmen | 21,904.04 | | |
| | | | | Current Period Ch | 21,904.04 | 24,232.66 | -2,328.62 |
| | 3/31/13 | | | Ending Balance | | | -24,232.66 |

Payment made in March

**7** Note that the ending balance on 2/28/13 equals the payment made in March.

**8** Scroll down to account 2330 Federal Payroll Taxes and note the 0 current balance as shown in Figure 8.27.

**Figure 8.27**

Partial View of Account 2330 from the General Ledger

| Account ID Account Description | Date | Reference | Jrnl | Trans Description | Debit Amt | Credit Amt | Balance |
|---|---|---|---|---|---|---|---|
| | 1/31/13 | 1014 | PRJ | Pat Ng | | 60.26 | |
| | 1/31/13 | 1014 | PRJ | Pat Ng | | 60.26 | |
| | | | | Current Period Ch | | 2,990.86 | -2,990.86 |
| | 2/1/13 | | | Beginning Balance | | | -2,990.86 |
| | 2/28/13 | 1025 | PRJ | Donna Chandler | | 258.33 | |
| | 2/28/13 | 1025 | PRJ | Donna Chandler | | 60.42 | |
| | 2/28/13 | 1025 | PRJ | Donna Chandler | | 463.00 | |
| | 2/28/13 | 1025 | PRJ | Donna Chandler | | 60.42 | |
| | 2/28/13 | 1025 | PRJ | Donna Chandler | | 258.33 | |
| | 2/28/13 | 1026 | PRJ | Karen Wilson | | 258.33 | |
| | 2/28/13 | 1026 | PRJ | Karen Wilson | | 60.42 | |
| | 2/28/13 | 1026 | PRJ | Karen Wilson | | 258.33 | |
| | 2/28/13 | 1026 | PRJ | Karen Wilson | | 60.42 | |
| | 2/28/13 | 1026 | PRJ | Karen Wilson | | 710.00 | |
| | 2/28/13 | 1027 | PRJ | Ryder Zacovic | | 13.70 | |
| | 2/28/13 | 1027 | PRJ | Ryder Zacovic | | 13.70 | |
| | 2/28/13 | 1027 | PRJ | Ryder Zacovic | | 58.59 | |
| | 2/28/13 | 1027 | PRJ | Ryder Zacovic | | 129.47 | |
| | 2/28/13 | 1027 | PRJ | Ryder Zacovic | | 58.59 | |
| | 2/28/13 | 1028 | PRJ | Pat Ng | | 17.75 | |
| | 2/28/13 | 1028 | PRJ | Pat Ng | | 75.89 | |
| | 2/28/13 | 1028 | PRJ | Pat Ng | | 17.75 | |
| | 2/28/13 | 1028 | PRJ | Pat Ng | | 75.89 | |
| | 2/28/13 | 1028 | PRJ | Pat Ng | | 167.69 | |
| | | | | Current Period Ch | | 3,077.02 | -3,077.02 |
| | 3/1/13 | | | Beginning Balance | | | -6,067.88 |
| | 3/29/13 | 1035 | CDJ | U.S. Treasury - Fe | 6,067.88 | | |
| | | | | Current Period Ch | 6,067.88 | | 6,067.88 |
| | 3/31/13 | | | **Ending Balance** | | | |

**Wild Water Sports, Inc. 8**
**General Ledger**
**For the Period From Jan 1, 2013 to Mar 31, 2013**
Filter Criteria includes: Report order is by ID. Report is printed with shortened descriptions and in Detail Format.

Note the 0 ending balance as the payment (check 1035) equaled the beginning balance

**9**  Scroll down to accounts 2340 FUTA and 2360 SUTA Payable, also noting the 0 current balances.

**10** Click **Close** to close the General Ledger report.

**11** Close the Select a Report or Form window as well.

It's important to note that Florida does not have a state income tax and thus no state income tax is withheld. Employers must pay state unemployment taxes (SUTA), which is all that is reflected here. In other states, where state income taxes are withheld, the company will be required to withhold state income taxes and then remit them periodically.

"All that is left for March is for us to record checks written for expenses and to record payroll," Karen states. "Our expenses are about the same each month, so you shouldn't see too much variation in what you did the last two months. We didn't have much in the way of service this month, and so Pat didn't work and Ryder just worked the hours we recorded earlier."

## To record end-of-the-month expenses:

1  Click **Write Checks** from the Banking center, and then select **New Check**.

2  Type **1036** as the Check Number.

3  Type **3/30/13** as the date.

4  Select **11600** Central Florida Gas & Electric as the Vendor ID.

5  Type **1050** as the amount.

6  Note that account **6400** should already be selected from the Account drop-down list. If it is not, select it now.

7  Click **Save**.

8  Type **1037** as the Check Number if it is not already there.

9  Type **3/30/13** as the Check Date if it is not already there.

10  Select **11700** Verizon as the Vendor ID.

11  Type **1500** as the amount.

12  Note that account **6500** should already be selected from the Account drop-down list. If it is not, select it now.

13  Click **Save**, and then click **Close**.

## To record end-of-the-month payroll:

1  Click **Pay Employees** from the Employees & Payroll center, and then select **Enter Payroll for One Employee**.

2  Type **1038** as the Check Number.

3  Type **3/31/13** as the Check Date and **3/31/13** as the Pay Period Ends date.

4  Enter the following payroll information. (*Note:* Pat Ng did not work this period.)

|  | Employee | | |
| Tax or Withholding | Chandler | Wilson | Zacovic |
| --- | --- | --- | --- |
| Check Number | 1038 | 1039 | 1040 |
| Earnings | 4,166.67 | 4,166.67 | 600.00 |
| Federal Withholding | −463.00 | −710.00 | −82.20 |
| Social Security Employee | −258.33 | −258.33 | −37.20 |
| Medicare Employee | −60.42 | −60.42 | −8.70 |
| Social Security Company | 258.33 | 258.33 | 37.20 |
| Medicare Company | 60.42 | 60.42 | 8.70 |
| Federal Unemployment | 33.33 | 33.33 | 4.80 |
| FL Unemployment Company | 112.50 | 112.50 | 16.20 |
| Check Amount | 3,384.92 | 3,137.92 | 471.90 |

5  When you are finished, close the Payroll Entry window.

# Recording Noncash Investing and Financing Activities

Although noncash investing and financing activities do not affect the cash position of a company, they do have an impact on a firm's financial position. One example of such an activity was Wild Water Sports' purchase of computer equipment in March that was completely financed with long-term debt (a $5,000 note payable to Staples with no interest and no payment due until 10/1/13). Karen explains the nature of this transaction to you and demonstrates how it should be recorded.

## To record the purchase of equipment with long-term debt:

**1**   From the Tasks menu, click **General Journal Entry**.

**2**   Create the journal entry shown in Figure 8.28.

**Figure 8.28**

Journal Entry to Record the Purchase of Equipment in Exchange for a Note Payable

Date: Mar 31, 2013    ☐ Reverse Transaction
Reference: 7

| GL Account | Description | Debit | Credit | Job |
|---|---|---|---|---|
| 1500 | Purchase of equipment for note payable | 5,000.00 | | |
| 2700 | Purchase of equipment for note payable | | 5,000.00 | |
| | | | | |
| | | | | |
| | | | | |
| | | | | |
| | | | | |
| | | | | |
| | | | | |
| | | | | |
| | Totals: | 5,000.00 | 5,000.00 | |
| | Out of Balance: | 0.00 | | |

**3**   Click **Save** and then click **Close**.

# Evaluate a Firm's Performance and Financial Position

Once again, the best way to evaluate a firm's performance and financial position at this point is to generate an income statement and balance sheet. Karen suggests you do this for the entire three months ending March 31, 2013 (the first quarter of 2013), and prepare a find transactions report like you did last month.

## To prepare a standard income statement and a balance sheet for March:

**1** Set the system date to **3/31/13**.

**2** From the Reports & Forms menu, click **Financial Statements.**

**3** Double-click <**Standard**> **Income Statement** from the Select a Report or Form window.

**4** Uncheck the **Print Page Numbers** and **Show Zero Amounts** check boxes.

**5** Click **OK** to view the income statement for March as shown in Figure 8.29.

**Figure 8.29**

Income Statement for March 2013

Wild Water Sports, Inc. 8
Income Statement
For the Three Months Ending March 31, 2013

| | Current Month | | | Year to Date | |
|---|---|---|---|---|---|
| **Revenues** | | | | | |
| Sales Income | $    369,750.00 | 99.18 | $ | 702,500.00 | 98.97 |
| Service Income | 2,740.00 | 0.73 | | 6,685.00 | 0.94 |
| Parts Income | 320.00 | 0.09 | | 610.00 | 0.09 |
| | | | | | |
| Total Revenues | 372,810.00 | 100.00 | | 709,795.00 | 100.00 |
| | | | | | |
| **Cost of Sales** | | | | | |
| Cost of Sales | 296,056.00 | 79.41 | | 562,488.00 | 79.25 |
| | | | | | |
| Total Cost of Sales | 296,056.00 | 79.41 | | 562,488.00 | 79.25 |
| | | | | | |
| Gross Profit | 76,754.00 | 20.59 | | 147,307.00 | 20.75 |
| | | | | | |
| **Expenses** | | | | | |
| Wages Expense | 8,933.34 | 2.40 | | 29,641.02 | 4.18 |
| Payroll Tax Expense | 996.06 | 0.27 | | 3,304.94 | 0.47 |
| Utilities Expense | 1,050.00 | 0.28 | | 2,870.00 | 0.40 |
| Telephone Expense | 1,500.00 | 0.40 | | 5,020.00 | 0.71 |
| Other Office Expense | 0.00 | 0.00 | | 4,500.00 | 0.63 |
| Advertising Expense | 0.00 | 0.00 | | 2,700.00 | 0.38 |
| Interest Expense | 5,958.60 | 1.60 | | 5,958.60 | 0.84 |
| Gain/Loss - Sale of Assets Exp | (3,000.00) | (0.80) | | (3,000.00) | (0.42) |
| | | | | | |
| Total Expenses | 15,438.00 | 4.14 | | 50,994.56 | 7.18 |
| | | | | | |
| Net Income | $    61,316.00 | 16.45 | $ | 96,312.44 | 13.57 |

**6** Click **Print** from the button bar and then **OK** to print this statement.

**7** Click **Close**.

**8** Double-click <**Standard**> **Balance Sheet** from the Select a Report or Form window.

**9** Make sure the **Print Page Numbers** and **Show Zero Amounts** check boxes are unchecked.

**10** Click **OK** to view the balance sheet for March as shown in Figures 8.30 and 8.31.

**Figure 8.30**

Assets Section of the Balance Sheet as of March 31, 2013

Wild Water Sports, Inc. 8
Balance Sheet
March 31, 2013

ASSETS

| Current Assets | | |
|---|---|---|
| Checking Account | $ 47,392.43 | |
| Short-Term Investments | 38,000.00 | |
| Accounts Receivable | 320,707.73 | |
| Inventory | 295,600.00 | |
| Inventory Parts | 2,112.00 | |
| Prepaid Expenses | 46,000.00 | |
| | | |
| Total Current Assets | | 749,812.16 |
| | | |
| Property and Equipment | | |
| Property and Equipment | 295,000.00 | |
| Accum. Depreciation - Prop&Eqt | (7,500.00) | |
| | | |
| Total Property and Equipment | | 287,500.00 |
| | | |
| Other Assets | | |
| | | |
| Total Other Assets | | 0.00 |
| | | |
| Total Assets | $ | 1,037,312.16 |

**Figure 8.31**

Liabilities and Capital Section of the Balance Sheet as of March 31, 2013

Wild Water Sports, Inc. 8
Balance Sheet
March 31, 2013

LIABILITIES AND CAPITAL

| Current Liabilities | | |
|---|---|---|
| Accounts Payable | $ 216,200.00 | |
| Sales Tax Payable | 24,232.66 | |
| Federal Payroll Taxes Payable | 2,622.00 | |
| FUTA Payable | 71.46 | |
| SUTA Payable | 241.20 | |
| | | |
| Total Current Liabilities | | 243,367.32 |
| | | |
| Long-Term Liabilities | | |
| Long Term Debt-Noncurrent | 297,632.40 | |
| | | |
| Total Long-Term Liabilities | | 297,632.40 |
| | | |
| Total Liabilities | | 540,999.72 |
| | | |
| Capital | | |
| Common Stock | 400,000.00 | |
| Net Income | 96,312.44 | |
| | | |
| Total Capital | | 496,312.44 |
| | | |
| Total Liabilities & Capital | $ | 1,037,312.16 |

**11** Click **Print** from the button bar and then **OK** to print this statement.

**12** Click **Close**.

## To prepare a find transactions report for March:

**1**  Click **Company Reports** from the Select a Report or Form window.

**2**  Double-click **Find Transactions Report**.

**3**  If your system date is still set at **3/31/13**, the report you get will only show you transactions recorded on 3/31/13. To change the report to reflect all transactions recorded in March 2013, click the **Options** button on the Report button bar.

**4**  Change the From date to **3/1/13** and then click **OK**.

**5**  Click **Print** from the Report button bar and then click **OK** to print. The report shown in Figure 8.32 should appear.

**6**  Click **Save**.

**7**  Type **Find Transactions Report 3/13** as the new name of the report and then click **Save**.

**8**  Click **Close** to close the report and then close the Select a Report or Form window.

## Figure 8.32

Find Transactions Report

**Wild Water Sports, Inc. 8**
**Find Transactions Report**
**For the Period From Mar 1, 2013 to Mar 31, 2013**
Filter Criteria includes: 1) All Transaction Types. Report order is by Date.

| Date | Type | Reference | ID | Name | Amount |
|------|------|-----------|-----|------|--------|
| 3/1/13 | Payment | 1029 | 11025 | Bank of Florida | 4,717.81 |
| 3/1/13 | Payment | 1030 | 11025 | Bank of Florida | 4,717.81 |
| 3/6/13 | Payment | 101 | 11025 | Bank of Florida | 300,000.00 |
| 3/6/13 | Payment | 1031 | 11030 | Bank of Orlando | 387,690.58 |
| 3/6/13 | Purchase | MB23987 | 10000 | Malibu Boats | 90,400.00 |
| 3/7/13 | General Journal Entry | 5 | | | 3,000.00 |
| 3/7/13 | Sale/Invoice | 10011 | 50009 | Fantasy Sports | 120,345.00 |
| 3/8/13 | Purchase Order | 4005 | 10000 | Malibu Boats | 83,200.00 |
| 3/11/13 | Time Ticket | 000042 | 003 | Ryder Zacovic | |
| 3/12/13 | Purchase Order | 4006 | 10200 | Tige Boats | 133,000.00 |
| 3/12/13 | Purchase Order | 4007 | 10100 | MB Sports | 52,000.00 |
| 3/12/13 | Receipt | 8593 | 50011 | Sonia Garcia | 51,120.00 |
| 3/12/13 | Sales Order | 1 | 50010 | Spirit Adventures | 69,225.00 |
| 3/12/13 | Time Ticket | 000045 | 003 | Ryder Zacovic | 150.00 |
| 3/12/13 | Time Ticket | 000046 | 003 | Ryder Zacovic | 1,000.00 |
| 3/13/13 | Time Ticket | 000047 | 003 | Ryder Zacovic | 375.00 |
| 3/14/13 | Time Ticket | 000043 | 003 | Ryder Zacovic | |
| 3/15/13 | Purchase | MB24002 | 10000 | Malibu Boats | 83,200.00 |
| 3/15/13 | Time Ticket | 000044 | 003 | Ryder Zacovic | |
| 3/19/13 | Sale/Invoice | 10010 | 50002 | Buena Vista Water Sports | 1,964.93 |
| 3/19/13 | Time Ticket | 000048 | 003 | Ryder Zacovic | 320.00 |
| 3/20/13 | Time Ticket | 000049 | 003 | Ryder Zacovic | 320.00 |
| 3/20/13 | Time Ticket | 000050 | 003 | Ryder Zacovic | 350.00 |
| 3/21/13 | Time Ticket | 000051 | 003 | Ryder Zacovic | 225.00 |
| 3/22/13 | Payment | 1032 | 10000 | Malibu Boats | 90,400.00 |
| 3/22/13 | Receipt | 9152 | 50001 | Orlando Water Sports | 5,300.00 |
| 3/22/13 | Time Ticket | 000052 | 003 | Ryder Zacovic | |
| 3/23/13 | Sale/Invoice | 10012 | 50004 | Freebirds | 138,450.00 |
| 3/23/13 | Sale/Invoice | 10013 | 50005 | Florida Sports Camp | 83,868.75 |
| 3/26/13 | Sale/Invoice | 10008 | 50006 | Performance Rentals | 1,293.98 |
| 3/28/13 | Purchase | T02398 | 10200 | Tige Boats | 133,000.00 |
| 3/29/13 | General Journal Entry | 6 | | | 40,000.00 |

**Wild Water Sports, Inc. 8**
**Find Transactions Report**
**For the Period From Mar 1, 2013 to Mar 31, 2013**
Filter Criteria includes: 1) All Transaction Types. Report order is by Date.

| Date | Type | Reference | ID | Name | Amount |
|------|------|-----------|------|------|--------|
| 3/29/13 | Payment | 1033 | 12000 | Florida Department of Revenue | 21,904.04 |
| 3/29/13 | Payment | 1034 | 12000 | Florida Department of Revenue | 559.10 |
| 3/29/13 | Payment | 1035 | 12100 | U.S. Treasury | 6,233.53 |
| 3/29/13 | Receipt | 741 | 50002 | Buena Vista Water Sports | 1,964.93 |
| 3/30/13 | Payment | 1036 | 11600 | Central Florida Gas & Electric | 1,050.00 |
| 3/30/13 | Payment | 1037 | 11700 | Verizon | 1,500.00 |
| 3/31/13 | General Journal Entry | 7 | | | 5,000.00 |
| 3/31/13 | Payroll Entry | 1038 | 001 | Donna Chandler | 3,384.92 |
| 3/31/13 | Payroll Entry | 1039 | 002 | Karen Wilson | 3,137.92 |
| 3/31/13 | Payroll Entry | 1040 | 003 | Ryder Zacovic | 471.90 |
| 3/31/13 | Receipt | 8774 | 50006 | Performance Rentals | 10,000.00 |
| | | | | **Report Total:** | **1,934,840.2** |
| | | | | **Number of Transactions:** 43 | |

**Figure 8.32**

Continued

"Not bad for our first three months," Karen comments. "But we still need to accrue some revenues and expenses, adjust some prepaid assets and unearned revenue, and record depreciation."

# End Note

You've now helped Karen understand even more of Peachtree's features, including how to record the repayment of loans, sale of investments, receipt of inventory items and related bills, credit sales, and the receipt of payments on account.

## Business Events Summary

| Business Event | Process Steps | Page |
|----------------|---------------|------|
| Pay loan | Use Write Checks from the Banking center | 246 |
| Transfer funds | Use Write Checks from the Banking center | 248 |
| Pay off loan | Use Write Checks from the Banking center | 248 |
| Sell investment | Use General Journal Entry from the Company center | 251 |
| Update vendor records | Use Vendors from the Vendors & Purchases center | 252 |
| Order inventory | Use Purchase Order from the Vendors & Purchases center | 253 |
| Receive inventory and bill | Use Receive Inventory from the Inventory & Services center | 254 |
| Update customer records | Use Customers from the Customers & Sales center | 255 |
| Create a new job | Use Jobs from the Customers & Sales center | 255 |
| Enter time information | Use Time and Expense Tickets from the Employees & Payroll center | 256 |

| Business Event | Process Steps | Page |
|---|---|---|
| Invoice customer for job-related work | Use Sales Invoices from the Customers & Sales center | 257 |
| Sell merchandise for cash | Use Receive Money from the Customers & Sales center | 260 |
| Sell merchandise on account | Use Sales Invoices from the Customers & Sales center | 261 |
| Apply deposits received | Use Sales Invoices from the Customers & Sales center | 261 |
| Receive deposits from customers | Use Receive Money from the Customers & Sales center | 264 |
| Pay bills | Use Payment Manager from the Analysis menu | 265 |
| Receive collections on account | Use Receive Money from the Customers & Sales center | 266 |
| Transfer funds between accounts | Use General Journal Entry from Company center | 268 |
| Determine sales and payroll tax liability | Print Taxable/Exempt Sales report and Payroll Register report | 268 |
| Pay sales and payroll taxes | Use Write Checks from the Banking center | 268 |
| Pay expenses | Use Write Checks from the Banking center | 273 |
| Pay employees | Use Pay Employees from the Employees & Payroll center | 273 |
| Purchase a fixed asset with long-term debt | Use General Journal Entry from the Company center | 274 |
| Evaluate a firm's performance | Use View All Financial Statements from the Company center | 275 |

## Chapter 8 Questions

**1** What information, contained in a loan amortization schedule, is part of the payment information recorded in Peachtree?

**2** How does a firm account for the transfer of funds from one bank to another bank in Peachtree?

**3** How do you update vendor records for changes in terms?

**4** Consider this statement: "Peachtree records revenue when an invoice is generated, even though cash has not been received." Is this practice acceptable? Why or why not?

**5** How do you record the receipt of inventory and the related bill in Peachtree?

**6** How is time accumulated on jobs?

**7** How did Wild Water know how much time to bill customers for service rendered?

**8** How does Peachtree warn you from recording a sale to a customer in excess of the customer's credit limit?

**9** What information does the Payment Manager provide?

**10** What are noncash investing and financing activities, and how are they recorded in Peachtree?

## Chapter 8 Exercises

### Chapter 8 Exercise 1
### FINANCING ACTIVITIES

Restore the file **Boston Catering Ch 8** found on the text CD or download it from the text website. Set the system date to **8/1/10** and the period to **Period 2 – 08/01/10–08/31/10**. Add the following transactions and then print a standard balance sheet as of 8/31/10.

a. On 8/2/10 the company wrote check #1509 to CitiBank (Vendor ID: CITI) for $926.29 as an installment on notes payable, $416.67 of which was for interest expense (Account ID: 527, Description: Interest, Type: Expense).

b. On 8/2/10 the company wrote check #1510 to Bank of America (Vendor ID: BA) for $610.32 as an installment on notes payable ($166.67 of which was for interest expense).

c. On 8/3/10 the company electronically transferred $20,000 from the Bank of America checking account to the short-term investments account.

*Chapter 8 Exercise 2*

## INVESTING ACTIVITIES

Restore the file **Boston Catering Ch 8** found on the text CD or download it from the text Website. Do *not* use the file created in Exercise 1 above. Set the system date to **8/1/10** and the period to **Period 2 – 08/01/10–08/31/10**. Add the following transactions and then print a standard balance sheet as of 8/31/10.

a.  On 8/6/10 the company purchased some additional equipment from a restaurant that closed the previous month. The equipment was valued at $10,000 for which the company signed a two-year 6% note payable to Evian Sprinter with no payment due until maturity.

b.  On 8/9/10 the company purchased furniture from Outlet Tool Supply for $1,000 using check 1511.

*Chapter 8 Exercise 3*

## OPERATING ACTIVITIES—PURCHASES AND PAYMENTS FROM/TO VENDORS

Restore the file **Boston Catering Ch 8** found on the text CD or download it from the text Website. Do *not* use the file created in the exercises above. Set the System date to **8/1/10** and the period to **Period 2 – 08/01/10–08/31/10**. Add the following transactions and then print a standard balance sheet as of 8/31/10.

a.  On 8/5/10 the company ordered 48 bottles of a new item (Item ID: W400) Vintage Brut from Domain Chandon (Vendor ID: DC), 1 California Drive, Yountville, CA 94599 terms net 30, on purchase order 104. This champagne costs $36 per bottle, sells for $48 per bottle, and uses the average cost method.

b.  On 8/6/10 the company paid a bill due US Food Service as of 7/30/10 assigning check number 1513.

c.  On 8/26/10 the company received the 48 bottles of item W400 from Domain Chandon along with invoice 23092 due in 30 days.

*Chapter 8 Exercise 4*

## OPERATING ACTIVITIES—EXPENSES AND SALES

Restore the file **Boston Catering Ch 8** found on the text CD or download it from the text Website. Do *not* use the file created in the exercises above. Set the system date to **8/1/10** and the period to **Period 2 – 08/01/10–08/31/10**. Add the following transactions and then print a standard balance sheet as of 8/31/10 and a standard income statement for the month ended 8/31/10.

a.  On 8/6/10 the company contracted with a new customer, Boston College (Customer ID: BC), terms net 15 that is subject to sales tax. The company anticipates many future catering engagements with this customer and thus created a new job (Job ID: 001, Description: Event 1).

b.  On 8/15/10 the company paid rent to New England Property Management on check 1513 for $3,000. (Be sure to record this as rent expense.)

c. On 8/16/10 the company contracted with MIT. The company anticipates many future engagements with this customer and thus created a new job (Job ID: 002, Description: Dean Bumble).

d. On 8/21/10 the company paid all bills due by 8/31/10 to Fiddlehead Cellars, Sanford Winery, and US Food Service using checks 1514–1516.

e. During the month of August Kyle Hain worked 10 hours and Amy Casey worked 9 hours on 8/15 during the Boston College Event 1 party as wait staff. Kyle worked 12 hours and Amy worked 10 hours on 8/29 during the MIT Dean Bumble party as wait staff. Otherwise they did not work. Payroll checks are issued on 8/31/10 starting with check #1517. Paycheck information is shown below. (*Note*: No premium is paid for overtime.)

| Pay/Tax/Withholding | Chambers | Hain | Casey |
|---|---|---|---|
| Hours | n/a | 22 | 19 |
| Rate | $0,000 | $ 16.00 | $ 18.00 |
| Gross pay | 4,166.67 | 352.00 | 342.00 |
| Federal withholding | 570.83 | 48.22 | 46.85 |
| Social Security employee | 258.33 | 21.82 | 21.20 |
| Medicare employee | 60.42 | 5.10 | 4.96 |
| MA withholding | 283.99 | 5.92 | 6.68 |
| Social Security employer | 258.33 | 21.82 | 21.20 |
| Medicare company | 60.42 | 5.10 | 4.96 |
| Federal unemployment | 33.33 | 2.82 | 2.74 |
| MA disability insurance | 0.42 | 0.04 | 0.03 |
| MA unemployment | 125.00 | 10.56 | 10.26 |
| Check amount | 2,993.10 | 270.94 | 262.31 |

f. On 8/15/10 the company catered the Boston College Event 1 party. On 8/16/10 the company invoiced Boston College using invoice number 1123. It used 30 bottles of W100 and served 150 heavy appetizers (A100). Authorization of an over-the-credit-limit sale was received.

g. On 8/29/10 the company catered the MIT Dean Bumble party. On 8/30/10 the company invoiced MIT using invoice number 1124. It used 45 bottles of W201 and served 200 light appetizers (A200). Authorization of an over-the-credit-limit sale was received. This is a taxable sale.

h. On 8/31/10 the company received a bill from US Food Service for $800 in food purchases on invoice 2349 for the Boston College event. A bill for the MIT party food purchases was expected next month.

i. On 8/31/10 the company paid sales tax due as of 8/31/10 using check 1520.

j. On 8/31/10 the company paid payroll liabilities due as of 7/31/10 using checks 1521 and 1522. (*Hint:* Boston Catering records all state and federal payroll tax payable into one account. State payroll taxes are paid to the Massachusetts Dept of Revenue and federal payroll taxes are paid to the IRS using Vendor ID: IRS. Use the payroll register report to determine amounts paid to each. Total of both checks should be $2,232.28.)

# Chapter 8 Assignments

## Chapter 8 Assignment 1

# ADDING MORE INFORMATION: WILD WATER SPORTS

Restore the file **Wild Water Sports, Inc. 8A** found on the text CD or download it from the text Website and then add the following business events in chronological order. Be sure to set the system date to **4/1/13** and the accounting period to **Period 4 – 04/01/13–04/30/13**.

| Event Number | Date | Business Event |
|---|---|---|
| 1 | 4/2/13 | Wrote Check No. 1041 for $4,717.81 as payment 3 on loan to the Bank of Florida. See loan amortization schedule in Figure 8.1 for interest and principal breakdown. |
| 2 | 4/3/13 | Received $92,095 as payment on account from Fantasy Sports on its Check No. 234 for Wild Water's Sales Receipt SR0014. |
| 3 | 4/5/13 | Deposited payment received from Fantasy Sports on Deposit Ticket ID 14. |
| 4 | 4/5/13 | Paid Malibu Boats bill by writing Check No. 1042 for $83,200. |
| 5 | 4/5/13 | Created Purchase Order No. 4008 to Tige to purchase one Tige 22v (item 301) and one Tige 24v (item 302) for showroom floor inventory to be shipped via Best Way. |
| 6 | 4/6/13 | Received one MB 220V and bill (Invoice MB23049) on Purchase Order No. 4007 from MB Sports. |
| 7 | 4/9/13 | Received $1,293.98 as payment on account from Performance Rentals on its Check No. 987 for Wild Water's Sales Receipt SR0015. |
| 8 | 4/9/13 | Accepted a new job (3008) to service a boat owned by Seth Blackman. |
| 9 | 4/12 through 4/16 | Pat Ng worked four hours on each day, April 12, 14, 15, and 16, doing office work. He worked two hours performing an engine service and three hours cleaning on Job No. 3008 on April 13, which were billed at the activity rate. |
| 10 | 4/9/13 | Recorded the sale of Apple Computer stock, originally purchased for $25,000 for a loss of $2,000 with journal entry 8. (Just record the loss as the proceeds remained in the short-term investments account.) |
| 11 | 4/12/13 | Deposited payment received from Performance Rentals using Deposit Ticket ID 15. |
| 12 | 4/12/13 | Created Invoice 10014 to Spirit Adventures to record sale of an MB 220V from sales order 105, terms net 30, for $69,225, including tax. Authorization for this over-the-credit-limit sale was received. |
| 13 | 4/13/13 | Created Invoice 10015 to Seth Blackman for service under Job No. 3008 and five quarts of oil, one air filter, and one oil filter, terms net 30, for $585.75, including tax. |
| 14 | 4/13/13 | Created Purchase Order No. 4009 to MB Sports to purchase one MB 220V (item 402) and one MB B52 V23 Team Edition (item 401) for showroom floor inventory shipped Best Way. |
| 15 | 4/14/13 | Received $83,868.75 as payment on account from Florida Sports Camp on its Check No. 8741 using sales receipt SR0016. |
| 16 | 4/15/13 | Deposited payment received from Florida Sports Camp using Deposit Ticket ID 16. |

| Event Number | Date | Business Event |
|---|---|---|
| 17 | 4/15/13 | Recorded the transfer of $20,000 from short-term investments to checking with journal entry 9. |
| 18 | 4/15/13 | Paid Tige Boats bill by writing Check No. 1043 for $133,000. |
| 19 | 4/19/13 | Accepted a new job (3009) to paint a boat owned by Fantasy Sports. |
| 20 | 4/19/13 | Ryder Zacovic worked six hours on each day, April 20 through April 23, which were nonbillable office work. He worked eight hours painting and repairing on Job No. 3009 on April 19, which are billed at the activity rate. |
| 21 | 4/19/13 | Created Invoice 10016 to High Flying Fun (a new customer with ID 50012 subject to Florida sales tax) to record sale of one Tige 24v (item 302) and one Malibu WakeSetter XTI (item 206), terms net 15 and a credit limit of $200,000, for customer pickup for a total of $167,737.50, including tax. |
| 22 | 4/19/13 | Created Sales Receipt SR0017 to Orlando Water Sports to record the sale of one Malibu Sunsetter LXi (item 201) in exchange for its Check No. 10005 in the amount of $63,900. |
| 23 | 4/19/13 | Deposited payment received from Orlando Water Sports using Deposit Ticket ID 17. |
| 24 | 4/20/13 | Created Invoice 10017 to Fantasy Sports for service under Job No. 3009 in the amount of $681.60. Authorization for this over-the-credit-limit sale was received. |
| 25 | 4/22/13 | Created Purchase Order No. 4010 to Malibu Boats to purchase one Malibu Sportster LX (item 202) for Freebirds, one Malibu Sunscape LSV (item 203) for Buena Vista Water Sports, and one Malibu WakeSetter VLX (item 205) and one Malibu Vride (item 204) for showroom floor inventory shipped via Best Way. Recorded sales order 106 for Freebirds and 107 for Buena Vista Water Sports, both for customer pickup on May 10. (*Note:* This sale is subject to sales tax.) |
| 26 | 4/22/13 | Received all items ordered on Purchase Order No. 4009 from MB Sports. Also received its Invoice MB234987. |
| 27 | 4/23/13 | Received all items ordered and bill on Purchase Order No. 4008 from Tige Boats. Also received its Invoice T023948. |
| 28 | 4/23/13 | Created Invoice 10018 to Half Moon Sports (a new customer with ID 50013 subject to Florida sales tax) to record sale of one MB 220V (item 402), terms net 15 and a credit limit of $75,000 for customer pickup. |
| 29 | 4/26/13 | Purchased another computer, printer, and other electronic equipment from Staples for $12,000, again completely financed with a note payable with no interest and no payment due until 11/1/14. Record this transaction using journal entry 10. |
| 30 | 4/27/13 | Created and printed a payroll register for the month of March. Paid payroll tax liabilities accrued as of 3/31/13 of $2,934.66 using Check No. 1044 to the Florida Department of Revenue for $241.20 and Check No. 1045 for $2,693.46 to the U.S. Treasury. (*Note:* Record the entire payment to the U.S. Treasury to Federal Payroll Taxes Payable even though some portion of the payment should be recorded to FUTA Payable.) |
| 31 | 4/27/13 | Paid sales tax liability as of 3/31/13 of $24,232.66 to the Florida Department of Revenue using Check No. 1046. |
| 32 | 4/27/13 | Wrote Check No. 1047 to Central Florida Gas & Electric for $1,250 for utilities expense. |
| 33 | 4/27/13 | Wrote Check No. 1048 to Verizon for $1,800 for telephone expense. |
| 34 | 4/27/13 | Wrote Check No. 1049 to Brian Szulczewski for $3,000 for advertising expense. |

| Event Number | Date | Business Event |
|---|---|---|
| 35 | 4/27/13 | Pat Ng performed four hours of office work each day (Monday–Friday) for the week of 4/1, and eight hours of office work each day (Monday–Friday) for the week of 4/22, in addition to the hours already recorded above. |
| 36 | 4/27/13 | Ryder Zacovic performed four hours of office work each day (Monday–Friday) for the week of 4/1, and eight hours of office work each day from 4/24 to 4/28, in addition to the hours already recorded above. |
| 37 | 4/30/13 | Received $681.60 as payment on account from Fantasy Sports on its Check No. 1874 using Wild Water's Sales Receipt SR0018. |
| 38 | 4/30/13 | Received $585.75 as payment on account from Seth Blackman on his Check No. 1547 using Wild Water's Sales Receipt SR0019. |
| 39 | 4/30/13 | Received $13,000 as a deposit from Freebirds on its Check No. 2514 toward the purchase of a Malibu Sportster LX ordered 4/22. (*Note*: Do not apply this amount to its existing balance). Use Wild Water's Sales Receipt SR0020. |
| 40 | 4/30/13 | Received $16,250 as a deposit from Buena Vista Water Sports on its Check No. 8742 toward the purchase of a Malibu Sunscape LSV ordered 4/22. Use Wild Water's Sales Receipt SR0021. |
| 41 | 4/30/13 √ | Deposited $30,517.35 of checks received 4/30 into checking account using Deposit Ticket ID 18. |
| 42 | 4/30/13 | Process payroll per the information provided in Table 8.1 starting with Check No. 1050. (Be sure to change the pay period date.) |

### Table 8.1

Payroll Information for Wild Water Sports

| | Employee | | | |
|---|---|---|---|---|
| Tax or Withholding | Donna | Karen | Ryder | Pat |
| Check Number | 1050 | 1051 | 1052 | 1053 |
| Earnings | 4,166.67 | 4,166.67 | 1,380.00 | 1,458.00 |
| Federal Withholding | −463.00 | −710.00 | −189.06 | −199.75 |
| Social Security Employee | −258.33 | −258.33 | −85.56 | −90.40 |
| Medicare Employee | −60.42 | −60.42 | −20.01 | −21.14 |
| Social Security Company | 258.33 | 258.33 | 85.56 | 90.40 |
| Medicare Company | 60.42 | 60.42 | 20.01 | 21.14 |
| Federal Unemployment | 0 | 0 | 11.04 | 11.66 |
| State Unemployment | 0 | 0 | 37.26 | 39.37 |
| Check Amount | 3,384.92 | 3,137.92 | 1,085.37 | 1,146.71 |

Print the following with no page numbers and no zero amounts and with the accounting period set to **Period 4:**

a.   Standard income statement

b.   Standard balance sheet

c.   Find transactions report for the period April 1 through April 30, 2013

*Chapter 8 Assignment 2*

# ADDING MORE INFORMATION: CENTRAL COAST CELLULAR

Restore the file **Central Coast Cellular Ch 8** found on the text CD or download it from the text Website. Change the system date to **1/1/09** and the accounting period to **Period 1 – 01/01/09–01/31/09**. Add the following business events:

| Event Number | Date | Business Event |
|---|---|---|
| 1 | 1/20/09 | The company received a shipment of phones from Nokia on Purchase Order No. 102. Items were received and Invoice 209387 was recorded due in 30 days. |
| 2 | 1/21/09 | The company invoiced the City of San Luis Obispo, using Invoice 10001 for 20 Nokia 8290 phones, 15 Nokia 8890 phones, 30 hours of consulting time, and 35 commissions earned on cell phone contracts (cell phone contracts is a new service item ID = COM, name = Commissions, valued at $50 per contract, and recorded to a new income account titled Commissions, ID = 4050). |
| 3 | 1/22/09 | The company purchased equipment in the amount of $95,000 cash from Kyle Equipment, Inc. (a new vendor with ID = KYLE) using Check No. 3008. (*Hint:* This is equipment, a long-lived asset, and thus you need to record this purchase as an asset to Account 1500.) |
| 4 | 1/24/09 | The company paid the Ericsson bill of $6,500 with Check No. 3009. |
| 5 | 1/31/09 | The company paid the semimonthly payroll starting with Check No. 3010 for the period of January 16 to January 31, 2009. Megan Paulson worked 85 hours during the period. Payroll tax information is shown in Table 8.2. |

| | Employee | | |
|---|---|---|---|
| Tax or Withholding | Rodriguez | Bruner | Paulson |
| Check Number | 3010 | 3011 | 3012 |
| Gross Pay/Hours | $2,000.00 | $1,500.00 | 85 |
| Federal Withholding | −300.00 | −225.00 | −153.00 |
| Social Security Employee | −124.00 | −93.00 | −63.24 |
| Medicare Employee | −29.00 | −21.75 | −14.79 |
| CA – Withholding | −100.00 | −75.00 | −51.00 |
| CA – Disability Employee | −10.00 | −7.50 | −5.10 |
| Social Security Company | 124.00 | 93.00 | 63.24 |
| Medicare Company | 29.00 | 21.75 | 14.79 |
| Federal Unemployment | 6.40 | 4.80 | 3.26 |
| CA – Unemployment (SUI) | 24.00 | 18.00 | 12.24 |
| California Employee Training Tax | 2.00 | 1.50 | 1.02 |
| Check Amount | 1,437.00 | 1,077.75 | 732.87 |

**Table 8.2**

Payroll Information for Central Coast Cellular

Print the following with no page numbers and no zero amounts:

a. Standard income statement for the one month ending January 31, 2009

b. Standard balance sheet as of January 31, 2009

c. Find transactions report for the period January 20 through January 31, 2009

service

## Chapter 8 Assignment 3

# ADDING MORE INFORMATION: SANTA BARBARA SAILING

Restore the file **Santa Barbara Sailing Ch 8** found on the text CD or download it from the text Website and then add the following business events after you set the system date to **7/1/12:**

| Event Number | Date | Business Event |
|---|---|---|
| 1 | 7/17/12 | Deposited three checks that had been collected earlier in the week into the checking account using Deposit Ticket ID 3 for a total of $20,243.60. |
| 2 | 7/17/12 | Hired a new employee, Jack Sparrow (ID: JS), to serve as a charter boat captain. Jack is single and earns $25 per hour but is billed out to customers at $50 per hour (a new activity item, ID: Charter, description: Charter Boat Captain, with a new income type account, ID: 4020, description: Charter Income). His Social Security number is 999-23-8722, and his address is 1 Black Pearl Road, Montecito, CA 93109. He is paid semimonthly like all employees, but his time is all billable to customers. Maximum billing is eight hours per day. |
| 3 | 7/18/12 | Borrowed an additional $50,000 from the Bank of the Caribbean at 7% interest due in monthly installments over the next three years. Deposited these funds directly into the company's checking account. Use JE #2. |
| 4 | 7/18/12 | Collected a $5,000 deposit from Raytheon on its MasterCard (Ref. 9852) as deposit on a charter with Captain Jack Sparrow using the CAT 50 for 10 days. The company's policy for credit customers is to collect a deposit in advance and then bill customers when they return. Raytheon is given net 15 terms. Deposited this advance the same day on Deposit Ticket ID 4. |
| 5 | 7/21/12 | Rented the CAT 42 to a new customer, Santa Barbara News-Press (ID: 104, located at 715 Anacapa Street, Santa Barbara, CA 93101), for one week, terms net 15. Collected a $2,500 check (Check No. 0932) as deposit, which was deposited into the bank the next day. The company's policy for credit customers is to collect a deposit in advance and then bill customers when they return. |
| 6 | 7/21/12 | Rented the CAT 28 to Deckers for seven days using Sales Receipt 10005 and collected Visa payment (Ref. 3241) for $1,663.20. |
| 7 | 7/22/12 | Deposited Santa Barbara News-Press and Deckers amounts on Deposit Ticket ID 5. |
| 8 | 7/25/12 | Rented the CAT 32 to a new customer, Barry Cohen (ID: 105, located at 398 Alameda Padre Serra, Santa Barbara, CA 93105, terms: C.O.D.), for 14 days using Sales Receipt 10006 and collected MasterCard payment (Ref. 2344) for $4,158.00. |
| 9 | 7/27/12 | Captain Jack returns in the evening with the Raytheon charter and records his 10 days of work at eight hours per day from 7/18/12 to 7/27/12. |
| 10 | 7/30/12 | Paid utilities expenses of $1,500 to Edison (new vendor with ID: 204) using Check No. 107. |
| 11 | 7/30/12 | Paid telephone expenses of $1,200 to Verizon (new vendor with ID: 205) using Check No. 108. |

| Event Number | Date | Business Event |
|---|---|---|
| 12 | 7/30/12 | Paid maintenance and repairs expenses of $3,000 to Harbor Marineworks (new vendor with ID: 206, located at 122 Harbor Way, Santa Barbara, CA 93109) using Check No. 109. |
| 13 | 7/30/12 | The company bills Raytheon for 10 days of Charter Boat Captain and 10 days of CAT 50 use, terms net 30, using Invoice 7002. Applied deposit received to this invoice. (Be sure to combine hours into one line item on the invoice.) Received authorization for an over-the-credit-limit taxable sale. |
| 14 | 7/30/12 | Made a payment of $2,940.93 to Bank of America (new vendor with ID: 207) with Check No. 110 as an installment on the long-term note payable of $264,900. ($1,324.50 of this payment represented interest expense, a new expense account with ID: 6180.) |
| 15 | 7/31/12 | Received a $3,400 bill from Creative Resource Group (a new vendor with ID 208) on its Invoice 320, for advertising services provided in July. Terms net 30. (*Hint:* Use Enter Bills to record this transaction. Payment is not made until next month.) |
| 16 | 7/31/12 | Paid employees for the period 7/16/12–7/31/12. Nathan Snyder and Jeanne Wine worked 33 and 42 hours, respectively, during that period. Jack Sparrow has already recorded his timesheet. Start with Check No. 111. Payroll tax information is shown in Table 8.3. |

**Table 8.3**

Payroll Information for Santa Barbara Sailing

| | Employee | | | |
|---|---|---|---|---|
| Tax or Withholding | Dutton | Wine | Snyder | Sparrow |
| Wage | 2,708.33 | 756.00 | 264.00 | 2,000.00 |
| Federal Withholding | −514.58 | −143.64 | −50.16 | −380.00 |
| Social Security Employee | −167.92 | −46.87 | −16.37 | −124.00 |
| Medicare Employee | −39.27 | −10.96 | −3.83 | −29.00 |
| CA – Income Tax | −216.67 | −60.48 | −21.12 | −160.00 |
| CA – Disability | −16.25 | −4.54 | −1.58 | −12.00 |
| Check Amount | 1,753.64 | 489.51 | 170.94 | 1,295.00 |
| Social Security Employer | 167.92 | 46.87 | 16.37 | 124.00 |
| Medicare Employer | 39.27 | 10.96 | 3.83 | 29.00 |
| Federal Unemployment | 21.67 | 6.05 | 2.11 | 16.00 |
| CA – Unemployment | 92.08 | 25.70 | 8.98 | 68.00 |
| CA Employment Training Tax | 2.71 | 0.76 | 0.26 | 2.00 |

Print the following as of 7/31/12 with no page numbers and no zero amounts:

a. Standard income statement

b. Standard balance sheet

c. Standard statement of cash flows

d. Find transactions report for the period 7/17/12 through 7/31/12

*sole proprietorship*

*service*

## Chapter 8 Cases

### *Chapter 8 Case Problem 1*
## FOREVER YOUNG

In Chapter 7, you added some business events to your file for **Forever Young**. Make a copy of that file and use that copy to enter the following business events after you set the system date to **1/1/08**:

| Event Number | Date | Business Event |
|---|---|---|
| 1 | 1/16/08 | Sebastian ran into an old friend, Larry Rice, at one of his speaking engagements and decided to hire Larry to speak with him at selected events. Larry agreed to work on an hourly basis at $500 per hour and Sebastian planned to bill Larry's time to customers at $750 per hour to cover overhead costs. Larry's Social Security number is 133-20-7357, his Employee ID is 503, he's married, and is subject to all California taxes. He'll be paid semimonthly like other employees. Be sure to set up a new Activity Item ID: 004, description: Professional Services, rate: $750, to Account ID: 4000 Consulting Income, non-taxable. |
| 2 | 1/17/08 | Signed a contract with Microsoft (a new customer with ID: 100006 and terms net 30) to provide a full-day seminar (Item 001) on 1/25/08 at Microsoft's sales convention with Mr. Rice speaking for two hours (Item 004). (Use Sales Order 1004.) Received a $2,000 deposit on Microsoft's Check No. 09380991, which was deposited that day on Deposit Ticket ID: 005. |
| 3 | 1/19/08 | Spoke at the Adobe officers' retreat, providing a full-day seminar, previously recorded as Sales Order 1003. Prepared Invoice 503, applied the previous credit, and received the remaining $5,000 due on Adobe's Check No. 698903, which was immediately deposited into the company's checking account that day using Deposit Ticket ID: 006. |
| 4 | 1/21/08 | Borrowed $50,000 on a three-year 7% note payable from Wells Fargo Bank. Funds were deposited into the company's checking account. (Use journal entry reference: 2 and create a new Notes Payable Account ID: 220.) |
| 5 | 1/22/08 | Wrote Check No. 7 for $6,000 to Westwood Design and Production (a new vendor with Vendor ID: 200005) to purchase brochures to promote future speaking engagements. Sebastian expects these brochures to last two years and be used equally each month. (*Hint:* Create a new Prepaid Expenses other current asset type of account with ID: 1300.) |
| 6 | 1/25/08 | Provided a full-day seminar at the Microsoft sales convention where Mr. Rice spoke for two hours. |
| 7 | 1/28/08 | Prepared Invoice 504 to Microsoft billing it for the full-day seminar and Mr. Rice's time (Sales Order 1004), applied the previous credit, and e-mailed the invoice to Microsoft's accounting department. |
| 8 | 1/30/08 | Wrote Check No. 8 to Global Travel (new vendor with Vendor ID: 200006) for $5,600 in travel expenses (Account ID: 6300). |
| 9 | 1/30/08 | Wrote Check No. 9 to Hertz (new vendor with Vendor ID: 200007) for $800 in automobile expenses (Account ID: 5800). |
| 10 | 1/30/08 | Wrote Check No. 10 to Cingular Wireless (new vendor with Vendor ID: 200008) for $500 for telephone expenses (Account ID: 6250). |

| Event Number | Date | Business Event |
|---|---|---|
| 11 | 1/31/08 | Paid semimonthly payroll starting with Check No. 11 for the period 1/16/08 to 1/31/08. Payroll tax information is shown in Table 8.4. Anne Sunshine worked 45 hours during this period, and Larry Rice worked 2 hours. |
| 12 | 1/31/08 | Signed a contract with ITP Thomson (new customer with Customer ID: 100007, terms net 30) to provide a full-day seminar on 2/12/08 at ITP's sales convention with Mr. Rice speaking for three hours using Sales Order 1005. Received a $3,000 deposit on ITP's Check No. 15474, which was deposited the next day. |
| 13 | 1/31/08 | Wrote Check No. 14 to Sebastian Young (new vendor with Vendor ID: 200009) for $5,000 as an owner's draw. (*Note:* This is an equity account that gets closed at year end. Use Account ID: 3055.) |

| | Employee | | |
|---|---|---|---|
| Tax or Withholding | Sunshine | Rice | Walsh |
| Wage | 900.00 | 1,000.00 | 3,333.33 |
| Federal Withholding | −171.00 | −190.00 | −633.33 |
| Social Security Employee | −55.80 | −62.00 | −206.67 |
| Medicare Employee | −13.05 | −14.50 | −48.33 |
| CA – Income Tax | −72.00 | −80.00 | −266.67 |
| CA – Disability | −5.40 | −6.00 | −20.00 |
| Check Amount | 582.75 | 647.50 | 2,158.33 |
| Social Security Employer | 55.80 | 62.00 | 206.67 |
| Medicare Employer | 13.05 | 14.50 | 48.33 |
| Federal Unemployment | 7.20 | 8.00 | 26.67 |
| CA – Unemployment | 30.60 | 34.00 | 113.33 |
| CA Employment Training Tax | 0.90 | 1.00 | 3.33 |

**Table 8.4**

Payroll Taxes and Withholding for Employees from January 16, 2008, through January 31, 2008

Print the following as of 1/31/08 with no page numbers and no zero amounts:

a.   Standard income statement

b.   Standard balance sheet

c.   Standard statement of cash flows

d.   Find transactions report for the period 1/16/08 through 1/31/08

## *Chapter 8 Case Problem 2*
## OCEAN VIEW FLOWERS

Restore the backup you made for **Ocean View Flowers** in Chapter 7 into a new company folder. (Do not restore this backup into an existing folder.) Change the company name to include Ch 8 at the end so that the new company name is **Ocean View Flowers Ch 8**. Change the system date to **2/1/08** and the accounting period to **Period 2 – 02/01/08–02/28/08**. Add the following business events:

*merchandising*

| Table 8.5 | Anthuriums | Quantity Ordered | Cost | Sales Price |
|---|---|---|---|---|
| Purchase Order No. 2 Information | Bright Red (ID = BRA) | 700 | 20.00 | 35.00 |
| | Peach (ID = PA) | 800 | 22.00 | 40.00 |
| | White (ID = WA) | 600 | 27.00 | 50.00 |

| Event Number | Date | Business Event |
|---|---|---|
| 1 | 2/1/08 | The company repaid a portion of the long-term debt it borrowed from Santa Barbara Bank & Trust with regular checking account Check No. 119 in the amount of $1,000. (All of this payment was principal, and none was interest.) |
| 2 | 2/4/08 | The company prepaid a one-year liability insurance policy to State Farm Insurance (new vendor with ID = SFI) with Union Bank Check No. 120 in the amount of $2,500. (The transaction was properly recorded to Prepaid Expenses.) |
| 3 | 2/5/08 | The company created Purchase Order No. 2 to Vordale Farms for the items shown in Table 8.5 to be purchased on terms net 30. All Anthuriums are to be recorded in Account 40100 – Anthurium Sales, an income account type, which you will have to create. (Use average cost.) |
| 4 | 2/8/08 | The company cashed in $5,000 of its $25,000 certificate of deposit early and received $5,200, which was deposited into the regular checking account. The $200 difference represents interest revenue and should be recorded with journal entry 3. (Be sure to change the company's interest income account title to **Interest Revenue** before entering this transaction.) |
| 5 | 2/12/08 | The company received the bills shown in Table 8.6. (Accept any terms changes and add any new vendors necessary.) |
| 6 | 2/15/08 | The company paid payroll. All employees worked the entire period. Kelly Gusland worked 62 hours. Margie Conner worked 72 hours. Checks were written using the regular checking account starting with Check No. 121. Payroll taxes and withholding for employees are shown in Table 8.7. |
| 7 | 2/18/08 | The company received items and entered the bill (Invoice VF323 from Purchase Order No. 2 to Vordale Farms on terms net 30). |
| 8 | 2/22/08 | The company created invoices to customers as shown in Table 8.8. |
| 9 | 2/25/08 | The company paid the GTE and Edison bills using Union Bank Check Nos. 126 and 127. |
| 10 | 2/26/08 | The company received Check No. AD32908 for $9,000 as payment on account from Latin Ladies. The check was deposited using Deposit Ticket ID 1. |
| 11 | 2/26/08 | The company purchased a warehouse and land for $300,000 ($30,000 of the purchase price is attributable to the land). A cash payment using Check No. 128 for $30,000 was made to Hawaiian Farms to pay for the land. The warehouse was purchased for $270,000 by signing a long-term note payable to the Bank of California, which then remitted the $270,000 to Hawaiian Farms. Use journal entry 4 to record the warehouse purchase. |
| 12 | 2/26/08 | The company paid payroll for the period ended February 29, 2008. All employees worked the entire period. Kelly Gusland worked 50 hours. Margie Conner worked 45 hours. Checks were written using the regular checking account starting with Check No. 129. (Do not print these checks.) Payroll taxes and withholding for employees are shown in Table 8.9. |

| Vendor | Invoice Number | Amount | Terms | Expense |
|---|---|---|---|---|
| GTE (GTE) | 654654 | 250 | Net 30 | Telephone |
| Edison (E) | 79411 | 300 | Net 30 | Utilities |
| FlowerMart (FM) | 914222 | 60 | Net 30 | Supplies |

**Table 8.6**

Bills Received

| | Employee | | | | |
|---|---|---|---|---|---|
| Tax or Withholding | Thomas | Gusland | Conner | McAninch | Comstock |
| Check Number | 121 | 122 | 123 | 124 | 125 |
| Salary/Hours | 2,916.67 | 62 | 72 | 2,500.00 | 2,083.34 |
| Federal Withholding | −667.00 | −123.00 | −113.00 | −402.00 | −286.00 |
| Social Security Employee | −180.83 | −57.66 | −53.57 | −155.00 | −129.17 |
| Medicare Employee | −42.30 | −13.48 | −12.53 | −36.25 | −30.20 |
| CA – Withholding | −192.30 | −20.93 | −8.60 | −153.55 | −61.86 |
| CA – Disability Employee | −14.58 | −4.65 | −4.32 | −12.50 | −10.42 |
| Social Security Company | 180.83 | 57.66 | 53.57 | 155.00 | 129.17 |
| Medicare Company | 42.30 | 13.48 | 12.53 | 36.25 | 30.20 |
| Federal Unemployment | 9.33 | 7.44 | 6.91 | 16.00 | 16.67 |
| CA – Unemployment | 0.58 | 0.46 | 0.43 | 1.00 | 1.05 |
| California Employee | | | | | |
|   Training Tax | 1.17 | 0.93 | 0.86 | 2.00 | 2.08 |
| Check Amount | 1,819.66 | 710.28 | 671.98 | 1,740.70 | 1,565.69 |

**Table 8.7**

Payroll Taxes and Withholding for Employees from February 1, 2008, through February 15, 2008

| Customer | Invoice Number | Item Sold | Quantity | Terms | Invoice Amount |
|---|---|---|---|---|---|
| Latin Ladies | 10001 | Calistoga Sun Daylilies | 400 | Net 30 | 9,000 |
| | | Caribbean Pink Sands | 100 | | |
| California Beauties | 10002 | White Anthuriums | 500 | Net 30 | 25,000 |
| FTD | 10003 | Bright Red Anthuriums | 300 | Net 30 | 10,500 |

**Table 8.8**

Customer Invoices

| | Employee | | | | |
|---|---|---|---|---|---|
| Tax or Withholding | Thomas | Gusland | Conner | McAninch | Comstock |
| Check Number | 129 | 130 | 131 | 132 | 133 |
| Salary/Hours | 2,916.67 | 50 | 45 | 2,500.00 | 2,083.34 |
| Federal Withholding | −667.00 | −96.00 | −64.00 | −402.00 | −286.00 |
| Social Security Employee | −180.83 | −46.50 | −33.48 | −155.00 | −129.17 |
| Medicare Employee | −42.30 | −10.88 | −7.83 | −36.25 | −30.20 |
| CA – Withholding | −192.30 | −13.32 | 0.00 | −153.55 | −61.86 |
| CA – Disability Employee | −14.58 | −3.75 | −2.70 | −12.50 | −10.42 |
| Social Security Company | 180.83 | 46.50 | 33.48 | 155.00 | 129.17 |
| Medicare Company | 42.30 | 10.88 | 7.83 | 36.25 | 30.20 |
| Federal Unemployment | 0.00 | 6.00 | 4.32 | 0.00 | 6.00 |
| CA – Unemployment (SUI) | 0.00 | 0.38 | 0.27 | 0.00 | 0.37 |
| California Employee | | | | | |
|   Training Tax | 0.00 | 0.75 | 0.54 | 0.00 | 0.75 |
| Check Amount | 1,819.66 | 579.55 | 431.99 | 1,740.70 | 1,565.69 |

**Table 8.9**

Payroll Taxes and With holding for Employees from February 16, 2008, through February 29, 2008

### Requirements

This is a continuous case in that the next chapter will use the work you've accomplished here as the basis for recording additional business events. After you've printed the following reports, create a backup of this file and store it on some type of external medium (flash drive, Internet site, CD, disk, etc.). The backup file should be named **Ocean View Flowers Ch 8** for easy identification later. You'll be restoring this file in the next chapter. Print the following with no page numbers and no zero amounts:

a. Standard balance sheet

b. Standard income statement

c. Statement of cash flows

d. Find transactions report for the period 2/1/08 to 2/29/08

### Chapter 8 Case Problem 3
# ALOHA PROPERTY MANAGEMENT

Restore the backup you made for Aloha in Chapter 7 into a new company folder. (Do not restore this backup into an existing folder.) Change the company name to include Ch 8 at the end so that the new company name is **Aloha Property Management Ch 8**. Change the system date to **2/1/08**. Add the following business events:

| Event Number | Date | Business Event |
|---|---|---|
| 1 | 2/1/08 | Wrote Check No. 994 for $31,000 to GMAC Mortgage (ID = GMAC) as an installment payment on a 7% loan payable. (Interest Expense, $22,604; Notes Payable Noncurrent, $8,396.) |
| 2 | 2/1/08 | Recorded Invoice 7511 for rental of Moana Units 1, 3, 4 and Villa Units 1 and 4 for one week to Pixar (ID = PX). Applied $14,000 of the advance payment to this invoice, noted terms due on receipt, and recorded receipt of balance owed of $14,080. (When you apply credits, type **14000** in the column Amt. to Use and then click **Done**.) Deposited Pixar Check No. 38771 for $14,080 into regular checking account using Deposit Ticket ID 006. |
| 3 | 2/4/08 | Received payment on account from Apple Computer of $25,000 on its Check No. 987426. Deposited check into regular checking account using Deposit Ticket ID 007. |
| 4 | 2/4/08 | Received a bill from Reilly Custodial for maintenance expenses of $3,500 with terms of net 15 on its Invoice AB1725. |
| 5 | 2/5/08 | Collected a $15,000 deposit (on Check No. Z100333) from new customer American Airlines (AA) using Deposit Ticket ID 008. |
| 6 | 2/7/08 | Received a bill from Blue Sky Pools (its Invoice 3600) for maintenance expenses of $1,800. (Blue Sky may have changed Aloha's credit terms to net 15.) |
| 7 | 2/8/08 | Recorded Invoice 7512 for rental of Moana Unit 4 and Villa Units 1 and 4 for one week to Pixar. Applied $10,000 of Pixar's advance payment to this invoice, noted terms due on receipt, and recorded receipt of balance owed of $11,840. |

| Event Number | Date | Business Event |
|---|---|---|
| 8 | 2/8/08 | Deposited Pixar check number 39087 for $11,840 into checking account using Deposit Ticket ID 009. |
| 9 | 2/8/08 | Recorded Sales Receipt 5119 for rent of Moana Units 1, 2, and 3 for one week each. Collected American Express payment (ref 2390832389) in full of $8,840 from new customer Accenture (ACC). |
| 10 | 2/8/08 | Deposited Accenture's American Express credit card payment of $8,840 into the checking account. |
| 11 | 2/11/08 | Received a bill from Pacific Electric for utilities expenses of $2,600 with terms of net 15 on its Invoice Q33789. |
| 12 | 2/15/08 | Recorded Invoice 7513 for rental of Moana Unit 3 and Villa Unit 4 for one week to Exxon. Applied Exxon's advance payment to this invoice, noted terms due on receipt, and recorded receipt of balance owed of $5,275 from Exxon's Check No. 943098. |
| 13 | 2/15/08 | Deposited Exxon's check for $5,275 into checking account. |
| 14 | 2/18/08 | Received invoice 3987 from Service Connection (SC) (a new vendor) for repairs expense of $5,200. Terms are net 15. |
| 15 | 2/20/08 | Received a bill from Sunset Media for advertising of $1,450 on its Invoice 4392. Terms are net 30. |
| 16 | 2/22/08 | Recorded Invoice 7514 for rental of all units for one week to Boeing, terms net 30. Invoice total $39,728. |
| 17 | 2/25/08 | Collected a $3,250 deposit on its Check No. 83546 from new customer UC Los Angeles (UCLA). |
| 18 | 2/26/08 | Collected a $7,500 deposit on its Check No. 75624 from new customer UC Berkely (UCB). |
| 19 | 2/26/08 | Deposited both checks into checking account. |
| 20 | 2/27/08 | Paid all bills due on or before 2/28/08 for a total of $9,700 using Check Nos. 995–997. Note that even though there are four bills that require payment, two are to the same vendor (Blue Sky Pools) and thus only three checks are required. |
| 21 | 2/28/08 | Paid sales tax due as of 1/31/08 of $2,128 with Check No. 998. |
| 22 | 2/28/08 | Paid payroll tax liabilities due as of 1/31/08. $2,756.51 in federal taxes are paid to the U.S. Treasury. $640.44 in total state taxes are all paid to the State of Hawaii Department of Taxation using ID 874525. (*Note:* The company has a dispute with the state unemployment system and has been directed not to remit the $277.50 owed as of 1/31/08.) Use Check Nos. 999 and 1000. (*Hint:* Remember to use the Payroll Register to determine these amounts. Add up all federal amounts and then all state amounts less the state unemployment amount owing as of 1/31/08.) |
| 23 | 2/29/08 | Process payroll per the information provided in Table 8.10 starting with Check No. 1001. |

### Table 8.10

Payroll Information for Aloha
Property Management

| Pay/Tax/Withholding | Employee | |
| --- | --- | --- |
| | Aki | Castillo |
| Hours | n/a | 160 |
| Rate | 75,000 | 20.00 |
| Gross Pay | 6,250.00 | 3,200.00 |
| Federal Withholding | −856.25 | −438.40 |
| Social Security Employee | −387.50 | −198.40 |
| Medicare Employee | −90.63 | −46.40 |
| HI Withholding | −442.33 | −210.53 |
| HI Disability | −1.25 | −0.64 |
| Social Security Employer | 387.50 | 198.40 |
| Medicare Company | 90.63 | 46.40 |
| Federal Unemployment | 50.00 | 25.60 |
| HI Unemployment | 187.50 | 96.00 |
| HI E & T | 0.63 | 0.32 |
| Check Amount | 4,472.04 | 2,305.63 |

*Requirements*

This is a continuous case in that the next chapter will use the work you've accomplished here as the basis for recording additional business events. After you've printed the following reports, create a backup of this file and store it on some type of external medium (flash drive, Internet site, CD, disk, etc.). The backup file should be named **Aloha Property Management Ch 8** for easy identification later. You'll be restoring this file in the next chapter. Print the following with no page numbers and no zero amounts:

a.   Standard balance sheet

b.   Standard income statement

c.   Statement of cash flows

d.   Find transactions report for the period 2/1/08 to 2/29/08

# Adjusting Entries and Bank Reconciliations

# 9

## *Case:* Wild Water Sports, Inc.

Karen has recorded the majority of Wild Water's financing, investing, and operating activities for January through April 2013. To help her prepare financial statements for the first quarter, she asks you to prepare any necessary adjusting entries for the period January 1 through March 31, 2013.

"Some people have trouble with adjusting entries," you remark, "but I'm not one of them. I was always helping my classmates understand these types of journal entries. Why don't I give them a try?"

"Okay with me," Karen responds. "Traditional journal entries are available in Peachtree as you've already seen." Karen explains that in Peachtree the most common adjusting entries—accruing expenses, accruing revenue, recording asset expirations, and recording liability reductions—can be made by using the General Journal Entry item in the Company center.

## Accruing Expenses

Wild Water Sports had a long-term liability of $383,800 when Karen and Donna made their initial investment. That loan was paid off along with accrued interest on March 6, 2013. The remaining balance in the loan payable account represents three different loans. The first, a $250,000, five-year, 5% loan from the Bank of Florida, was made on January 4, 2013. The second was a $50,000, three-year, 6% loan from CitiBank that was made on January 2, 2013. The third was just recently acquired when the company purchased a computer from Staples for $5,000. In March, the company made two payments on the Bank of Florida loan.

**Video Demonstration**

*Demo 9A - Accruing expenses*

According to the loan amortization schedule (see Figure 8.1), a payment of $4,717.81 is due to be made at the beginning of April on the $250,000 loan of which $1,010.97 represents interest owed. (*Note:* This payment was made in Chapter 8, on April 2, using Check No. 1041.) As of March 31, 2013, that interest should be included in interest expense for March. Payments are due annually on the $50,000 loan. Thus, as of March 31, 2013, the company owes $750 of interest calculated as **Principal** × **Rate** × **Time** ($50,000 × 6% × 3/12). The Staples loan bears no interest.

"Peachtree does not automatically assign journal entry numbers for reference," Karen points out. "The journal numbers we'll assign for March 31 adjustments may follow journal entries used for April business events. What's important is the date specified in the journal."

"Okay," you respond. "I'll take the information provided and create the adjustment necessary for interest expense as of March 31."

### To accrue interest expense:

1  Start the Peachtree program.

2  Restore the Wild Water Sports, Inc. 9 file from your Data Files CD or download it from the Internet.

3  Set the system date to **3/31/13** and the accounting period to **Period 3**.

4  From the Tasks menu, click **General Journal Entry**.

5  The journal entry date should already indicate Mar 31, 2013.

6  Type **11** as the Reference.

7  Select **6725** – Interest Expense as the first account.

8  Type **To accrue interest expense on long-term debt** in the Description text box.

9  Type **1010.97** as the amount in the Debit column. This will increase interest expense (an expense account).

10  Click the magnifying glass in the second row in the GL Account column and then click **New** to create a new account. Create a new account by typing ID = **2200**, Description = **Accrued Interest Payable**, and Account Type = **Other Current Liabilities**, click **Save**, and then click **Close**.

11  Select **2200** – Accrued Interest Payable as the second account and then press **[Tab]**.

12  Accept **To accrue interest expense on long-term debt** in the Description text box for this row.

**13**  Type **1010.97** as the amount in the Credit column. This will increase accrued interest payable. The resulting journal entry should look like Figure 9.1.

| GL Account | Description | Debit | Credit | Job |
|---|---|---|---|---|
| 6725 | To accrue interest expense on long-term debt | 1,010.97 | | |
| 2200 | To accrue interest expense on long-term debt | | 1,010.97 | |
| | | | | |
| | | | | |
| | | | | |
| | | | | |
| | | | | |
| | | | | |
| | | | | |
| | | | | |
| | Totals: | 1,010.97 | 1,010.97 | |
| | Out of Balance: | 0.00 | | |

Date: Mar 31, 2013   ☐ Reverse Transaction
Reference: 11

**Figure 9.1**

Accruing Interest Expense

**14**  Click **Save**.

**15**  Accept **12** as the Reference.

**16**  Select **6725 – Interest Expense** as the first account.

**17**  Type **To accrue interest expense on long-term debt** in the Description text box.

**18**  Type **750** as the amount in the Debit column.

**19**  Select **2200 – Accrued Interest Payable** as the second account and then press **[Tab]**.

**20**  Accept **To accrue interest expense on long-term debt** in the Description text box for this row.

**21**  Type **750** as the amount in the Credit column.

**22**  Click **Save** and then click **Close**.

Karen explains that this process properly reflects interest expenses in the correct accounting period (first quarter of 2013) and establishes the liability as of March 31, 2013. However, in April, when the company pays the next installment on the $250,000 loan, Karen will have to remember that the interest has already been accrued.

"Either that, or we can reverse the adjustment as of April 1 and then just record the next payment as we've done in the past with a portion of the payment going to interest expense and a portion going to reduce the loan principal," Karen suggests.

"I like that idea," you answer. "Do we do the same for the $50,000 loan?"

"No," Karen responds. "The $50,000 loan is on an annual payment plan, and if we reversed the journal entry as of April 1, we'd have to reestablish it as of March 31 and accrue more interest for the second quarter. I suggest we reverse the first accrual only."

Karen explains that reversing a journal entry can be accomplished in one of two ways. One alternative is to actually create the reversing journal entry in the next period: in this case on April 1. A second and more common alternative is to use the automatic reversal process provided in Peachtree. This process is generated when you click the **Reverse Transaction** check box available on every journal entry.

"This is confusing," you say.

"I know," Karen answers. "Let me walk you through this. First off, I'll go back and edit the journal entry we just recorded to accrue interest via journal entry 11 for $1,010.97. All I have to do is place a check in the **Reverse Transaction** check box, and a journal entry, the exact opposite of journal entry 11, will appear on the first of the month following our original entry. Since the original entry was 3/31/13, the reversing journal entry will appear as 4/1/13 and use the same reference number: 11."

## To reverse an accrual entry:

**1**  From the Tasks menu, click **General Journal Entry**.

**2**  Click the **arrows** to go back through recorded journal entries until you find journal entry 11.

**3**  Click in the **Reverse Transaction** check box as shown in Figure 9.2.

**Figure 9.2**

Reversing an Entry

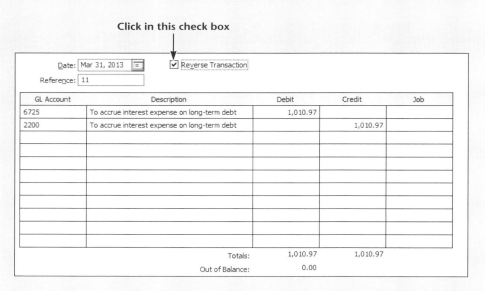

**4**  Click **Save** and then click **Close**.

"After this entry was recorded on April 1, the accrued interest payable balance was 0 and interest expense for April has a credit balance of $1,010.97." Now, Karen explains, "when we record the next payment on this loan, we can use the amortization schedule to record the interest paid and the reduction of principal. The payment will reduce cash and increase interest expense by $1,010.97, creating a balance of 0 in interest expense for April. If we need to provide GAAP-based financial statements in April, we'll need to accrue interest owed at April 30. Let me show you what the general ledger accounts look like after these entries."

### To view the effects of the interest accrual and related reversal:

**1**   From the Reports & Forms menu, click **General Ledger**, then double-click **General Ledger.**

**2**   Click the **Options** button and change the To: date of the report to **Period 4** so that the report will reflect transactions affecting general ledger accounts for both Periods 3 and 4 and then click **OK**.

**3**   Scroll down the General Ledger report to account 2200. See Figure 9.3.

This is the original
entry increasing the liability

| Account ID<br>Account Description | Date | Reference | Jrnl | Trans Description | Debit Amt | Credit Amt | Balance |
|---|---|---|---|---|---|---|---|
| 2200 | 3/1/13 | | | Beginning Balance | | | |
| Accrued Interest Payable | 3/31/13 | 11 | GEN | To accrue interest | | 1,010.97 | |
| | 3/31/13 | 12 | GEN | To accrue interest | | 750.00 | |
| | | | | Current Period Ch | | 1,760.97 | -1,760.97 |
| | 4/1/13 | | | Beginning Balance | | | -1,760.97 |
| | 4/1/13 | 11 | GEN | To accrue interest | 1,010.97 | | |
| | | | | Current Period Ch | 1,010.97 | | 1,010.97 |
| | 4/30/13 | | | **Ending Balance** | | | **-750.00** |

This is the automatic reversing
entry decreasing the liability

**Figure 9.3**

Account 2200 for Periods 3 and 4

**4**   Now scroll down the General Ledger report to account 6725. See Figure 9.4. After viewing the report, click the Close Box to close the report.

This is the original
entry increasing the
expense

| Account ID<br>Account Description | Date | Reference | Jrnl | Trans Description | Debit Amt | Credit Amt | Balance |
|---|---|---|---|---|---|---|---|
| 6725 | 3/1/13 | | | Beginning Balance | | | |
| Interest Expense | 3/1/13 | 1029 | CDJ | Bank of Florida - In | 1,041.67 | | |
| | 3/1/13 | 1030 | CDJ | Bank of Florida - In | 1,026.35 | | |
| | 3/6/13 | 1031 | CDJ | Bank of Orlando - I | 3,890.58 | | |
| | 3/31/13 | 11 | GEN | To accrue interest | 1,010.97 | | |
| | 3/31/13 | 12 | GEN | To accrue interest | 750.00 | | |
| | | | | Current Period Ch | 7,719.57 | | 7,719.57 |
| | 4/1/13 | | | Beginning Balance | | | 7,719.57 |
| | 4/1/13 | 11 | GEN | To accrue interest | | 1,010.97 | |
| | 4/2/13 | 1041 | CDJ | Bank of Florida - In | 1,010.97 | | |
| | | | | Current Period Ch | 1,010.97 | 1,010.97 | |
| | 4/30/13 | | | **Ending Balance** | | | **7,719.57** |

This is the automatic
reversing entry
decreasing the expense

Note the payment we made on 4/2 with check 1041 for interest owed as of 3/31. The net effect of the reversal and payment is 0 for April.

**Figure 9.4**

Account 6725 for Periods 3 and 4

# Accruing Revenue

*Video Demonstration*

*Demo 9B - Accruing expenses*

Karen tells you that she can also use journal entries to record revenue earned on investments. She points out that during the quarter the company had some short-term investments with ETrade that earned money market interest if they were not invested in stock. The interest is paid quarterly. Since no interest was paid during the quarter, no interest revenue has been recorded. After checking with ETrade's investment advisor, Karen learns that $1,890.41 of interest revenue was earned but unpaid as of March 31, 2013. She decides to accept Peachtree's description of interest revenue as interest income.

---

### To accrue interest revenue:

**1**  From the Tasks menu, click **General Journal Entry**.

**2**  The journal entry date should already indicate Mar 31, 2013.

**3**  Type **13** as the Reference.

**4**  Select **1030** – Short-Term Investments as the first account.

**5**  Type **To accrue interest revenue on short-term investments** in the Description text box.

**6**  Type **1890.41** as the amount in the Debit column.

**7**  Select **4100** – Interest Income as the second account.

**8**  Type **1890.41** as the amount in the Credit column.

**9**  Click **Save**.

---

"I thought we were going to record more interest revenue," you say. "Why did we choose to record this as interest income?"

"Peachtree doesn't follow the accounting convention of recording interest revenue," Karen points out. "Peachtree was originally created as a tool for businesses preparing tax returns, and the Internal Revenue Service (IRS) uses the income reference for interest instead of revenue. Rather than changing the account title, we'll just use interest income."

"Another issue we have to address is whether any products were delivered to customers but not recorded as sales at the end of the month," Karen comments. "For example, our records show that we delivered a boat to Spirit Adventures on March 31, but we didn't invoice the company until April 2. Thus, as of March 31, 2013, we need to accrue that additional revenue, sales tax, and cost of goods sold."

"Don't you also have to reduce inventory since our records show that boat in inventory March 31?" you ask.

"Exactly." Karen answers, "Plus, since this transaction is recorded as an invoice in April, we'll need to reverse this accrual entry on April 1."

## To adjust for sales occurring in March but not invoiced until April:

**1**  Accept **3/31/13** as the journal entry date.

**2**  Place a check in the **Reverse Transaction** check box.

**3**  Accept **14** as the Reference.

**4**  Select **1100** – Accounts Receivable as the first account.

**5**  Type **To accrue revenue and costs of sales** in the Description text box.

**6**  Type **69225** as the amount in the Debit column. Press **[Tab]** three times.

**7**  Select **4000** – Sales Income as the second account. Press **[Tab]** two times.

**8**  Type **65000** as the amount in the Credit column. Press **[Tab]** two times.

**9**  Select **2310** – Sales Tax Payable as the third account. Press **[Tab]** three times.

**10**  Type **4225** as the amount in the Credit column. Press **[Tab]** two times.

**11**  Select **5000** – Cost of Sales as the fourth account. Press **[Tab]** two times.

**12**  Type **52000** as the amount in the Debit column. Press **[Tab]** three times.

**13**  Select **1200** – Inventory as the fifth account. Press **[Tab]** three times.

**14**  Type **52000** as the amount in the Credit column. Your journal entry should look like Figure 9.5.

| | | | | |
|---|---|---|---|---|
| Date: Mar 31, 2013 | | ☑ Reverse Transaction | | |
| Reference: 14 | | | | |

| GL Account | Description | Debit | Credit | Job |
|---|---|---|---|---|
| 1100 | To accrue revenue and cost of sales | 69,225.00 | | |
| 4000 | To accrue revenue and cost of sales | | 65,000.00 | |
| 2310 | To accrue revenue and cost of sales | | 4,225.00 | |
| 5000 | To accrue revenue and cost of sales | 52,000.00 | | |
| 1200 | To accrue revenue and cost of sales | | 52,000.00 | |
| | | | | |
| | | | | |
| | | | | |
| | | | | |
| | | | | |
| | | | | |
| | Totals: | 121,225.00 | 121,225.00 | |
| | Out of Balance: | 0.00 | | |

**Figure 9.5**

Accruing Sales Revenue

**15**  Click **Save** and then click **Close**.

"Where did you get the cost of goods sold and inventory asset information?" you ask.

"I got it from our list of items, which provides the sales price, income account, and cost," Karen answers. "When we accrue the sales revenue, we must also accrue the related cost of goods sold."

"How about the sales tax payable?" you ask. "Why didn't we just use our normal sales tax payable account?"

"I didn't use the normal sales tax payable account because that account is tied to the payment of sales tax and this accrual is for our records only. When the invoice is recorded in April, the normal sales tax account will be increased."

Karen explains that this is another case where it is best to reverse this accrual the first of the next month so that when the actual invoice is recorded in April, it will be offset by the previous accrual.

"This accrual accounting process is a lot of work!" you comment.

"Yes," Karen agrees. "But at least we get a picture of our performance and financial position based on when events occur, not just when we get around to recording them."

## Recording Expenses Incurred but Previously Deferred

*Video Demonstration*

*Demo 9C - Recording expenses previously deferred*

The adjustments that you and Karen just recorded accounted for previously unrecorded transactions. Now Karen wants to show you how to record adjustments that affect previously recorded business activity, such as the prepayment of expenses and the purchase of fixed assets.

On February 1, 2013, Wild Water Sports paid $24,000 to Coe Marketing for a one-year advertising campaign. Since this payment represented an expenditure that benefited more than the one accounting period, it was correctly recorded to prepaid expenses, an asset account.

On March 31, 2013, two months of the time period covered by the ad campaign had expired. Thus, two-twelfths of the cost ($4,000) should be recorded as advertising expense and the prepaid advertising account reduced accordingly. Each month thereafter, one-twelfth of the cost ($2,000) should be recorded as advertising expense and the prepaid expense account reduced accordingly.

### To adjust prepaid expenses for advertising consumed:

1   From the Tasks menu, click **General Journal Entry**.

2   Accept **3/31/13** as the journal entry date.

3   Type **15** as the Reference.

4   Select **6600** – Advertising Expense as the first account.

5   Type **To adjust prepaid expenses for advertising consumed** in the Description text box.

6   Type **4000** as the amount in the Debit column.

7   Select **1400** – Prepaid Expenses as the second account.

8   Type **4000** as the amount in the Credit column.

9   Click **Save**.

On January 29, 2013, Wild Water Sports paid $22,000 to Manchester Insurance for a one-year liability insurance policy covering it for the calendar year

2013. Once again, since this payment represented an expenditure that benefited more than one accounting period, it was correctly recorded to prepaid expenses, an asset account.

On March 31, 2013, three months of the time period covered by the insurance policy had expired. Thus, three-twelfths of the cost ($5,500) should be recorded as insurance expense and the prepaid expense account reduced accordingly. Each month thereafter, one-twelfth of the cost ($1,833.33) should be recorded as insurance expense and the prepaid insurance account reduced accordingly.

---

## To adjust prepaid expenses:

**1**  Accept **3/31/13** as the journal entry date.

**2**  Accept **16** as the Reference.

**3**  Select **6950** – Insurance Expense as the first account.

**4**  Type **To adjust prepaid expenses for insurance consumed** in the Description text box.

**5**  Type **5500** as the amount in the Debit column.

**6**  Select **1400** – Prepaid Expenses as the second account.

**7**  Type **5500** as the amount in the Credit column.

**8**  Click **Save**.

---

A similar adjustment called *depreciation* is needed to allocate the cost of previously recorded depreciable plant and equipment assets. Wild Water Sports has one account for all property, plant, and equipment. Depreciation on said plant and equipment is usually accumulated in a separate contra-asset account on the balance sheet for control purposes.

While Peachtree does have a separate module available to track individual assets and calculate depreciation, Karen has chosen not to use this feature. Instead, she maintains a separate spreadsheet to track when assets were purchased, how much depreciation should be recorded, and when assets are sold. Her analysis indicates that $10,333 of depreciation should be recorded as of March 31, 2013, to reflect depreciation for the first quarter of 2013. Of that balance, $5,583 is related to equipment, $2,500 is related to furniture and fixtures, and $2,250 is related to the truck.

---

## To record depreciation expense:

**1**  Accept **3/31/13** as the journal entry date.

**2**  Accept **17** as the Reference.

**3**  Select **7050** – Depreciation Expense as the first account.

**4**  Type **To depreciate assets** in the Description text box.

**5**  Type **10333** as the amount in the Debit column.

**6** Select **1900 – Accum. Depreciation - Prop&Eqt** as the second account.

**7** Type **10333** as the amount in the Credit column.

**8** Click **Save** and then click **Close**.

You find the above procedures very straightforward but are curious about the financial statement impact of these adjusting entries so far. You wonder if Peachtree provides a way to view financial statements so you can see what effect these adjustments have had. Karen tells you that Peachtree does have such a feature—you can view financial statements at any time without having to post entries. She suggests that you look at the balance sheet as of March 31, 2013, to see the effect of these adjustments on the balance sheet.

### To examine the balance sheet as of March 31, 2013:

**1** Click **Reports & Forms**, click **Financial Statements**, and then double-click **Balance Sheet**.

**2** Make sure the **Print Page Numbers** and **Show Zero Amounts** check boxes are unchecked and then click **OK**.

**3** View the assets section of the balance sheet as shown in Figure 9.6.

**Figure 9.6**

Asset Portion of the Balance Sheet after Adjusting Entries So Far

Wild Water Sports, Inc. 9
Balance Sheet
March 31, 2013

ASSETS

| | | |
|---|---|---|
| Current Assets | | |
| Checking Account | $ 47,392.43 | |
| Short-Term Investments | 39,890.41 | |
| Accounts Receivable | 389,932.73 | |
| Inventory | 243,600.00 | |
| Inventory Parts | 2,112.00 | |
| Prepaid Expenses | 36,500.00 | |
| Total Current Assets | | 759,427.57 |
| Property and Equipment | | |
| Property and Equipment | 295,000.00 | |
| Accum. Depreciation - Prop&Eqt | (17,833.00) | |
| Total Property and Equipment | | 277,167.00 |
| Other Assets | | |
| Total Other Assets | | 0.00 |
| Total Assets | | $ 1,036,594.57 |

**4** Close all windows.

Karen notes that the ending balance in prepaid expenses ($36,500) is made up of two items: prepaid advertising ($20,000) and prepaid insurance ($16,500). The prepaid advertising as of March 31, 2013, makes sense since 10 months of the ad campaign are left (10 months × $2,000 per month = $20,000). She also notes that the balance in prepaid insurance as of March 31, 2013, also makes sense since 9 months of insurance coverage are left (9 months × $1,833.33 per month = $16,500). She also notes the new balances in the accumulated depreciation accounts.

Having tackled prepaid asset and depreciable asset adjustments, you and Karen are now ready to move on to the last adjustment category—adjusting unearned revenue.

## Adjusting for Unearned Revenue

On March 31, 2013, Wild Water Sports received $10,000 from its customer Performance Rentals as a deposit on a boat in stock. On this date, Performance Rentals had an existing balance outstanding, but you and Karen chose to account for this as a separate transaction and not apply this payment to the amount due. As described in Chapter 8, Karen recorded this transaction by increasing the checking account and decreasing Performance Rental's accounts receivable. Karen has decided to reclassify it as unearned revenue, a liability, on March 31, 2013. Here's why: Cash has been received, but the boat has not been delivered. Thus, on March 31, you need to reclassify the $10,000 to an unearned revenue account (a liability). When the company actually sells the boat to Performance Rentals in a future period, Wild Water will create an invoice, decrease the liability, and increase sales revenue.

*Demo 9D - Recording revenues previously deferred*

The effect of this adjusting journal entry is to increase accounts receivable and increase unearned revenue (in our case an account called Customer Deposits), reflecting the fact that Wild Water still has a balance owed by Performance Rentals of $1,293.98 and owes Performance Rentals $10,000 if it doesn't deliver the boat on which Performance placed the deposit. Karen chooses to automatically reverse this entry in the next accounting period, which will reallocate this $10,000 as a credit to accounts receivable and remove it from customer deposits. However, she warns you that reversing this entry assumes that in the next accounting period a sale will take place and this $10,000 credit will be offset against an increase in accounts receivable from the sale. If this doesn't occur in April, you will need to reclassify the $10,000 as unearned revenue (customer deposit) again.

---

**To reclassify the $10,000 as unearned revenue (customer deposit) at 3/31/13:**

1  From the Tasks menu, click **General Journal Entry**.

2  Accept **3/31/13** as the journal entry date.

3  Type **18** as the Reference.

4   Place a check in the **Reverse Transaction** check box.

5   Select **1100** – Accounts Receivable as the first account.

6   Type **To reclassify amounts to unearned revenue** in the Description text box.

7   Type **10000** as the amount in the Debit column.

8   Select **2400** – Customer Deposits as the second account.

9   Type **10000** as the amount in the Credit column.

10  Click **Save** and then close the General Journal window.

"I always like to print out a copy of my adjustments to make sure every-thing was recorded correctly," Karen comments. "Peachtree has a journal fea-ture that we can use to print just those transactions occurring on March 31 and April 1 so we can see the effects of our adjustments."

**To print the journal for March 31 and April 1:**

1   Click **Reports & Forms** from the Peachtree menu, click **General Ledger**, and then double-click **General Journal**.

2   Click the **Options** button.

3   Uncheck the **Include accounts with zero amounts** box.

4   Uncheck the **Shorten Description** check box.

5   Type **3/31/13** in the From text box.

6   Type **4/1/13** in the To text box.

7   Click **OK**.

8   Resize the Reference, Trans Description, and any other columns you'd like so that your report fits on one page.

9   Click the **Print** button and then click **OK** to print the general journal. Your printout should look like Figure 9.7.

10  Click **Close** to close the Journal window.

11  Click **No** when asked if you want to save this report as modified.

12  Close the Select a Report or Form window.

**Figure 9.7**

General Journal Entries from 3/31 and 4/1

**Wild Water Sports, Inc. 9**
**General Journal**
**For the Period From Mar 31, 2013 to Apr 1, 2013**

Filter Criteria includes: Report order is by Date. Report is printed in Detail Format.

| Date | Account ID | Reference | Trans Description | Debit Amt | Credit Amt |
|------|-----------|-----------|-------------------|-----------|------------|
| 3/31/13 | 6725 | 11 | To accrue interest expense on long-term debt | 1,010.97 | |
| | 2200 | | To accrue interest expense on long-term debt | | 1,010.97 |
| 3/31/13 | 6725 | 12 | To accrue interest expense on long-term debt | 750.00 | |
| | 2200 | | To accrue interest expense on long-term debt | | 750.00 |
| 3/31/13 | 1030 | 13 | To accrue interest revenue on short-term investments | 1,890.41 | |
| | 4100 | | To accrue interest revenue on short-term investments | | 1,890.41 |
| 3/31/13 | 1100 | 14 | To accrue revenue and cost of sales | 69,225.00 | |
| | 4000 | | To accrue revenue and cost of sales | | 65,000.00 |
| | 2310 | | To accrue revenue and cost of sales | | 4,225.00 |
| | 5000 | | To accrue revenue and cost of sales | 52,000.00 | |
| | 1200 | | To accrue revenue and cost of sales | | 52,000.00 |
| 3/31/13 | 6600 | 15 | To adjust prepaid expenses for advertising consumed | 4,000.00 | |
| | 1400 | | To adjust prepaid expenses for advertising consumed | | 4,000.00 |
| 3/31/13 | 6950 | 16 | To adjust prepaid expenses for insurance consumed | 5,500.00 | |
| | 1400 | | To adjust prepaid expenses for insurance consumed | | 5,500.00 |
| 3/31/13 | 7050 | 17 | To depreciate assets | 10,333.00 | |
| | 1900 | | To depreciate assets | | 10,333.00 |
| 3/31/13 | 1100 | 18 | To reclassify amounts to unearned revenue | 10,000.00 | |
| | 2400 | | To reclassify amounts to unearned revenue | | 10,000.00 |
| 3/31/13 | 1500 | 7 | Purchase of equipment for note payable | 5,000.00 | |
| | 2700 | | Purchase of equipment for note payable | | 5,000.00 |
| 4/1/13 | 6725 | 11 | To accrue interest expense on long-term debt | | 1,010.97 |
| | 2200 | | To accrue interest expense on long-term debt | 1,010.97 | |
| 4/1/13 | 1100 | 14 | To accrue revenue and cost of sales | | 69,225.00 |
| | 4000 | | To accrue revenue and cost of sales | 65,000.00 | |
| | 2310 | | To accrue revenue and cost of sales | 4,225.00 | |
| | 5000 | | To accrue revenue and cost of sales | | 52,000.00 |
| | 1200 | | To accrue revenue and cost of sales | 52,000.00 | |
| 4/1/13 | 1100 | 18 | To reclassify amounts to unearned revenue | | 10,000.00 |
| | 2400 | | To reclassify amounts to unearned revenue | 10,000.00 | |
| | | **Total** | | **291,945.35** | **291,945.35** |

Karen explains that most of these journals represent the adjustments you just made and seem to be in order. She points out that each transaction has a transaction number, a type, a date, a journal number (if applicable), names, accounts, debits, and credits.

# Preparing a Bank Reconciliation and Recording Related Adjustments

Every month, the Bank of Florida sends Wild Water Sports a bank account statement that lists all deposits received by the bank and all checks and payments that have cleared the bank as of the date of the statement. You and Karen examine the bank statements for the months of January, February, and March, which indicate an ending balance of $37,172.24 as of March 31, 2013. Normally, you would reconcile your statement each month, but you've been a little busy these last couple of months. You now turn your attention toward reconciling that balance with the balance reported by Peachtree. You note that Peachtree indicates an ending checking account balance of $47,392.43 at that same date. You believe that most of the difference between these two amounts is probably attributable to "outstanding checks" that Wild Water Sports has written but that the bank hasn't yet paid, deposits it has recorded that have not been received by the bank, bank service charges, and interest income.

A review of all three statements shows that all checks recorded by Wild Water Sports have been paid by the bank except payroll checks written on March 30, 2013, totaling $6,994.74. All deposits recorded by the company have been received by the bank except one dated March 29, 2013, for $7,264.93 and one dated March 31, 2013, for $10,000.00. Bank charges per the bank statement total $75, which has not yet been recorded by the company. Interest income credited to the company's bank account in the amount of $125 also has not yet been recorded by the company.

The only adjustments created in this bank reconciliation were the recognition of bank service fees and interest income. Peachtree automatically records these in the checking account. Once reconciled, Peachtree also inserts a check mark in the check register next to each transaction that has cleared the bank.

## To reconcile the bank statement as of 3/31/13:

1 From the Banking center, click **Reconcile Accounts**.

2 Select **1020** as the Account to Reconcile.

3 Accept **3/31/13** as the Statement Date.

4 Select **All** from the Show drop-down list.

5 Type **37172.24** as the Statement Ending Balance (box at bottom right of screen).

6 Type **125** as the Interest Income, accept **3/31/13** as the Date, and type **4100** as the Account.

7 Type **75** as the Service Charges, accept **3/31/13** as the Date, and type **6850** as the Account.

8 Place a check mark next to all of the checks, payments, and service charges except Check Nos. 1038, 1039, and 1040. (These are the payroll checks issued 3/30/13 that have not yet cleared the bank.)

9 Place a check mark next to all of the Deposits, Interest, and Other Credits except the deposit 13 of $7,264.93 dated 3/29/13 and the $10,000.00 deposit 12 dated 3/31/13.

**10** Click in the **Date** column title to sort these transactions in descending date order (latest to earliest).

**11** Scroll to the top of the listing. Your screen should look like Figure 9.8.

**Figure 9.8**

Account Reconciliation

Note unreconciled difference here

**12** Note the unreconciled difference of 0.00 in the lower-right corner of the window.

**13** Click **OK** to complete the reconciliation.

**14** Click **Reports & Forms, Account Reconciliation**, and then double-click **Account Reconciliation** from the Select a Report or Form window. Your window should look like Figure 9.9.

**Figure 9.9**

Account Reconciliation Report
for Account 1020 as of
March 31, 2013

**Wild Water Sports, Inc. 9**
**Account Reconciliation**
**As of Mar 31, 2013**
**1020 - Checking Account**
**Bank Statement Date: March 31, 2013**
Filter Criteria includes: Report is printed in Detail Format.

| | | | | |
|---|---|---|---|---|
| Beginning GL Balance | | | | 164,775.11 |
| Add: Cash Receipts | | | | 68,384.93 |
| Less: Cash Disbursements | | | | (225,767.61) |
| Add (Less) Other | | | | 40,050.00 |
| Ending GL Balance | | | | 47,442.43 |
| Ending Bank Balance | | | | 37,172.24 |
| Add back deposits in transi | | | | |
| | Mar 31, 2013 | 12 | 10,000.00 | |
| | Mar 29, 2013 | 13 | 7,264.93 | |
| Total deposits in transit | | | | 17,264.93 |
| (Less) outstanding checks | | | | |
| | Mar 31, 2013 | 1038 | (3,384.92) | |
| | Mar 31, 2013 | 1039 | (3,137.92) | |
| | Mar 31, 2013 | 1040 | (471.90) | |
| Total outstanding checks | | | | (6,994.74) |
| Add (Less) Other | | | | |
| Total other | | | | |
| Unreconciled difference | | | | 0.00 |
| Ending GL Balance | | | | 47,442.43 |

**15**   Click **Print** and then click **OK** to print this reconciliation.

**16**   Close all open windows.

# Evaluate a Firm's Performance and Financial Position

Once again, the best way to evaluate a firm's performance and financial position at this point is to generate an income statement and balance sheet. Karen suggests you do this for the entire three months ending March 31, 2013 (the first quarter of 2013), and prepare a find transactions report like you did last month.

## To prepare a standard income statement and a balance sheet for March:

1  Be sure the system date is set to **3/31/13**.

2  Click **Reports & Forms** and then click **Financial Statements.**

3  Double-click <**Standard**> **Income Stmnt** from the Select a Report or Form window.

4  Uncheck the **Print Page Numbers** and **Show Zero Amounts** check boxes.

5  Click **OK** to view the income statement for March as shown in Figure 9.10.

**Figure 9.10**

Income Statement for March 2013 after Adjusting Entries and Bank Reconciliation

Wild Water Sports, Inc. 9
Income Statement
For the Three Months Ending March 31, 2013

|  | Current Month |  | Year to Date |  |
|---|---|---|---|---|
| **Revenues** |  |  |  |  |
| Sales Income | $ 434,750.00 | 98.85 | $ 767,500.00 | 98.80 |
| Service Income | 2,740.00 | 0.62 | 6,685.00 | 0.86 |
| Parts Income | 320.00 | 0.07 | 610.00 | 0.08 |
| Interest Income | 2,015.41 | 0.46 | 2,015.41 | 0.26 |
| Total Revenues | 439,825.41 | 100.00 | 776,810.41 | 100.00 |
| **Cost of Sales** |  |  |  |  |
| Cost of Sales | 348,056.00 | 79.14 | 614,488.00 | 79.10 |
| Total Cost of Sales | 348,056.00 | 79.14 | 614,488.00 | 79.10 |
| Gross Profit | 91,769.41 | 20.86 | 162,322.41 | 20.90 |
| **Expenses** |  |  |  |  |
| Wages Expense | 8,933.34 | 2.03 | 29,641.02 | 3.82 |
| Payroll Tax Expense | 996.06 | 0.23 | 3,304.94 | 0.43 |
| Utilities Expense | 1,050.00 | 0.24 | 2,870.00 | 0.37 |
| Telephone Expense | 1,500.00 | 0.34 | 5,020.00 | 0.65 |
| Other Office Expense | 0.00 | 0.00 | 4,500.00 | 0.58 |
| Advertising Expense | 4,000.00 | 0.91 | 6,700.00 | 0.86 |
| Interest Expense | 7,719.57 | 1.76 | 7,719.57 | 0.99 |
| Service Charge Expense | 75.00 | 0.02 | 75.00 | 0.01 |
| Insurance Expense | 5,500.00 | 1.25 | 5,500.00 | 0.71 |
| Depreciation Expense | 10,333.00 | 2.35 | 10,333.00 | 1.33 |
| Gain/Loss - Sale of Assets Exp | (3,000.00) | (0.68) | (3,000.00) | (0.39) |
| Total Expenses | 37,106.97 | 8.44 | 72,663.53 | 9.35 |
| Net Income | $ 54,662.44 | 12.43 | $ 89,658.88 | 11.54 |

6  Click **Print** from the button bar and then **OK** to print this statement.

**7**   Click **Close**.

**8**   Double-click <**Standard**> **Balance Sheet** from the Select a Report or Form window.

**9**   Make sure the **Print Page Numbers** and **Show Zero Amounts** check boxes are unchecked.

**10**   Click **OK** to view the balance sheet for March as shown in Figure 9.11.

**Figure 9.11**

Balance Sheet as of March 31, 2013, after Adjusting Entries and Bank Reconciliation

Wild Water Sports, Inc. 9
Balance Sheet
March 31, 2013

### ASSETS

Current Assets
| | | |
|---|---|---|
| Checking Account | $ 47,442.43 | |
| Short-Term Investments | 39,890.41 | |
| Accounts Receivable | 399,932.73 | |
| Inventory | 243,600.00 | |
| Inventory Parts | 2,112.00 | |
| Prepaid Expenses | 36,500.00 | |
| Total Current Assets | | 769,477.57 |

Property and Equipment
| | | |
|---|---|---|
| Property and Equipment | 295,000.00 | |
| Accum. Depreciation - Prop&Eqt | (17,833.00) | |
| Total Property and Equipment | | 277,167.00 |

Other Assets

| | | |
|---|---|---|
| Total Other Assets | | 0.00 |
| Total Assets | | $ 1,046,644.57 |

### LIABILITIES AND CAPITAL

Current Liabilities
| | | |
|---|---|---|
| Accounts Payable | $ 216,200.00 | |
| Accrued Interest Payable | 1,760.97 | |
| Sales Tax Payable | 28,457.66 | |
| Federal Payroll Taxes Payable | 2,622.00 | |
| FUTA Payable | 71.46 | |
| SUTA Payable | 241.20 | |
| Customer Deposits | 10,000.00 | |
| Total Current Liabilities | | 259,353.29 |

Long-Term Liabilities
| | | |
|---|---|---|
| Long Term Debt-Noncurrent | 297,632.40 | |
| Total Long-Term Liabilities | | 297,632.40 |
| Total Liabilities | | 556,985.69 |

Capital
| | | |
|---|---|---|
| Common Stock | 400,000.00 | |
| Net Income | 89,658.88 | |
| Total Capital | | 489,658.88 |
| Total Liabilities & Capital | | $ 1,046,644.57 |

**11**  Click **Print** from the button bar and then **OK** to print this statement.

**12**  Close all windows.

## To prepare a find transactions report for March 31:

**1**  Click **Reports & Forms** and then click **Company**.

**2**  Double-click **Find Transactions Report 3/13**.
*Trouble?* If this report isn't shown, you probably forgot to save it as requested. If so, change the report to reflect all transactions recorded in March 2013 by clicking the **Options** button on the Report button bar. Change the From date to **3/1/13** and then click **OK**.

**3**  Click **Print** from the Report button bar and then click **OK** to print. The report shown in Figure 9.12 should appear.

**Wild Water Sports, Inc. 9**
**Find Transactions Report**
**For the Period From Mar 31, 2013 to Mar 31, 2013**
Filter Criteria includes: 1) All Transaction Types. Report order is by Date.

| Date | Type | Reference | ID | Name | Amount |
|------|------|-----------|-----|------|--------|
| 3/31/13 | General Journal Entry | 03/31/13 | | | 75.00 |
| 3/31/13 | General Journal Entry | 03/31/13 | | | 125.00 |
| 3/31/13 | General Journal Entry | 11 | | | 1,010.97 |
| 3/31/13 | General Journal Entry | 12 | | | 750.00 |
| 3/31/13 | General Journal Entry | 13 | | | 1,890.41 |
| 3/31/13 | General Journal Entry | 14 | | | 121,225.00 |
| 3/31/13 | General Journal Entry | 15 | | | 4,000.00 |
| 3/31/13 | General Journal Entry | 16 | | | 5,500.00 |
| 3/31/13 | General Journal Entry | 17 | | | 10,333.00 |
| 3/31/13 | General Journal Entry | 18 | | | 10,000.00 |
| 3/31/13 | General Journal Entry | 7 | | | 5,000.00 |
| 3/31/13 | Payroll Entry | 1038 | 001 | Donna Chandler | 3,384.92 |
| 3/31/13 | Payroll Entry | 1039 | 002 | Karen Wilson | 3,137.92 |
| 3/31/13 | Payroll Entry | 1040 | 003 | Ryder Zacovic | 471.90 |
| 3/31/13 | Receipt | 8774 | 50006 | Performance Rentals | 10,000.00 |
| | | | | **Report Total:** | **176,904.12** |
| | | | | **Number of Transactions:**  15 | |

**Figure 9.12**

Find Transactions Report for March 31, 2013

**4**  Click **Close** to close the report and then close the Select a Report or Form window.

# End Note

You've now helped Karen record various adjustments, including accrued expenses, accrued revenues, expiration of prepaid and depreciable assets, creation of unearned revenue, and reconciliation of bank accounts.

## Business Events Summary

| Business Event | Process Steps | Page |
|---|---|---|
| Accrue expenses | Use General Journal Entry from the Company center | 298 |
| Reversing an accrual entry | Use General Journal Entry from the Company center | 300 |
| Accrue revenue | Use General Journal Entry from the Company center | 302 |
| Adjusting prepaid expenses | Use General Journal Entry from the Company center | 304 |
| Record depreciation | Use General Journal Entry from the Company center | 305 |
| Adjusting unearned revenue | Use General Journal Entry from the Company center | 307 |
| Reconcile bank accounts | Use Reconcile Accounts from the Banking center | 310 |

## Chapter 9 Questions

**1**  What is the typical formula used to calculate interest?

**2**  Give an example of accrued revenue other than the examples given in this chapter. Explain how this example of accrued revenue would be adjusted using journal entries.

**3**  Give an example of an accrued expense other than the example given in this chapter. Explain how this example of an accrued expense would be adjusted using journal entries.

**4**  Give an example of asset expiration other than the example given in this chapter. Explain how this example would be adjusted using journal entries.

**5**  Give an example of unearned revenue and explain the process for period-end adjustments involving unearned revenue.

**6**  Explain how to access general journal entries.

**7**  What center would you use to start bank reconciliations?

**8**  What account is typically used to record service charges?

**9**  When you've finished reconciling a bank account, what should be the difference between the ending balance and the cleared balance?

**10**  What information is included in the account reconciliation report?

## Chapter 9 Exercises

### Chapter 9 Exercises 1

### ACCRUING EXPENSES

Restore the file Boston Catering Ch 9 found on the text CD or download it from the text website. Set the system date to **9/30/10** and the period to **Period 3 – 09/01/10–09/30/10**. Make the following adjustments and then print an income statement and balance sheet for the period 7/1/10 through 9/30/10 so that you view an income statement for July, August, and September 2010 and a balance sheet as of 7/31/10, 8/31/10, and 9/30/10. (You may need to refer to prior chapters to remember how to create these comparative financial statements.)

a.  Accrue interest expense and the related accrued interest payable (new account) as of 7/31/10, 8/31/10, and 9/30/10 based on the following schedules. (Note that on 8/2/10 the company made the July payments of 926.29 and 610.32 and on 9/1/10 the company made the August payments of 926.29 and 610.32. Record the later two payments with check numbers 1523 to CitiBank and 1524 to Bank of America.)

| Month | Payment | Interest | Principal | Balance |
|---|---|---|---|---|
| | | | | $ 50,000.00 |
| Jul 2010 | $926.29 | $ 416.67 | $509.63 | $ 49,490.37 |
| Aug 2010 | $926.29 | $ 412.42 | $513.87 | $ 48,976.50 |
| Sep 2010 | $926.29 | $ 408.14 | $518.15 | $ 48,458.35 |

| Month | Payment | Interest | Principal | Balance |
|---|---|---|---|---|
| | | | | $ 25,000.00 |
| Jul 2010 | $610.32 | $ 166.67 | $443.66 | $ 24,556.34 |
| Aug 2010 | $610.32 | $ 163.71 | $446.61 | $ 24,109.73 |
| Sep 2010 | $610.32 | $ 160.73 | $449.59 | $ 23,660.14 |

| Month | Payment | Interest | Principal | Balance |
|---|---|---|---|---|
| | | | | $ 10,000.00 |
| Aug 2010 | $0 | $ 50.00 | $0 | $ 10,000.00 |
| Sep 2010 | $0 | $ 50.00 | $0 | $ 10,000.00 |

b. Reverse accrued interest expense for the first two loans on 8/1/10 and 9/1/10 as appropriate. Do not reverse accrued interest expense on the $10,000 loan.

## Chapter 9 Exercise 2
## ACCRUING REVENUE

Restore the file Boston Catering Ch 9 found on the text CD or download it from the text website. Do not use the file created in Exercise 1 above. Set the system date to **9/30/10** and the period to **Period 3 – 09/01/10–09/30/10**. Make the following adjustments and then print an income statement and balance sheet for the period 7/1/10 through 9/30/10 so that you view an income statement for July, August, and September 2010 and a balance sheet as of 7/31/10, 8/31/10, and 9/30/10. (You may need to refer to prior chapters to remember how to create these comparative financial statements.)

a. Accrue interest income (a new income type account with Account ID: 450) as of 7/31/10 of $11 to the short-term investments account. Interest is paid at the end of every calendar quarter.

b. On 8/1/10 reverse the interest income accrual you made above.

c. Accrue interest income as of 8/31/10 of $115 to the short-term investments account.

d. On 9/1/10 reverse the interest income accrual you made above.

e. On 9/1/10 the company billed Fidelity Investments on invoice 1125 for a catering engagement held on 8/31/10 for 200 Fall Suppers (Item Code S300) resulting in $13,000 in catering sales and $650 in sales tax, which were billed on account (total $13,650). The food purchases of $4,000 were set up as accounts payable to US Food Service. Accrue this revenue and expense as of 8/31/10.

f. On 9/1/10 reverse the revenue and expense accrual made above.

g. On 9/1/10 record the invoice described in (e) above.

h. On 9/1/10 record check 1512 to US Food Service for $4,000 in food purchases. (*Hint:* record in account 502.)

*Chapter 9 Exercise 3*

## RECORDING EXPENSES INCURRED BUT PREVIOUSLY DEFERRED

Restore the file **Boston Catering Ch 9** found on the text CD or download it from the text website. Do not use the file created in the exercises above. Set the system date to **9/30/10** and the period to **Period 3 – 09/01/10–09/30/10**. Make the following adjustments and then print an income statement and balance sheet for the period 7/1/10 through 9/30/10 so that you view an income statement for July, August, and September 2010 and a balance sheet as of 7/31/10, 8/31/10, and 9/30/10. (You may need to refer to prior chapters to remember how to create these comparative financial statements.)

a.  The $3,000 prepaid insurance balance recorded as of 6/30/10 represented three months of insurance premiums, which expire equally in July, August, and September.

b.  Depreciation expense was $1,000, $1,075, and $1,350 for the months of July, August, and September.

*Chapter 9 Exercise 4*

## PREPARING BANK RECONCILIATION

Restore the file **Boston Catering Ch 9** found on the text CD or download it from the text website. Do not use the file created in the exercises above. Reconcile the Bank of America checking account and then print an account reconciliation for each month. (Be sure to set the account to **Account ID: 100**.)

a.  Set the system date to **7/31/10** and the period to **Period 1 – 07/01/10–07/31/10**. The 7/31/10 Bank of America bank statement shows an ending balance of $78,881 with service charges of $39. All deposits made in July were received by the bank except those made on 7/31/10, which were received by the bank on 8/1/10. All checks written in July were cashed by the bank except check numbers 1505 through 1508, which cleared the bank in August.

b.  Set the system date to **8/31/10** and the period to **Period 2 – 08/01/10–08/31/10**. The 8/31/10 Bank of America bank statement shows an ending balance of $54,036.64 with service charges of $45. All deposits made in August were received by the bank. All checks written in August were cashed by the bank except check numbers 1517 through 1522.

## Chapter 9 Assignments

*Chapter 9 Assignment 1*

## ADDING MORE INFORMATION: WILD WATER SPORTS

Restore the file **Wild Water Sports, Inc. 9A** found on the text CD or download it from the text Website and then add the following transactions in chronological order. Be sure to set the system date to **4/30/13** and the accounting period to **Period 4 – 04/01/13–04/30/13**.

*merchandising*

| Event # | Date | Adjustment |
|---|---|---|
| 1 | 5/1 | Invoice 10019 was recorded on this date for the sale of a Malibu Sportster LX (item 202) to Alisa Hay for $52,000 plus tax. (Even though this isn't an adjusting entry, record it in Peachtree to illustrate how the accrual and reversal work.) |
| 2 | 4/30 | Accrue interest expense of $995.52 on the $250,000 loan as per the amortization schedule in Figure 8.1. Use journal entry 19. Don't forget to reverse the entry. |
| 3 | 4/30 | Accrue interest expense of $250 on the $50,000 loan. No reversal required. Use journal entry 20. |
| 4 | 4/30 | Accrue interest income of $100 on short-term investments. Use journal entry 21. |
| 5 | 4/30 | Records show that the company delivered a Malibu Sportster LX to Alisa Hay on April 30 but the company didn't invoice her until May 1 (see event 1 above.). The boat was sold for $52,000 and cost $41,600. Sales tax in the amount of $3,380 was collected on 5/1 from the sale. Create journal entry 22 to adjust for this event. Be sure to indicate this transaction should be reversed in the next accounting period. |
| 6 | 4/30 | Adjust prepaid expenses ($2,000 for advertising and $1,833.33 for insurance) in April similar to what you did for March in the chapter. Use journal entries 23 and 24. |
| 7 | 4/30 | Record depreciation expense of $3,870 for the month of April: for equipment, for furniture, and for the truck. Use journal entry 25. |
| 8 | 4/30 | Reclassify the deposit of $16,250 received from Buena Vista Water Sports on 4/30/13 to Customer Deposits (unearned revenue). Reclassify the $10,000 Performance Rentals deposit as well. Use journal entry 26 and remember to reverse this journal entry next period. |
| 9 | 4/30 | The Bank of Florida bank statement as of 4/30 has an ending balance of $54,475.03. All checks cleared the bank account except Check Nos. 1050 to 1053. All deposits cleared the bank account except the $30,517.35 deposit made 4/30. The bank statement shows interest income of $35 and bank charges of $25. |

Print the following with no page numbers and no zero amounts and with the accounting period set to **Period 4**:

a.  Standard income statement for April 2013

b.  Standard balance sheet for April 30, 2013

c.  Account reconciliation report for the checking account as of April 30, 2013

d.  General journal from April 30 to May 1, 2013 (fit on one page)

## Chapter 9 Assignment 2

# ADDING MORE INFORMATION: CENTRAL COAST CELLULAR

Restore the file **Central Coast Cellular Ch 9** found on the text CD or download it from the text Website. Change the system date to **1/31/09** and the accounting period to **Period 1 – 01/01/09–01/31/09**. Add the following adjusting journal entries and perform the bank reconciliation. (*Note:* The company has chosen not to provide journal entry reference numbers.)

| Event # | Date | Adjustment |
|---------|------|-----------|
| 1 | 1/31 | Record depreciation expense of $1,000 for equipment and $500 for office furniture. |
| 2 | 1/31 | Accrue interest expense of $950. (Create a new interest expense account with ID = 6925 and a new accrued interest payable account with ID = 2050.) Set this entry up to automatically reverse the next accounting period. |
| 3 | 1/31 | Reclassify the credit balance of $10,000 in the City of San Luis Obispo account to unearned revenue (Customer Deposits). |
| 4 | 1/31 | The bank statement dated January 31, 2009, indicated a bank balance of $133,640.49, with all checks clearing except Check Nos. 3010, 3011, and 3012. All deposits cleared. A bank service charge of $80 was reported. Reconcile the bank statement. |

Print the following with no page numbers and no zero amounts:

a.  Standard income statement for January 2009

b.  Standard balance sheet for January 31, 2009

c.  Account reconciliation report for the checking account as of January 31, 2009

d.  General journal from January 30 to February 1, 2009 (fit on one page)

## *Chapter 9 Assignment 3*
## ADDING MORE INFORMATION: SANTA BARBARA SAILING

Restore the file **Santa Barbara Sailing Ch 9** found on the text CD or download it from the text Website. Add the following adjustments and bank reconciliation after you set the system date to **7/31/12**:

*service*

| Event # | Date | Adjustment |
|---------|------|-----------|
| 1 | 7/31/12 | Adjust Prepaid Expenses (Account ID: 1400) for $2,000 to Rent or Lease Expense (Account ID: 6300) with journal entry 5. |
| 2 | 7/31/12 | Accrue Interest Expense (Account ID: 6180) on the $50,000 Bank of Caribbean loan for $134.25 to Accrued Interest Payable (a new other current liability account with Account ID: 2200) with journal entry 6. |
| 3 | 7/31/12 | Record Depreciation Expense (Account ID: 7050) for the month of $5,750 with journal entry 7. |
| 4 | 7/31/12 | The boat rented to Barry Cohen for 14 days was paid in advance and recorded as $3,850 in Rental Income. Of this amount, only half ($1,925) was earned as of 7/31/12. Reduce Rental Income accordingly and increase Unearned Revenue (a new other current liability account with Account ID: 2100) with journal entry 8. (*Note:* This is different from the example provided in the text where you were reclassifying an advance to unearned revenue. In this case, you are actually debiting revenue and crediting a liability for revenue you have not yet earned.) |
| 5 | 8/1/12 | Make all appropriate reversing journal entries. (This should include just the interest expense and unearned revenue adjustments.) |
| 6 | 7/31/12 | The bank statement dated 7/31/12 indicated a bank balance of $122,206.74 with all checks clearing except numbers 111–114. The bank deducted a service charge of $43 and added interest income of $70. All deposits were accounted for except the receipt of $4,158 from Barry Cohen, which had not yet been deposited. |

Print the following as of 7/31/12 with no page numbers and no zero amounts:

a.   Standard income statement

b.   Standard balance sheet

c.   Account reconciliation report for the checking account

d.   General journal from 7/31/12 to 8/1/12 (fit on one page)

## Chapter 9 Cases

### Chapter 9 Case Problem 1

## FOREVER YOUNG

*sole proprietorship*

*service*

Restore the backup you made of **Forever Young** in Chapter 9 into a new company folder. (Do not restore this backup into an existing folder.) Change the company name to include Ch 9 at the end so that the new company name is **Forever Young Ch 9**. Add the following adjustments and bank reconciliation after you set the system date to **1/31/08**:

| Event # | Date | Adjustment |
|---|---|---|
| 1 | 1/31/08 | Record the use of Supplies (Account ID: 1200) for January using journal entry 1. (Assume supplies are used evenly throughout the 6 month period they were purchased for and that they are expensed to a new account, Office Supplies Expense, Account ID: 6225.) |
| 2 | 1/31/08 | Accrue interest expense on the Wells Fargo note payable of $96 using journal entry 2. (Create two new accounts: Interest Expense with Account ID: 5900 and Accrued Interest Payable with Account ID: 2050.) |
| 3 | 1/31/08 | Record the use of brochures for January using journal entry 3, creating a new Advertising Expense account with Account ID: 5700. (*Hint:* Look at how this transaction was described and recorded in the previous chapter.) |
| 4 | 1/31/08 | Reclassify ITP's deposit to a new account Customer Deposits with Account ID: 2400 using journal entry 4. (*Hint:* Look at how this transaction was described and recorded in the previous chapter.) |
| 5 | 1/31/08 | Record Depreciation Expense (new expense account with Account ID: 5850) to Accumulated Depreciation (a new fixed asset account with Account ID: 1510) of $67 for the month using journal entry 5. |
| 6 | 2/1/08 | Make all appropriate reversing journal entries. |
| 7 | 1/31/08 | Create the following new accounts: Account ID 5825, Description: Bank Fees, Account Type: Expenses, and Account ID: 4100, Description: Interest Income, Account Type: Income. |
| 8 | 1/31/08 | The bank statement dated 1/31/08 indicated a bank balance of $63,233.82 with all checks clearing except numbers 11–14. The bank charged a fee of $25 and provided interest income of $115. All deposits were accounted for except the $3,000 received on 1/31/08, which has not yet been deposited. |

This is a continuous case in that the next chapter will use the work you've accomplished here as the basis for recording additional business events. After you've printed the following reports, create a backup of this file on some type of external medium (flash drive, Internet site, CD, disk, etc.). The backup should be named **Forever Young Ch 9** for easy identification later. You'll be restoring this file in the next chapter. Print the following as of 1/31/08 with no page numbers and no zero amounts:

a.   Standard income statement

b.   Standard balance sheet

c.   Account reconciliation report for the checking account

d.   General journal from 1/31/08 to 2/1/08 (fit on one page)

*merchandising*

## Chapter 9 Case Problem 2

# OCEAN VIEW FLOWERS

Restore the backup you made for **Ocean View Flowers** in Chapter 9 into a new company folder. (Do not restore this backup into an existing folder.) Change the company name to include Ch 9 at the end so that the new company name is **Ocean View Flowers Ch 9**. Add the following adjustments and bank reconciliation:

| Event # | Date | Adjustment |
|---|---|---|
| 1 | 1/31 | Change the system date to **1/31/08** and the accounting period to **Period 1 – 01/01/08–01/31/08**. The January bank statement reported an ending balance for the regular checking account of $76,340.29, bank service charges of $45, and interest revenue of $100 as of January 31, 2008. Deposits for $100,000, $50,000, $6,600, and $22,200 were received by the bank. Check Nos. 101–110 were paid by the bank. Reconcile the bank statement. |
| 2 | 2/29 | Change the system date to **2/29/08** and the accounting period to **Period 2 – 02/01/08–02/29/08**. Accrue loan interest expense of $3,190 on the $319,000 loan for two months' interest to an account called Accrued Expenses (an existing current liability account with ID = 23000). Use journal entry 5. Reverse this transaction next period. |
| 3 | 2/29 | Accrue interest revenue of $800 on a certificate of deposit with journal entry 6. (Record this to a new account called Accrued Interest Receivable, another current asset account, with ID = 11100.) Reverse this transaction next period. |
| 4 | 2/29 | Prepaid insurance of $100 expired for each month: January and February 2008. Use journal entry 7. |
| 5 | 2/29 | Record depreciation expense of $3,100: $2,000 for the building, $600 for the computer equipment, and $500 for the office equipment. Use journal entry 8. |
| 6 | 2/29 | Reclassify the deposit received from FTD on 1/28/08 to unearned revenue (a new current liability account called Customer Deposits with ID = 24300). Use journal entry 9 and reverse this transaction next period. (*Hint:* Create a Receipts List to view the receipts received in January.) |
| 7 | 2/29 | A review of the shipping records indicates that a shipment that occurred on 2/28 was not invoiced until 3/3. Invoice 10004, recorded in the next accounting period, billed California Beauties $16,000 for 800 Calistoga Sun Daylilies, $7,200 for 300 Almond Puff Daylilies, and $20,000 for 500 Peach Anthuriums (cost: $22,600). Use journal entry 10 and reverse this transaction next period. |

| Event # | Date | Adjustment |
|---|---|---|
| 8 | 2/29 | The February bank statement reported an ending balance of $65,579.61, bank service charges of $55, and interest revenue of $75 as of February 29, 2008. Deposits for $5,000 and $5,200 were received by the bank. Check Nos. 111–127 were paid by the bank. |

This is a continuous case in that the next chapter will use the work you've accomplished here as the basis for recording additional business events. After you've printed the following reports, create a backup of this file and store it on some type of external medium (flash drive, Internet site, CD, disk, etc.). The backup file should be named **Ocean View Flowers Ch 9** for easy identification later. You'll be restoring this file in the next chapter. Print the following with no page numbers and no zero amounts:

a.   Standard income statement for February 2008

b.   Standard balance sheet for February 29, 2008

c.   Account reconciliation report for the checking account as of January 31, 2008 (You will have to set the accounting period to **Period 1** to print this reconciliation.)

d.   Account reconciliation report for the checking account as of February 29, 2008 (You will have to set the accounting period back to **Period 2** to print this reconciliation.)

e.   General journal from February 29 through March 1, 2008 (fit on one page)

## *Chapter 9 Case Problem 3*
## ALOHA PROPERTY MANAGEMENT

Restore the backup you made for **Aloha** in Chapter 9 into a new company folder. (Do not restore this backup into an existing folder.) Change the company name to include Ch 9 at the end so that the new company name is **Aloha Property Management Ch 9**. Change the system date to **2/29/08** and the accounting period to **Period 2 – 02/01/08–02/29/08**. Add the following adjustments and bank reconciliation. (*Note:* The company has chosen not to provide journal entry reference numbers.)

| Event # | Date | Adjustment |
|---|---|---|
| 1 | 2/29 | Accrue interest expense of $22,555 on the $3,875,000 loan to account 23000 Accrued Expenses. Reverse this entry. |
| 2 | 2/29 | Accrue interest income of $210 on short-term investments. |
| 3 | 2/29 | Adjust prepaid insurance for January and February 2008 to insurance expense. (*Hint:* Go to the original entry, recorded in Chapter 7, to determine the amount of the adjustment.) |
| 4 | 2/29 | Record depreciation expense of $34,612 for the months of January and February 2008: $13,334 for the Moana building, $20,000 for the Villa building, and $1,278 for the furniture. |

| Event # | Date | Adjustment |
|---------|------|------------|
| 5 | 2/29 | Reclassify the deposits received from American Airlines, UCLA, and UCB on 2/5/08, 2/25/08, and 2/26/08, respectively, to unearned revenue (a new current liability account, Customer Deposits, numbered 24400). (*Hint:* Create a Receipts List to view the receipts received in February.) Do not reverse this entry. |
| 6 | 2/29 | Complete the bank reconciliation. The Bank of Hawaii bank statement as of 2/29 has an ending balance of $115,292.39 for the regular checking account. All checks cleared the bank account except Check Nos. 998 through 1002. All deposits cleared the bank account except the $10,750 deposit made 2/26. The bank statement shows interest income of $175 and bank charges of $35. |

This is a continuous case in that the next chapter will use the work you've accomplished here as the basis for recording additional business events. After you've printed the following reports, create a backup of this file and store it on some type of external medium (flash drive, Internet site, CD, disk, etc.). The backup file should be named **Aloha Property Management Ch 9** for easy identification later. You'll be restoring this file in the next chapter. Print the following with no page numbers and no zero amounts:

a.   Standard income statement for the two months ending February 2008

b.   Standard balance sheet for February 29, 2008

c.   Account reconciliation report for the checking account as of February 29, 2008

d.   General journal from February 29 through March 1, 2008 (fit on one page)

# Budgeting

*In this Chapter, you will:*

- Create budgets for revenues.
- Create budgets for expenses.
- Create a budgeted income statement.
- Create a budgeted versus actual income statement.
- Create a budget for assets, liabilities, and equities.
- Create a budgeted balance sheet.
- Create a budgeted versus actual balance sheet.

## *Case:* Wild Water Sports, Inc.

Today, Donna asks you and Karen to prepare financial statements for the first quarter of the year. She reminds you that you have already recorded all of the transactions for January through April, so you're ready to prepare the statements as of the end of the first quarter, March 31. "But preparing the statements is just half the job," Karen points out. "We have to be able to interpret these statements. How will we know if the company is doing well?"

Donna is quick to respond, "At the beginning of the year, I used a spreadsheet program to establish budgets for the year. I can compare the actual results shown in the statements you prepare with these budgets."

"Doesn't Peachtree have a budgeting feature?" you ask.

"You're right!" exclaims Donna. "I didn't use that feature, but now that you mention it, I should have. Would the two of you mind entering my budget estimates into Peachtree as well?"

"Not at all," you respond.

After Donna leaves, Karen explains to you that Peachtree allows you to set up a budget for an account or for a customer within an account. To do this, you enter budgeted amounts for the income statement accounts or balance sheet accounts you wish to track.

"Are you able to track actual versus budgeted amounts?" you ask.

"Yes," Karen replies. "I'll show you how to use Peachtree's budget reports to examine the budget by itself, as well as how to compare Wild Water Sports' actual results to its budgeted amounts."

You have another question. "Can we create different budgets based on different assumptions in Peachtree?"

"No," Karen answers. "Peachtree allows you to have a different budget for different fiscal years, but you may have only one budget per fiscal year."

Karen explains that Peachtree allows you to set up budgets for specific accounts within financial statements or for all specific financial statements. While it is easier to budget for specific accounts, it might be more useful to prepare a budgeted income statement or budgeted balance sheet.

To begin, Karen suggests that you print Donna's spreadsheet budget and then the two of you can establish the monthly budget for revenues.

## Budgeting Revenues

*Video Demonstration*

***Demo 10A - Budgeting revenues***

Peachtree provides a Maintain Budgets window to enter budget information. In this window, you specify the fiscal year, the account, and the corresponding amounts for each month. As you fill in this information, you are setting up a budget for a single account, such as a balance sheet or an income statement account.

You also ask about Peachtree's use of the term *income* instead of *revenues* for products and services. Karen reminds you that although *revenues* is the traditional accounting term for these items, Peachtree has chosen to classify them as "income" in the Type section of the chart of accounts.

Donna's budget predicts revenue of $200,000 in January 2013, with an increase of $50,000 each month throughout the year. Service and parts revenue is expected to remain constant, at $3,000 and $500 per month, respectively, throughout the year.

### To create a budget for specific revenues:

1   Start the Peachtree program.

2   Restore the **Wild Water Sports, Inc. 10** file from your Data Files CD or download it from the Internet.

3   Set the system date to **3/31/13** and the accounting period to **Period 3**.

4   Click **Budgets** from the Maintain menu.

5   Click the **Edit** menu and then click **Quick Action Buttons** to remove the check from this item and disable Quick Action Buttons. (These can be more of an obstacle than an aid.)

6   Select **Income Statement Accounts** from the Type drop-down list.

7   Select **01/01/13–12/31/13** from the View Fiscal Year drop-down list. A partial view of the resulting Maintain Budgets window is shown in Figure 10.1.

**Figure 10.1**

Partial View of the Maintain Budgets Window

**8**　Click in the cell at the intersection of the 1/31/13 column and the 4000 – Sales Income row. Type **200000**.

**9**　Continue entering budgeted amounts for revenues until your window looks like Figure 10.2.

Click here, for example, and then drag the mouse left or right to increase or decrease the column width

**Figure 10.2**

Revenue Budget

| Account ID | Account Name | Total | 1/31/13 | 2/28/13 | 3/31/13 | 4/30/13 | |
|---|---|---|---|---|---|---|---|
| 4000 | Sales Income | 1,100,000.00 | 200,000.00 | 250,000.00 | 300,000.00 | 350,000.00 | |
| 4010 | Service Income | 12,000.00 | 3,000.00 | 3,000.00 | 3,000.00 | 3,000.00 | |
| 4030 | Parts Income | 2,000.00 | 500.00 | 500.00 | 500.00 | 500.00 | |
| 4100 | Interest Income | 0.00 | 0.00 | 0.00 | 0.00 | 0.00 | |
| 4200 | Finance Charge Income | 0.00 | 0.00 | 0.00 | 0.00 | 0.00 | |
| 4300 | Other Income | 0.00 | 0.00 | 0.00 | 0.00 | 0.00 | |
| 4900 | Sales Discounts | 0.00 | 0.00 | 0.00 | 0.00 | 0.00 | |
| 5000 | Cost of Sales | 0.00 | 0.00 | 0.00 | 0.00 | 0.00 | |
| 5100 | Cost of Sales-Freight | 0.00 | 0.00 | 0.00 | 0.00 | 0.00 | |
| 5400 | Cost of Sales-Salary & ' | 0.00 | 0.00 | 0.00 | 0.00 | 0.00 | |
| 5900 | Inventory Adjustments | 0.00 | 0.00 | 0.00 | 0.00 | 0.00 | |
| 6000 | Wages Expense | 0.00 | 0.00 | 0.00 | 0.00 | 0.00 | |

**10**　*Trouble?* You may have to adjust the column widths to view the amounts. Click the line dividing a column title as shown in Figure 10.2 and then drag the mouse left or right to increase or decrease the column width.

Now you're ready to set up budgeted amounts for expenses.

# Budgeting Expenses

The budget for Wild Water Sports cost of goods sold depends on product sales. Donna estimated that product cost should amount to approximately 80% of sales since the company marks up the cost of boats 25% above their cost. Thus, as budgeted sales increase, so should budgeted cost of sales. Karen recalls that in January you set up the budget to include sales of $200,000. Thus, expected cost of sales should be 80% of the total January sales of $200,000, or $160,000. Each month thereafter, Donna expects sales to increase by $50,000. Accordingly, the related cost of goods sold should increase monthly by 80% of $50,000, or $40,000.

Karen expects wages expense, the largest budgeted expense item for Wild Water Sports, to remain constant at $12,000 per month throughout the year. Depreciation expenses are expected to be $3,500 per month, insurance expenses $2,000 per month, other office expenses $1,000 per month, marketing and advertising expense $2,500 per month, interest expense $2,800 per month, telephone expenses $2,100 per month, and utilities $900 per month.

## To create a budget for specific expenses:

**1** Click in the cell at the intersection of the first column and the 5000 – Cost of Sales row. Type **160000** ($200,000 × 80%).

**2** Type **200000, 240000**, and **280000** as the Cost of Sales for February, March, and April, respectively.

**3** Enter budgeted expenses for January as follows:

| Account ID | Amount |
| --- | --- |
| 6000 | 12,000 |
| 6400 | 900 |
| 6500 | 2,100 |
| 6550 | 1,000 |
| 6600 | 2,500 |
| 6725 | 2,800 |
| 6950 | 2,000 |
| 7050 | 3,500 |

**4** Click and drag to select all budgeted amounts for January between Wages Expense and Depreciation Expense.

**5** Right-click the selected cells and select **Copy** from the shortcut menu as shown in Figure 10.3

**6** Click and drag to select all budgeted amounts for February between Wages Expense and Depreciation Expense.

**7** Right-click the selected cells and select **Paste** from the shortcut menu.

**8** Repeat steps 6 and 7 for March and April since budgeted expenses for these items are identical for all four months being budgeted. Your completed expense budget should look like Figure 10.4.

**9** Click **Save** to save all these budgeted amounts.

| Account ID | Account Name | Total | 1/31/13 | 2/28/13 | 3/31/13 | 4/30/13 |
|---|---|---|---|---|---|---|
| 6000 | Wages Expense | 12,000.00 | 12,000.00 | 0.00 | 0.00 | 0.00 |
| 6050 | Employee Benefit Prog | 0.00 | 0.00 | 0.00 | 0.00 | 0.00 |
| 6100 | Payroll Tax Expense | 0.00 | 0.00 | 0.00 | 0.00 | 0.00 |
| 6150 | Bad Debt Expense | 0.00 | 0.00 | 0.00 | 0.00 | 0.00 |
| 6200 | Income Tax Expense | 0.00 | 0.00 | 0.00 | 0.00 | 0.00 |
| 6250 | Other Taxes Expense | 0.00 | 0.00 | 0.00 | 0.00 | 0.00 |
| 6300 | Rent or Lease Expense | 0.00 | 0.00 | 0.00 | 0.00 | 0.00 |
| 6350 | Maintenance & Repairs | 0.00 | 0.00 | 0.00 | 0.00 | 0.00 |
| 6400 | Utilities Expense | 900.00 | 900.00 | 0.00 | 0.00 | 0.00 |
| 6450 | Office Supplies Expens | 0.00 | 0.00 | 0.00 | 0.00 | 0.00 |
| 6500 | Telephone Expense | 2,100.00 | 2,100.00 | 0.00 | 0.00 | 0.00 |
| 6550 | Other Office Expense | 1,000.00 | 1,0 | | | |
| 6600 | Advertising Expense | 2,500.00 | 2,5 | | | |
| 6650 | Commissions and Fees | 0.00 | | | | |
| 6700 | Franchise Fees Expense | 0.00 | | | | |
| 6725 | Interest Expense | 2,800.00 | 2,8 | | | |
| 6750 | Equipment Rental Expe | 0.00 | | | | |
| 6800 | Freight Expense | 0.00 | | | | |
| 6850 | Service Charge Expense | 0.00 | | | | |
| 6900 | Purchase Disc-Expense | 0.00 | | | | |
| 6950 | Insurance Expense | 2,000.00 | 2,0 | | | |
| 7000 | Over and Short Expens | 0.00 | | | | |
| 7050 | Depreciation Expense | 3,500.00 | 3,5 | | | |
| 7100 | Gain/Loss - Sale of Ass | 0.00 | | | | |

Context menu:
- Select ▶
- Cut    Ctrl+X
- Copy    Ctrl+C
- Paste    Ctrl+V
- Clear Text    Del
- Allocate Total Amount
- Adjust Amount
- Round to Nearest ▶
- Quick Action Buttons
- What's This?

**Figure 10.3**

Copying Budget Cells

| Account ID | Account Name | Total | 1/31/13 | 2/28/13 | 3/31/13 | 4/30/13 |
|---|---|---|---|---|---|---|
| 5000 | Cost of Sales | 880,000.00 | 160,000.00 | 200,000.00 | 240,000.00 | 280,000.00 |
| 5100 | Cost of Sales-Freight | 0.00 | 0.00 | 0.00 | 0.00 | 0.00 |
| 5400 | Cost of Sales-Salary & | 0.00 | 0.00 | 0.00 | 0.00 | 0.00 |
| 5900 | Inventory Adjustments | 0.00 | 0.00 | 0.00 | 0.00 | 0.00 |
| 6000 | Wages Expense | 48,000.00 | 12,000.00 | 12,000.00 | 12,000.00 | 12,000.00 |
| 6050 | Employee Benefit Prog | 0.00 | 0.00 | 0.00 | 0.00 | 0.00 |
| 6100 | Payroll Tax Expense | 0.00 | 0.00 | 0.00 | 0.00 | 0.00 |
| 6150 | Bad Debt Expense | 0.00 | 0.00 | 0.00 | 0.00 | 0.00 |
| 6200 | Income Tax Expense | 0.00 | 0.00 | 0.00 | 0.00 | 0.00 |
| 6250 | Other Taxes Expense | 0.00 | 0.00 | 0.00 | 0.00 | 0.00 |
| 6300 | Rent or Lease Expense | 0.00 | 0.00 | 0.00 | 0.00 | 0.00 |
| 6350 | Maintenance & Repairs | 0.00 | 0.00 | 0.00 | 0.00 | 0.00 |
| 6400 | Utilities Expense | 3,600.00 | 900.00 | 900.00 | 900.00 | 900.00 |
| 6450 | Office Supplies Expens | 0.00 | 0.00 | 0.00 | 0.00 | 0.00 |
| 6500 | Telephone Expense | 8,400.00 | 2,100.00 | 2,100.00 | 2,100.00 | 2,100.00 |
| 6550 | Other Office Expense | 4,000.00 | 1,000.00 | 1,000.00 | 1,000.00 | 1,000.00 |
| 6600 | Advertising Expense | 10,000.00 | 2,500.00 | 2,500.00 | 2,500.00 | 2,500.00 |
| 6650 | Commissions and Fees | 0.00 | 0.00 | 0.00 | 0.00 | 0.00 |
| 6700 | Franchise Fees Expense | 0.00 | 0.00 | 0.00 | 0.00 | 0.00 |
| 6725 | Interest Expense | 11,200.00 | 2,800.00 | 2,800.00 | 2,800.00 | 2,800.00 |
| 6750 | Equipment Rental Expe | 0.00 | 0.00 | 0.00 | 0.00 | 0.00 |
| 6800 | Freight Expense | 0.00 | 0.00 | 0.00 | 0.00 | 0.00 |
| 6850 | Service Charge Expense | 0.00 | 0.00 | 0.00 | 0.00 | 0.00 |
| 6900 | Purchase Disc-Expense | 0.00 | 0.00 | 0.00 | 0.00 | 0.00 |
| 6950 | Insurance Expense | 8,000.00 | 2,000.00 | 2,000.00 | 2,000.00 | 2,000.00 |
| 7000 | Over and Short Expens | 0.00 | 0.00 | 0.00 | 0.00 | 0.00 |
| 7050 | Depreciation Expense | 14,000.00 | 3,500.00 | 3,500.00 | 3,500.00 | 3,500.00 |
| 7100 | Gain/Loss - Sale of Ass | 0.00 | 0.00 | 0.00 | 0.00 | 0.00 |

**Figure 10.4**

Budgeted Expenses

    Now that all of the detail income and expense amounts have been created for the budget, you can create a budgeted income statement.

# Budgeted Income Statement

Now that Karen has entered budgetary information for several specific income statement accounts, she is curious to see a complete budget. Thus, she will create and print a budgeted income statement for the first quarter of 2013.

## To create and print a budgeted income statement:

1    Click **Reports** from the button toolbar (located near the top of the Maintain Budgets window) and then select **Budget**.

2    Click **Options** from the button toolbar.

3    Select **Per End (3/31/13)** from the To: drop-down list.

4    Uncheck the **Include accounts with zero amounts** check box and then click **OK**. The resulting Budget is then displayed as shown in Figure 10.5.

**Figure 10.5**

Budgeted Income Statement

### Wild Water Sports, Inc. 10
### Budget
### For the Period From Jan 1, 2013 to Mar 31, 2013

Filter Criteria includes: 1) Types: Income Statement Accounts; 2) Active Accounts.

| Account ID | Account Description | 1/31/13 | 2/28/13 | 3/31/13 | YTD Total |
|---|---|---|---|---|---|
| 4000 | Sales Income | 200,000.00 | 250,000.00 | 300,000.00 | 750,000.00 |
| 4010 | Service Income | 3,000.00 | 3,000.00 | 3,000.00 | 9,000.00 |
| 4030 | Parts Income | 500.00 | 500.00 | 500.00 | 1,500.00 |
| 5000 | Cost of Sales | 160,000.00 | 200,000.00 | 240,000.00 | 600,000.00 |
| 6000 | Wages Expense | 12,000.00 | 12,000.00 | 12,000.00 | 36,000.00 |
| 6400 | Utilities Expense | 900.00 | 900.00 | 900.00 | 2,700.00 |
| 6500 | Telephone Expense | 2,100.00 | 2,100.00 | 2,100.00 | 6,300.00 |
| 6550 | Other Office Expense | 1,000.00 | 1,000.00 | 1,000.00 | 3,000.00 |
| 6600 | Advertising Expense | 2,500.00 | 2,500.00 | 2,500.00 | 7,500.00 |
| 6725 | Interest Expense | 2,800.00 | 2,800.00 | 2,800.00 | 8,400.00 |
| 6950 | Insurance Expense | 2,000.00 | 2,000.00 | 2,000.00 | 6,000.00 |
| 7050 | Depreciation Expense | 3,500.00 | 3,500.00 | 3,500.00 | 10,500.00 |
| | | | | | |
| | Revenue | 203,500.00 | 253,500.00 | 303,500.00 | 760,500.00 |
| | - Cost of Sales | -160,000.00 | -200,000.00 | -240,000.00 | -600,000.00 |
| | | | | | |
| | Gross Profit | 43,500.00 | 53,500.00 | 63,500.00 | 160,500.00 |
| | - Expenses | -26,800.00 | -26,800.00 | -26,800.00 | -80,400.00 |
| | | | | | |
| | Net Income | 16,700.00 | 26,700.00 | 36,700.00 | 80,100.00 |

5    Click **Print** and then click **OK** to print this budgeted income statement.

6    Click **Close** to close the budgeted income statement.

7    Close the Maintain Budgets window.

Karen explains that the above report just describes the current budget but does not compare that budget with actual results from the quarter ended March 31, 2013. She suggests that you create a budgeted versus actual report for the quarter ending March 31, 2013, showing only quarterly amounts.

"Why not monthly?" you ask.

"Remember we only made our adjusting entries at the end of March," Karen reminds you. "We didn't make adjusting entries at the end of January and February. As a result, our budgeted versus actual analysis on a monthly basis would reveal all sorts of discrepancies. Take insurance, for example. We budgeted insurance expense of $2,000 per month for January, February, and March. Our actual insurance expense will only be recorded in March when we made an adjusting entry for prepaid insurance. Thus, we'll be under budget in January and February and over budget in March just because of when we recorded our adjustments."

"Then why don't we make adjusting entries every month?" you ask.

"Good question," Karen answers. "We could, but it would take lots of time. Instead, we'll just produce financial statements every quarter, since that's when the bank wants to see how we're doing."

---

## To create and print a budgeted versus actual report for the first quarter of 2013:

**1** Click **Reports & Forms**, select **Financial Statements**, and then double-click <**Standard**> **Income/Budget**.

**2** Uncheck the **Print Page Numbers** and **Show Zero Amounts** check boxes and then click **OK**. The resulting Income Statement Compared with Budget is then displayed as shown in Figure 10.6.

Wild Water Sports, Inc. 10
Income Statement
Compared with Budget
For the Three Months Ending March 31, 2013

| | Current Month Actual | Current Month Budget | Current Month Variance | Year to Date Actual | Year to Date Budget | Year to Date Variance |
|---|---|---|---|---|---|---|
| **Revenues** | | | | | | |
| Sales Income | $ 434,750.00 | $ 300,000.00 | 134,750.00 $ | 767,500.00 $ | 750,000.00 | 17,500.00 |
| Service Income | 2,740.00 | 3,000.00 | (260.00) | 6,685.00 | 9,000.00 | (2,315.00) |
| Parts Income | 320.00 | 500.00 | (180.00) | 610.00 | 1,500.00 | (890.00) |
| Interest Income | 2,015.41 | 0.00 | 2,015.41 | 2,015.41 | 0.00 | 2,015.41 |
| | | | | | | |
| Total Revenues | 439,825.41 | 303,500.00 | 136,325.41 | 776,810.41 | 760,500.00 | 16,310.41 |
| | | | | | | |
| **Cost of Sales** | | | | | | |
| Cost of Sales | 348,056.00 | 240,000.00 | 108,056.00 | 614,488.00 | 600,000.00 | 14,488.00 |
| | | | | | | |
| Total Cost of Sales | 348,056.00 | 240,000.00 | 108,056.00 | 614,488.00 | 600,000.00 | 14,488.00 |
| | | | | | | |
| Gross Profit | 91,769.41 | 63,500.00 | 28,269.41 | 162,322.41 | 160,500.00 | 1,822.41 |
| | | | | | | |
| **Expenses** | | | | | | |
| Wages Expense | 8,933.34 | 12,000.00 | (3,066.66) | 29,641.02 | 36,000.00 | (6,358.98) |
| Payroll Tax Expense | 996.06 | 0.00 | 996.06 | 3,304.94 | 0.00 | 3,304.94 |
| Utilities Expense | 1,050.00 | 900.00 | 150.00 | 2,870.00 | 2,700.00 | 170.00 |
| Telephone Expense | 1,500.00 | 2,100.00 | (600.00) | 5,020.00 | 6,300.00 | (1,280.00) |
| Other Office Expense | 0.00 | 1,000.00 | (1,000.00) | 4,500.00 | 3,000.00 | 1,500.00 |
| Advertising Expense | 4,000.00 | 2,500.00 | 1,500.00 | 6,700.00 | 7,500.00 | (800.00) |
| Interest Expense | 7,719.57 | 2,800.00 | 4,919.57 | 7,719.57 | 8,400.00 | (680.43) |
| Service Charge Expense | 75.00 | 0.00 | 75.00 | 75.00 | 0.00 | 75.00 |
| Insurance Expense | 5,500.00 | 2,000.00 | 3,500.00 | 5,500.00 | 6,000.00 | (500.00) |
| Depreciation Expense | 10,333.00 | 3,500.00 | 6,833.00 | 10,333.00 | 10,500.00 | (167.00) |
| Gain/Loss - Sale of Assets Exp | (3,000.00) | 0.00 | (3,000.00) | (3,000.00) | 0.00 | (3,000.00) |
| | | | | | | |
| Total Expenses | 37,106.97 | 26,800.00 | 10,306.97 | 72,663.53 | 80,400.00 | (7,736.47) |
| | | | | | | |
| Net Income | $ 54,662.44 $ | 36,700.00 | 17,962.44 $ | 89,658.88 $ | 80,100.00 | 9,558.88 |

**Figure 10.6**

Budgeted Versus Actual Income Statement

**3** Click **Print** and then click **OK** to print this report.

**4** Click **Close** to close the report.

Karen points out that, based on the budgeted versus actual report, the company is doing pretty well. She'll ask Donna about budgeting for bank service charges and other income since neither was included in the budget. She also wants to investigate the actual office expenses, which, according to the report, were 50% over budget.

# Budgeting Assets, Liabilities, and Equities

Karen explains to you that creating specific budgets for assets, liabilities, and stockholders' equity accounts is not a simple task. First, you cannot complete this task until the budget for revenues and expenses has been established. This is due to the relationship that exists between net income and retained earnings. Budgeted retained earnings are dependent on net income/net loss. That is, budgeted retained earnings must be increased by monthly net income and decreased by monthly net losses, if any.

Second, budgets for accounts receivable are dependent on sales, while budgets for inventory and accounts payable are dependent on cost of sales and projected sales. Budgeted accumulated depreciation accounts are increased by monthly depreciation expenses. Fortunately for you and Karen, Donna has already created this budget in her spreadsheet program.

Donna's budget for assets had forecasts for the cash financing activities of issuing more stock, offering credit terms to customers, buying more inventory for the showroom, temporarily investing some cash, and then eventually paying down some debt. She also planned to increase accounts payable by getting suppliers to offer credit terms as well.

Before you get started on the current period budget, you need to create budgeted beginning balances as of the start of the year (1/1/13), which, of course, should be the same balances you ended up with the previous year (12/31/12).

## To create beginning balances as of 1/1/13:

1 Click Budgets from the Maintain menu again, and then select **Balance Sheet Accounts** from the Type drop-down list.

2 Select **01/01/2012 – 12/31/2012** from the View Fiscal Year drop-down list.

3 Click in the cell at the intersection of the 12/31/12 column and the 1020 – Checking Account row. Type **25000**. Remember, even though these amounts represent ending balances, they also represent changes from the previous balances, which were all $0.

4 Continue by entering, in the 12/31/12 column, the following amounts (from the beginning balances established when you first created the Wild Water Sports file) for each account as specified:

| Account ID | Amount |
|---|---|
| 1020 | 25,000 |
| 1100 | 96,300 |
| 1200 | 372,000 |
| 1500 | 75,000 |
| 1900 | 7,500 |
| 2000 | 77,000 |
| 2700 | 383,800 |
| 3930 | 100,000 |

**5** Click **Save**. Your window should look like Figure 10.7.

| Account ID | Account Name | Total | 12/31/12 |
|---|---|---|---|
| 1010 | Cash on Hand | 0.00 | 0.00 |
| 1020 | Checking Account | 25,000.00 | 25,000.00 |
| 1030 | Short-Term Investment | 0.00 | 0.00 |
| 1100 | Accounts Receivable | 96,300.00 | 96,300.00 |
| 1150 | Allowance for Doubtful | 0.00 | 0.00 |
| 1200 | Inventory | 372,000.00 | 372,000.00 |
| 1230 | Inventory Parts | 0.00 | 0.00 |
| 1400 | Prepaid Expenses | 0.00 | 0.00 |
| 1500 | Property and Equipmer | 75,000.00 | 75,000.00 |
| 1900 | Accum. Depreciation - F | 7,500.00 | 7,500.00 |
| 2000 | Accounts Payable | 77,000.00 | 77,000.00 |
| 2200 | Accrued Interest Payab | 0.00 | 0.00 |
| 2310 | Sales Tax Payable | 0.00 | 0.00 |
| 2320 | Deductions Payable | 0.00 | 0.00 |
| 2330 | Federal Payroll Taxes P | 0.00 | 0.00 |
| 2340 | FUTA Payable | 0.00 | 0.00 |
| 2350 | State Payroll Taxes Pay | 0.00 | 0.00 |
| 2360 | SUTA Payable | 0.00 | 0.00 |
| 2370 | Local Taxes Payable | 0.00 | 0.00 |
| 2380 | Income Taxes Payable | 0.00 | 0.00 |
| 2400 | Customer Deposits | 0.00 | 0.00 |
| 2500 | Current Portion Long-T | 0.00 | 0.00 |
| 2700 | Long Term Debt-Noncu | 383,800.00 | 383,800.00 |
| 3910 | Retained Earnings | 0.00 | 0.00 |
| 3920 | Paid-in Capital | 0.00 | 0.00 |
| 3930 | Common Stock | 100,000.00 | 100,000.00 |
| 3940 | Dividends Paid | 0.00 | 0.00 |

**Figure 10.7**

You have now established budgeted beginning balances for the current fiscal year. Karen suggests that you complete the current year budgeted changes one step at a time—first entering the budget for assets, then the budget for liabilities, and then the budget for stockholders' equity. You agree with her suggestion and remind her that the budgeted amounts for these accounts are the changes expected for the period, not the ending balances expected for each quarter. For now, you'll just be creating budgeted changes for assets at the end of March 2013.

## To create a budget for assets:

**1** With the Maintain Budgets window open, select **Balance Sheet Accounts** from the Type drop-down list.

**2** Select **01/01/2013 – 12/31/2013** from the View Fiscal Year drop-down list.

**3** Click in the cell at the intersection of the 3/31/13 column and the 1020 – Checking Account row. Type **9250**.

**4** Continue by entering the following amounts for each account as specified:

| Account ID | Amount |
|---|---|
| 1020 | 9,250 |
| 1030 | 50,000 |
| 1100 | 303,700 |
| 1200 | −172,000 |
| 1230 | 2,000 |
| 1400 | 36,500 |
| 1500 | 220,000 |
| 1900 | 10,250 |

**5** Your window should look like Figure 10.8.

**Figure 10.8**

Budgeted Change in Assets

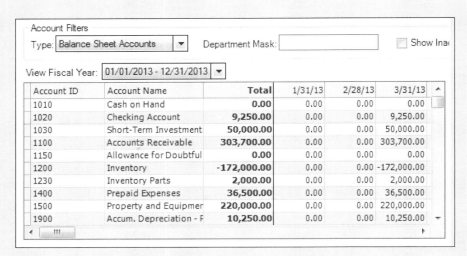

The liabilities and stockholders' equity items are less numerous and include accounts payable, loans payable, common stock, and retained earnings, to name a few. Loans payable was relatively easy to predict, as the owners of Wild Water Sports planned initially to borrow funds when they first opened and then to pay down some of that debt when they took on another investor and sold some inventory. Common stock was also easy since Donna and Karen knew what they were going to invest and had already planned on a fourth investor. Retained earnings were linked to Donna's estimate for net income, and since they started the year with no retained earnings, ending retained earnings as of March 31 had to equal their budgeted net income since they hadn't planned to distribute any earnings via dividends. Once again, these budgeted amounts are predicted changes in account balances, not ending balances.

## To create a budget for liabilities and stockholders' equity:

**1** Scroll down the Maintain Budgets window until Accounts Payable is the top account shown.

**2** Click in the cell at the intersection of the 3/31/13 column and the 2000 – Accounts Payable row. Type **123000**.

**3** Continue by entering the following amounts for each account as specified:

| Account ID | Amount |
|------------|--------:|
| 2000 | 123,000 |
| 2200 | 1,500 |
| 2310 | 15,400 |
| 2330 | 2,650 |
| 2340 | 100 |
| 2360 | 250 |
| 2700 | −83,800 |
| 3930 | 300,000 |

**4** Your window should look like Figure 10.9.

**Figure 10.9**

Budgeted Liabilities and Stockholders' Equity

**5** Click **Save**.

Now that all of the detailed asset, liability, and stockholders' equity amounts have been created for the budget, you can create a budgeted balance sheet.

# Budgeted Balance Sheet

Now that Karen has entered budgetary information for several specific balance sheet accounts, she is curious to see a complete budget. Thus, she will create and print a budgeted balance sheet for the quarter ended March 31, 2013.

## To create and print a budgeted balance sheet:

1  Click **Reports** from the button toolbar and then select **Budget**.

2  Click **Options** from the button toolbar.

3  Select **Per Start (3/1/13)** from the From: drop-down list.

4  Select **Per End (3/31/13)** from the To: drop-down list.

5  Uncheck the **Include accounts with zero amounts** check box.

6  Click **OK**.

7  Adjust the size of the columns by clicking the blue lines in between the columns. The resulting budget should look like Figure 10.10.

**Figure 10.10**

Budgeted Balance Sheet

**Wild Water Sports, Inc. 10**
**Budget**
**For the Period From Mar 1, 2013 to Mar 31, 2013**
Filter Criteria includes: 1) Types: Balance Sheet Accounts; 2) Active Accounts.

| Account ID | Account Description | 3/31/13 | YTD Total |
|---|---|---|---|
| 1020 | Checking Account | 9,250.00 | 9,250.00 |
| 1030 | Short-Term Investments | 50,000.00 | 50,000.00 |
| 1100 | Accounts Receivable | 303,700.00 | 303,700.00 |
| 1200 | Inventory | -172,000.00 | -172,000.00 |
| 1230 | Inventory Parts | 2,000.00 | 2,000.00 |
| 1400 | Prepaid Expenses | 36,500.00 | 36,500.00 |
| 1500 | Property and Equipment | 220,000.00 | 220,000.00 |
| 1900 | Accum. Depreciation - Pro | 10,250.00 | 10,250.00 |
| 2000 | Accounts Payable | 123,000.00 | 123,000.00 |
| 2200 | Accrued Interest Payable | 1,500.00 | 1,500.00 |
| 2310 | Sales Tax Payable | 15,400.00 | 15,400.00 |
| 2330 | Federal Payroll Taxes Paya | 2,650.00 | 2,650.00 |
| 2340 | FUTA Payable | 100.00 | 100.00 |
| 2360 | SUTA Payable | 250.00 | 250.00 |
| 2700 | Long Term Debt-Noncurre | -83,800.00 | -83,800.00 |
| 3930 | Common Stock | 300,000.00 | 300,000.00 |
|  |  |  |  |
|  | **Assets** | **439,200.00** | **439,200.00** |
|  | **Liabilities** | **59,100.00** | **59,100.00** |
|  | **Equity** | **300,000.00** | **300,000.00** |

8  Click **Print** and then click **OK** to print this budget.

9  Click **Close** to close the Report window.

"That doesn't look right," you say. "Assets don't equal liabilities plus equities!"

"You're correct," Karen responds. "I found that disconcerting as well. Since we had no beginning retained earnings, our ending retained earnings should be our current period income less dividends, which were zero. However, this budget also is linked to our budget for income, which estimated net income of $80,100. Thus, ending retained earnings will be beginning retained earnings ($0) plus net income ($80,100) for a total of $80,100. When ending retained earnings is added to common stock, the change in total equity will equal

$380,100. Now the balance sheet equation works: Change in Assets ($439,200) = Change in Liabilities ($59,100) + Change in Equity ($380,100).

Karen explains that once again the above report just describes the current budget but does not compare that budget with actual results from the quarter ended March 31, 2013. She suggests that you create a budgeted versus actual report for the balance sheet just like you did for the income statement as of the quarter ended March 31, 2013.

While getting ready to create this report, you discover that Peachtree doesn't have a predefined budgeted versus actual report for the balance sheet. However, Karen says she can quickly modify the existing standard balance sheet to add budget, variance, and percent variance columns.

---

**To create and print a balance sheet budgeted versus actual report as of the first quarter of 2013:**

1 Click the **Reports & Forms** menu, select **Financial Statements**, and then double-click <**Standard**> **Balance Sheet**.

2 Uncheck the **Print Page Numbers** and **Show Zero Amounts** check boxes and then click **OK**.

3 Click **Save**.

4 Type **Balance Sheet/Budget** in the Name text box and then click **Save**.

5 Click **Design** and then double-click on the text **Balance Sheet**.

6 Type **Budget Versus Actual** in front of the words **Balance Sheet** in the Text to Print text box and then click **OK**.

7 Double-click the **Text – Body** row that contains the text **ASSETS**, select **Left of Column** from the Alignment drop-down list, and then click **OK**.

8 Double-click the **Text – Body** row that contains the text **LIABILITIES AND CAPITAL**, select **Left of Column** from the Alignment drop-down list, and then click **OK**.

9 Double-click on the text **Net Balance Current Period** shown as the second column title.

10 Click in the first row where column 1 is described. Type **30** in the Width text box.

11 Click in the second row where column 2 is described. Type **20** in the Width text box.

12 Click **Alignment Options**, select the **Data and Totals aligned in the column** option button, and then click **OK**.

13 Click in the third row of the Column Description text box and check the **Print** check box. Select **Balance** from the Contents drop-down list. Type **20** in the Width text box and place a check in the **Format/$** check box.

14 Select **Center of Column** from the Align Title drop-down list.

15 Select **Budget** from the Qualifier drop-down list. Your window should look like Figure 10.11.

**Figure 10.11**

Modifying the Column
Description

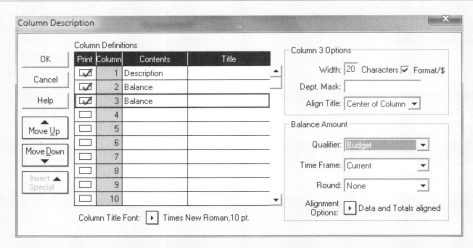

16  Click in the fourth row of the Column Description text box and check the **Print** check box. Select **Formula** from the Contents drop-down list. Type **20** in the Width text box.

17  Type **Actual** as the Title of Column 2, type **Budget** as the Title of Column 3, and then type **Variance** as the Title of Column 4.

18  Select **Center of Column** from the Align Title drop-down list.

19  Input the Formula Activity as shown in Figure 10.12.

**Figure 10.12**

Creating a Variance Formula

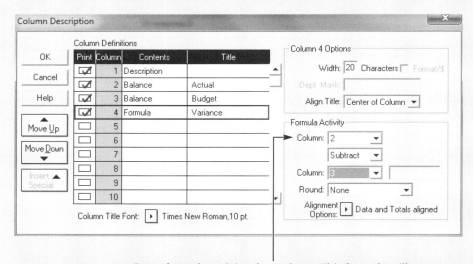

Enter formula activity shown here. This formula will
subtract budget figures in column 3 from actual figures
in column 2 and display the result which will give us the
variance between actual and budget

20  Click **OK**.

21  Click **Preview** and then click **OK**. The assets section of your report should look like Figure 10.13, and the liabilities and capital section of your report should look like Figure 10.14.

**Figure 10.13**

Assets Section of the Budgeted versus Actual Balance Sheet

```
                    Wild Water Sports, Inc. 10
                 Budget Versus Actual Balance Sheet
                         March 31, 2013

                        Actual          Budget          Variance
Current Assets
Checking Account      $    47,442.43 $   34,250.00       13,192.43
Short-Term Investments     39,890.41     50,000.00      (10,109.59)
Accounts Receivable       399,932.73    400,000.00          (67.27)
Inventory                 243,600.00    200,000.00       43,600.00
Inventory Parts             2,112.00      2,000.00          112.00
Prepaid Expenses           36,500.00     36,500.00            0.00

Total Current Assets      769,477.57    722,750.00       46,727.57

Property and Equipment
Property and Equipment    295,000.00    295,000.00            0.00
Accum. Depreciation - Prop&Eqt (17,833.00) (17,750.00)     (83.00)

Total Property and Equipment 277,167.00 277,250.00         (83.00)

Other Assets

Total Other Assets              0.00          0.00            0.00

Total Assets          $ 1,046,644.57 $ 1,000,000.00       46,644.57
```

**Figure 10.14**

Liabilities and Capital Section of the Budgeted versus Actual Balance Sheet

```
                    Wild Water Sports, Inc. 10
                 Budget Versus Actual Balance Sheet
                         March 31, 2013

                        Actual          Budget          Variance
LIABILITIES AND CAPITAL

Current Liabilities
Accounts Payable      $   216,200.00 $  200,000.00       16,200.00
Accrued Interest Payable    1,760.97      1,500.00          260.97
Sales Tax Payable          28,457.66     15,400.00       13,057.66
Federal Payroll Taxes Payable 2,622.00    2,650.00          (28.00)
FUTA Payable                   71.46        100.00          (28.54)
SUTA Payable                  241.20        250.00           (8.80)
Customer Deposits          10,000.00          0.00       10,000.00

Total Current Liabilities 259,353.29    219,900.00       39,453.29

Long-Term Liabilities
Long Term Debt-Noncurrent 297,632.40    300,000.00       (2,367.60)

Total Long-Term Liabilities 297,632.40  300,000.00       (2,367.60)

Total Liabilities         556,985.69    519,900.00       37,085.69

Capital
Common Stock              400,000.00    400,000.00            0.00
Net Income                 89,658.88     80,100.00        9,558.88

Total Capital             489,658.88    480,100.00        9,558.88

Total Liabilities & Capital $ 1,046,644.57 $ 1,000,000.00 46,644.57
```

**22** Click **Save** and then click **Print** and then **OK** to print this report.

Karen points out that, based on the budgeted versus actual report, the company is right on target. She'll ask Donna about budgeting for the customer deposit account since it was included in the budget. She does want to investigate the inventory asset account, which was $43,600 over budget, and sales tax payable, which was $13,057.66 over budget.

## Business Events Summary

| Business Event | Process Steps | Page |
| --- | --- | --- |
| Budgeting revenues | Use Budgets from the Company center | 328 |
| Budgeting expenses | Use Budgets from the Company center | 330 |
| Budgeting assets, liabilities, and equities | Use Budgets from the Company center | 334 |

# End Note

You and Karen have now entered all budgetary information for the first quarter of 2013. Donna can make changes to the budget at any time if additional information becomes available, and Peachtree will automatically update any related budget report.

## Chapter 10 Questions

**1**  Explain how the budgeting process is accomplished in Peachtree.

**2**  Can multiple budgets be created in Peachtree? Explain.

**3**  In Peachtree, do the terms *revenues* and *income* mean the same thing?

**4**  How do you set up the budget for just income accounts?

**5**  Explain the typical relationship between cost of goods sold and sales in the budgeting process.

**6**  Compare the process of budgeting revenues and expenses with the process of budgeting assets, liabilities, and owner's equity and explain how this information is included in the Peachtree budgeting process.

**7**  Explain the typical relationship between accumulated depreciation and depreciation expense in the budgeting process and how this information is included in the Peachtree budgeting process.

**8**  Can you copy and paste in Peachtree budgets?

**9**  Does Peachtree have a built-in budgeted versus actual income statement and balance sheet?

**10**  Explain the typical relationship between retained earnings and net income/loss in the budgeting process. How is this information included in the Peachtree budgeting process?

## Chapter 10 Exercises

### Chapter 10 Exercise 1
## BUDGETING REVENUES AND EXPENSES

Restore the file **Boston Catering Ch 10 (Backup)** found on the text CD or download it from the text website. Enter budgeted revenues and expenses described below and then print the profit & loss budget overview and profit & loss budget vs. actual reports for the month ended July 2010.

*merchandising*

a.  Budgeted revenues for July include bar sales of $2,000 and catering sales of $20,000.

b.  Budgeted expenses for July include bar purchases of $1,400, food purchases of $2,500, interest expense of $600, depreciation expense of $1,000, insurance expense of $1,000, payroll expenses of $6,000, and rent expense of $3,000.

### Chapter 10 Exercise 2
## BUDGETING ASSETS, LIABILITIES, AND EQUITIES

Restore the file **Boston Catering Ch 10 (Backup)** found on the text CD or download it from the text website. Do not use the file created in the exercises above. Enter budgeted assets, liabilities, and equities described below and then print the balance sheet budget overview and balance sheet budget versus actual reports.

a. Budgeted assets as of July 31, 2010, include cash in bank (Bank of America) $80,000, short-term investments $5,000, accounts receivable $20,000, inventory $5,000, furniture and equipment $76,500, and accumulated depreciation $3,000.

b. Budgeted liabilities as of July 31, 2010, include accounts payable $10,000, payroll liabilities $2,000, notes payable (Bank of America) $25,000, and notes payable (CitiBank) $50,000.

c. Budgeted equities as of July 31, 2010, include common stock $90,000 and retained earnings $6,500.

## Chapter 10 Assignments

### Chapter 10 Assignment 1

## ADDING MORE INFORMATION: WILD WATER SPORTS

*merchandising*

Restore the file **Wild Water Sports, Inc. 10A** found on the text CD or download it from the text website. Be sure to set the system date to **4/30/13** and the accounting period to **Period 4 – 04/01/13–04/30/13** and then modify the existing April budget as follows: Sales income for April is expected to be 10% higher than what is budgeted in March. Cost of goods sold for April is still estimated at 80% of sales. Wages expenses for April are expected to be $15,000. Changes in assets, liabilities, and equities are as follows:

| Account ID | Amount |
|---|---|
| 1020 | 25,750 |
| 1030 | −20,000 |
| 1100 | 100,000 |
| 1200 | 90,000 |
| 1400 | −4,250 |
| 1500 | 12,000 |
| 1900 | 3,500 |
| 2000 | 145,200 |
| 2200 | 500 |
| 2310 | 14,600 |

Print the following with no page numbers and no zero amounts and with the accounting period set to **Period 4:**

a. Budgeted income statement for the four months ended in April (*Hint*: The range is from 1/1/13 to 4/30/13.)

b. Budgeted versus actual income statement for April

c. Budgeted balance sheet for April

d. Budgeted versus actual balance sheet for April

*Chapter 10 Assignment 2*

## ADDING MORE INFORMATION: CENTRAL COAST CELLULAR

Restore the file **Central Coast Cellular Ch 10** found on the text CD or download it from the text website. Change the system date to **1/1/09** and the accounting period to **Period 1 – 01/01/09–01/31/09**. Add the following budget information:

*merchandising*

Commissions of $2,000 are expected each month for the first quarter. Sales income of $18,000 is expected in January, increasing to $23,800 in February and to $29,680 in March. Cost of sales is estimated at $5,000, $7,500, and $10,000 for January, February, and March, respectively. Bank service charges and depreciation of $80 and $1,500, respectively, are expected each month. Loan interest expense and rent of $1,000 and $3,000, respectively, are expected each month. Wages expenses of $10,000 are expected in January, increasing by $2,000 each month thereafter. Telephone expenses of $500 are expected in January, increasing $100 each month thereafter. Utilities expenses of $300 are expected in January, increasing 5% each month thereafter.

Changes in assets, liabilities, and equities during January are as follows:

| Account ID | Amount |
| --- | --- |
| 1020 | 130,000 |
| 1100 | 14,000 |
| 1200 | 18,000 |
| 1300 | 68,500 |
| 1400 | 3,000 |
| 1410 | 3,000 |
| 1500 | 115,000 |
| 1900 | 1,500 |
| 2000 | 24,380 |
| 2050 | 1,000 |
| 2310 | 2,000 |
| 2330 | 3,000 |
| 2350 | 1,000 |
| 2700 | 120,000 |
| 3930 | 200,000 |

Print the following with no page numbers and no zero amounts:

a.  Budgeted income statement for the quarter (1/1/09–3/31/09)

b.  Budgeted versus actual income statement for January

c.  Budgeted balance sheet for January

d.  Budgeted versus actual balance sheet for January

*service*

## Chapter 10 Assignment 3

# ADDING MORE INFORMATION: SANTA BARBARA SAILING

Restore the file **Santa Barbara Sailing Ch 10** found on the text CD or download it from the text website. Add the following budget information after you set the system date to **7/31/12**:

Rental income is expected to be $30,000 in July, increasing 10% each month during the quarter. Charter income is expected to be $5,000 in July, increasing $1,000 per month thereafter. Expenses are budgeted as follows and are expected to remain constant for the next three months.

| | |
|---|---|
| Wages Expense | 9,000 |
| Payroll Tax Expense | 1,000 |
| Interest Expense | 1,000 |
| Rent or Lease Expense | 2,000 |
| Maintenance and Repairs Expense | 2,500 |
| Utilities Expense | 1,200 |
| Telephone Expense | 1,300 |
| Advertising Expense | 3,500 |
| Depreciation Expense | 5,750 |

Budgeted assets, liabilities, and equities as of 7/31/12 are as follows:

| | |
|---|---|
| Checking | 115,000 |
| Accounts Receivable | 4,000 |
| Prepaid Expenses | 22,000 |
| Property and Equipment | 352,500 |
| Accumulated Depreciation – Property and Equipment | 5,750 |
| Accounts Payable | 4,000 |
| Payroll Taxes Payable | 4,500 |
| Sales Tax Payable | 4,000 |
| Long-Term Debt – Noncurrent | 317,500 |
| Common Stock | 150,000 |

Print the following with no page numbers and no zero amounts:

a.  Budgeted income statement for the quarter (7/1/12–9/30/12)

b.  Budgeted versus actual income statement for July 12

c.  Budgeted balance sheet for July 12

d.  Budgeted versus actual balance sheet for July 12

# Chapter 10 Cases

## *Chapter 10 Case Problem 1*

## FOREVER YOUNG

Restore the backup you made of **Forever Young** in Chapter 9 into a new company folder. (Do not restore this backup into an existing folder.) Change the company name to include Ch 10 at the end so that the new company name is **Forever Young Ch 10**. Add the following budget information after you set the system date to **1/31/08**.

service

sole proprietorship

Consulting income is expected to be $40,000 in January, increasing $5,000 per month thereafter. Expenses are budgeted as follows and are expected to remain constant for the next three months:

| | |
|---|---|
| Advertising Expense | 500 |
| Automobile | 1,000 |
| Depreciation Expense | 100 |
| Interest Expense | 100 |
| Payroll Expenses | 10,000 |
| Professional Fees | 4,000 |
| Rent | 3,800 |
| Telephone | 500 |
| Travel | 7,000 |

Budgeted assets, liabilities, and equities as of 1/31/08 are as follows:

| | |
|---|---|
| Checking | 63,000 |
| Accounts Receivable | 15,000 |
| Supplies | 2,100 |
| Prepaid Expenses | 5,000 |
| Furniture and Equipment | 4,000 |
| Accumulated Depreciation | 100 |
| Security Deposit | 4,000 |
| Payroll Liabilities | 5,000 |
| Notes Payable | 50,000 |
| Owner's Equity | 25,000 |

This is a continuous case in that the next chapter will use the work you've accomplished here as the basis for recording additional business events. After you've printed the following reports, create a backup of this file on some type of external medium (flash drive, Internet site, CD, disk, etc.). The backup should be named **Forever Young Ch 10** for easy identification later. You'll be restoring this file in the next chapter. Print the following with no page numbers and no zero amounts:

a. Budgeted income statement for the quarter (1/1/08–3/31/08) like that created in the chapter and illustrated in Figure 10.5

b. Budgeted versus actual income statement for January 2008 like that created in the chapter and illustrated in Figure 10.6

c. Budgeted balance sheet for January 2008 like that created in the chapter and illustrated in Figure 10.10

d. Budgeted versus actual balance sheet for January 2008 like that created in the chapter and illustrated in Figures 10.13 and 10.14

## Chapter 10 Case Problem 2

# OCEAN VIEW FLOWERS

merchandising

Restore the backup you made for **Ocean View Flowers** in Chapter 9 into a new company folder. (Do not restore this backup into an existing folder.) Change the company name to include Ch 10 at the end so that the new company name is **Ocean View Flowers Ch 10**. Enter the following budget information:

| Account ID | January | February |
|---|---|---|
| 40000 | 30,000 | 30,000 |
| 40100 | 5,000 | 50,000 |
| 40600 | 500 | 1,000 |
| 50000 | 16,000 | 42,000 |
| 64500 | 1,500 | 1,500 |
| 67500 | 100 | 100 |
| 68000 | 1,600 | 1,600 |
| 69000 | 500 | 500 |
| 74500 | 1,400 | 1,400 |
| 77100 | 400 | 400 |
| 77500 | 20,000 | 20,000 |
| 78000 | 300 | 300 |

Changes in assets, liabilities, and equities during January and February are as follows:

| Account ID | January | February |
|---|---|---|
| 10200 | 70,000 | −34,000 |
| 10700 | 25,000 | −5,000 |
| 11000 | 0 | 80,000 |
| 12000 | 20,000 | 0 |
| 14300 | 2,000 | 0 |
| 15000 | 20,000 | |
| 15100 | 15,000 | |
| 15500 | 0 | 270,000 |
| 16900 | 0 | 30,000 |
| 17000 | 0 | 500 |
| 17100 | 0 | 500 |
| 17500 | 0 | 2,000 |
| 20000 | 1,300 | 47,800 |
| 23400 | 6,000 | 6,000 |
| 23600 | 1,000 | 1,000 |
| 27000 | 50,000 | 270,000 |
| 39003 | 100,000 | 0 |

This is a continuous case in that the next chapter will use the work you've accomplished here as the basis for recording additional business events. After you've printed the following reports, create a backup of this file and store it on some type of external medium (flash drive, Internet site, CD, disk, etc.). The backup file should be named **Ocean View Flowers Ch 10** for easy identification later. You'll be restoring this file in the next chapter. Print the following with no page numbers and no zero amounts:

a.  Budgeted income statement for February

b.  Budgeted versus actual income statement for February

c.   Budgeted balance sheet for January and February

d.   Budgeted versus actual balance sheet for February

## Chapter 10 Case Problem 3

# ALOHA PROPERTY MANAGEMENT

*service*

Restore the backup you made for **Aloha** in Chapter 9 into a new company folder. (Do not restore this backup into an existing folder.) Change the company name to include Ch 10 at the end so that the new company name is **Aloha Property Management Ch 10.** Use that file to enter the following budget information for January and February. Be sure to change the system date to **1/1/08** and the accounting period to **Period 1**.

Rental income is expected to be $60,000 in January and $100,000 in February. Advertising is expected to be $12,500 in January (for an initial advertising campaign) and then $1,500 per month thereafter. Depreciation should be about $17,000 per month. Other expenses per month include insurance $2,000, interest $23,000, maintenance $4,650, repairs $2,500, telephone $4,000, wages $10,000, and utilities $3,000.

Balances as of 12/31/07 were as follows:

| Account ID | Amount |
|---|---|
| 10200 | 15,000 |
| 11000 | 101,000 |
| 15500 | 5,000,000 |
| 17500 | 1,200,000 |
| 20000 | 6,300 |
| 27000 | 3,875,000 |
| 39003 | 10,000 |
| 39005 | 24,700 |

Changes in assets, liabilities, and equities during January and February are as follows:

| Account ID | January | February |
|---|---|---|
| 10200 | 53,000 | 49,000 |
| 10700 | 40,000 | 10,000 |
| 11000 | -88,000 | 45,000 |
| 14000 | 20,000 | 5,000 |
| 15000 | 19,000 | 0 |
| 17000 | 0 | 1,000 |
| 17500 | 0 | 33,000 |
| 20000 | 3,650 | 750 |
| 23000 | 0 | 25,000 |
| 23100 | 5,000 | 4,000 |
| 23400 | 2,800 | 3,000 |
| 23600 | 1,200 | 1,300 |
| 24400 | 0 | 24,000 |
| 27000 | 0 | -15,400 |
| 39003 | 50,000 | 0 |

This is a continuous case in that the next chapter will use the work you've accomplished here as the basis for recording additional business events. After you've printed the following reports, create a backup of this file and store it on some type of external medium (flash drive, Internet site, CD, disk, etc.). The backup file should be named **Aloha Property Management Ch 10** for easy identification later. You'll be restoring this file in the next chapter. Print the following with no page numbers and no zero amounts:

a.   Budgeted income statement for the two months ended in February

b.   Budgeted versus actual income statement for the two months ended in February

c.   Budgeted balance sheet for January and February

d.   Budgeted versus actual balance sheet for February

# Reporting Business Activities

*In this Chapter, you will:*

- Create an income statement, a statement of retained earnings, a balance sheet, and a statement of cash flows.
- Create additional reports for analysis of sales and purchases.
- Create additional reports managing accounts receivable, accounts payable, and inventory.
- Export reports to Excel.

## *Case:* Wild Water Sports, Inc.

Now that you have entered the budget information for Wild Water Sports' first year and have entered in the first four months of operating, investing, and financing transactions as well as adjustments, you are ready to prepare financial statements to send to the bank for Wild Water Sports' first three months. Donna has asked you and Karen to prepare these statements and to provide any additional information that will help her better understand Wild Water's financial performance. You and Karen decide that you'll create a set of financial statements that includes the income statement, statement of retained earnings, balance sheet, and statement of cash flows.

In addition, you agree to provide Donna some related supporting schedules that are already built into Peachtree such as an inventory profitability report, a report of items sold to customers, and a report of items purchased from vendors. These will give Donna a better idea of the company's profitability and operating activities and support the numbers reported on the company's income statement.

"What about support for the numbers on the balance sheet?" you ask.

"We'll also create some detailed reports using Peachtree's analysis tools such as the Collections Manager, Payment Manager, and Financial Manager." Karen answers.

Karen suggests you help her create an aging of accounts receivable report, which will support the accounts receivable balance on the balance sheet; an inventory valuation report, which will support the inventory balance on the balance sheet; and an aging of accounts payable report, which will support the accounts payable balance on the balance sheet. In addition, she suggests that printing key ratios and key balances found in the Financial Manager will help with an analysis of the company's financial position.

"Sounds like Peachtree saves hours of work," you remark. "Let's get started."

## Creating a Set of Financial Statements

Karen decides to create one customized income statement for the three-month period ended March 31 without examining each month separately, because adjustments were made only as of March 31.

**Video Demonstration**

**Demo 11A - *Creating a customized statement of income and retained earnings***

Karen explains that Peachtree enables you to create reports for any period you desire. It also lets you create separate columns for a time segment—such as a day, a week, four weeks, a month, a quarter, and so on—within each period. At the end of the fiscal year, Karen will create an income statement report for the year with separate columns for each quarter.

Karen decides to modify the Income/Earnings report available in Peachtree to include just a year-to-date column and % of Total Revenues column.

"Do we have to go through this customization effort every time?" you ask.

"No," Karen replies. "Peachtree has a save feature that can 'save' or retain the customization—what columns we want, what period, what layout, and so on. That way, the next time we want a similar report, it will be available from a report list."

### To create and save a customized income and retained earnings statement:

1  Start the Peachtree program.

2  Restore the **Wild Water Sports, Inc 11** file from your Data Files CD or download it from the Internet.

3  Set the system date to **3/31/13** and the accounting period to **Period 3**.

4  Click **Reports & Forms**, click **Financial Statements**, and then double-click <**Standard**> **Income/Earnings**.

5  Uncheck the **Print Page Numbers** and **Show Zero Amounts** check boxes and then click **OK**.

6  Click the **Design** button.

7  Double-click the **Net Activity Current** column description.

8  Uncheck the **Print** check boxes for rows 2 and 3.

9  Remove the title from row 4.

10  Type **% of Total Revenues** as the title for row 5.

11  Change the width of column 5 to **25**. The Column Description window should now look like Figure 11.1.

12  Click **OK**.

13  Double-click the **Net Balance Current** column description.

14  Uncheck the **Print** check boxes for rows 2 and 3.

15  Change the width of column 5 to **25** and then click **OK**.

16  Double-click the **Net Activity Current** column description.

17  Uncheck the **Print** check boxes for rows 2 and 3.

18  Change the width of column 5 to **25** and then click **OK**.

19  Click **Preview** and then click **OK**. Your modified income and retained earnings statement should look like Figure 11.2.

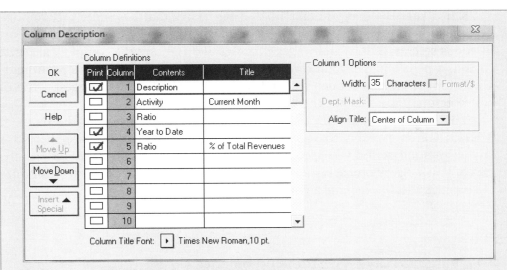

**Figure 11.1**

Modified Column Description

---

Wild Water Sports, Inc. 11
Statement of Income and Retained Earnings
For the Three Months Ending March 31, 2013

**Figure 11.2**

Modified Income and Retained
Earnings Statement

|  |  | % of Total Revenues |
|---|---|---|
| **Revenues** | | |
| Sales Income | 767,500.00 | 98.80 |
| Service Income | 6,685.00 | 0.86 |
| Parts Income | 610.00 | 0.08 |
| Interest Income | 2,015.41 | 0.26 |
| Total Revenues | 776,810.41 | 100.00 |
| **Cost of Sales** | | |
| Cost of Sales | 614,488.00 | 79.10 |
| Total Cost of Sales | 614,488.00 | 79.10 |
| Gross Profit | 162,322.41 | 20.90 |
| **Expenses** | | |
| Wages Expense | 29,641.02 | 3.82 |
| Payroll Tax Expense | 3,304.94 | 0.43 |
| Utilities Expense | 2,870.00 | 0.37 |
| Telephone Expense | 5,020.00 | 0.65 |
| Other Office Expense | 4,500.00 | 0.58 |
| Advertising Expense | 6,700.00 | 0.86 |
| Interest Expense | 7,719.57 | 0.99 |
| Service Charge Expense | 75.00 | 0.01 |
| Insurance Expense | 5,500.00 | 0.71 |
| Depreciation Expense | 10,333.00 | 1.33 |
| Gain/Loss - Sale of Assets Exp | (3,000.00) | (0.39) |
| Total Expenses | 72,663.53 | 9.35 |
| Net Income | 89,658.88 | 11.54 |
| Beginning Retained Earnings | 0.00 | |
| Adjustments To Date | 0.00 | |
| Ending Retained Earnings | 89,658.88 | |

**20** Click **Save**, type **Income/Earnings** as the new name of this statement, and then click **Save**.

**21** Click **Print** and then click **OK**.

**22** Click **Close**. Leave the Select a Report of Form window open.

Karen suggests that you take note of the % of Total Revenues column. She explains how this column reports each item's percentage of total revenue. Cost of goods sold at 79.10% and wages expenses at 3.82% are the company's largest costs as a percentage of total revenue. Notice also that Wild Water's profit margin ratio (net income divided by total revenue) is 11.54%. You suggest a cup of coffee before you come back to customize a balance sheet.

You return to your office to create the balance sheet Donna needs as of 3/31/13. Karen explains to you that Peachtree can prepare balance sheets for any accounting period you specify. Since Donna needs results as of 3/31/13, the two of you start by preparing a standard balance sheet. You decide to customize the balance sheet to include a percentage column.

*Video Demonstration*

*Demo 11B - Creating a
customized balance sheet*

### To create and save a customized balance sheet:

1    Double-click <**Standard**> **Balance Sheet** from the Select a Report or Form window.

2    Uncheck the **Print Page Numbers** and **Show Zero Amounts** check boxes and then click **OK**.

3    Click the **Design** button.

4    Double-click the **Net Balance Current Period** column description.

5    Change the column width of column 2 to **15**.

6    Set the Alignment Options of column 2 to **Data and Totals aligned in the column**.

7    Add a third row with **Ratio** as the Contents description and % as the Title. Be sure to check the Print box.

8    Set the column width of column 3 to **8**.

9    Select **Center of Column** from the Align Title drop-down list for the new row.

10   Select **2** as the Use Column.

11   Click the arrow next to Account Range.

12   Select **1010** as the From Account Range, select **1900** as the To Account Range, and then click **OK**. (This, in effect, selects all asset accounts.)

13   Click **OK** to close the Column Description window.

14   Set the Assets and Liabilities and Capital text body rows to a **Left of Column** Alignment.

15   Click **Preview** and then click **OK**. Your new balance sheet should look like Figures 11.3 and 11.4.

**Figure 11.3**

Modified Balance Sheet—Assets Section

```
                    Wild Water Sports, Inc. 11
                        Balance Sheet
                        March 31, 2013

                                                          %
ASSETS

Current Assets
  Checking Account              $        47,442.43       4.53
  Short-Term Investments                 39,890.41       3.81
  Accounts Receivable                   399,932.73      38.21
  Inventory                             243,600.00      23.27
  Inventory Parts                         2,112.00       0.20
  Prepaid Expenses                       36,500.00       3.49
                                      _____

  Total Current Assets                  769,477.57      73.52

Property and Equipment
  Property and Equipment                295,000.00      28.19
  Accum. Depreciation - Prop&Eqt        (17,833.00)     (1.70)
                                      _____

  Total Property and Equipment          277,167.00      26.48

Other Assets
                                      _____

  Total Other Assets                          0.00       0.00

  Total Assets                $       1,046,644.57     100.00
                                      ============
```

**16** Click **Print** and then click **OK**.

**17** Click **Save**. Type **Balance Sheet** as the name of this new financial statement and then click **Save**.

**18** Click **Close**.

## Figure 11.4

Modified Balance Sheet—
Liabilities and Capital Section

Wild Water Sports, Inc. 11
Balance Sheet
March 31, 2013

| | | | % |
|---|---|---|---|
| **LIABILITIES AND CAPITAL** | | | |
| | | | |
| Current Liabilities | | | |
| Accounts Payable | $ | 216,200.00 | 20.66 |
| Accrued Interest Payable | | 1,760.97 | 0.17 |
| Sales Tax Payable | | 28,457.66 | 2.72 |
| Federal Payroll Taxes Payable | | 2,622.00 | 0.25 |
| FUTA Payable | | 71.46 | 0.01 |
| SUTA Payable | | 241.20 | 0.02 |
| Customer Deposits | | 10,000.00 | 0.96 |
| | | | |
| Total Current Liabilities | | 259,353.29 | 24.78 |
| | | | |
| Long-Term Liabilities | | | |
| Long Term Debt-Noncurrent | | 297,632.40 | 28.44 |
| | | | |
| Total Long-Term Liabilities | | 297,632.40 | 28.44 |
| | | | |
| Total Liabilities | | 556,985.69 | 53.22 |
| | | | |
| Capital | | | |
| Common Stock | | 400,000.00 | 38.22 |
| Net Income | | 89,658.88 | 8.57 |
| | | | |
| Total Capital | | 489,658.88 | 46.78 |
| | | | |
| Total Liabilities & Capital | $ | 1,046,644.57 | 100.00 |

Donna notices that Peachtree includes a line item called "Net Income" in the Capital section. Standard accounting practice does not allow inclusion of such an income statement category in a balance sheet. Usually, this net income is included in the retained earnings account.

Karen comments that at first she thought the percentage column was the same as the one shown in the income statement: the percentage each item is to the total revenue (what Peachtree calls "income"). But now she sees that this column shows the percentage of total assets. For example, the checking account is 4.53% of Wild Water Sports' total assets, and accounts receivable is 38.21% of total assets. She comments that it looks like a large portion of those assets came from accounts payable (20.66%) and loans payable (28.44%), and most of the balance is from capital (46.78%).

The last financial statement required is a statement of cash flow for the quarter. Karen explains that she'll have to modify this statement as well since all she wants is cash flow for the quarter, not for the month and the quarter, which is what the standard cash flow report provides.

## To create and save a modified statement of cash flows:

**1** Double-click <**Standard**> **Cash Flow** from the Select a Report or Form window.

**2** Uncheck the **Print Page Numbers** and **Show Zero Amounts** check boxes and then click **OK**.

**3** Click the **Design** button.

**4** Double-click the **Net Activity Current** column description.

**5** Uncheck the **Print** check box from row 2.

**6** Delete the title from row 3 and then click **OK**.

**7** Do the same for all other sections of the statement of cash flows.

**8** Click **Preview** and then click **OK**. Your statement of cash flows should look like Figure 11.5.

**9** Click **Print** and then click **OK**.

**10** Click **Save**. Type **Cash Flow** as the name of this new financial statement and then click **Save**.

**11** Click **Close**.

## Figure 11.5

Modified Statement of Cash Flow

Wild Water Sports, Inc. 11
Statement of Cash Flow
For the three Months Ended March 31, 2013

| | | |
|---|---|---:|
| Cash Flows from operating activities | | |
| Net Income | $ | 89,658.88 |
| Adjustments to reconcile net income to net cash provided by operating activities | | |
| Accum. Depreciation - Prop&Eqt | | 10,333.00 |
| Accounts Receivable | | (303,632.73) |
| Inventory | | 128,400.00 |
| Inventory Parts | | (2,112.00) |
| Prepaid Expenses | | (36,500.00) |
| Accounts Payable | | 139,200.00 |
| Accrued Interest Payable | | 1,760.97 |
| Sales Tax Payable | | 28,457.66 |
| Federal Payroll Taxes Payable | | 2,622.00 |
| FUTA Payable | | 71.46 |
| SUTA Payable | | 241.20 |
| Customer Deposits | | 10,000.00 |
| | | |
| Total Adjustments | | (21,158.44) |
| | | |
| Net Cash provided by Operations | | 68,500.44 |
| | | |
| Cash Flows from investing activities | | |
| Used For | | |
| Property and Equipment | | (220,000.00) |
| | | |
| Net cash used in investing | | (220,000.00) |
| | | |
| Cash Flows from financing activities | | |
| Proceeds From | | |
| Long Term Debt-Noncurrent | | 305,000.00 |
| Common Stock | | 300,000.00 |
| Used For | | |
| Long Term Debt-Noncurrent | | (391,167.60) |
| | | |
| Net cash used in financing | | 213,832.40 |
| | | |
| Net increase <decrease> in cash | $ | 62,332.84 |
| | | |
| | | |
| Summary | | |
| Cash Balance at End of Period | $ | 87,332.84 |
| Cash Balance at Beg of Period | | (25,000.00) |
| | | |
| Net Increase <Decrease> in Cash | $ | 62,332.84 |

In addition to the basic set of financial statements, Karen now plans to create some supporting schedules and graphs.

# Creating Additional Reports for Analysis of Sales and Purchases

"This is very helpful information," Donna comments as she quickly skims the customized income and retained earnings statement, balance sheet, statement of cash flows, and budgeted versus actual reports you previously created. "I can see Wild Water's financial position, and how we stand in relation to where I thought we'd be. Can I see a bit more detail?" she asks. "I'm afraid I might miss something when I look at just the financial statements."

Both you and Karen agree that some additional detail would be helpful. In particular, Donna is anxious to know more about product sales and related costs. It is clear that one standard report that might be helpful is Peachtree's inventory profitability report. This report identifies each item sold during the period, how many were sold, what they cost, what gross profit was earned, the percentage of gross profit to sales, and the percentage of total sales provided by each item.

### To create an inventory profitability report:

1 Click **Reports & Forms**, click **Inventory**, and then double-click **Inventory Profitability Report** from the Select a Report or Form window.

2 Click the **Options** button.

3 Uncheck the **Include Items with no activity** check box.

4 Select **Period 1 (1/1/13)** in the From drop-down list and then click **OK**.

5 Click the **Columns** button.

6 Uncheck the **Show** check box in row 1 next to Item ID and then click **OK**.

7 Click **Print** and then click **OK**. Your report should look like Figure 11.6.

**Wild Water Sports, Inc. 11**
**Inventory Profitability Report**
**For the Period From Jan 1, 2013 to Mar 31, 2013**
Filter Criteria includes: 1) Stock/Assembly. Report order is by ID. Report is printed with shortened descriptions.

| Item Description | Units Sold | Sales($) | Cost($) | Gross Profit($) | Gross Profit(% | % of Tot |
|---|---|---|---|---|---|---|
| Malibu Sportster LX | 1.00 | 52,000.00 | 41,600.00 | 10,400.00 | 20.00 | 7.40 |
| Malibu Sunscape LSV | 3.00 | 195,000.00 | 156,000.00 | 39,000.00 | 20.00 | 27.73 |
| Malibu Vride | 2.00 | 96,000.00 | 76,800.00 | 19,200.00 | 20.00 | 13.65 |
| Malibu WakeSetter VLX | 1.00 | 57,000.00 | 45,600.00 | 11,400.00 | 20.00 | 8.11 |
| Malibu WakeSetter XTI | 1.00 | 70,000.00 | 56,000.00 | 14,000.00 | 20.00 | 9.96 |
| Tige 22v | 2.00 | 157,500.00 | 126,000.00 | 31,500.00 | 20.00 | 22.40 |
| Tige 24v | | | | | | |
| MB B52 V23 Team Edition | 1.00 | 75,000.00 | 60,000.00 | 15,000.00 | 20.00 | 10.67 |
| Engine Oil | 9.00 | 45.00 | 36.00 | 9.00 | 20.00 | 0.01 |
| Oil Filter | 2.00 | 30.00 | 24.00 | 6.00 | 20.00 | |
| Tune-up Parts | 2.00 | 500.00 | 400.00 | 100.00 | 20.00 | 0.07 |
| Air Filter | 1.00 | 35.00 | 28.00 | 7.00 | 20.00 | |
| | 25.00 | 703,110.00 | 562,488.00 | 140,622.00 | | 100.00 |

### Figure 11.6

Inventory Profitability Report for the Quarter Ended 3/31/13

> **8**  Click **Save**. Type **1st Qtr Inv. Profitability** as the name of this new report and then click **Save**.
>
> **9**  Close both the newly saved report and the Select a Report or Form windows.

"Shouldn't the total sales shown on this report equal the revenues reported from the sales of boats and parts on the income statement?" you ask. "When I add the two revenue accounts (sales income of $767,500 and parts income of $610) from the income statement, I get $768,110. However, the inventory profitability report only shows $703,110, a $65,000 difference."

"That difference is the accrual adjusting entry (#14) we made at the end of March," Karen says. "Many of the detailed reports generated by Peachtree are based on typical source documents like invoices and exclude adjusting entries like the adjusting entry I just referred to." Karen creates the following reconciliation to explain the difference:

| | |
|---|---:|
| Sales as reported on the income statement | $768,110.00 |
| Adjusting entry #14 | 65,000.00 |
| Sales as reported on the inventory profitability report | $703,110.00 |

Another report Karen thinks might be interesting is the items sold to customers report for the quarter. This report identifies how many items were sold to each customer, the dollar amount of those sales, the cost of those sales, the gross profit on those sales, and the gross profit percentage.

### To create an items sold to customers report:

> **1**  Click **Reports & Forms**, click **Accounts Receivable**, and then double-click **Items Sold to Customers** from the Select a Report or Form window.
>
> **2**  Click the **Options** button.
>
> **3**  Type **1/1/13** in the From drop-down list.
>
> **4**  Place a check in the **Summarize report** check box and then click **OK**.
>
> **5**  Click the **Columns** button.
>
> **6**  Uncheck the **Show** check box in row 1 next to Customer ID and then click **OK**.
>
> **7**  Click **Print** and then click **OK**. Your report should look like Figure 11.7.

**Wild Water Sports, Inc. 11**
**Items Sold to Customers**
**For the Period From Jan 1, 2013 to Mar 31, 2013**
Filter Criteria includes: Report order is by Customer ID, Item ID. Report is printed in Summary Format.

| Name | Qty | Amount | Cost of Sales | Gross Profit | Gross Margin |
|---|---|---|---|---|---|
| Orlando Water Sports | 5.00 | 1,250.00 | 200.00 | 1,050.00 | 84.00 |
| Buena Vista Water Sports | 16.00 | 1,845.00 | 256.00 | 1,589.00 | 86.12 |
| Walking on Water | 1.00 | 57,000.00 | 45,600.00 | 11,400.00 | 20.00 |
| Freebirds | 9.00 | 130,845.00 | 104,000.00 | 26,845.00 | 20.52 |
| Florida Sports Camp | 9.00 | 150,325.00 | 119,000.00 | 31,325.00 | 20.84 |
| Performance Rentals | 15.00 | 154,965.00 | 123,000.00 | 31,965.00 | 20.63 |
| Seth Blackman | 1.00 | 52,000.00 | 41,600.00 | 10,400.00 | 20.00 |
| Alisa Hay | 12.00 | 565.00 | 32.00 | 533.00 | 94.34 |
| Fantasy Sports | 2.00 | 113,000.00 | 90,400.00 | 22,600.00 | 20.00 |
| Sonia Garcia | 1.00 | 48,000.00 | 38,400.00 | 9,600.00 | 20.00 |
| **Report Totals** | **71.00** | **709,795.00** | **562,488.00** | **147,307.00** | **20.75** |

**Figure 11.7**

Items Sold to Customers for the Quarter

**8**  Click **Save**. Type **1st Qtr Items Sold** as the name of this new report and then click **Save**.

**9**  Close both the newly saved report and the Select a Report or Form windows.

Once again, you have to reconcile this report to revenues reported on the income statement. This report includes revenues from the sales of boats and parts as well as revenues from services provided. The total revenue report from these items on the income statement for the quarter was $774,795 (sales income of $767,500 + parts income of $610 + service income of $6,685). Once again, the difference between the total revenue shown on the items sold to customers report of $709,795 and the total revenue reported on the income statement of $774,795 is the $65,000 accrual discussed previously. Karen creates the following reconciliation:

| | |
|---|---|
| Sales as reported on the income statement | $774,795.00 |
| Adjusting entry #14 | 65,000.00 |
| Sales as reported on the inventory profitability report | $709,795.00 |

A third report Karen thinks might be interesting is the items purchased from vendors report for the quarter.

## To create an items purchased from vendors report:

1 Click **Reports & Forms**, click **Accounts Payable**, and then double-click **Items Purchased from Vendors** from the Select a Report or Form window.

2 Click the **Options** button.

3 Type **1/1/13** in the From drop-down list.

4 Click **Vendor ID** in the Select a filter section.

5 Select **10000** in the From drop-down list for Vendor ID and **10200** in the To drop-down list for Vendor ID to restrict the list of vendors to only those whose Vendor IDs are between 10000 and 10200. This will give you a list of just those vendors from whom the company purchases inventory. Click **OK**.

6 Click the **Columns** button.

7 Uncheck the Show check box in row 1 next to Vendor ID and in row 7 next to Item ID and then click **OK**.

8 Click **Print** and then click **OK**. Your report should look like Figure 11.8.

**Figure 11.8**

Items Purchased from Vendors for the Quarter

| Wild Water Sports, Inc. 11 | | | |
|---|---|---|---|
| Items Purchased from Vendors | | | |
| For the Period From Jan 1, 2013 to Mar 31, 2013 | | | |
| Filter Criteria includes: 1) Vendor IDs from 10000 to 10200. Report order is by Vendor ID, Item ID. Report is printed in Detail Format. | | | |
| **Name** | **Item Description** | **Qty** | **Amount** |
| Malibu Boats | Malibu Sportster LX | 2.00 | 83,200.00 |
| | Malibu Sunscape LSV | 1.00 | 52,000.00 |
| | Malibu Vride | 1.00 | 38,400.00 |
| | Malibu WakeSetter XTI | 1.00 | 56,000.00 |
| | | 5.00 | 229,600.00 |
| MB Sports | MB B52 V23 Team Edition | 1.00 | 60,000.00 |
| | | 1.00 | 60,000.00 |
| Tige Boats | Tige 22v | 2.00 | 126,000.00 |
| | Tige 24v | 1.00 | 70,000.00 |
| | | 3.00 | 196,000.00 |
| **Report Totals** | | 9.00 | 485,600.00 |

9 Click **Save**. Type **1st Qtr Items Purchased** as the name of this new report and then click **Save**.

10 Click **Close** and close the Select a Report or Form window.

When you show Donna these reports, she comments that they will be very helpful. But she wants to see even more information derived from the financial statements—specifically, she wants to see detailed reports on accounts receivable, accounts payable, and inventory.

# Creating Additional Reports for Managing Accounts Receivable, Accounts Payable, Inventory, and Your Business

With Peachtree, you can generate many supporting reports for the financial statements—what accountants consider traditional support in the form of schedules. Karen reads through Peachtree Help and discovers several reports that Peachtree generates that will help Donna—the collection aging report, payment aging report, financial manager reports, and an inventory valuation report. The collection aging report stratifies the amounts owed by customers by the number of days outstanding. The older the balance, the more likely it won't be collected. The payment aging report stratifies the amounts owed by the company to its vendors by the number of days outstanding. The financial manager report provides key financial ratios and balances. The inventory valuation report identifies the items remaining in inventory as of a particular date. It specifies the quantity on hand, the items' value (cost), and the percentage of inventory value by item.

## To create the collection aging and payment aging reports:

**1**  Click **Analysis** and then click **Collection Manager**.

**2**  Select the **Numeric** Display option button to see the collection aging report in Figure 11.9.

Click here for numeric version of report

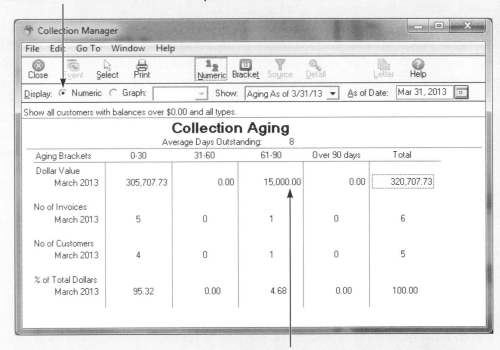

**Figure 11.9**

Collection Aging Report

Note this past due balance for follow-up

**3**  Click **Print** to print this report and then click **Close** to close this window.

**4** Click **Analysis** and then click **Payment Manager**.

**5** Select the **Numeric** Display option button to see the payment aging report in Figure 11.10.

**Figure 11.10**

Payment Aging Report

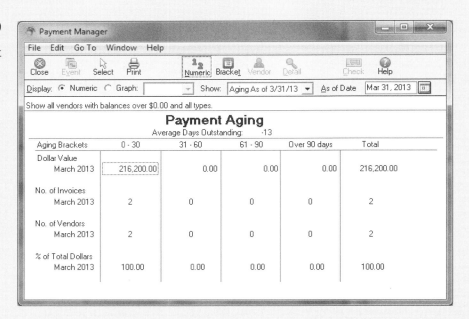

**6** Click **Print** to print this report and then click **Close** to close this window.

Karen reminds you that these two reports will also have to be reconciled to the accounts receivable and accounts payable amounts as reported on the balance sheet. The balance sheet reported accounts receivable of $399,932.73, while the collection aging report stated total accounts receivable of $320,707.73. The difference is partially attributed to the accrual of revenue and related amounts to be collected for sales tax. The remaining difference is attributed to a journal entry created to reclassify $10,000 received as a deposit on account to unearned revenue. Karen creates the following reconciliation:

| | |
|---|---|
| Accounts receivable as reported on the balance sheet | $399,932.73 |
| Adjusting entry #18 to reclassify unearned revenue | 10,000.00 |
| Adjusting entry #14 | 69,225.00 |
| Accounts receivable as reported on the collection aging report | $320,707.73 |

When you compare the preceding payable aging report and the accounts payable balance per the financial statement, you note that both amounts agree.

"This won't always be the case," Karen explains. "If we had made an adjusting entry to accrue some expenses, the balance in the payable aging report would have been different from the balance in accounts payable as reported on the balance sheet, and thus we would have had to create a reconciliation to explain the difference."

Karen notes the past due balances from a customer and will follow up tomorrow. She notes the accounts payable balance is current as of 3/31/13. She explains that the last analysis report she wants to create will provide typical financial management information like profitability ratios and liquidity ratios like the current ratio.

## To create the financial manager report:

**1** Click **Analysis** and then click **Financial Manager**.

**2** Select the **Business Summary** Display option button to see the ratios report in Figure 11.11.

**Figure 11.11**

Financial Manager Business Summary Report

**3** Click **Print** to print this report.

**4** Select the **Key Balances** Display option button to see the report in Figure 11.12.

**Figure 11.12**

Financial Manager Key Balances Report

**5** Click **Print** to print this report and then click **Close** to close this window.

Karen believes that both the business summary and the key balances reports will help Donna negotiate with the bank and give her quick access to ratios and balances. She needs one more report to help her identify the detail behind the balance sheet inventory amount.

## To create the inventory valuation report:

**1** Click **Reports & Forms**, click **Inventory**, and then click **Inventory Valuation Report**.

**2** Click **Options** and then uncheck the **Shorten Description** and **Include Items with no quantity on hand**.

**3** Click **Columns** in the Other Options section and uncheck the **Show** check box for the first two rows, Item ID and Item Class, and for the fourth row, Stocking U/M and then click **OK**.

**4** Resize the Item Description column by dragging the blue column separators, until all text is included.

**5** The inventory valuation report should look like Figure 11.13.

**Figure 11.13**

Inventory Valuation Report

### Wild Water Sports, Inc. 11
### Inventory Valuation Report
### As of Mar 31, 2013

Filter Criteria includes: 1) Stock/Assembly. Report order is by ID.

| Item Description | Cost Method | Qty on Hand | Item Value | Avg Cost | % of Inv Value |
|---|---|---|---|---|---|
| Malibu Sunsetter LXi | Average | 1.00 | 48,000.00 | 48000.00 | 16.12 |
| Malibu Sportster LX | Average | 2.00 | 83,200.00 | 41600.00 | 27.95 |
| Malibu Vride | Average | 1.00 | 38,400.00 | 38400.00 | 12.90 |
| Malibu WakeSetter XTI | Average | 1.00 | 56,000.00 | 56000.00 | 18.81 |
| Tige 24v | Average | 1.00 | 70,000.00 | 70000.00 | 23.51 |
| Engine Oil | Average | 141.00 | 564.00 | 4.00 | 0.19 |
| Oil Filter | Average | 23.00 | 276.00 | 12.00 | 0.09 |
| Tune-up Parts | Average | 3.00 | 600.00 | 200.00 | 0.20 |
| Air Filter | Average | 24.00 | 672.00 | 28.00 | 0.23 |
| | | | 297,712.00 | | 100.00 |

**6** Click **Print** and then click **OK** to print this report.

**7** Click **Close** and then click **No** when asked if you want to save changes.

**8** **Close** the Select a Report or Form window.

Karen notes that, once again, the balance in this report doesn't equal the amount reported as inventory on the general ledger of $245,712 (in the inventory and inventory parts accounts). The difference between the two is the $52,000 accrual on March 31, 2013, where inventory was reduced and cost of goods sold was charged for $52,000. Karen creates the following reconciliation:

| | |
|---|---|
| Inventory and inventory parts as reported on the balance sheet | $245,712.00 |
| Adjusting entry #14 | 52,000.00 |
| Inventory as reported on the inventory valuation report | $297,712.00 |

To help understand all of these reconciliations, Karen prepared the following summary reconciliation for all accounts:

| | A/R | Inventory | A/P | Sales (Items Sold to Cust.) | Sales (Inv. Profit) |
|---|---|---|---|---|---|
| As reported on the financial statement | 399,932.73 | 245,712.00 | 216,200.00 | 774,795.00 | 768,110.00 |
| Adjusting entry | (10,000.00) | — | — | — | — |
| Adjusting entry | (69,225.00) | 52,000.00 | — | (65,000.00) | (65,000.00) |
| As reported on the supporting schedule | 320,707.73 | 297,712.00 | 216,200.00 | 709,795.00 | 703,110.00 |

# Exporting Reports to Excel

*Video Demonstration*

*Demo 11D - Exporting reports to Excel*

Karen explains that in Peachtree you can export any reports you create to Microsoft's Excel spreadsheet program.

"Why export to Microsoft Excel when Peachtree gives us so many report options?" you ask.

Karen explains that, occasionally, she may need to change a report's appearance or contents in ways that are not available within Peachtree. Since the changes you make in Excel do not affect your Peachtree data, you are free to customize a report as needed or even change report data to run "what if" scenarios.

Karen reads through Peachtree Help and discovers that exporting a report to Excel is as simple as clicking a new button on the report's button bar. She suggests that the two of you experiment with this feature by exporting a standard income statement. (*Note*: Karen has Excel 2010, and the instructions provided here match Excel 2010. If you are using Excel 2003 or 2007, you can still export the file, but the formatting instructions may be different.)

---

### To export the standard income statement to Excel 2010:

1 Click **Reports & Forms**, click **Financial Statements**, and then double-click <**Standard**> **Income Stmnt**.

2 Uncheck the **Print Page Numbers** and the **Show Zero Amounts** check boxes and then click **OK**.

3 Click **Excel**.

4 Select the **Create a new Microsoft Excel workbook** option button under File option.

5 Check the **Use freeze panes** check box under Excel options.

6 Select the **Raw data layout** option button under Report layout option.

7 Select the **Send header to Page Setup** in Excel option button.

**8** Click **OK** to see the Excel report created in Figure 11.14. (*Hint*: Excel may have to be closed for this to work!)

## Figure 11.14

Excel 2010 Format Income Statement

Quick Access Toolbar

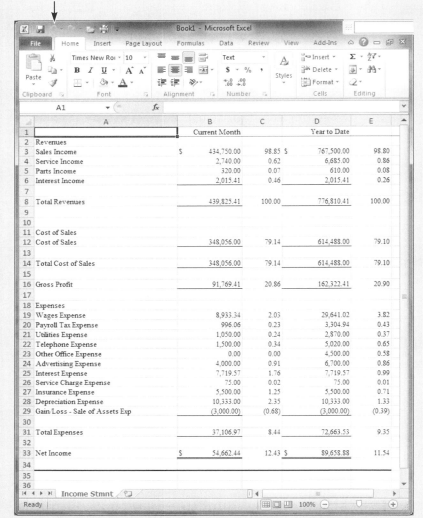

Screenshot © 2011 Microsoft Corporation. Microsoft® Excel® is a registered trademark of the Microsoft Corporation in the United States and/or other countries.

**9** In Excel, click the **Page Layout** tab, click **Orientation**, and then select **Portrait**.

**10** Select cell **C3** in the report just exported. Note that the export process has created not only a spreadsheet with values but also one with formulas.

**11** Click the **Print Preview** icon from the Quick Access Toolbar. (*Note*: If it is not there, right-click the **Quick Access Toolbar** and then select **Customize Quick Access Toolbar** to add the Print Preview icon.)

**12** Click **Page Setup** and then click the **Sheet** tab in the Page Setup window. Place a check mark in the **Gridlines** and **Row and column headings** check boxes. (This will enable the printing of gridlines and row and column headings.)

**13**  Click the **Page** tab, click the **Fit to:** option button to scale printing to one page wide and one page tall, and then click **OK**.

**14**  Click **Print** in the Excel Print Preview window and then click **OK** in the Print window to print the Excel document you just created. Your spreadsheet should look like Figure 11.15.

Wild Water Sports, Inc. 11
Income Statement
For the Three Months Ending March 31, 2013

| | A | B | C | D | E |
|---|---|---|---|---|---|
| 1 | | Current Month | | Year to Date | |
| 2 | Revenues | | | | |
| 3 | Sales Income | $ 434,750.00 | 98.85 | $ 767,500.00 | 98.80 |
| 4 | Service Income | 2,740.00 | 0.62 | 6,685.00 | 0.86 |
| 5 | Parts Income | 320.00 | 0.07 | 610.00 | 0.08 |
| 6 | Interest Income | 2,015.41 | 0.46 | 2,015.41 | 0.26 |
| 7 | | | | | |
| 8 | Total Revenues | 439,825.41 | 100.00 | 776,810.41 | 100.00 |
| 9 | | | | | |
| 10 | | | | | |
| 11 | Cost of Sales | | | | |
| 12 | Cost of Sales | 348,056.00 | 79.14 | 614,488.00 | 79.10 |
| 13 | | | | | |
| 14 | Total Cost of Sales | 348,056.00 | 79.14 | 614,488.00 | 79.10 |
| 15 | | | | | |
| 16 | Gross Profit | 91,769.41 | 20.86 | 162,322.41 | 20.90 |
| 17 | | | | | |
| 18 | Expenses | | | | |
| 19 | Wages Expense | 8,933.34 | 2.03 | 29,641.02 | 3.82 |
| 20 | Payroll Tax Expense | 998.06 | 0.23 | 3,504.94 | 0.45 |
| 21 | Utilities Expense | 1,050.00 | 0.24 | 2,870.00 | 0.37 |
| 22 | Telephone Expense | 1,500.00 | 0.34 | 5,020.00 | 0.65 |
| 23 | Other Office Expense | 0.00 | 0.00 | 4,500.00 | 0.58 |
| 24 | Advertising Expense | 4,000.00 | 0.91 | 6,700.00 | 0.86 |
| 25 | Interest Expense | 7,719.57 | 1.76 | 7,719.57 | 0.99 |
| 26 | Service Charge Expense | 75.00 | 0.02 | 75.00 | 0.01 |
| 27 | Insurance Expense | 5,500.00 | 1.25 | 5,500.00 | 0.71 |
| 28 | Depreciation Expense | 10,333.00 | 2.35 | 10,333.00 | 1.33 |
| 29 | Gain/Loss - Sale of Assets Exp | (3,000.00) | (0.68) | (3,000.00) | (0.39) |
| 30 | | | | | |
| 31 | Total Expenses | 37,106.97 | 8.44 | 72,663.53 | 9.35 |
| 32 | | | | | |
| 33 | Net Income | $ 54,662.44 | 12.43 | $ 89,658.88 | 11.54 |
| 34 | | | | | |

**Figure 11.15**

Printed Excel 2010 Document

**15**  Exit the Excel program.

**16**  Click **No** to not save the spreadsheet since it will no longer be used.

**17**  Close all windows in Peachtree.

"The steps to create the Excel document are the same in Peachtree regardless of whether you are using Excel 2010, 2007, or 2003?" you comment.

"Exactly," Karen responds. "The differences are just in the Excel program steps and the resulting file looks the same whether you used Excel 2010, 2007, or 2003."

# End Note

You've completed the reports for Donna and decide to deliver them to her office. After quickly skimming each report, she compliments you and Karen on your fine work and you turn to walk back to your office.

As you walk back to your office, you comment, "That was a pretty good review of the accounting basics and now I've learned to use a computerized accounting system. Life is good!"

## Business Events Summary

| Business Event | Process Steps | Page |
|---|---|---|
| Creating customized financial statements | Use Design from within a report | 352 |
| Creating additional reports for analysis | Use the Reports & Forms menu | 359 |
| Creating additional reports for management | Use the Analysis menu | 363 |
| Exporting reports to Excel | Use Excel from within a report | 367 |

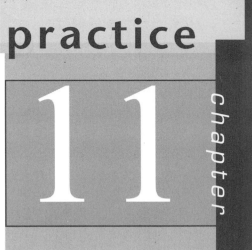

## Chapter 11 Questions

1  Identify the three supporting schedules that support the operating activities of a company reported on the income statement as illustrated in this chapter.

2  Identify the four supporting schedules that support the balance sheet as illustrated in this chapter.

3  How is the profit margin ratio calculated?

4  What are the steps necessary to create a % of Total Assets column in the balance sheet?

5  Once created, what does the % of Total Assets column mean?

6  What information does the inventory profitability report provide?

7  What information does the items sold to customers report provide?

8  What information does the collection aging report provide?

9  What information does the payment aging report provide?

10  What information does the inventory valuation report provide?

## Chapter 11 Exercises

### Chapter 11 Exercise 1

## MODIFIED FINANCIAL STATEMENTS

Restore the file **Boston Catering Ch 11** found on the text CD or download it from the text website and create the following reports for the period 7/1/10 through 9/30/10 like you did in the chapter. (Don't forget to set the system date.)

a.  Statement of Income and Retained Earnings for the three months ending September 30, 2010, with a % of Total Revenues column.

b.  Balance Sheet as of September 30, 2010, with a % of Total Assets column.

c.  Statement of Cash Flow for the three months ended September 30, 2010.

### Chapter 11 Exercise 2

## ADDITIONAL REPORTS

Restore the file **Boston Catering Ch 11** found on the text CD or download it from the text website and create the following reports for the period 7/1/10 through 9/30/10 in a manner similar to that used in the chapter. Be sure to set the system date to **9/30/10** and the period to **Period 3 – 09/01/10–09/30/10.**

a.  Inventory profitability report

b.  Items sold to customers report

c.  Items purchased from vendors report (click the Summarize report checkbox)

d.  Collections aging report

e.  Payment aging report

f.  Financial manager business summary report

g.  Financial manager key balances report

h.  Inventory valuation report

## *Chapter 11 Exercise 3*
## EXPORT TO EXCEL

Restore the file **Boston Catering Ch 11** found on the text CD or download it from the text website.

a.  Create a standard income statement report for the month of September 2010.

b.  Export the report created in (a) above to Excel in a manner similar to that used in the chapter.

c.  Print the resulting Excel worksheet with gridlines and row and column headlines.

## Chapter 11 Assignments

### *Chapter 11 Assignment 1*
### ADDING MORE INFORMATION: WILD WATER SPORTS

Restore the file **Wild Water Sports, Inc 11A** found on the text CD or download it from the text website. Be sure to set the system date to **4/30/13** and the accounting period to **Period 4 – 04/01/13–04/30/13** and then create, save, and print the following reports with no page numbers and without zero balance accounts (just like you did in the chapter):

a.  Statement of income and retained earnings for the four months ending April 30, 2013, with a % of Total Revenues column

b.  Balance sheet as of April 30, 2013, with a % column

c.  Statement of cash flows (with no current month) for the four months ending April 30, 2013

d.  Inventory profitability report for the four months ending April 30, 2013

e.  Items sold to customers report for the four months ending April 30, 2013

f.  Items purchased from vendors report for the four months ending April 30, 2013, from only those vendors who sell Wild Water inventory

g.  Collection aging report as of April 30, 2013

h.  Payment aging report as of April 30, 2013

i.  Business summary report as of April 30, 2013

j.  Key balances report as of April 30, 2013

k.  Inventory valuation report as of April 30, 2013

l.  Export the inventory profitability report you created to Excel and then print the Excel spreadsheet from Excel with row and column headers and gridlines in landscape orientation

m.  Prepare a summary reconciliation to explain any differences between the supporting schedules and the financial statements you just created like the one created in the chapter

## Chapter 11 Assignment 2

## ADDING MORE INFORMATION: CENTRAL COAST CELLULAR

Restore the file **Central Coast Cellular Ch 11** found on the text CD or download it from the text website. Change the system date to **1/31/09** and the accounting period to **Period 1 – 01/01/09–01/31/09** and then create, save, and print the following reports with no page numbers and without zero balance accounts (as you did in the chapter):

a.  Statement of income and retained earnings for January 2009 with a % of Total Revenues column

b.  Balance sheet as of January 31, 2009, with a % column

c.  Statement of cash flows for January 2009

d.  Inventory profitability report for January 2009

e.  Items sold to customers report for January 2009

f.  Items purchased from vendors report for January 2009 for all vendors

g.  Collection aging report as of January 31, 2009

h.  Payment aging report as of January 31, 2009

i.  Business summary report as of January 31, 2009

j.  Key balances report as of January 31, 2009

k.  Inventory valuation report as of January 31, 2009

l.  Export the inventory profitability report you created to Excel and then print the Excel spreadsheet from Excel with row and column headers and gridlines in landscape orientation

m.  Reconciliation of financial statement amounts and supporting schedules

## Chapter 11 Assignment 3

## ADDING MORE INFORMATION: SANTA BARBARA SAILING

Restore the file **Santa Barbara Sailing Ch 11** found on the text CD or download it from the text website. Change the system date to **7/31/12** and the accounting period to **Period 7 – 07/01/12–07/31/12** and then create, save, and print the following reports with no page numbers and without zero balance accounts (as you did in the chapter). (*Note*: Since this is a service company, no inventory profitability, inventory valuation, or items purchased from vendors reports are required.)

a. Statement of income and retained earnings for the month ended 7/31/12 with a % of Total Revenues column like you did in the chapter

b. Balance sheet as of 7/31/12 with a % column like you did in the chapter

c. Statement of cash flows for the seven months ended 7/31/12 as you did in the chapter

d. Summarized report of items sold to customers report for the month ended 7/31/12 (uncheck the **Show** check boxes for the Customer ID, Cost of Sales, Gross Profit, and Gross Margin columns)

e. Collection aging report as of 7/31/12 (numeric display)

f. Payment aging report as of 7/31/12

g. Business summary report as of 7/31/12

h. Key balances report as of 7/31/12

i. Export the statement of income and retained earnings you created to Excel and then print the Excel spreadsheet from Excel with row and column headers and gridlines in portrait orientation (use the Fit to 1 page width option)

j. Prepare a summary reconciliation to explain any differences between the supporting schedules and the financial statements you just created like the one created in the chapter

## Chapter 11 Cases

### Chapter 11 Case Problem 1

## FOREVER YOUNG

service

sole proprietorship

Restore the backup you made for **Forever Young** in Chapter 10 into a new company folder. (Do not restore this backup into an existing folder.) Change the company name to include Ch 11 at the end so that the new company name is **Forever Young Ch 11**. Change the system date to **1/31/08** and the accounting period to **Period 1 – 01/01/08–01/31/08** and then create, save, and print the following reports with no page numbers and without zero balance accounts (as you did in the chapter). (*Note*: Since this is a service company, no inventory profitability, inventory valuation, or items purchased from vendors reports are required.)

a. Statement of income and retained earnings for the month ended 1/31/08 with a % of Total Revenues column

b. Balance sheet as of 1/31/08 with a % column

c. Statement of cash flows for the month ended 1/31/08

d. Items sold to customers report for the month ended 1/31/08 (uncheck the **Show** check boxes for the Customer ID, Cost of Sales, Gross Profit, and Gross Margin columns)

e. Collection aging report as of 1/31/08

f. Payment aging report as of 1/31/08

g. Business summary report as of 1/31/08

h.  Key balances report as of 1/31/08

i.  Export the statement of income and retained earnings you created above to Excel and then print the Excel spreadsheet from Excel with row and column headers and gridlines in portrait orientation (use the Fit to 1 page width option)

j.  Prepare a summary reconciliation to explain any differences between the supporting schedules and the financial statements you just created like the one created in the chapter

## *Chapter 11 Case Problem 2*
# OCEAN VIEW FLOWERS

*merchandising*

Restore the backup you made for **Ocean View Flowers** in Chapter 10 into a new company folder. (Do not restore this backup into an existing folder.) Change the company name to include Ch 11 at the end so that the new company name is **Ocean View Flowers Ch 11**. Change the system date to **2/29/08** and the accounting period to **Period 2 – 02/01/08–02/29/08** and then create and print the following reports with no page numbers and without zero balance accounts (as you did in the chapter):

a.  Statement of income and retained earnings for the two months ending February 29, 2008, with a % of Total Revenues column

b.  Balance sheet as of February 29, 2008, with a % column

c.  Statement of cash flows for the two months ending February 29, 2008

d.  Inventory profitability report for the two months ending February 29, 2008

e.  Items sold to customers report for the two months ending February 29, 2008

f.  Items purchased from vendors report for the two months ending February 29, 2008

g.  Collection aging report as of February 29, 2008

h.  Payment aging report as of February 29, 2008

i.  Business summary report as of February 29, 2008

j.  Key balances report as of February 29, 2008

k.  Inventory valuation report as of February 29, 2008

l.  Export the inventory valuation report you created to Excel and then print the Excel spreadsheet from Excel with row and column headers and gridlines in landscape orientation

m.  Prepare a summary reconciliation to explain any differences between the supporting schedules and the financial statements you just created like the one created in the chapter

## Chapter 11 Case Problem 3

# ALOHA PROPERTY MANAGEMENT

*service*

Restore the backup you made for **Aloha** in Chapter 10 into a new company folder. (Do not restore this backup into an existing folder.) Change the company name to include Ch 11 at the end so that the new company name is **Aloha Property Management Ch 11**. Change the system date to **2/29/08** and the accounting period to **Period 2 – 02/01/08–02/29/08** and then create, save, and print the following reports with no page numbers and without zero balance accounts (like you did in the chapter). (*Note*: Since this is a service company, no inventory profitability, inventory valuation, or items purchased from vendors reports are required.)

a.   Statement of income and retained earnings for the two months ending February 29, 2008, with a % of Total Revenues column

b.   Balance sheet as of February 29, 2008, with a % column

c.   Statement of cash flows for the two months ending February 29, 2008

d.   Items sold to customers report for the two months ending February 29, 2008 (uncheck the **Show** check boxes for both the Customer ID and the Item ID fields, then check the **Item Description Show** check box with the item Description field selected, click the **Move UP** button until the Item Description field is right below the Name field)

e.   Collection aging report as of February 29, 2008

f.   Payment aging report as of February 29, 2008

g.   Business summary report as of February 29, 2008

h.   Key balances report as of February 29, 2008

i.   Export the statement of income and retained earnings report you created to Excel and then print the Excel spreadsheet from Excel with row and column headers and gridlines in portrait orientation (use the Fit to 1 page width option)

## Comprehensive Problems

## Comprehensive Problem 1: SPORTS CITY

Restore the file **Sports City** found on the text CD or download it from the text website. Be sure to set the system date to **1/31/07** and the accounting period to **Period 1 – 01/01/07–01/31/07**. The previous accountant had used a different computer accounting system. You chose to convert that work to Peachtree, and the file you just restored is the result of that effort. You note the existing sales tax rate already present in the Peachtree file is 8%. Now you need to record the following additional business transactions in chronological order (remember, dates are in the month of January 2007).

## Chronological List of Business Events

| Event # | Date | Business Event |
|---------|------|----------------|
| 1 | 1/16 | Purchased office supplies from vendor Office Max for $250 with Check No. 4 recording this as supplies expense. |
| 2 | 1/16 | Received terms net 10 days from Nike and Wilson Sporting Goods. Update vendor records accordingly. |
| 3 | 1/17 | Received items and entered a bill (Invoice 23423) from Nike for a previously recorded Purchase Order No. 1 (terms net 10). |
| 4 | 1/18 | Received items and entered a bill (Invoice 984) from Wilson Sporting Goods for a previously recorded Purchase Order No. 2 (terms net 10). |
| 5 | 1/19 | Hired a new employee, ID AF, Anne Franks, 112 East Fir #3, Lompoc, CA 93436, a single woman, Social Security number 233-89-4232. She will earn an hourly wage of $8.00, is paid semimonthly like all employees, and is subject to all payroll taxes, including the training tax. |
| 6 | 1/22 | Received a $400 payment on account from Cabrillo High School (its Check No. 354), which is grouped with other undeposited funds. (Used Sales Receipt SR 001.) |
| 7 | 1/23 | Invoiced Buena Vista Elementary (a new subject to sales tax customer with ID Buena Vista, 300 Aldeberan St., Vandenberg Village, CA 93436, and terms due in 5 days and a credit limit of $3,000) for 100 shirts and 5 footballs with Invoice 3. |
| 8 | 1/23 | Received a $600 payment on account (its Check No. 0933, Sports City's Sales Receipt SR 002) from Lompoc High School, which is also grouped with other undeposited funds. |
| 9 | 1/24 | Borrowed $10,000 from Mid-State Bank with a short-term note payable. Use journal entry 1 and create a new short-term notes payable account. |
| 10 | 1/25 | Wrote checks to pay all bills due by 1/31/07 using Check Nos. 5–9 for a total of $18,994. (This excludes the state sales taxes owed.) |
| 11 | 1/29 | Deposited by mail all previously received but undeposited payments, totaling $1,000, to Mid-State Bank with Deposit Ticket ID 0001. |
| 12 | 1/31 | Recorded depreciation of $2,000 on furniture and fixtures with journal entry 2. |
| 13 | 1/31 | Recorded the expiration of $3,000 in prepaid rent with journal entry 3. |
| 14 | 1/31 | Reclassified the advance payment made by Arroyo Grande High School to unearned revenue (a new other current liability account with ID 2300) with journal entry 4. |
| 15 | 1/31 | Paid all employees for the pay period 1/16–1/31. Ms. Franks worked 75 hours during this period. (See the following tax information table.) |
| 16 | 1/31 | Reconciled the bank account. The ending bank balance per the statement is $5,333.52. The bank charged a $40 service charge. Check Nos. 10, 11, and 12 for the January 31 payroll do not appear on the statement, nor does the $1,000 deposited by mail on January 29. |

|  | Sam Snead | Kelly Flowers | Anne Franks |
|---|---|---|---|
| Check Number | 10 | 11 | 12 |
| Gross Pay | 1,458.33 | 1,250.00 | 600.00 |
| Federal Withholding | −244.00 | −147.00 | −73.00 |
| Social Security Employee | −90.41 | −77.50 | −37.20 |
| Social Security Employer | 90.41 | 77.50 | 37.20 |
| Medicare Employee | −21.14 | −18.12 | −8.70 |
| Medicare Employer | 21.14 | 18.12 | 8.70 |
| CA—Withholding | −57.39 | −40.72 | −7.66 |
| CA—Disability Employee | −7.29 | −6.25 | −3.00 |
| CA—Training Tax | 1.46 | 1.25 | 0.60 |
| Federal Unemployment | 11.66 | 10.00 | 4.80 |
| CA—Unemployment | 0.73 | 0.62 | 0.30 |
| Check Amount | 1,038.10 | 960.41 | 470.44 |

Budget information for January through March 2007 is as follows. (*Note*: You are to round budget data to the nearest whole dollar.)

| Account | January 07 | Following |
|---|---|---|
| Sales | $10,000 | 15% increase each month thereafter |
| Cost of Sales | $ 6,000 | 60% of sales |
| Depreciation | $ 2,000 | Constant each month thereafter |
| Payroll | $ 6,500 | $500 increase each month thereafter |
| Rent | $ 3,000 | Constant each month thereafter |
| Telephone | $   100 | 5% increase each month thereafter |
| Utilities | $   200 | 5% increase each month thereafter |

Create, save, and print the following reports with no page numbers and without zero balance accounts (as you did in this and previous chapters):

a.  Account reconciliation report of Mid-State Bank checking account for January 2007

b.  Budgeted income statement accounts for January through March 2007

c.  Budgeted versus actual income statement for January 2007

d.  Statement of income and retained earnings for January 2007 with a % of Total Revenues column

e.  Balance sheet as of January 31, 2007, with a % column

f.  Statement of cash flows for January 2007

g.  Inventory profitability report for January 2007

h.  Items sold to customers report for January 2007 (print in detail, not summary, format)

i.  Items purchased from vendors report for January 2007 (print in detail, not summary, format)

j.  Collection aging report as of January 31, 2007

k.  Payment aging report as of January 31, 2007

l.  Business summary report as of January 31, 2007

m.  Key balances report as of January 31, 2007

n.  Inventory valuation report as of January 31, 2007

o. Export the inventory profitability report you created to Excel and then print the Excel spreadsheet from Excel with row and column headers and gridlines in landscape orientation

p. Prepare a summary reconciliation to explain any differences between the supporting schedules and the financial statements you just created like the one created in the chapter

## Comprehensive Problem 2: PACIFIC BREW INC.

Restore the backup you made for **Pacific Brew Inc.** in Chapter 7 into a new company folder. (Do not restore this backup into an existing folder.) Change the company name to include Ch 11 at the end so that the new company name is **Pacific Brew Ch 11**. Change the system date to **1/1/08** and the accounting period to **Period 1 – 01/01/08–01/31/08**. Add the following business events:

*merchandising*

*Chronological List of Business Events*

| Event # | Date | Business Event |
|---|---|---|
| 1 | 1/17 | Received all items ordered on Purchase Order No. 1003 to Lost Coast (terms net 30) on its Invoice LC9873. |
| 2 | 1/17 | Received Invoice 2039480 from Staples (a new vendor with Vendor ID "S") for $2,500 of office supplies purchased on account terms net 15. These supplies will be used over the next six months; thus, you will need to create an office supplies (ID 1300 other current asset) account. |
| 3 | 1/17 | Using Purchase Order No. 1004, ordered 1,000 of Item 402, 1,500 of Item 403, and 2,000 of Item 404 for Best Way delivery, terms net 30, from Lost Coast. |
| 4 | 1/18 | Using Purchase Order No. 1005, ordered 750 each of Items 302, 303, 304, and 305 for Best Way delivery, terms net 30, from Mad River. |
| 5 | 1/18 | The manager believes the company charges too little for its products and increases all product prices 50%. (Use Peachtree Help to find out how to change item sales prices by calculating new item prices for a range of items. Adjust Price Level 1 by increasing the current price by 50% with no rounding. Be careful to only do this once! For example, the new price for Item 302 should be $9.00, and the new price for Item 402 should be $9.38.) |
| 6 | 1/21 | Changed terms for vendor Humboldt to the standard net 30 days. Then using Purchase Order No. 1006, ordered 500 each of Items 502, 506, and 507 for Best Way delivery, from Humboldt. |
| 7 | 1/21 | Received and shipped via Best Way an order to Bon Jovi's for 200 units of Item 302, 150 units of Item 303, and 100 units of Item 507. Invoice 7001 was generated to bill the customer on net 30 terms. |
| 8 | 1/22 | Received and shipped via Best Way an order to Ocean Grove for 100 units each of Items 302, 304, and 305. Invoice 7002 was generated to bill the customer on net 30 terms. |
| 9 | 1/23 | Received and shipped via Best Way an order to Avalon Bistro for 150 units each of Items 502, 506, and 507. Invoice 7003 was generated to bill the customer on net 30 terms. |
| 10 | 1/24 | Received all items ordered and entered a bill (Invoice 098732) from Purchase Order No. 1004 to Lost Coast. |

| Event # | Date | Business Event |
|---------|------|----------------|
| 11 | 1/24 | Received Invoice 232 from Verizon (a new vendor with ID = V) for telephone services for the month of January in the amount of $500, terms net 10. |
| 12 | 1/24 | Received Invoice 121223 from the City of Arcata (a new vendor with ID = CA) for utility services for the month of January in the amount of $1,500, terms net 10. |
| 13 | 1/25 | Received Check No. 9388 as payment on account from Bon Jovi's of $4,575 on Invoice 7001, which will be deposited later in the week. |
| 14 | 1/28 | Received Check No. 1233334 as an advance on future orders from River House in the amount of $1,200, which will be deposited later. |
| 15 | 1/29 | Deposited $5,775 in checks received earlier to Wells Fargo using Deposit Ticket ID A4007. |
| 16 | 1/30 | Modified terms for Mad River to net 15 from net due. Received all items ordered and entered Invoice 82798 from Purchase Order No. 1005 to Mad River. |
| 17 | 1/30 | Paid bills from Verizon, City of Arcata, and Staples for a total of $4,500, assigning Check Nos. 110, 111, and 112, respectively. |
| 18 | 1/30 | Received and shipped an order (SR 5007) to Hole in the Wall for 250 units each of Items 303, 305, and 404. Payment of $7,032.50 (with its Check No. 3232) was deposited and mailed to Wells Fargo Bank that same day using Deposit Ticket ID A4008. |
| 19 | 1/30 | Paid employees. Duarte worked 83 hours, and Lopez worked 79 hours during the period. See tax information in the table on the next page. |
| 20 | 1/31 | Recorded depreciation of $800 for the month with journal entry 2. |
| 21 | 1/31 | Recorded the use of office supplies of $400 with journal entry 3. |
| 22 | 1/31 | Reclassified the $1,200 payment from River House to customer deposits with journal entry 4. |
| 23 | 1/31 | Accrued interest income on the certificate of deposit short-term investment of $2,000 with journal entry 5. |
| 24 | 1/31 | Accrued interest expense on the long-term note payable of $2,600 with journal entry 6. (*Hint*: You'll have to create a new interest expense account ID = 6875 and a new accrued interest payable account ID = 2390.) |
| 25 | 1/31 | Reconciled the Wells Fargo bank account. No bank service charges were noted on the bank statement. The ending bank balance was $28,673.30. All deposits were recorded by the bank except the $7,032.50 deposit recorded 1/30/08. All checks cleared the bank except those issued on 1/31/08 for payroll. |
| 26 | 1/31 | Budgeted income statement account information for January through March is as follows: Sales income of $35,000 is expected in January, increasing $5,000 each month thereafter. Cost of goods sales of $15,000 is expected in January, increasing $2,500 each month thereafter. Depreciation, interest, rent, and office supplies expenses are expected to remain constant at $1,000, $2,000, $2,500, and $500, respectively. Telephone expenses of $450 are budgeted for January and are expected to increase $50 each month thereafter. Wages expenses are budgeted at $8,500 for January and February and then $10,000 for March. Utilities expense is budgeted at $1,200 for January and is expected to increase by 5% each month thereafter. Interest income of $1,500 is expected each month. |

| Event # | Date | Business Event |
|---------|------|----------------|
| 27 | 1/31 | Budgeted balance sheet account information for January is as follows: |

| | |
|---|---:|
| Checking Account | $40,000 |
| Certificates of Deposit | 30,000 |
| Accounts Receivable | 10,000 |
| Inventory | 45,000 |
| Office Supplies | 2,000 |
| PP & E | 23,000 |
| Accounts Payable | 50,650 |
| Federal Payroll Taxes Payable | 3,000 |
| State Payroll Taxes Payable | 1,000 |
| Notes Payable | 40,000 |
| Common Stock | 50,000 |

| | Duarte | Lopez | Patrick |
|---|---:|---:|---:|
| Check Number | 113 | 114 | 115 |
| Gross Pay | 913.00 | 948.00 | 2,083.33 |
| Federal Withholding | −125.08 | −129.88 | −285.42 |
| Social Security Employee | −56.61 | −58.78 | −129.17 |
| Medicare Employee | −13.24 | −13.75 | −30.21 |
| CA–Withholding | −50.22 | −52.14 | −114.58 |
| CA–Disability | −4.57 | −4.74 | −10.42 |
| CA–Employment Training Tax | 0.91 | 0.95 | 2.08 |
| Social Security Employer | 56.61 | 58.78 | 129.17 |
| Medicare Company | 13.24 | 13.75 | 30.21 |
| Federal Unemployment | 7.30 | 7.58 | 16.67 |
| CA–Company Unemployment | 27.39 | 28.44 | 62.50 |
| Check Amount | 663.28 | 688.71 | 1,513.53 |

Create and print the following reports with no page numbers and without zero balance accounts (like you did in this and previous chapters):

a. Bank reconciliation report for January 2008

b. Budgeted income statement accounts for January through March 2008 with a YTD column

c. Budgeted versus actual income statement for the month of January 2008

d. Budgeted balance sheet accounts for January through March 2008 with a YTD column

e. Budgeted versus actual balance sheet for the month ended January 2008 with Budget, Variance, and % Variance columns

f. Statement of income and retained earnings for the month of January 2008 with a % of Total Revenues column

g. Balance sheet as of 1/31/08 with a % column

h. Statement of cash flows for the month of January 2008 with no YTD column

i. Inventory profitability report for the month of January 2008

j. Items sold to customers report for the month of January 2008 in summary format without Customer ID

k.  Items purchased from vendors report for the month of January 2008 in summary format without Vendor ID

l.   Collection aging report as of 1/31/08

m.  Payment aging report as of 1/31/08

n.  Business summary report as of 1/31/08

o.  Key balances report as of 1/31/08

p.  Inventory valuation report as of 1/31/08 without Item ID, Item Class, Cost Method, and Stocking U/M

q.  Export the inventory profitability report you created to Excel and then print the Excel spreadsheet from Excel with row and column headers and gridlines in landscape orientation

r.   Prepare a summary reconciliation to explain any differences between the supporting schedules and the financial statements you just created like the one created in the chapter

## Comprehensive Problem 3: SUNSET SPAS INC.

*merchandising*

Restore the backup you made for **Sunset Spas Inc.** in Chapter 7 into a new company folder. (Do not restore this backup into an existing folder.) Change the company name to include Ch 11 at the end so that the new company name is **Sunset Spas Ch 11**. Change the system date to **1/1/07** and the accounting period to **Period 1 – 01/01/07–01/31/07**. Add the following business events:

*Chronological List of Business Events*

| Event # | Date | Business Events |
|---|---|---|
| 1 | 1/17 | Paid $18,000 in liability insurance for the year to Hartford Insurance (new vendor with ID = HI) using Check No. 110. (*Hint*: Record this as Prepaid Expenses.) |
| 2 | 1/17 | Received Invoice A4900 from Staples (new vendor with ID = ST) for $500 in office supplies purchased on account, which are expected to be consumed in this month. Terms are net 30. |
| 3 | 1/17 | Received net 30 terms from Cal Spas, changed the default shipper for this vendor to Cust. Pickup, and increased Sunset's credit limit with Cal Spas to $50,000. |
| 4 | 1/17 | Using Purchase Order No. 5003, ordered one each of Items 301, 302, and 303 for immediate delivery, terms net 30, from Cal Spas. |
| 5 | 1/18 | Created a new customer: Landmark Landscaping, ID = LL, address = 8500 Ridgefield Place, San Diego, CA 92129, shipping = Cust. Pickup, payment terms net 15, Sales Tax = Tax, and a credit limit of $25,000. |
| 6 | 1/18 | Sold two of Item 302 to Landmark Landscaping with six hours of installation on Invoice 10001. |
| 7 | 1/19 | Granted terms of net 15 to customer Marriott Hotels, changed the default shipper for this customer to Cust. Pickup, and changed Sunset's credit limit with Marriott to $50,000. |
| 8 | 1/19 | Sold two of Item 202 and one of Item 302 to Marriott Hotels with 15 hours of installation on Invoice 10002, payment terms net 15. |
| 9 | 1/19 | Applied the Marriott Hotels prepayment received on 1/16/07 to Invoice 10002. |

| Event # | Date | Business Events |
|---------|------|-----------------|
| 10 | 1/20 | Hired a new employee, Walton Perez, ID = WP, 530 Miramar Rd., Apt 230, San Diego, CA 92145, a single man, Social Security number 323-99-2394. He will earn an hourly wage of $9.00, is paid semimonthly, and is subject to all payroll taxes. He will start work 2/1/07. |
| 11 | 1/22 | Purchased equipment for installation and support of spa services from Outlet Tool Supply (a new vendor with ID OTS, shipper = Cust. Pickup, terms net 30, credit limit $30,000) for $25,000. Received Outlet's Invoice 92378 with 30-day terms. (Record as Equipment.) |
| 12 | 1/22 | Received and deposited (Deposit Ticket ID = 906) a $3,500 check (Check No. 9098) from a new customer, Kristen's Spa Resort (ID = KSR and shipper = Cust. Pickup), for work to be performed next month. |
| 13 | 1/23 | Received a $23,000 invoice (Invoice 982223) from the City of San Diego (ID = SD) for licenses payable with terms net 15. |
| 14 | 1/24 | Changed terms for Pam's Designs (a customer) to net 15 with a credit limit of $70,000 and shipper = Cust. Pickup. |
| 15 | 1/24 | Sold six of Item 203 to Pam's Designs with 18 hours of installation on Invoice 10003, payment terms net 15. |
| 16 | 1/25 | Received a $1,400 bill (Invoice 309) from Verizon (new vendor with ID = V) for telephone installation services, terms net 15. |
| 17 | 1/26 | Received shipment from Cal Spas (Sunset's Purchase Order No. 5003, Cal Spas' Invoice 2987). All items were received. (Terms are net 30.) |
| 18 | 1/29 | Received $5,000 payment (Landmark's Check No. 3098) on account from Landmark Landscaping, which was deposited into the checking account with Deposit Ticket ID 907. |
| 19 | 1/30 | Paid two bills in full: City of San Diego and Verizon using Check Nos. 111 and 112, respectively. |
| 20 | 1/31 | Paid employees. Sanchez worked 84 hours, and Lee worked 67 hours during the period. Start with Check No. 113. See tax information in the table on the next page. |
| 21 | 1/31 | Accrued $3,000 in additional telephone services provided by Verizon to accounts payable for which a bill had not yet been received. Set up for reversal next month. (Use journal entry 3.) |
| 22 | 1/31 | Recorded the expiration of one month's prepaid insurance. (Use journal entry 4.) |
| 23 | 1/31 | Reclassified Kristen's Spa Resort prepayment of $3,500 and Landmark's prepayment of $5,000 as customer deposits for reversal next month. (Use journal entry 5.) |
| 24 | 1/31 | Recorded depreciation expense of $1,750 ($1,500 on equipment, $250 on furniture). (Use journal entry 6.) |
| 25 | 1/31 | Accrued interest expense on a note payable for $1,000 to a liability account called accrued expenses for reversal next month. (Use journal entry 7.) |
| 26 | 1/31 | Accrued interest income to short-term investments for $75 for reversal next month. (Use journal entry 8.) |
| 27 | 1/31 | Accrued revenue and related cost of goods sold for a shipment that took place 1/31/07 but was invoiced in February. The sale was to Pam's Design and represented two Item 201 spas, which were sold for $7,000 each, sales tax of $1,085, and which cost Sunset $5,000 each. (Use journal entry 9.) |

| Event # | Date | Business Events |
|---------|------|-----------------|
| 28 | 1/31 | Reconciled the bank account. There were no bank service charges. The bank statement balance was $34,793.43 at 1/31/07. Check Nos. 104, 113, 114, and 115 had not been paid according to the bank statement. One deposit, made on 1/29/07 for $5,000, was not reflected on the bank statement. |
| 29 | 1/31 | Income and expense budget information for January through March is as follows: Merchandise sales of $170,000 are expected in January, increasing $10,000 per month thereafter. Service sales of $10,000 are expected in January, increasing $1,000 per month thereafter. Cost of goods sold is expected to be 75% of merchandise sales. Depreciation, insurance, interest, supplies, rent, and telephone are expected to remain constant at $1,800, $1,500, $1,000, $500, $3,000, and $1,500, respectively. A one-time license fee of $20,000 was expected for January. Salaries expenses are estimated at $10,000 per month. |
| 30 | 1/31 | Asset, liability, and equity budget information for January is as follows: |

| | |
|---|---|
| Checking | $ 31,850 |
| Accounts Receivable | 100,000 |
| Inventory | 150,000 |
| Prepaid Expenses | 15,000 |
| Short-Term Investments | 30,000 |
| Furniture | 4,500 |
| Equipment | 37,400 |
| Accum. Depreciation Furniture | −250 |
| Accum. Depreciation Equipment | −1,500 |
| Deposits | 3,000 |
| Accounts Payable | 29,800 |
| Sales Tax Payable | 15,000 |
| Federal Payroll Taxes Payable | 2,500 |
| State Payroll Taxes Payable | 500 |
| Customer Deposits | 9,000 |
| Notes Payable | 200,000 |
| Common Stock | 100,000 |

| Pay/Tax/Withholding | Christopher | Sanchez | Lee |
|---------------------|-------------|---------|------|
| Hours | n/a | 84 | 67 |
| Check Number | 113 | 114 | 115 |
| Annual Salary or Hourly Rate | 60,000.00 | 13.00 | 12.00 |
| Gross Pay | 2,500.00 | 1,092.00 | 804.00 |
| Federal Withholding | −342.50 | −149.60 | −110.15 |
| Social Security Employee | −155.00 | −67.70 | −49.85 |
| Medicare Employee | −36.25 | −15.83 | −11.66 |
| CA–Withholding | −137.50 | −60.06 | −44.22 |
| CA–Disability | −12.50 | −5.46 | −4.02 |
| CA–Employment Training Tax | 2.50 | 1.09 | 0.80 |
| Social Security Employer | 155.00 | 67.70 | 49.85 |
| Medicare Company | 36.25 | 15.83 | 11.66 |
| Federal Unemployment | 20.00 | 8.74 | 6.43 |
| CA–Unemployment | 6.25 | 2.73 | 2.01 |
| Check Amount | 1,816.25 | 793.35 | 584.10 |

Create and print the following reports with no page numbers and without zero balance accounts (like you did in this and previous chapters):

a. Bank reconciliation report for January 2007

b. Budgeted income statement accounts for January through March 2007 with a YTD column

c. Budgeted versus actual income statement for the month of January 2007

d. Budgeted balance sheet accounts for January through March 2007 with a YTD column

e. Budgeted versus actual balance sheet for the month ended January 2007 with Budget, Variance, and % Variance columns

f. Statement of income and retained earnings for the month of January 2007 with a % of Total Revenues column

g. Balance sheet as of 1/31/07 with a % column

h. Statement of cash flows for the month of January 2007 with no YTD column

i. Inventory profitability report for the month of January 2007

j. Items sold to customers report for the month of January 2007 in detail format without Customer ID

k. Items purchased from vendors report for the month of January 2007 in summary format without Vendor ID

l. Collection aging report as of 1/31/07

m. Payment aging report as of 1/31/07

n. Business summary report as of 1/31/07

o. Key balances report as of 1/31/07

p. Inventory valuation report as of 1/31/07 without Item ID, Item Class, Cost Method, and Stocking U/M

q. Export the inventory profitability report you created to Excel and then print the Excel spreadsheet from Excel with row and column headers and gridlines in landscape orientation

r. Prepare a summary reconciliation to explain any differences between the supporting schedules and the financial statements you just created like the one created in the chapter

## Comprehensive Problem 4: BRIDGETTE SWEET PHOTOGRAPHY

Restore the backup you made for **Bridgette Sweet Photography** in Chapter 7 into a new company folder. (Do not restore this backup into an existing folder.) Change the company name to include Ch 11 at the end so that the new company name is **Bridgette Sweet Photography Ch 11**. Change the system date to **2/1/13** and the accounting period to **Period 2 – 02/01/13–02/28/13**. Add the following business events:

*merchandising*

*Chronological List of Business Events*

| Event # | Date | Business Event |
|---------|------|----------------|
| 1 | 2/1/13 | Transferred funds from checking into a new short-term investments account (GL Account 10600) with E-Trade in the amount of $7,000 using journal entry 18. |
| 2 | 2/4/13 | Wrote check 9851 for $1,800 to GEICO (new vendor with Vendor ID: GEICO and Name GEICO Insurance) to prepay auto insurance for one year beginning 2/1/13. |
| 3 | 2/5/13 | Received and deposited check 2309 (Deposit ticket ID: 325) from a new customer Ipad, Inc. (Customer ID: IPAD) in the amount of $12,000. Created two new jobs 436 (IPAD) and 437 for Boss Design (Customer ID: BD), a new customer. Both new jobs are for photo shoots. |
| 4 | 2/6/13 | Received and deposited check 9432 (Deposit ticket ID: 326) as payment on account from Foster Corporation in the amount of $3,000. |
| 5 | 2/7/13 | Received invoice 19328089 from Chicago Electric (new vendor with Vendor ID: CE and Name Chicago Electric) for utilities consumed in January 2013. Paid $234 with check 9852 charging it to utilities expense. |
| 6 | 2/8/13 | Wrote check 9853 for $370.53 to Bank of Chicago (new vendor with Vendor ID: BC and Name Bank of Chicago) as payment of note payable. This was the payment due 1/31/13 of which $70 was applied to interest expense. |
| 7 | Various | Created new timesheets for all employees as per the schedule shown below these events. Remember, Bridgette bills her time based on an activity rate while all other employees bill their time based on their employee rate. |
| 8 | 2/15/13 | Created purchase order 6415 to US Photo for 100 prints for job 435 and 200 prints and 5 albums for job 436. Prints cost $21 and albums cost $75 each. Items are for customer pickup. All items ordered on this purchase order were picked up on 2/19 with US Photo invoice 10622. Created purchase order 6416 to Peterson Framing for 20 frames at a cost of $150 each for inventory to be shipped via Airborne. Frames were received on 2/16 with an invoice 8926. |
| 9 | 2/20/13 | Invoiced customer KW for photo shoot time and expenses and 10 frames on invoice 10210. Applied payment received on 1/30 against this invoice. Invoiced customer IPAD for photo shoot time and expenses and 12 frames on invoice 10211. Applied payment received on 2/5 against this invoice. Both customers are charged sales tax. |
| 10 | 2/22/13 | Received and deposited check 974123 as payment on account from BW in the amount of $4,346.10 and check 23908 for $10,000 as advance payment on future services from Foster Corporation. (Deposit ticket ID: 327.) |
| 11 | 2/27/13 | Paid sales tax owed as of 1/31/13 to the Illinois Department of Revenue using check 9854. |
| 12 | 2/28/13 | Paid employees with checks 9855–9857 based on the table shown after all events. Pay bills due as of 2/28/13 for a total amount of $10,100 using checks 9858–9859. |
| 13 | 2/28/13 | Reconciled the regular checking account as of 2/28/13. Checks 9854–9859 have not yet cleared and deposit ticket 326 does not appear on the bank statement. Bank charges amount to $60. The statement ending balance is $22,438.75. |

| Event # | Date | Business Event |
|---|---|---|
| 14 | 2/28/13 | On 3/4/13 the company created invoice 10212 to Customer ID: BD for job 437. No prints or albums were ordered but 5 frames were delivered on 2/28. Timesheets indicate hours had been incurred and sales tax was collected. Record this invoice on 3/4/13 and accrue sales and the cost of goods sold as of 2/28/13 using journal entry reference 19. |
| 15 | 1/31/13 and 2/28/13 | Accrued utility expense as of 1/31/13 related to January but paid on 2/7 with check 9852 using journal entry reference 20. Accrue interest expense related to 1/31/13 but paid on 2/8 with check 9853 using journal entry reference 21. (*Hint*: Accrue in January and set up for reversal in February using the liability account accrued expenses.) Also accrue utility expense of $250 and interest expense of $68.25 on 2/28/13 using journal entry references 22 and 23, respectively. (*Hint*: Accrue in February and set up for reversal in March using the liability account accrued expenses.) |
| 16 | 2/28/13 | Adjusted prepaid expenses for one month of insurance expense based on the previously deferred cost incurred on 2/4 using journal entry reference 24. |
| 17 | 2/28/13 | Adjusted accounts receivable for the $10,000 received from Foster Corporation on 2/22/13 to unearned revenue (a new other current liability account 24700) using journal entry reference 25. |
| 18 | 1/31/13 and 2/28/13 | Recorded depreciation expense of $450 each for January and February ($250 for furniture and $200 for equipment) using journal entry references 26 and 27. |
| 19 | 2/28/13 | Recorded loss on sale of short-term investments (as other income) of $300 using journal entry reference 28. |
| 20 | 2/28/13 | Budget data is shown in a table below. |

## *Employee Timesheet Information*

| Date | Customer/Job ID | Activity | Billing Status | Sweet | Garrett | Pease |
|---|---|---|---|---|---|---|
| 2/01 | Administrative | 2000 | Non-Billable | | 6 | 6 |
| 2/02 | KW/435 | 1000 | Billable | 8 | 8 | 7 |
| 2/11 | Administrative | 2000 | Non-Billable | | 8 | 8 |
| 2/12 | Administrative | 2000 | Non-Billable | | 8 | 8 |
| 2/15 | IPAD/436 | 1010 | Billable | 8 | 8 | 8 |
| 2/22 | Administrative | 2000 | Non-Billable | | 6 | 8 |
| 2/23 | BD/437 | 1010 | Billable | 12 | 7 | 5 |
| Total | | | | 28 | 51 | 50 |

## *Employee Payroll Information*

| Pay/Tax/Withholding | Sweet | Garrett | Pease |
|---|---|---|---|
| Hours | n/a | 51 | 50 |
| Salary/Hourly Rate | $60,000.00 | $   25.00 | $   20.00 |
| Gross Pay | 5,000.00 | 1,275.00 | 1,000.00 |
| Federal Withholding | −685.00 | −174.68 | −137.00 |
| Social Security Employee | −310.00 | −79.05 | −62.00 |
| Medicare Employee | −72.50 | −18.49 | −14.50 |
| State Withholding | −347.33 | −64.23 | −43.33 |
| Social Security Employer | 310.00 | 79.05 | 62.00 |
| Medicare Company | 72.50 | 18.49 | 14.50 |

| Pay/Tax/Withholding | Sweet | Garrett | Pease |
|---|---|---|---|
| Federal Unemployment | 40.00 | 10.20 | 8.00 |
| State Unemployment | 150.00 | 38.25 | 30.00 |
| Check Amount | 3,585.17 | 938.55 | 743.17 |

*Budget Data*

| Income Statement Budget Data | January | February |
|---|---|---|
| Photographic Sales | 5,000 | 5,000 |
| Weddings Income | 3,000 | 3,000 |
| Corporate Income | 4,000 | 4,000 |
| Sales-Frames | 15,000 | 18,000 |
| Other Income | 0 | 0 |
| Cost of Orders | 5,000 | 5,000 |
| Cost of Frames | 7,500 | 9,000 |
| Bank Charges | 0 | 0 |
| Depreciation Expense | 450 | 450 |
| Insurance Expense | 150 | 150 |
| Interest Expense | 80 | 80 |
| Payroll Tax Expense | 850 | 850 |
| Rent or Lease Expense | 1,750 | 1,750 |
| Salaries Expense | 5,000 | 5,000 |
| Wages Expense | 1,500 | 2,000 |
| Utilities Expense | 200 | 225 |

| Balance Sheet Budget Data | December | January | February |
|---|---|---|---|
| Regular Checking Account | 9,000 | 1,970 | 1,030 |
| Short-Term Investments | 0 | 0 | 7,000 |
| Accounts Receivable | 26,000 | 10,000 | 8,000 |
| Inventory Frames | 3,000 | -2,000 | -100 |
| Furniture and Fixtures | 10,000 | 0 | 0 |
| Equipment | 5,000 | 5,000 | 0 |
| Accumulated Depreciation Furniture and Fixtures | 2,000 | 250 | 250 |
| Accumulated Depreciation Equipment | 1,000 | 200 | 200 |
| Accounts Payable | 4,000 | 6,000 | 5,985 |
| Sales Tax Payable | 0 | 1,500 | 1,500 |
| Federal Payroll Taxes Payable | 0 | 2,500 | 2,500 |
| Notes Payable—Noncurrent | 12,000 | 0 | 0 |
| Common Stock | 15,000 | 0 | 0 |
| Retained Earnings | 19,000 | 0 | 0 |

Create and print the following reports with no page numbers and without zero balance accounts (like you did in this and previous chapters):

a. Bank reconciliation report for January 2013

b. Budgeted income statement accounts with balances for January through February 2013 with a YTD column

c. Budgeted versus actual income statement for January through February 2013

d. Budgeted balance sheet accounts for January through February 2013 with a YTD column

e.  Budgeted versus actual balance sheet for the month ended February 2013 with Actual, Budget, and Variance, columns

f.  Standard statement of income and retained earnings for the 2 months ended February 2013

g.  Customized balance sheet as of 2/28/13 with a % of Total Assets column

h.  Standard statement of cash flows for the two months ended February 2013

i.  Inventory profitability report for the month of February 2013

j.  Items sold to customers report for the month of February 2013 in summary format without Customer ID

k.  Items purchased from vendors report for the two months ended February 2013 in summary format without Vendor ID

l.  Collection aging report as of 1/31/13 displayed numerically

m.  Payment aging report as of 1/31/13 displayed numerically

n.  Business summary report as of 1/31/13

o.  Key balances report as of 1/31/13

p.  Inventory valuation report as of 1/31/13

q.  Export the inventory profitability report you created to Excel and then print the Excel spreadsheet from Excel with row and column headers and gridlines in landscape orientation

## Comprehensive Problem 5: CRYSTAL CLEAR POOL SERVICE

Restore the backup you made for **Crystal Clear Pool Service** in Chapter 7 into a new company folder. (Do not restore this backup into an existing folder.) Change the company name to include Ch 11 at the end so that the new company name is **Crystal Clear Pool Service Ch 11**. Change the system date to **11/1/12** and the accounting period to **Period 2 – 11/01/12–11/30/12**. Add the following business events:

*merchandising*

*Chronological List of Business Events*

| Event # | Date | Business Event |
|---------|---------|----------------|
| 1 | 11/1/12 | Invoiced customers 100–103 40 hours each for pool services to be rendered in November using invoice numbers 10139–10142 with sales tax. |
| 2 | 11/5/12 | Received following payments from customers on account and deposited amounts using deposit ticket ID 90: check 8852 from customer 100 for $5,777, check 124891 from customer 101 for $7,300, VISA payment 6579514 from customer 102 for $5,300. |
| 3 | 11/6/12 | Created purchase order 45 to Cactus Pool Supply for the purchase of $1,850 in parts needed for repair work being completed for Adobe Grand (Customer ID: 103) on a new job ID 262 Pool repairs. Also created purchase order 46 to Sun Systems for the purchase of $1,200 in parts needed for repair work to be done for Hilton Resorts (Customer ID: 101) on a new job ID 263 Pool Repairs. |

| Event # | Date | Business Event |
|---------|------|----------------|
| 4 | 11/9/12 | Received parts ordered on purchase order 45 from Cactus Pool Supply on its invoice 585421 and purchase order 46 from Sun Systems on its invoice 2323. |
| 5 | 11/12/12 | Completed job 262 and invoiced the customer on invoice number 10143 for 10 hours in pool repairs and for parts reimbursement for a total of $3,286. |
| 6 | 11/13/12 | Purchased cleaning supplies from Cactus Pool Supply in the amount of $1,200 using check 295 and charged the purchase to a new other current asset account ID: 145 and description: Supplies. |
| 7 | 11/14/12 | Paid rent expense to Century 21 Leasing using check 296 for $1,789. |
| 8 | 11/15/12 | Wrote check 297 to Goldman Sachs (a new vendor with ID 205) for $5,000 as a short-term investment (a new account with ID 110 and account type cash). |
| 9 | 11/26/12 | Invoiced customers 100–103 for pool supplies consumed in November using invoice numbers 10144–10147 with sales tax. Customer 100—20 units of chlorine, 9 units of pool shock, and 4 units of pool algaecide. Customer 101—22 units of chlorine, 9 units of pool shock, and 3 units of pool algaecide. Customer 102—16 units of chlorine, 7 units of pool shock, and 3 units of pool algaecide. Customer 103—28 units of chlorine, 15 units of pool shock, and 8 units of pool algaecide. |
| 10 | 11/29/12 | Paid bills due as of 11/30/12 for a total amount of $3,200 using check 298. Received following payments from customers on account and deposited amounts using deposit ticket ID 91: check 8944 from customer 100 for $5,300, check 125600 from customer 101 for $5,300, VISA payment 6558411 from customer 102 for $5,777, and $4,000 from new customer Sheraton of Sedona (ID: 104) on check 301000 as an advance payment on a new job 264 for pool repairs to be completed in December. |
| 11 | 11/29/12 | Paid sales tax owed as of 10/31/12 to the Arizona Dept. of Revenue using check 299. |
| 12 | 11/30/12 | Paid employees with checks 300–301 based on the table below. |
| 13 | 11/30/12 | Reconciled the regular checking account as of 11/30/12. Checks 298, 300, and 301 have not yet cleared and deposit ticket 91 does not appear on the bank statement. Bank service charges (a new type expenses account with ID 605 and description Bank Charges) amount to $23. The statement ending balance is $14,563.46. |
| 14 | 11/30/12 | On 12/3/12 the company created invoice 10148 to Customer ID: 101 for job 263, which was completed on 11/30/12 after incurring 5 hours in pool repairs and for parts reimbursement for a total of $1,934.50 including sales tax. Record this invoice on 12/3/12 and accrue accounts receivable, pool services revenue, parts revenue, and sales tax payable as of 11/30/12 using journal entry reference 123. (*Note*: Cost of goods sold and inventory do not need to be accrued since cost of goods sold is charged in this business when parts are received and purchased.) |
| 15 | 10/31/12 and 11/30/12 | Accrued utility expense of $500 and $550 for 10/31/12 and 11/30/12, respectively, but paid in December using journal entry references 124 and 125. Accrue interest expense of $117 and $115 for 10/31/12 and 11/30/12, respectively, but paid in December using journal entry references 126 and 127. (*Hint*: Don't set either of these up for reversal since they were not paid until December. Do set up a new current liability type account called Accrued Liabilities with ID: 230 and a new expenses type account called Interest Expense with ID: 615) |

| Event # | Date | Business Event |
|---|---|---|
| 16 | 10/31/12 and 11/30/12 | Adjusted prepaid expenses to insurance expense (a new expenses type account with ID 612) $500 for both October and November using journal entry references 128 and 129. Adjust supplies to supplies expense for $350 of supplies used in November. No supplies were used in October. |
| 17 | 11/30/12 | Adjusted accounts receivable for the $4,000 received from Sheraton of Sedona to unearned revenue (a new other current liability account ID: 240) using journal entry reference 131. |
| 18 | 10/31/12 and 11/30/12 | Recorded depreciation expense of $200 each for October and November using journal entry references 132 and 133. |
| 19 | 11/30/12 | Recorded decline in market value of short-term investments (record in new account type income with description Unrealized Loss ID: 450) of $600 using journal entry reference 134. |
| 20 | | Budget data is shown in a table below. |

## Employee Payroll Data

| Pay/Tax/Withholding | Patrick | Singh |
|---|---|---|
| Hours | 155 | 162 |
| Rate | $ 18.00 | $ 20.00 |
| Gross Pay | 2,790.00 | 3,240.00 |
| Federal Withholding | −382.23 | −443.88 |
| Social Security Employee | −172.98 | −200.88 |
| Medicare Employee | −40.46 | −46.98 |
| State Withholding | −111.60 | −129.60 |
| Social Security Employer | 172.98 | 200.88 |
| Medicare Company | 40.46 | 46.98 |
| Federal Unemployment | 22.32 | 25.92 |
| State Unemployment | 111.60 | 129.60 |
| Check Amount | 2,082.73 | 2,418.66 |

## Budget Data

| Income Statement Budget Data | October | November |
|---|---|---|
| Pool Service Revenue | 20,000 | 20,000 |
| Pool Supplies Revenue | 2,000 | 2,000 |
| Parts Revenue | 2,000 | 2,000 |
| Cost of Supplies/Parts Sold | 4,000 | 4,000 |
| Depreciation Expense | 200 | 200 |
| Insurance Expense | 500 | 500 |
| Interest Expense | 100 | 100 |
| Payroll Tax Expense | 750 | 750 |
| Rent Expense | 1,800 | 1,800 |
| Supplies Expense | 200 | 200 |
| Utilities Expense | 500 | 500 |
| Wages Expense | 5,500 | 5,500 |

| Balance Sheet Budget Data | September | October | November |
|---|---|---|---|
| Checking | 8,000 | −4,300 | 22,700 |
| Short-Term Investments | | | 5,000 |
| Accounts Receivable | 15,000 | 15,000 | −5,000 |
| Inventory | 5,000 | −1,000 | −2,000 |
| Prepaid Expenses | 3,000 | −500 | −500 |
| Equipment | 22,000 | | |
| Accumulated Depreciation Equipment | 2,000 | 200 | 200 |
| Accounts Payable | 6,500 | −5,450 | 7,550 |
| Payroll Taxes Payable | | 2,000 | 2,000 |
| Sales Tax Payable | | 1,500 | |
| Accrued Liabilities | | 500 | |
| Notes Payable | 20,000 | | |
| Owner's Capital | 18,000 | | |
| Retained Earnings | 6,500 | | |

Create and print the following reports with no page numbers and without zero balance accounts (like you did in this and previous chapters):

a.  Bank reconciliation report for November 2012

b.  Budgeted income statement accounts with balances for October through November 2012 with a YTD column

c.  Budgeted versus actual income statement for October through November 2012

d.  Budgeted balance sheet accounts for October through November 2012 with a YTD column

e.  Budgeted versus actual balance sheet for the month ended November 2012 with Actual, Budget, and Variance columns

f.  Standard statement of income and retained earnings for the two months ended November 2012

g.  Export the statement of income and retained earnings report you just created to Excel and then print the Excel spreadsheet with row and column headers and gridlines in landscape orientation

h.  Customized balance sheet as of 11/30/12 with a % of Total Assets column

i.  Standard statement of cash flows for the two months ended 11/30/12

j.  Inventory profitability report for the month of November 2012

k.  Items sold to customers report for the month of November 2012 in normal not summary format without Customer ID

l.  Items purchased from vendors report for the two months ended 11/30/12 in summary format without Vendor ID

m.  Collection aging report as of 11/30/12 displayed numerically

n.  Payment aging report as of 11/30/12 displayed numerically

o.  Business summary report as of 11/30/12

p.  Key balances report as of 11/30/12

q.  Inventory valuation report as of 11/30/12

# Payroll Taxes

Learning Objectives

*In this Appendix, you will:*

- Calculate federal income tax withholding.
- Calculate Social Security and Medicare taxes.
- Calculate federal unemployment taxes.
- Learn about state income and unemployment taxes.

## Overview

Throughout this text, you have been provided information for employee payroll tax withholding and employer payroll tax expenses. Peachtree has the ability to calculate each of these for you; however, the company charges an annual fee to do so. Some businesses will find this service very valuable and worth the cost, and some will not. Payroll tax computations are not straightforward. They are, in fact, quite convoluted and dependent on all sorts of exceptions and rules. For example, federal income tax withholding is dependent on employees' income; whether they are being paid weekly, biweekly, semimonthly, monthly, etc.; the number of exemptions they claim; and their filing status: married, single, head of household, etc.

This appendix is designed to provide you a basic overview of the payroll tax conundrum and is focused on federal taxes only, as each state has its own rules for income tax withholding, unemployment, etc. Examples used are based on 2008 tax tables and law since the process is the same regardless of the tax year and tax tables.

## Federal Income Tax Withholding

As previously mentioned, federal income tax withholding is dependent on employees' income; whether they are being paid weekly, biweekly, semimonthly, monthly, etc.; the number of exemptions they claim; and their filing status: married, single, head of household, etc. Guiding employers in this regard is Circular E (Employer's Tax Guide) and the Circular E Supplement (Employer's Supplemental Tax Guide), which can be found online at the Internal Revenue Service Websites at **http://www.irs.gov/pub/irs-pdf/p15.pdf** and **http://www.irs.gov/pub/irs-pdf/p15a.pdf**, respectively.

The IRS provides tables in this document to compute the specific amount to be withheld from each employee. It also provides a percentage method, which is much easier to produce for our purposes. Employees must supply employers with payroll tax information each year such as their filing status—married, single, head of household—and the number of exemptions they are claiming.

## The steps necessary for computation of an employee's federal income tax withholding are as follows:

**1** Determine the frequency of wage payments: weekly, biweekly, semi-monthly, monthly, etc.

**2** Determine the employee's filing status.

**3** Based on the above, choose the appropriate table for Percentage Method of Withholding found in Figure A1.1.

### Figure A1.1

Tables for Percentage Method of Withholding from the Employer's Supplemental Tax Guide

## Alternative 1.—Tables for Percentage Method Withholding Computations
(For Wages Paid in 2008)

### Table A(1)—WEEKLY PAYROLL PERIOD (Amount for each allowance claimed is $67.31)

| **Single Person** | | | | **Married Person** | | | |
| If the wage in excess of allowance amount is: | | The income tax to be withheld is: | | If the wage in excess of allowance amount is: | | The income tax to be withheld is: | |
| Over— | But not over— | Of such wage— | From product | Over— | But not over— | Of such wage— | From product |
| $0 | —$51 | 0% | $0 | $0 | —$154 | 0% | $0 |
| $51 | —$198 | 10% less | $5.10 | $154 | —$453 | 10% less | $15.40 |
| $198 | —$653 | 15% less | $15.00 | $453 | —$1,388 | 15% less | $38.05 |
| $653 | —$1,533 | 25% less | $80.30 | $1,388 | —$2,651 | 25% less | $176.85 |
| $1,533 | —$3,202 | 28% less | $126.29 | $2,651 | —$3,994 | 28% less | $256.38 |
| $3,202 | —$6,916 | 33% less | $286.39 | $3,994 | —$7,021 | 33% less | $456.08 |
| $6,916 | | 35% less | $424.71 | $7,021 | — | 35% less | $596.50 |

### Table B(1)—BIWEEKLY PAYROLL PERIOD (Amount for each allowance claimed is $134.62)

| **Single Person** | | | | **Married Person** | | | |
| If the wage in excess of allowance amount is: | | The income tax to be withheld is: | | If the wage in excess of allowance amount is: | | The income tax to be withheld is: | |
| Over— | But not over— | Of such wage— | From product | Over— | But not over— | Of such wage— | From product |
| $0 | —$102 | 0% | $0 | $0 | —$308 | 0% | $0 |
| $102 | —$396 | 10% less | $10.20 | $308 | —$906 | 10% less | $30.80 |
| $396 | —$1,306 | 15% less | $30.00 | $906 | —$2,775 | 15% less | $76.10 |
| $1,306 | —$3,066 | 25% less | $160.60 | $2,775 | —$5,302 | 25% less | $353.60 |
| $3,066 | —$6,404 | 28% less | $252.58 | $5,302 | —$7,988 | 28% less | $512.66 |
| $6,404 | —$13,833 | 33% less | $572.78 | $7,988 | —$14,042 | 33% less | $912.066 |
| $13,833 | — | 35% less | $849.44 | $14,042 | — | 35% less | $1,192.90 |

### Table C(1)—SEMIMONTHLY PAYROLL PERIOD (Amount for each allowance claimed is $145.83)

| **Single Person** | | | | **Married Person** | | | |
| If the wage in excess of allowance amount is: | | The income tax to be withheld is: | | If the wage in excess of allowance amount is: | | The income tax to be withheld is: | |
| Over— | But not over— | Of such wage— | From product | Over— | But not over— | Of such wage— | From product |
| $0 | —$110 | 0% | $0 | $0 | —$333 | 0% | $0 |
| $110 | —$429 | 10% less | $11.00 | $333 | —$981 | 10% less | $33.30 |
| $429 | —$1,415 | 15% less | $32.45 | $981 | —$3,006 | 15% less | $82.35 |
| $1,415 | —$3,322 | 25% less | $173.95 | $3,006 | —$5,744 | 25% less | $382.95 |
| $3,322 | —$6,938 | 28% less | $273.61 | $5,744 | —$8,654 | 28% less | $555.27 |
| $6,938 | —$14,985 | 33% less | $620.51 | $8,654 | —$15,213 | 33% less | $987.97 |
| $14,985 | | 35% less | $920.21 | $15,213 | — | 35% less | $1,292.23 |

### Table D(1)—MONTHLY PAYROLL PERIOD (Amount for each allowance claimed is $291.67)

| **Single Person** | | | | **Married Person** | | | |
| If the wage in excess of allowance amount is: | | The income tax to be withheld is: | | If the wage in excess of allowance amount is: | | The income tax to be withheld is: | |
| Over— | But not over— | Of such wage— | From product | Over— | But not over— | Of such wage— | From product |
| $0 | —$221 | 0% | $0 | $0 | —$667 | 0% | $0 |
| $221 | —$858 | 10% less | $22.10 | $667 | —$1,963 | 10% less | $66.70 |
| $858 | —$2,830 | 15% less | $65.00 | $1,963 | —$6,013 | 15% less | $164.85 |
| $2,830 | —$6,644 | 25% less | $348.00 | $6,013 | —$11,488 | 25% less | $766.15 |
| $6,644 | —$13,875 | 28% less | $547.32 | $11,488 | —$17,308 | 28% less | $1,110.79 |
| $13,875 | —$29,971 | 33% less | $1,214.07 | $17,308 | —$30,425 | 33% less | $1,976.19 |
| $29,971 | | 35% less | $1,840.49 | $30,425 | | 35% less | $2,584.69 |

### Table E(1)—DAILY or MISCELLANEOUS PAYROLL PERIOD
(Amount for each allowance claimed for such period is $13.46)

| **Single Person** | | | | **Married Person** | | | |
| If the wage in excess of allowance amount divided by the number of days in the pay period is: | | The income tax to be withheld multiplied by the number of days in such period is: | | If the wage in excess of allowance amount divided by the number of days in the pay period is: | | The income tax to be withheld multiplied by the number of days in such period is: | |
| Over— | But not over— | Of such wage— | From product | Over— | But not over— | Of such wage— | From product |
| $0.00 | —$10.20 | 0% | $0 | $0 | —$30.80 | 0% | $0 |
| $10.20 | —$39.60 | 10% less | $1.02 | $30.80 | —$90.60 | 10% less | $3.08 |
| $39.60 | —$130.60 | 15% less | $3.00 | $90.60 | —$277.50 | 15% less | $7.61 |
| $130.60 | —$306.60 | 25% less | $16.06 | $277.50 | —$530.20 | 25% less | $35.36 |
| $306.60 | —$640.40 | 28% less | $25.26 | $530.20 | —$798.80 | 28% less | $51.26 |
| $640.40 | —$1,383.30 | 33% less | $57.28 | $798.80 | —$1,404.20 | 33% less | $91.19 |
| $1,383.30 | — | 35% less | $84.95 | $1,404.20 | — | 35% less | $119.28 |

**Note.**— The adjustment factors may be reduced by one–half cent (e.g., 7.50 to 7.495; 69.38 to 69.375) to eliminate separate half rounding operations.

The first two brackets of these tables may be combined, provided zero withholding is used to credit withholding amounts computed by the combined bracket rates, for example, $0 to $51 and $51 to $198 combined to read, "Over $0, But not over $198."

The employee's excess wage (gross wage less amount for allowances claimed) is used with the applicable percentage rates and subtraction factors to calculate the amount of income tax withheld.

**4**   Determine the amount of wage payment.

**5**   Determine the number of employee withholding allowances.

**6**   Use Figure A1.1 to calculate the value of one withholding allowance.

**7**   Compute the employee's withholding amount by multiplying the employee's withholding allowances by the value of one withholding allowance determined above.

**8**   Calculate the net wages by subtracting the employee's withholding amount determined above from his or her wage payment.

**9**   Using net wages determined above, calculate the required federal income tax withholding using the table you selected from Figure A1.1.

For example, a single employee, claiming two withholding allowances, is paid $600 weekly.

## To calculate the federal income tax withholding:

**1**   Frequency of wage payments: **weekly**.

**2**   Employee's filing status: **single**.

**3**   Appropriate table for Percentage Method of Withholding: **Table A(1)**.

**4**   Amount of wage payment: **600**.

**5**   Number of employee withholding allowances: **2**.

**6**   Value of one withholding allowance: **67.31**.

**7**   Employee's withholding amount: $2 \times 67.31 =$ **134.62**.

**8**   Net wages: $600.00 - 134.62 =$ **465.38**.

**9**   Required federal income tax withholding: $(15\% \times 465.38) - 15.00 =$ **54.81**.

A second example, a married employee, claiming three withholding allowances, is paid $1,500 semimonthly.

## To calculate the federal income tax withholding:

**1**   Frequency of wage payments: **semimonthly**.

**2**   Employee's filing status: **married**.

**3**   Appropriate table for Percentage Method of Withholding: **Table C(1)**.

**4**  Amount of wage payment: **1,500**.

**5**  Number of employee withholding allowances: **3**.

**6**  Value of one withholding allowance: **145.83**.

**7**  Employee's withholding amount: $3 \times 145.83 = $ **437.49**.

**8**  Net wages: $1,500.00 - 437.49 = $ **1062.51**.

**9**  Required federal income tax withholding: $(1,062.51 \times 15\%) - 82.35 = $ **77.03**.

A third example, a married employee, claiming five withholding allowances, is paid $8,000 monthly.

## To calculate the federal income tax withholding:

**1**  Frequency of wage payments: **monthly**.

**2**  Employee's filing status: **married**.

**3**  Appropriate table for Percentage Method of Withholding: **Table D(1)**.

**4**  Amount of wage payment: **8,000**.

**5**  Number of employee withholding allowances: **5**.

**6**  Value of one withholding allowance: **291.67**.

**7**  Employee's withholding amount: $5 \times 291.67 = $ **1,458.35**.

**8**  Net wages: $8,000 - 1,458.35 = $ **6,541.65**.

**9**  Required federal income tax withholding: $(6,541.65 \times 25\%) - 766.15 = $ **869.26**.

# Social Security and Medicare Taxes

The Federal Insurance Contributions Act (FICA) provides for a federal system of old-age, survivors, disability, and hospital insurance. The old-age, survivors, and disability insurance part is financed by the Social Security tax. The hospital insurance part is financed by the Medicare tax. Each of these taxes is reported separately. Generally, you are required to withhold Social Security and Medicare taxes from your employees' wages, and you must also pay a matching amount of these taxes. Certain types of wages and compensation are not subject to Social Security taxes. Generally, employee wages are subject to Social Security and Medicare taxes regardless of the employee's age or whether he or she is receiving Social Security benefits.

Social Security and Medicare taxes have different rates, and only the Social Security tax has a wage base limit. The wage base limit is the maximum wage that is subject to the tax for the year. Determine the amount of withholding for Social Security and Medicare taxes by multiplying each payment by the employee tax rate. There are no withholding allowances for Social Security and Medicare taxes. In 2009, the employee tax rate for Social Security is 6.2% (amount withheld). In 2011, the government reduced this withholding to 4.2% as a part of the stimulus package to spur spending during the recession. In 2012, the rate is scheduled to return to 6.2%. The employer tax rate for Social Security is also 6.2% (12.4% total). The 2007 wage base limit was $97,500. For 2008, the wage base limit is $102,000. The current employee tax rate for Medicare is 1.45% (amount withheld). The employer tax rate for Medicare tax is also 1.45% (2.9% total). There is no wage base limit for Medicare tax; all covered wages are subject to Medicare tax. Guiding employers in this regard is Circular E (Employer's Tax Guide), which can be found online at the Internal Revenue Service Website at **http://www.irs.gov/pub/irs-pdf/p15.pdf**.

## The steps necessary for computation of an employee's withholding and employer's computation of Social Security and Medicare taxes are as follows:

1 Determine the employee's cumulative earnings year to date prior to this paycheck.

2 Determine the amount of wage payment for the current period.

3 Determine if the employee's cumulative earnings exceed or are close to the Social Security wage base limit.

4 Calculate the Social Security tax by multiplying the appropriate wage payment by 6.2%.

5 Calculate the appropriate Medicare tax by multiplying the wage payment by 1.45%.

For example, in 2008, a single employee, claiming two withholding allowances, is paid $600 in the current week. Cumulative earnings to date are $3,000.

### To calculate the Social Security and Medicare tax:

1 Cumulative earnings year to date: **3,000**.

2 Wage payment: **600**.

3 Cumulative earnings compared to the Social Security wage base limit: **3,000 is less than 102,000**.

4 Social Security tax: $600 \times 6.2\% = $ **37.20**.

5 Medicare tax: $600 \times 1.45\% = $ **8.70**.

A second example, in 2008, a married employee, claiming three withholding allowances, is paid $1,500 semimonthly. Cumulative earnings to date are $6,000.

## To calculate the Social Security and Medicare tax:

1　Cumulative earnings year to date: **6,000**.

2　Wage payment: **1,500**.

3　Cumulative earnings compared to the Social Security wage base limit: **6,000 is less than 102,000**.

4　Social Security tax: $1,500 \times 6.2\% = $ **93.00**.

5　Medicare tax: $1,500 \times 1.45\% = $ **21.75**.

A third example, in 2008, a married employee, claiming five withholding allowances, is paid $8,000 monthly. Cumulative earnings to date are $100,000.

## To calculate the Social Security and Medicare tax:

1　Cumulative earnings year to date: **100,000**.

2　Wage payment: **8,000**.

3　Cumulative earnings compared to the Social Security wage base limit: **100,000 is less than 102,000 but close. Difference is 2,000**.

4　Social Security tax: $2,000 \times 6.2\% = $ **124.00** (since this will bring the employee up to the wage limit).

5　Medicare tax: $8,000 \times 1.45\% = $ **116.00**.

# Federal Unemployment Taxes

Use Form 940 (or Form 940-EZ) to report your annual Federal Unemployment Tax Act (FUTA) tax. FUTA tax, together with state unemployment systems, provides for payments of unemployment compensation to workers who have lost their jobs. Most employers pay both federal and state unemployment taxes. Only the employer pays FUTA tax. Do not collect or deduct it from your employees' wages. The tax, currently at 0.8%, applies to the first $7,000 you pay each employee in a year after subtracting any exempt payments. The $7,000 amount is the federal wage base. Your state wage base may be different. Instructions can currently be found at **http://www.irs.gov/pub/irs-pdf/i940.pdf**.

## The steps necessary for computation of the FUTA tax are as follows:

**1** Determine the employee's cumulative earnings year to date prior to this paycheck.

**2** Determine the amount of wage payment for the current period.

**3** Determine if the employee's cumulative earnings exceed or are close to the FUTA wage base limit.

**4** Calculate the FUTA tax by multiplying the appropriate wage payment by 0.8%.

For example, in 2008, a single employee, claiming two withholding allowances, is paid $600 in the current week. Cumulative earnings to date are $3,000.

### To calculate the FUTA tax:

**1** Cumulative earnings year to date: **3,000**.

**2** Wage payment: **600**.

**3** Cumulative earnings compared to the FUTA wage base limit: **3,000 is less than 7,000**.

**4** FUTA tax: $600 \times 0.8\% =$ **4.80**.

A second example, in 2008, a married employee, claiming three withholding allowances, is paid $1,500 semimonthly. Cumulative earnings to date are $6,000.

### To calculate the FUTA tax:

**1** Cumulative earnings year to date: **6,000**.

**2** Wage payment: **1,500**.

**3** Cumulative earnings compared to the FUTA wage base limit: **6,000 is less than 7,000 but close. Difference is 1,000**.

**4** FUTA tax: $1,000 \times 0.8\% =$ **8.00**.

A third example, in 2008, a married employee, claiming five withholding allowances, is paid $8,000 monthly. Cumulative earnings to date are $88,000.

**To calculate the FUTA tax:**

**1** Cumulative earnings year to date: **88,000**.

**2** Wage payment: **8,000**.

**3** Cumulative earnings compared to the FUTA wage base limit: **88,000 is more than 7,000**.

**4** FUTA tax: $0 \times 0.8\% =$ **0.00**.

## State Income Tax Withholding and Unemployment Taxes

Each state, of course, has its own rules for withholding state income taxes and computing the employer's cost for unemployment. Some states, Florida and Nevada for instance, do not have a state income tax. Other states, such as California and Hawaii, not only have state income taxes but also have training taxes.

Most of the state income tax computations are similar to the federal computations in that they have different tables for different filing status—single, married, etc.—and they have tables for exemption allowances. Rather than explain how to calculate taxes for each and every state in the union, I suggest you visit your local state tax agency to determine income tax and unemployment tax rates and requirements. Some Website references follow. (Remember, these sites were operational when this text was published. They may no longer be operational if the state moved them or reconfigured its Website.)

| | |
|---|---|
| California | **http://www.edd.ca.gov/** |
| Florida | **http://www.myflorida.com/dor/taxes/** |
| Hawaii | **http://hawaii.gov/tax/** |

## Appendix 1 Questions

**1**   What factors affect an employee's federal income tax withholding?

**2**   Where can employers get guidance on federal income tax withholding?

**3**   What do withholding allowances do to the computation of federal income tax withholding?

**4**   What does the Social Security tax finance?

**5**   What does the Medicare tax finance?

**6**   What is the Social Security tax rate?

**7**   Is there a wage base limit to the Social Security tax? If so, what is it for 2008?

**8**   What is the Medicare tax rate?

**9**   Is there a wage base limit to the Medicare tax? If so, what is it for 2008?

**10**   Who pays FUTA, and what is the current rate and computational structure?

## Appendix 1 Assignments

**1**   In 2008, a married employee, claiming one withholding allowance, is paid $800 in the current week. Cumulative earnings to date are $4,000. Calculate the following:

   a.   Federal income tax withholding

   b.   Employee Social Security taxes to be withheld

   c.   Employee Medicare taxes to be withheld

   d.   Employer Social Security tax

   e.   Employer Medicare tax

   f.   FUTA

**2**   In 2008, a single employee, claiming three withholding allowances, is paid $2,000 semimonthly. Cumulative earnings to date are $6,500. Calculate the following:

   a.   Federal income tax withholding

   b.   Employee Social Security taxes to be withheld

   c.   Employee Medicare taxes to be withheld

   d.   Employer Social Security tax

   e.   Employer Medicare tax

   f.   FUTA

**3**  In 2008, a single employee, claiming zero withholding allowances, is paid $10,000 monthly. Cumulative earnings to date are $95,000. Calculate the following:

a.  Federal income tax withholding

b.  Employee Social Security taxes to be withheld

c.  Employee Medicare taxes to be withheld

d.  Employer Social Security tax

e.  Employer Medicare tax

f.  FUTA

# Installing and Registering the Peachtree Application Software

## Overview

This text includes a disc containing the Peachtree application software that is subject to restrictions outside of Cengage Learning and the author's control. The installation and registration process was created by Sage, the software's publisher.

As this book is scheduled to go to the printer, Sage is changing the registration process for Peachtree Complete 2012. Users will no longer be provided with access codes. Instead, users will go to the Sage Website and register their software, where they'll receive a serial number to be used within the Peachtree software in order to activate it for the full trial period.

Complete instructions on installing and registering the software may be found at this book's companion Website. To access those instructions, please follow these steps:

1  Please direct your browser to: http://www.cengagebrain.com/shop/index.html

2  Enter "Using Peachtree Complete 2012" or the ISBN: 9781133627289 into the search menu.

3  Click on the "Access Now" link under the "Study Tools" heading.

4  A new window will open. The directions may be found under the "Book Resources" tab.

# index